DREAM VACATIONS

Frommer's Travel Experts Choose Their Favorite Places on Earth

Wiley Publishing, Inc.

Published by:

Wiley Publishing, Inc.

111 River St.
Hoboken, NJ 07030-5774

ISBN: 978-0-470-11335-6

Editors: Michael Spring and Melinda Quintero
Production Editor: Suzanna R. Thompson
Cartographers: Andrew Dolan, Andrew Murphy, Elizabeth Puhl, Guy Ruggiero, and Roberta Stockwell
Photo Editor: Richard H. Fox
Anniversary Logo Design: Richard Pacifico
Production by Wiley Indianapolis Composition Services
Interior Design by Vertigo Design NYC

Front cover photo: African elephant, Okavango Delta, Botswana (© Michael Melford/Getty Images)

For information on our other products and services or to obtain technical support, please contact our Customer Care Department within the U.S. at 800/762-2974, outside the U.S. at 317/572-3993 or fax 317/572-4002. Wiley also publishes its books in a variety of electronic formats. Some content that appears in print may not be available in electronic formats.

Manufactured in China

5   4   3   2   1

A Note on Prices

This book provides prices in U.S. dollars and British pounds. The rates of this exchange as this book went to press are listed in the table below. Exchange rates are constantly in flux; for up-to-the-minute information, consult a currency-conversion website such as www.oanda.com/convert/classic.

U.S. $	U.K. £	E.U. €	Canadian $	Australian $	New Zealand $
$1 equals	£0.53	0.77€	C$1.17	A$1.28	NZ$1.45

An Additional Note

Please be advised that travel information is subject to change at any time—and this is especially true of prices. We therefore suggest that you write or call ahead for confirmation when making your travel plans. The authors, editors, and publisher cannot be held responsible for the experiences of readers while traveling. Your safety is important to us, however, so we encourage you to stay alert and be aware of your surroundings. Keep a close eye on cameras, purses, and wallets, all favorite targets of thieves and pickpockets.

► *Lavender field, Provence, Pays de Valensole.*
© John Lawrence/Getty Images

A Note from the Publisher

Dream Vacations is several books in one. It's an inspirational book to get you on the road and an idea book to help you decide where to go. It's a photo book with gorgeous images that celebrate the world, reminding us how beautiful it can be. And it's a nostalgia book, awakening memories of great trips we've taken in the past.

Dream Vacations is also a guidebook with practical advice, so you can take these trips yourself. This is not just a book of dreams, but a guide to help you make those dreams come true.

The approach is simple. We asked 30 of Frommer's most seasoned authors—the ones who have been everywhere—to write about their favorite places on earth, the places they go to when they're *not* on assignment.

Some writers gave us one destination; others, a handful. Cities, villages, islands, monuments—we cover them all, in every corner of the globe. The results are idiosyncratic and intensely personal, which is not surprising: Frommer's writers are an independent lot who don't like to go where the crowds go—or who like to explore familiar places in fresh, unexpected ways.

The photos speak as loudly as the text. Our photo editor, Richard Fox, and I went through thousands of images, searching for those precious few that bring each destination to life. How many of these 93 places have I been to? Forty-seven. How about you? Wouldn't it be awful to have seen them all? Fortunately, there will always be new places to discover.

You'll notice that some writers have given you their e-mail addresses. I hope you'll contact them with your compliments or complaints; they want to hear from you. I'd love to hear from you, too, so send your thoughts my way at mspring@wiley.com.

As any savvy traveler knows, there's a high mortality rate among hotels and restaurants, so I encourage you to call ahead for the latest information. And get your travel safety updates from the U.S. State Department at www.state.gov. This is a dream book—we don't want any rude awakenings.

Have a great trip.

Michael Spring

Michael Spring, Publisher
Frommer's Travel Guides

CONTENTS

▼ *Château de Chenonceaux, Loire Valley.*
© Jon Arnold/DanitaDelimont.com

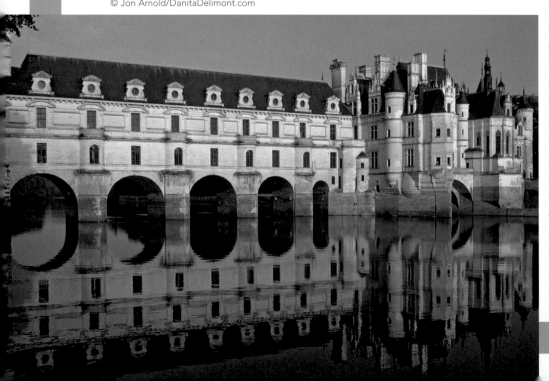

Skogafoss Waterfall, Iceland.
© Franz Aberham/Digital Vision/Getty Images

▶ *A giant tortoise—a familiar sight on the Galápagos.*
© James Martin/Getty Images

Man with wool spindle, Ladakh.
© Michael Spring

Petra, Jordan.
© SIME s.a.s./eStock Photo

A dune walk in the Namib-Naukluft National Park.
© Marc Abrahms Photography

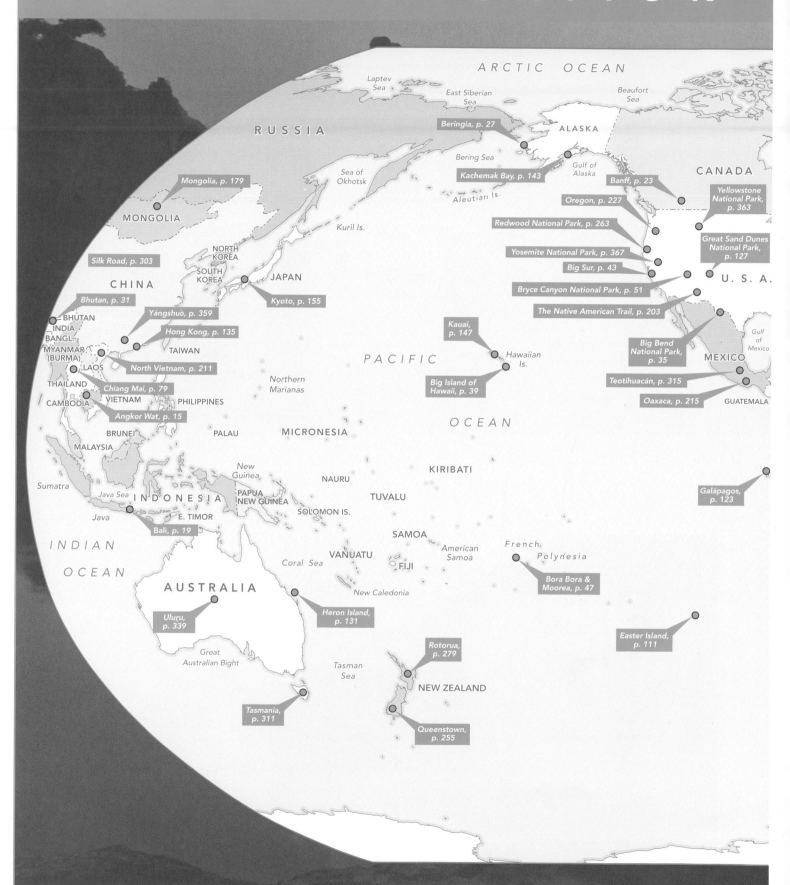

DREAM VACATION

ARCTIC OCEAN

Laptev Sea

East Siberian Sea

Beaufort Sea

RUSSIA

Beringia, p. 27

ALASKA

CANADA

Bering Sea

Gulf of Alaska

Kachemak Bay, p. 143

Mongolia, p. 179

Sea of Okhotsk

Aleutian Is.

Banff, p. 23

Oregon, p. 227

Yellowstone National Park, p. 363

MONGOLIA

Kuril Is.

Redwood National Park, p. 263

Great Sand Dunes National Park, p. 127

Silk Road, p. 303

NORTH KOREA

SOUTH KOREA

JAPAN

Yosemite National Park, p. 367

Big Sur, p. 43

U.S.A.

CHINA

Kyoto, p. 155

Bryce Canyon National Park, p. 51

Bhutan, p. 31

Yángshuò, p. 359

Kauai, p. 147

The Native American Trail, p. 203

BHUTAN

INDIA

Hong Kong, p. 135

TAIWAN

Hawaiian Is.

Gulf of Mexico

BANGL.

MYANMAR (BURMA)

LAOS

North Vietnam, p. 211

Big Island of Hawaii, p. 39

Big Bend National Park, p. 35

MEXICO

THAILAND

Chiang Mai, p. 79

VIETNAM

PACIFIC

Teotihuacán, p. 315

CAMBODIA

Angkor Wat, p. 15

PHILIPPINES

OCEAN

Oaxaca, p. 215

GUATEMALA

BRUNEI

PALAU

MICRONESIA

MALAYSIA

Sumatra

Northern Marianas

Java Sea

INDONESIA

New Guinea

NAURU

KIRIBATI

Java

PAPUA NEW GUINEA

Galápagos, p. 123

Bali, p. 19

E. TIMOR

SOLOMON IS.

TUVALU

INDIAN

SAMOA

OCEAN

Coral Sea

VANUATU

FIJI

American Samoa

French Polynesia

AUSTRALIA

New Caledonia

Bora Bora & Moorea, p. 47

Uluru, p. 339

Heron Island, p. 131

Great Australian Bight

Rotorua, p. 279

Easter Island, p. 111

Tasman Sea

NEW ZEALAND

Tasmania, p. 311

Queenstown, p. 255

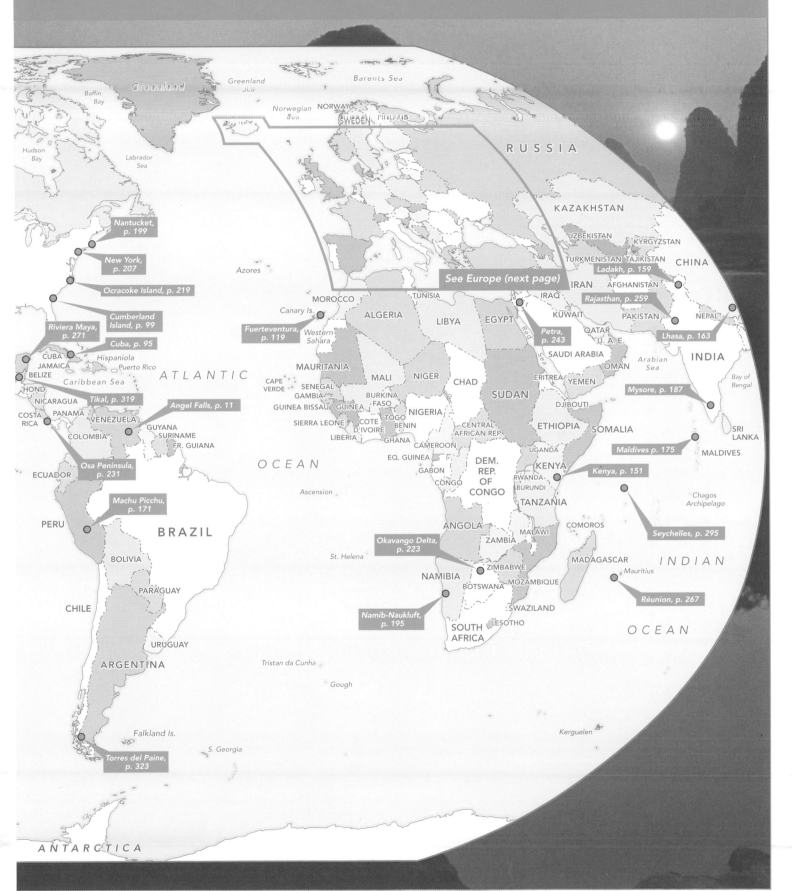

DESTINATIONS

Greenland

Baffin Bay

Greenland Sea

Barents Sea

Norwegian Sea

NORWAY

SWEDEN   FINLAND

RUSSIA

Hudson Bay

Labrador Sea

KAZAKHSTAN

UZBEKISTAN   KYRGYZSTAN

TURKMENISTAN   TAJIKISTAN   CHINA

Nantucket, p. 199

New York, p. 207

See Europe (next page)

Ladakh, p. 159

Ocracoke Island, p. 219

IRAN   AFGHANISTAN

Azores

MOROCCO   TUNISIA   IRAQ   **Rajasthan, p. 259**

Canary Is.

Cumberland Island, p. 99

ALGERIA   LIBYA   EGYPT   KUWAIT   PAKISTAN   NEPAL

Riviera Maya, p. 271

Fuerteventura, p. 119

Western Sahara

Petra, p. 243

QATAR

U.A.E.

Lhasa, p. 163

INDIA

Cuba, p. 95

CUBA   Hispaniola

JAMAICA   Puerto Rico

BELIZE

ATLANTIC

MAURITANIA   MALI   NIGER   CHAD   SAUDI ARABIA   OMAN   Arabian Sea

Bay of Bengal

HOND.   Caribbean Sea

CAPE VERDE   SENEGAL   ERITREA   YEMEN   **Mysore, p. 187**

NICARAGUA

GAMBIA   BURKINA FASO   SUDAN   DJIBOUTI

Tikal, p. 319   **Angel Falls, p. 11**

GUINEA BISSAU   GUINEA   NIGERIA   ETHIOPIA   SOMALIA   SRI LANKA

COSTA RICA   PANAMA   VENEZUELA

SIERRA LEONE   COTE D'IVOIRE   BENIN   CENTRAL AFRICAN REP.

COLOMBIA   GUYANA   SURINAME   FR. GUIANA

LIBERIA   GHANA   TOGO   CAMEROON   UGANDA   **Maldives p. 175**   MALDIVES

EQ. GUINEA   DEM. REP. OF CONGO   KENYA   **Kenya, p. 151**

Osa Peninsula, p. 231

ECUADOR

OCEAN

Ascension

GABON   CONGO   RWANDA   BURUNDI

TANZANIA

Chagos Archipelago

Machu Picchu, p. 171

PERU   BRAZIL

ANGOLA   MALAWI   COMOROS   **Seychelles, p. 295**

St. Helena

Okavango Delta, p. 223

ZAMBIA   MADAGASCAR   INDIAN

BOLIVIA

ZIMBABWE   Mauritius

NAMIBIA   BOTSWANA   MOZAMBIQUE

PARAGUAY

Réunion, p. 267

CHILE

Namib-Naukluft, p. 195

SWAZILAND

URUGUAY

SOUTH AFRICA   LESOTHO   OCEAN

ARGENTINA   Tristan da Cunha

Gough

Falkland Is.

Kerguelen

S. Georgia

Torres del Paine, p. 323

ANTARCTICA

Red Sea

Bahama

Red Sea

DREAM VACATION

Iceland, p. 139

ICELAND

Shetlands

Orkneys

Outer
Hebrides

The Scottish Highlands, p. 291

NORWAY

Gulf
of
Bothnia

SWEDEN

Vänern

Vättern

Gotland

NORTH
SEA

DENMARK

Ærø, p. 3

Bornholm

Öland

BALTIC
SEA

Donegal, p. 103

Connemara, p. 83

IRELAND

Irish
Sea

UNITED
KINGDOM

The Cotswolds, p. 87

Wadden Islands, p. 351

HOLLAND

POLAND

Wales, p. 355

Somerset, p. 307

Oxford, p. 235

English Channel

Channel Is.

BELGIUM

LUXEMBOURG

GERMANY

CZECH
REPUBLIC

SLOVAKIA

ATLANTIC
OCEAN

Paris, p. 239

Loire Valley, p. 167

FRANCE

Burgundy, p. 63

Bay of Biscay

SWITZERLAND

LIECHT.

L. Geneva

AUSTRIA

HUNGARY

Camino de
Santiago, p. 67

Zermatt, p. 371

Venice, p. 347

SLOVENIA

CROATIA

Chamonix, p. 75

The Duoro, p. 107

Provence, p. 251

MONACO

Portofino, p. 247

Adriatic

BOSNIA &
HERZEGOVINA

PORTUGAL

SPAIN

ANDORRA

Saint-Tropez, p. 283

Corsica

Tuscany, p. 335

Umbria, p. 343

Trogir,
p. 327

Sea

MONTENEGRO

ITALY

Rome, p. 275

Andalusia, p. 7

Balearic Is.

Menorca

Ibiza

Mallorca

Sardinia

Tyrrhenian Sea

Formentera, p. 115

MEDITERRANEAN SEA

Ionian
Sea

Morocco, p. 183

Tunisia, p. 331

Sicily, p. 299

MOROCCO

ALGERIA

TUNISIA

MALTA

DESTINATIONS

FINLAND

Lake
Onega

Lake
Ladoga

Gulf of Finland

ESTONIA

L. Peipus

RUSSIA

LATVIA

LITHUANIA

KALININGRAD
(RUSSIA)

BELARUS

KAZAKHSTAN

UKRAINE

Bucovina, p. 55

MOLDOVA

Sea of
Azov

Caspian
Sea

Crimea

ROMANIA

BLACK SEA

GEORGIA

AZERBAIJAN

SERBIA

Bulgaria, p. 59

ARMENIA

BULGARIA

MACEDONIA

Lake Van

ALBANIA

IRAN

GREECE

Aegean
Sea

TURKEY

Cappadocia, p. 71

Nafplion, p. 191

Santorini, p. 287

SYRIA

Crete, p. 91

Rhodes

IRAQ

Crete

CYPRUS

LEBANON

ÆRØ, DENMARK

An unspoiled island of beaches & storybook hamlets

The globetrotter Bennett Scott, who'd been everywhere, claimed that the town of Ærøskøbing was "one of the five places that one should see in the world." I feel that's an exaggeration, but it's still one of my favorite little towns in Europe, and if Scott succumbed to hyperbole to call attention to Ærøskøbing's quaint charms, I forgive him.

If the small Danish island of Ærø, off the southern coast of Funen, didn't exist, Hans Christian Andersen would have invented it. It's that special. Walt Disney might have gone through this town with a paintbrush and a bucket of rainbow colors.

Many of Denmark's offshore islands are dull and flat, with red-brick market towns best passed through hurriedly. But Ærø is a place at which you'll want to linger, wandering its sleepy one-lane roads, walking the cobblestone streets of its hamlets—or merely spending a day at the beach. The best sands are along the northern and eastern coastlines. Take your pick. Chances are, even in July, you'll end up with a strip of sand all to yourself for some serious skinny-dipping.

The place is small, so it's easy to get around—30km (8 miles) long and 8km (5 miles) at its widest point. The number of windswept "souls" is also small, no more than 7,000 hearty islanders, with less than 1,000 centered in the capital of Ærøskøbing itself.

There are only two towns on the island that could even be called that. If time is fleeting, explore only Ærøskøbing. But there is also the ancient seaport of Marstal, where mariners once set out to conquer the Seven Seas. It has a bustling marina and a shipyard that still makes some wooden vessels as in viking days.

The moment the ferry docks on Ærø, and you suck in the pristine air, you know something's different. The air is purer because more than three-quarters of Ærø is powered by renewable energy sources.

There are two things I really like about Ærø: its overwhelming sense of isolation, seemingly free of a world of terrorism and taxes, and its unhurried, provincial character. It's a place where doing nothing is an art form. I once sat for an hour on a beach, mesmerized by the swishing sound of an old windmill turning in the cool, salty Danish winds.

Small fishing harbors, wheat fields rippling in the winds, storybook hamlets of half-timbered houses, a dilapidated church or two from the Middle Ages, beer gardens filled with raucous laughter during the too-short weeks of summer, and yacht-filled marinas—these are the scenes that make Ærø the kind of island you search for—but rarely find—in all of Scandinavia. A local resident put it this way: "Our island didn't change after our seagoing heyday in the 17th century. We were too poor to modernize. When we finally started earning money centuries later, we were an antique, a valuable antique, and we learned there was money to be made from the visitors who wanted to see Denmark the way it used to be."

Ærø is like one of those old Michael J. Fox films about a return to the past. Just set back your watch 2 centuries as you disembark.

◀ *A windmill on the island of Ærø.*
© Yann Arthus-Bertrand/Corbis

SPECIAL MOMENTS

1 Ærøskøbing. Of all the little towns of Europe, I like best to wander through the higgledy-piggledy cobblestone streets of Ærø's capital, with its hollyhocks and half-timbered houses. It's like a well-preserved slice of 18th-century Denmark. In his traditional red jacket, the postman actually whistles as he makes his rounds (I'm not making that up); and the mayor, as he bicycles home from work, salutes all the townspeople. Both the postman and the mayor know every man, woman, and child in Ærøskøbing. But what are those little doggies seen in the private windows? They're actually pairs of ceramic dogs brought home by sailors after visits to the Far East. In Asia, prostitutes, as a cover, gave the ceramic dogs to sailors, pretending they were hawking souvenirs from within their boudoirs when, in fact, they were taking money for sex.

2 Bicycling. On the island of Ærø, cycling is a way of life.

Islanders have a right to be smug when some travel guides for cyclists view their island as the best biking terrain in Europe. The distances are mercifully short. The island, for the most part, is level, except for some small hills designed to build up your leg muscles. Picture it: With sea breezes blowing in your hair, you set out along undulating country roads. You pass, in review, thatched houses that look like the abode of Hansel and Gretel. You wave at a farmer hoeing rows of cabbages and red beets. Along the way, you cycle past graveyards where vikings were buried after a lifetime of raping and pillaging. The tourist office will supply you with a free bike map, outlining three idyllic routes, each signposted. Of the three, I prefer scenic route #91, beginning at the old port of Marstal and winding its way along the less densely populated southern coast as far as the hamlet of Søby.

3 Churches. Even if you haven't been near a church in decades, consider a visit to the seven churches of Ærø. Unique in Denmark, each church has its own character, many with a maritime decor. If you're biking around Ærø, break up the trip, as I do, by calling on at least three—my favorites—of these relics of yesterday. In Ærøskøbing, launch your quest at the **Ærøskøbing Church,** Lars Søndergade 43. Built in 1756, the church has saved a baptismal font from the 1200s and a pulpit from 1643. Moving southeast to the port of Marstal, call at **Marstal Church,** Kongensgade, which dates to 1738. The blue benches here are a symbol of the sea.

From Marstal, head west to the village of Store Rise in the southeastern section of Ærø. **Rise Church,** at Kirkeballevej, in this idyllic hamlet, was a Romanesque church until decorators and renovators arrived in the 1600s. A marked

footpath leads to **Tingstedet,** a Neolithic passage grave that's older than 5,000 years. This may also have been the site of a prehistoric fertility cult, so I can only imagine what transpired here.

4 **Shopping.** In summer, open-air markets are staged in both Ærøskøbing and Marstal. Ask at the tourist office for dates and times. But as you bicycle around, you'll find that the entire island is one vast shopping mart, with the highly creative islanders selling art, homemade and gift items, and foodstuff they raise themselves. More artists and craftspeople are drawn to Ærø than to any other island in Denmark. Some artists fashion their art out of the local stones, shells, and driftwood. As you move about, you can stop at any roadside stand that captures your fancy and negotiate with the stallkeepers. I've done this many times and always make my getaway feeling that I've made a "steal."

ABOUT THE AUTHOR

DARWIN PORTER is one of the world's most prolific travel writers. His books for Frommer's include guides to the Caribbean, Italy, France, Germany, and England. A Hollywood columnist and a celebrity biographer, Porter is also a radio broadcaster; his shows on American popular culture are heard in all 50 states.

YOUR TRIP

General Information: Before you go, contact the **Scandinavian Tourist Office—Visit Denmark** (655 3rd Ave., New York, NY, 10017; ☎ 212/885-9700; www.visitdenmark.com). On Ærø itself, drop in at **Ærøskøbing Turistbureau** (Vestergade 1B; ☎ 45-62/52-13-00; www.visitaeroe.dk). Pick up cycling maps here. **Getting There:** Ærø lies 29km (18 miles) across the water south of the city of Svendborg, which lies on the island of Funen. That's 176km (110 miles) west of Copenhagen. Hour-long car ferries depart Svendborg six times daily and bookings are made through **Det Aeroske Faergegraf-Ikselskab** by calling ☎ 45-62/52-40-00. **What to See & Do:** Rent a bike at **Pilebraekkens Cykler,** in Ærøskøbing, costing from $9 (£5) a day (Pillebraekken 11; ☎ 45-62/52-11-10). **Best Lodging:** For those who want to go first class, the only bet is **Hotel Aeroe Strand** in Marstal (Egehovedvej 4; ☎ 45-62/53-33-20; www.hotel-aeroestrand.dk; $157/£83 double). This is the island's largest hotel with the most spacious rooms and also boasts an indoor, heated pool. **Best Lodging Value:** My favorite nest is **Det Lille Hotel** in Ærøskøbing (Smedegate 33; ☎ 45-62/52-23-00; www.det-lille-hotel.dk; $117/£62 double). Big on charm, short on amenities (no private bathrooms), it was built in 1844 as the home of a sea captain. **Best Restaurant:** In Ærøskøbing, make it the 1780 **Restaurant Mumm** (Søndergade 12; ☎ 45-62/52-12-12; main courses $20–$32/£10–£17). The fresh fish is the best preparation. **Best Restaurant Value:** Paper plates and plastic forks but, oh, that smoked fish at **Ærøskøbing Røgeri** (Havnen; ☎ 45-62/52-40-07; platters $3–$4/£1.50–£2). **When to Go:** June to September is best, although it can sometimes be difficult to find lodging. Plan in advance.

◀ *A house in the town of Ærøskøbing.*
© John Elk III/Lonely Planet Images

ANDALUSIA, SPAIN

The heart of the Moorish kingdom for nearly 800 years

The sun in Andalusia, Spain's famed southern region, is not to be underestimated. It bakes olive groves and Costa del Sol beaches, and it sears blindingly white villages carved out of rocky bluffs. But the warmth and passion of the Andaluces, the wildly gregarious and hospitable people of the south, are every bit as intense.

Bizet may have been French, but he had the good sense to set his fiery opera *Carmen* in Seville, a seductive city renowned for its raven-haired beauties and boulevards lined with orange trees. Don Juan, the original Latin lover, came from Andalusia, as did Federico García Lorca, Spain's great poet and the author of *Blood Wedding.* Pablo Picasso was reared in Málaga along the coast.

Life in Andalusia is expressive, intensely felt. Flamenco, with its staccato rhythms and throaty *cante hondo* vocals that give voice to the suffering of a people, is the quintessential expression of Gypsy culture. Bullfights, those death-defying dramas of man versus beast, are at their most passionate and folkloric in the south.

During long siestas, Andaluces hide from the sun, but when they emerge, they seem incapable of resisting a crowded tapas joint or noisy bar. In the languid air of Andalusia, no one ever seems in a hurry, least of all to go home.

The Moors—Arab and Berber conquerors from North Africa—ruled Spain for nearly 800 years. In the south, they established the heart of their kingdom, Al-Andalus, and two of the most glorious monuments in western Europe: Granada's Alhambra, a monumental red castle in the foothills of the snowcapped Sierra Nevada, and the Great Mosque in Córdoba. García Lorca was deeply enamored of the region's Muslim roots, and Moorish culture's erudition and inscrutability infused his writing. The Moors created palaces and pools, fountains and fortresses. The bewitching Alhambra was their idealized earthly paradise.

The society the Moors presided over in medieval Spain was both lofty and practical but, in its unprecedented tolerance, unique. For 7 centuries, Muslims, Jews, and Christians lived and worked alongside one another. Language, culture, and religion intermingled. The Reconquest put a violent end to that, and the clash of cultures can be seen in side-by-side architecture that reveals the dominant power and bombast of the Christians and the delicate lyricism of the Moors. There is no better or sadder example than Córdoba's Great Mosque, where Catholics raised an ostentatious, gilded church inside a serene expanse of candy-cane-striped arches.

Luckily, Spain's magical mix of East and West survives. You feel it in the atmospheric old Jewish quarters of Santa Cruz in Seville and in La Judería in Córdoba. The Albaycín district in Granada thrives with Moroccan-style teahouses, Arab baths, and *cármenes*, 15th-century Moorish villas surrounded by sweet-smelling orchards. Diminutive *pueblos blancos*—whitewashed villages dotting the rolling hills between Seville and the sea—look as though they were transported in their entirety from North Africa.

Perhaps what one intuitively absorbs traveling through Andalusia is the dream of that long-ago, tolerant society. In flamenco, there's a word, *duende,* that speaks to the ineffable magic and mystery in the music. It's usually interpreted as "soul," and that's as good a definition as any for Andalusia.

◀ *The village of Caseras in Andalusia.*
© Jose Fuste Raga/Zefa/ Corbis

SPECIAL MOMENTS

1 **Imbibing Seville.** Exuberant and romantic Seville is unmatched for ambience. Though it possesses the world's largest Gothic cathedral and a magnificent *alcázar* (royal residence), it's the kind of place where you most want to make like a local and take it all in, at the easygoing pace that Sevillanos so well understand. Their hometown is the best spot in Spain to hit tapas bars, especially across the river in Triana, and wander the charming whitewashed alleyways of the Barrio de Santa Cruz. It's a feast for the senses, with the scent of orange trees and fresh flowers, and the sounds of church bells overlapping with the clip-clop of horses' hooves and flamenco resounding from within late-night flamenco clubs. If you can make it for supercharged Easter or April Fair celebrations, the greatest in Spain, even better.

2 **Grasping Granada's Moorish dream.** The Alhambra, created under the Nasrid dynasty in the 13th and 14th centuries, is so astonishing that it alone is worth a trip to Spain. Its murmuring fountains and regal palaces, and airs of elegance and harmony, provide clues to a little-understood, but sophisticated people. My favorite way to enjoy the Alhambra is away from the hordes that crowd its gates on a daily basis. By all means visit during the day and see the spectacular gardens and royal summer estate (the Generalife), but return at night for a much quieter and more intimate encounter. Spend an afternoon wandering through the serpentine streets of the hilly Albaycín district, the old Arab quarter, across the river, and find your way to the Mirador de San Nicolás. A small plaza in front of the church perfectly frames the Alhambra against the snowcapped ridges of the Sierra Nevada, a mesmerizing sight, especially at sunset, when the Alhambra glows red, or late at night, when it is exquisitely floodlit.

3 **Touring the *pueblos blancos.*** Andalusia's whitewashed, medieval villages—clustered in the mountainous region between Seville and the coast—are enchanting throwbacks, as notable for their spectacular settings as their dazzling whiteness and warrens of impenetrable, Arab-style alleyways. Several of these villages—Moorish defensive strongholds in their heyday—are perched on rugged, 1,524m (5,000-ft.) limestone slopes. Ronda, one of the oldest towns in Spain, clings tantalizingly to a cliff above a narrow 91m (350-ft.) chasm, with palatial mansions crowding the edges of the gorge. The birthplace of modern bullfighting, Ronda has Spain's oldest and most romantic bullring. The *pueblos* make for a perfect driving tour amid olive groves and rolling hills, and the villages are within easy reach of Andalusia's sherry wineries in Jerez and the relaxed beaches of the Costa de la Luz.

4 **Conjuring Córdoba's glorious past.** While the rest of Europe foundered in the Dark Ages, Córdoba thrived under the Moors and became Europe's most enlightened and populated city, replete with libraries, universities, and sophisticated architecture. Though today it strains the imagination to think of Córdoba as such an important center, its former greatness is revealed behind the walls of the Mezquita, or Great Mosque, which presents one of Spain's most stunning sights: an unending horizon of overlapped, candy-cane-striped arches. Córdoba is known as the city of patios for its spectacular flower-bedecked interior spaces, celebrated with an "open patio" festival every May. Córdoba's evocative old Jewish Quarter, La Judería, is the other great remnant of the past that thrives today: a pretty jumble of narrow, white-washed alleyways, tiled portraits of saints and Madonnas, potted plants and bougainvillea, and artisans' shops.

NEIL E. SCHLECHT is a graduate of Georgetown University's School of Foreign Service and holds master's degrees from the University of Texas at Austin. He has worked on development programs for the E.U. and authored a dozen travel guides and articles on two of his obsessions: tennis and wine. He has lived in Spain, Brazil, and Ecuador.

ABOUT THE AUTHOR

YOUR TRIP

General Information: Contact the **Tourist Office of Spain** (☎ 212/265-8822; www.spain.info) or visit www.andalucia.org. **Getting There:** Fly into Córdoba, Seville, or Granada or travel there by train from Madrid or Barcelona (☎ 34-90/224-34-02; www.renfe.es). Once there, a full tour of the *pueblos blancos* is practical only in a private automobile. **Best Lodging:** In Seville, **Hotel Alfonso XIII** (San Fernando 2; ☎ 888/625-5144 in the U.S., or 34-95/491-70-00 in Spain; www.hotel-alfonsoxiii.com; 534€–566€/$640–$680). In Granada, **Parador Nacional de San Francisco** (Real de la Alhambra s/n; ☎ 34-95/822-14-40; 250€/$300). **Best Lodging Value:** In Seville, **La Casa del Maestro** (Almudena 5; ☎ 34-95/450-00-07; www.lacasadelmaestro.com; 100€–116€/$120–$140). **La Casa Grande,** in Arcos de la Frontera (Maldonado 10; ☎ 34-95/670-39-30; www.lascasagrande.net; 65€–102€/$78–$122). In Granada, **Casa Horno del Oro** (Horno del Oro 6; ☎ 34-95/822-32-36; www.casahornodeloro.com; 90€–160€/$108–$192). **Best Restaurants:** In Seville, **Egaña Oriza** (San Fernando 41; ☎ 34-95/422-72-11; main courses 20€–58€/$24–$70). In Córdoba, **Bodegas Campos** (Calle de los Lineros 32; ☎ 34-95/749-75-00; main courses 14€–20€/$17–$24). In Ronda, **Tragabuches** (José Aparicio 1; ☎ 34-95/219-02-91; main courses 16€–34€/$19–$40). **Best Restaurant Value:** Seville's tapas bars in Triana, including **Kiosco de las Flores** (Betis s/n; ☎ 34-95/433-38-98) and **La Albariza** (Betis 6; ☎ 34-95/433-89-60). In Granada, **Antigua Bodega Castañeda** (Calle Elvira 5; ☎ 34-95/822-63-62; main courses 7€–12€/$8–$14). **When to Go:** Late spring and fall; avoid the intense heat of July and August.

◀ *La Mezquita Cathedral, Córdoba.*
© Jon Arnold/DanitaDelimont.com

ANGEL FALLS, VENEZUELA

A thunderous trip to the world's tallest waterfall

I've visited plenty of places on this planet that have literally taken my breath away. But my favorite memories—and photographs—of any single natural wonder remain those from my trips to Angel Falls—from the wet and wild ride upriver in a traditional dugout canoe, to my first sighting of the falls, to swimming in the small pool made by big rocks at its base.

Angel Falls is the world's tallest waterfall, over 15 times taller than Niagara. That in itself is impressive. However, Angel Falls is also set in a remote section of southeastern Venezuela, the Gran Sabana, whose forests and landscape are truly otherworldly. This is a vast area of virgin rainforest with towering tepuis spread all around. In fact, the tepuis of this region inspired Sir Arthur Conan Doyle's *The Lost World.*

Tepuis are unique geological formations, massive flat-topped limestone mesas with steep sides. They are geographically and biologically isolated, and boast an amazing variety of endemic flora and fauna. The sides drop off so perfectly vertical that the tepuis have become a major destination for base jumpers, who climb to the tops and leap off with just a parachute on their backs. In my mind, there are better ways to enjoy this region.

Angel Falls begins its plunge from the top of Auyántepui, or "Devil's Mountain," the largest of the tepuis. What follows is an uninterrupted drop of 807m (2,648 ft.). After that, the falls continue a little longer, for a total drop of just under a kilometer (3,212 ft.). During the height of the rainy season, Angel Falls is a raging torrent and you can get soaked near the base. At other times, a thin ribbon streams down, turning almost entirely to mist before hitting the ground.

Trips to Angel Falls depart from the tiny Pemón indigenous village of Canaima in the predawn penumbra. As you make your way up the Carrao and Churún rivers in a motorized *curiari,* or dugout canoe, the landscape comes alive. Tepuis emerge out of the darkness, taking shape and growing more and more impressive in size and beauty as dawn turns to day. The trip upriver includes the fording of several dicey rapids, and one major portage. In all, it's about 3 hours on the beautiful, black-colored river, with a break for breakfast, before the falls come into sight. After that, it's a 1-hour walk through dense forest to the pool at the foot of the falls. On one trip, my local Pemón guide made the hike barefoot, pointing out interesting facts about the flora and fauna along the way. Still, it can be wet and slippery, so bring sturdy footwear, and be careful.

Much of the fun of a visit to Angel Falls is the chance to stay at a small lodge on the shores of the Canaima lagoon, a beautiful black-water lagoon ringed by pink-sand beaches and fed by seven thundering waterfalls. I definitely recommend taking enough time to hike through the rainforests here, visit some local indigenous communities, and enjoy the other waterfalls close by.

◀ *Angel Falls.*
© Pablo Corral V/Corbis

SPECIAL MOMENTS

1 Beach time. Most people wouldn't think of heading over 640km (400 miles) inland to go lie on the beach, but the rivers around Angel Falls and Canaima have beautiful sections of riverside beach made up of fine sand. In many cases, the sand is a soft pink, almost the color of a flamingo. I like the beach at the base of El Sapo Falls, but local guides can find you plenty of others. The dry season, December through May, when the rivers are lowest, is the best time to take advantage of these remote freshwater jungle beaches, but you can find a patch of sand here throughout the year. However, don't expect to find any lounge chairs, beach umbrellas, or kids selling iced fresh coconuts.

2 Other falls. While Angel Falls is clearly the top draw here, I enjoy all of the waterfalls around the Canaima lagoon. Hacha Falls and Ucaima Falls can be seen from just about any spot along the shores of the lagoon. At a 15-minute hike up-hill from the village, you'll find a lookout on the top of Ucaima Falls. It's not Niagara, but it's a pretty good view. However, I like to hire a boat for a trip to El Sapo Falls, which is located behind Anatoly's Island. Come prepared to get wet, because you'll definitely want to make the short, slippery walk on the trail that leads into and behind this waterfall. Since I'm already wet, I always take a swim at the large, calm pool at the base. When I want to wander farther afield, I head downstream to the broad and powerful Yuri Falls, where there are good hiking trails through the forest.

3 Isla Ratoncito. Most people just get to see photos of Angel Falls. The majority of those that see it in person do so briefly out of the side of an airplane as part of a popular fly-by tour. The lucky ones get to actually visit the falls and bathe in the water at their base. But the luckiest of all are those who spend the night near the falls sleeping at a camp on Isla Ratoncito. This isn't

luxurious. In fact, you'll be sleeping in a hammock strung between poles in an open-air hut. But you will dream to the sound of rushing water and wake to the sight of Angel Falls.

4 Local crafts. Makunaima Arte Indígena is a Canaima gift shop with a broad and reasonably priced selection of local indigenous arts and crafts, including blowguns and darts made and still used by the local Pemón people. I brought mine home as a carry-on item years ago, but in this current age of heightened airport security, you should probably either have them ship it, or pack it securely in your checked baggage. You can also get baskets made by the remote Yanomami tribe, as well as quality jewelry, ceramics, and woodwork made by various regional tribes. My favorite items here are masks of the Piaroa people. These black-and-white ceramic masks feature long manes of "hair" made from dried reeds.

As a teen, **ELIOT GREENSPAN** read *On the Road* and was hooked. After hitchhiking in the Americas and sailing most of the Caribbean, he went on to earn a writing degree from the Jack Kerouac School for Disembodied Poetics. Since then, he has been writing guidebooks for Frommer's.

ABOUT THE AUTHOR

YOUR TRIP

General Information: I consider www.think-venezuela.net the best all-around general tourism site on Venezuela. For information on Angel Falls, try www.salto-angel.com. Almost all visitors come to Canaima as part of a pre-arranged package including meals, accommodations, and tours. Packages can be arranged with local lodges listed below or any number of agencies in Caracas or abroad. It's best to deal directly with the lodges and make reservations prior to arrival. If you decide to visit on your own, there are usually several local tour agencies waiting for incoming flights at the airport. **Getting There:** Angel Falls are 725km (450 miles) southeast of Caracas. **Avior** (☎ 58-0501/284-67737; www.avioairlines.com) and **Conviasa** (☎ 58-0500/266-84272; www.conviasa.aero) both have regular flights to Canaima, the gateway to Angel Falls. **Best Lodging: Jungle Rudy Campamento** (Parque Nacional Canaima, Sector Laguna de Canaima, Gran Sabana, Edificio Bolívar; ☎ 58-0286/ 962-2359, or 58-212/693-0618 in Caracas; www.junglerudy.com; $300–$400/£159–£212, including three meals and drinks). **Best Lodging Value:** Budget travelers can find several options for hanging a hammock, or sleeping in a rented hammock, for $5 to $10 (£3–£5.30) per person per night. Your best bet is to ask around the information desks at the airport upon arrival. Try the rustic **Campamento Tomás Bernal** (Isla Anatoly; ☎ 58-0414/854-8234; www.bernaltours.com; $40/£21 double, including three meals). Usually a representative of Bernal Tours is at the airport. **When to Go:** Trips to the falls are made from June through early December, with mid-October through late November being the best time to visit.

◀ *Angel Falls.*
© Juan Carlos Muñoz/AGE Fotostock, Inc.

ANGKOR WAT, CAMBODIA

A trip to the spiritual capital of the ancient Khmer Empire

'll never forget my first sunset at Angkor. An assortment of spiritual seekers and shutter clickers gathered high up on the temple ruins of Bakheng Hill. Someone played a flute; others chanted in Pali while tour groups took turns posing for pictures with the temples in the background. As the sun dropped low in the sky and turned the spires of Angkor Wat to gold, people conversed in subdued tones. Even the insidious clicks of cameras couldn't destroy the solemnity of the moment.

Whoever you are, whatever your interests, a visit to Angkor Wat will be a highlight of your trip to Southeast Asia. It is one of the most inspirational religious monuments in the world. The temple of Angkor Wat is one of the most famous and most beautiful here, but it's only one of numerous temple ruins spread over miles, and you will need at least a few days to explore the massive grounds. Angkor, the capital of the ancient Khmer Empire, was founded around the 9th century, reached its peak in the 12th, and declined in the 14th. It is really a collection of cities that were home to the Angkor kings, who reigned over a highly developed society in the heart of Indochina for some 400 years, starting in A.D. 800. The compound was rediscovered and reclaimed from the jungle only in the late 19th century. Today Angkor is a must-see on any itinerary of the region. An hour's flight from Ho Chi Minh City, and only 2 hours from Hanoi, it's easily included with trips to Vietnam.

For many years the Angkor temples were home to encampments of dangerous Khmer Rouge guerillas, and the temple sites were dotted with landmines. But Cambodia is relatively stable today, which means that the temples and the nearby support town of Siem Reap are at once more crowded and home to excellent amenities. You'll find five-star hotels just a short ride from the temple complex, as well as sophisticated restaurants serving local and international fare, shopping emporiums with decent goods, and an active, edgy nightlife catering to travelers from around the globe.

I've been to Angkor countless times, and, each time I go, I see something new—a new path, a new temple. My recommendation for temple touring: Get a guide. Sure, you'll be amazed by the temples whether you're with a guide or not, but without one it all starts looking like a big stone jungle gym. A guide can point out the nuances, the stories in stone, the eccentricities, and the fascinating history of the early Khmer people. A guide will take you to little-known nooks and crannies and steer you away from the crowds.

If you have time, buy the 3-day pass and spend at least a day with a guide, another day on your own playing "tomb raider," and the last day exploring sites farther afield. Bring extra film or lots of gigabytes for your camera because Angkor brings out the photographer in us all. And, at night, enjoy the club scene near the Old Market in Siem Reap: The way into the heart of a country is not just through its monuments to the past.

◄ *Angkor Thom at Angkor Wat (southern entrance).*
© David A. Harvey/ National Geographic/ Getty Images

15

SPECIAL MOMENTS

1 **Angkor Wat.** The largest and most uniquely designed of all the Angkor temples—it's featured on the Cambodian flag—is everyone's favorite. Catch it in the early morning or at sunset for maximum effect. Go with a guide to learn about the detailed frescoes on the first-floor gallery, including the "Churning of the Sea of Milk" story, which tells the Hindu creation myth. A rope guide wire has been placed along the steep steps up to the main *prang*, or tower, but you can still climb it freestyle if you feel plucky.

2 **Bakheng Hill.** You can go up by elephant or scramble up steep steps, but however you go, don't miss it. A prime sunset and sunrise viewpoint over Angkor Wat and other temples, Bakheng is also said to mirror mythical Mount Meru, birthplace of the Hindu gods. A Hindu temple in the form of a mountain, it was built in the 9th century and dedicated to Shiva.

3 **Angkor Thom and the Bayon.** The many large relief busts of Apsaras, Cambodia's mythical dancers, are Southeast Asia's Mona Lisas. See your first grinning Apsara, whose faces are modeled after Jayavarman, Angkor's greatest architect, on the entryway to the Angkor Thom compound. You'll find similar giant relief sculptures on any gate of the city and clustered around the central temple. If you are in Angkor for just half a day, do not miss the **Bayon**—the top deck is crowded with relief sculpture of the elusively grinning Jayavarman, and the sides are chiseled with epic tales of the Khmer people. On the north end of the Bayon, find more stunning relief sculpture at the Elephant Terraces.

4 **Four Temples. Ta Prohm** makes a tomb raider out of everyone. After years of neglect, the jungle reclaimed this 12th-century monastic site. But instead of clearing the overgrowth, as they did with other temples, the French archaeologists

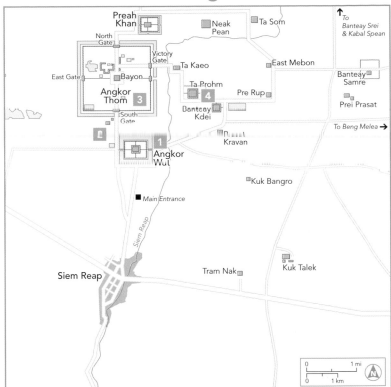

who found Ta Prohm fortuitously left it as it was. Massive Spoong trees and vines burst through the rock and cleave the temple walls, giving you the opportunity to experience the sense of wonder and discovery the early-19th-century explorers must have felt. The site is at its most serene in the early morning. A long, dusty road leads from the main temple site to another crumbling ruin, **Beng Melea,** this one a giant mound of rock with tunnels to explore and clambering galore. The interior area is to temple touring what the pit of plastic balls is to a Chuck E. Cheese restaurant: a big, fun pile of rubble great for trouncing around. Kids love this one. Get here in the morning and you'll have the place to yourself.

Another day trip outside the main compound takes you to **Banteay Srei,** a stunningly preserved Hindu temple with its own distinct architecture. Near **Kabal Spean** is the "River of a Thousand Linga" (linga are the phallic symbols representing the Hindu god Shiva).

CHARLES AGAR wrote a number of Frommer's titles on Southeast Asia, including *Frommer's Vietnam.* Born with "itchy feet," according to his grandma, he traveled and taught English in Asia before he started writing. He is currently a newspaper reporter in Aspen, Colorado. Contact him at www.charlesagar.com.

ABOUT THE AUTHOR

YOUR TRIP

General Information: Click on "Cambodia" at www.visit-mekong.com. **Getting There:** There are direct flights to Siem Reap—the support town for the Angkor Wat compound—from a number of international destinations, including the main Asian hubs. Many travelers include a trip to the quirky capital, Phnom Penh, or parts of southern Vietnam, with Angkor Wat itineraries. **Getting Around:** The temples are some 6km (3½ miles) north of Siem Reap. Tour the temples by rented car or in a shaded surrey pulled by a motorcycle. Arrange guide services with **Exotissimo** (☎ 855-063/964-323 in Siem Reap; www.exotissimo.com) or **Diethelm** (☎ 855-063/963-524 in Siem Reap; www.diethelmtravel.com). **Best Lodging: Raffles Grand Hotel D'Angkor** is the old colonial grand dame of Siem Reap, though the town now boasts loads of upmarket lodging (1 Vithei Charles de Gaulle; ☎ 855-063/963 888; http://siemreap.raffles. com; $310–$1,900/£164–£1,007). **Best Lodging Value: Angkor Village** is a good value and very comfortable (Wat Bo Rd., Siem Reap; ☎ 855-063/965-561; www.angkorvillage.com; $89–$165/£47–£87). **Best Restaurant:** The **FCC Angkor (Foreign Correspondent's Club)** is the place to see and be seen (Pokambor Ave.; ☎ 855-012/900-123; entrees $4–$18/£2–£10). **Best Restaurant Value:** Down an alley just north of the old market you'll find **Khmer Kitchen,** a no-fuss storefront with real-deal Khmer dishes and a hush-hush reputation (☎ 855-012/763-468; main courses $2–$3/£1–£2). For a very affordable and hearty meal at the temples, try **Sunrise Angkor,** behind and to the left of the Angkor Café (☎ 855-012/946-595). **When to Go:** It's always hot in Cambodia, but the dry season— December to April—is best.

◀ *Ta Prohm at Angkor Wat.*
© Tom Till/Getty Images

BALI, INDONESIA

Dreamy beaches & deep, green gorges of jaw-dropping beauty

First of all, Bali is not in the South Pacific. It's actually nestled between the Java Sea and the Indian Ocean. And while its residents do wear sarongs some of the time, they're considered somewhat formal wear—not at all the Dorothy Lamour look.

If Bali is not precisely the stuff of Hollywood movies or florid novels, don't fret; it's still as dreamy as you imagined. This is a pocket-sized island, so small you can practically drive from one end to the other in 2 or 3 hours, but so crammed with beauty, it practically bursts with it. Volcanic mountains tower above deep, green gorges and sculptured tiers of rice paddies, leading down to the sea. It's what most of us order up when we ask for paradise.

The Balinese culture is so rich, so layered, that expats who have lived here for decades say with a not-unhappy sigh, "The longer I stay, the less I understand it." It's a place where beauty is said to please the gods, and art is a devotional act entwined with daily life. As a result, music pours from doorways and streets are strewn with religious offerings in the form of delicate boxes made of banana leaves, bearing tiny portions of rice, petals, and incense. Because local religious belief holds that there is a spirit in everything, everything—rocks, trees, water—is imbued with meaning and life.

What you find in Bali depends largely on where you choose to go. There are delights for any tourist agenda. You can shop till you drop, swim and sun, climb to holy sites, visit villages largely untouched by time, and eat extremely well. You can be a conventional beach resort tourist living the high life on a rich person's budget, or get down and dirty, Euro-hippie style. You can travel all over the island or you can settle down in the village of Ubud, inhaling the fragrance of frangipani blossoms and watching the days turn to years.

If you're like me, you'll find some time to spend with the Balinese themselves. To come here and never get off the beach seems a waste of an extraordinary opportunity. At the same time, Bali does have some of the most stunning luxury hotels in the world, masterpieces of architecture and comfort, designed to blend into the landscape and often sensitively incorporating local aesthetic traditions. Once ensconced in one, it's not easy to leave. Still, I would consider forgoing that fancy hotel for a night or two and staying in a private home (or *losmen*), and getting to know your hosts up close. These can cost just a few dollars a night, including a huge breakfast.

Bali buffs mourn the island's loss of innocence. After all, Bali has been "discovered," and tourism now plays a major role in its economy. Worse, Bali was badly hurt by terrorist attacks in 2002 and 2005. While Indonesia is the fourth-largest Muslim nation in the world, Bali is Hindu and the attacks came from Islamist outsiders. The essential Bali, with its ritualized way of life, has not changed. The island's intense spirituality remains for anyone lucky enough to experience it.

◄ *Vendor selling batiks on Bali.*
© Jon Arnold/DanitaDelimont.com

SPECIAL MOMENTS

1   A religious celebration. The Balinese are deeply spiritual and their religion is seamlessly incorporated into every facet of their day-to-day existence. Over 90% of the population is Balinese Hindu. Practitioners focus on pleasing God through intricate aesthetic rituals and ceremonies. Daily life is governed by a series of rituals, from morning to night, from birth to death. Every home has a small shrine, and every village has at least three temples. Each morning you will see handmade banana leaf offerings, wafting incense, by every doorway and on every corner, to thank the gods and make the day go well. That's just the beginning. Almost every day, you can watch or join in at least one parade of gorgeously dressed Balinese, with towering offerings of meticulously arranged fruit and flowers balanced on their heads. You're welcome to fall in line as they head to a ceremony, perhaps a coming-of-age tooth filing, or a wedding, or even a cremation. All you need is to don a sarong and sash—they're for sale everywhere; carry them with you for special moments such as these!—and a respectful attitude. All the local theatrical performances—from gamelan music to the intricate ballets of the legong and barong dances—are actually religious rituals, and seeing them in context is a remarkable experience. Stand at the back at first, but don't be surprised if some locals soon pull you to the front and begin to share with you the mysteries of their extraordinary way of life.

2   Ubud. This engaging village, nestled between deep, green gorges of jaw-dropping beauty, is everyone's favorite place on Bali. It's the island's cultural center, the source of most of its best art. There is a lot of hustle that goes on, thanks to the shops that line the main drags, the personal drivers hyperventilating at the chance to drive a tourist around, and the New Age hucksters trying to take advantage of the genuine spiritual seekers. And yet all the surface confusion fades away after a few days, as you see past the noise to the continuing deep spiritual life of the community. Ubud is the perfect jumping-off point for sightseeing on the rest of the island, but don't be surprised if, after a very short time, you discover you have no interest in leaving.

3   Gunung Kawi. There are countless temples and other intriguing buildings in Bali, but these mysterious stone monuments, carved directly into a mountain face, are a can't-miss sight, though strangely not on the regular tourist

▶ *Rice terraces on Bali.*
© Craig J. Brown/Index Stock Imagery

track. To reach them, you have to climb down a steep flight of some 300 steps and then trek a bit alongside a small gorge and rushing river. Once there, you are faced with silent monoliths of unknown origin (probably cenotaphs honoring an 11th-c. king and his concubines). Awesome.

4 **Shopping.** Because arts and crafts are so intrinsic to the Balinese culture, there is an overwhelming amount of it for sale, from traditional stone and woodcarvings, to ceremonial masks, to paintings in styles both ancient and modern, to glorious hand-dyed itek and endek cloth. There's a certain amount of mass-produced junk to wade through—some of it actually pretty nifty—but if you keep a keen eye and cool head—especially when you're bargaining—you will come home with plenty of treasures to remind you of the unique magic of this place.

MARY HERCZOG's dream job was writing the Bali chapter for the first edition of *Frommer's Southeast Asia*. She writes a number of books for Frommer's, including *Frommer's Las Vegas*, *Frommer's Las Vegas Day by Day*, and *Frommer's New Orleans*. She is also a contributor to *California For Dummies*.

ABOUT THE AUTHOR

YOUR TRIP

General Information: Given the attacks in Bali, and other parts of Indonesia, U.S. travelers are strongly advised to check out the advice and any up-to-date warnings regarding vacation travel in Bali at the **U.S. State Department**'s website (http://travel.state.gov). For planning your trip, **Bali Paradise Online** (www.bali-paradise.com), **Bali Online** (www.indo.com), and **Bali Guide** (www.baliguide.com) are excellent online resources. For information on travel visas to Indonesia, visit **www.embassyofindonesia.org**. **Getting There:** Most visitors make a connection with Singapore, Bangkok, Taipei, Hong Kong, or Japan. For direct flights from Australia, try **Qantas** (www.qantas.com). **Best Lodging:** The **Four Seasons Jimbaran Bay** has deeply romantic accommodations styled on traditional Balinese bungalows, plus private plunge pools, all spread out along a magnificent ocean view (Jimbaran; ☎ 62-361/701010; www.fourseasons.com; $450/£239). **Best Lodging Value: Casa Luna,** set in a rice paddy just a few minutes' walk from the center of Ubud, is a high-end losmen with lovely rooms and a terrific breakfast (Jalan Raya Ubud; ☎ 62-361/973282; www.casalunabali.com; $38–$55/£20–£29). **Best Restaurant Value:** At **Satri's Warong,** order the banana-marinated chicken as required, a day in advance. You won't be sorry (Monkey Forest Rd., Ubud; ☎ 62-361/973279; $1–$14/50p–£7). **When to Go:** The rainy season lasts from October to April, but it's not the dampness of the rain (it usually hits in sharp bursts that last no more than an hour), but the humidity that gets you. The hottest months are from February to April, and the tourist high season is July, August, and the weeks surrounding Christmas and New Year's.

BANFF, CANADA

A world of high, lonely peaks, glacial lakes & grand hotels

I've logged in over 30,000 miles of cross-country road trips, mostly in the American West, and can tell you that few places compare to Alberta's Banff National Park (Banff NP), one of UNESCO's World Heritage Sites.

So many other wild northern places have all the same elements as Banff—a wilderness untamed by roads and trains, turquoise lakes, glaciers only minutes from parking areas, trails that take you through a diversity of biological zones—even grand hotels. Creede, Colorado, has the same arty, small-town feel as Banff, the town (pop. 7,600). Yosemite National Park has as magnificent a hotel. Yellowstone has better hot springs and many of the same animal sightings. Perhaps Banff's special appeal is that it offers all of these experiences, all of them eminently accessible and within an hour's drive of each other.

When people say "Banff," they can mean the national park, the town, or the region. Lake Louise is part of Banff NP; to make matters more confusing, the very small town of Lake Louise (pop. 1,500) is not on the lake. The Chateau Lake Louise is among the grandest sights on earth—which is why you should try to stay there and see the mountain reflected in the lake in the morning and evening.

What will attract you here during the day is often not the towns, and perhaps not even Lake Louise (is this treason to say?), with its busloads of visitors from 9am to 5pm, but the variety of outdoor experiences so close by: the high, lonely peaks; the glaciers and glacial lakes that have never found their way into tourist brochures; the countless trails; the grassy meadows so complex in color that you can only guess at the diversity of flora.

The "new" highway (Rte. 1) and the older Bow River Parkway that parallels it run through the park, cutting through a greenbelt that stretches from Yellowstone to the Yukon. The Canadian government must constantly weigh what's best for the park against what's best for its 4.3 million visitors. Banff is the only city in a Canadian park large enough to warrant a mayor. When you drive here, you'll find roads closed in the spring to give the elk space during calving season. Other areas are off-limits because they're prime wolf habitat. Expensive—and successful—wildlife corridors cross under or over Route 1, to provide safe passage; more than 37,000 animals, from voles to bears, have used the bridges and tunnels so far.

Both the Chateau Lake Louise and its sister, the Banff Springs Hotel, serve proper high tea with scones and clotted cream in rooms with floor-to-ceiling windows. No matter what the weather, the view is glorious. Both hotels are perfect home bases for playing outside (from kayaking to skiing), whatever the season. No time here outshines another. Spring is prime time for waterfalls. Summer brings a burst of wildflowers. Early fall, the bears come closer to town to gorge on the buffalo berry bushes that grow nearby. Later in the autumn, it's elk rutting season, when the sun turns the yellow aspen to gold in the late afternoon. In winter, the towns become fairylands with holiday lights and dry, sparkling snowflakes.

◀ *Babel Creek, Consolation Basin, Banff National Park.*
© Muench Photography Inc.

SPECIAL MOMENTS

1 Lake Louise at dawn and dusk. In the morning, the sky doesn't color as it does at sunset, but the quiet is profound, and often the still water reflects the mountain and its famous glacier. I love leaving early for the 3.4km (2.1-mile) hike (each way) to the Lake Agnes teahouse, especially in summer when the teahouse smells of warm baked goods. An hour before sunset is often a lovely—and quiet—time to take out a canoe. Happiness is stopping at the Chateau Lake Louise's deli, choosing your own sandwich fixings, and bringing supper along on the boat.

2 Peyto Lake. This lake was named for Bill Peyto, a colorful explorer who became one of the park's first wardens (similar to a ranger). This was said to be one of his favorite places. The trail from the parking lot at Bow Pass climbs gradually through sub-Alpine evergreens, and in just 10 or 15 minutes you're enjoying the views from an often windy overlook (bring a jacket). Most hikers stop here, but you should continue on for privacy and more spectacular views of the broad glacier that feeds the lake. A wide delta fans out from the glacier—a good lesson in glaciology. The lake, like Lake Louise, is turquoise from the rock-flour particles (fine dust from the glacier) suspended in it. Set off on one of the dirt paths, away from the pavement, for an even finer view.

3 The Columbia Icefields. Sure, it's touristy to go out on the glacier by "Ice Explorer," but the all-terrain, six-wheeled vehicles are part of the fun. Even on a summer day, the winds blowing off the headwall of the Athabasca Glacier (2 hr. north of Banff) can be intensely cold. The glacier is 365m (1,200 ft.) at its thickest. Just beyond the headwall lies the triple continental divide: a third flowing to the Arctic Ocean, a third to the Pacific, and a third to the Atlantic. To really appreciate the subtleties of the glacier—to see the bluish greens that make it so extraordinary—hire a guide for a 3- or 5-hour walking tour.

▶ *Lake Louise, Banff National Park.*
© Jon Arnold/DanitaDelimont.com

4 From Banff to the Columbia Icefields. Awesome. Magnificent. Words do not do justice to this road. There is never enough daylight to take in what this highway has to offer. Although the drive from Banff takes only 2½ hours, I've spent 9 hours or more on the road, getting out to explore Bow Lake, Johnston Canyon, Moraine Lake, or Parker Ridge. I've slowed for caribou crossing the road and bighorn sheep trying to flee the noise of cars. From the icefields, the parkway descends steeply into the Athabasca River drainage. From the parking area for Sunwapta Falls, you can crowd around the chain fence and peer at the turbulent falls, or take the half-hour hike to the equally impressive but less crowded Lower Sunwapta Falls. Athabasca Falls, farther north along the highway, is another must-see. Parks Canada estimates that about 14,000 cars pass through Lake Louise in the summer. Yet, in autumn, I've driven for long stretches without seeing another vehicle.

NAOMI BLACK has contributed to more than eight books on travel and food, including *Dude Ranches of the American West* and *The Ghost Town Storyteller*. Her articles have appeared in *Travel + Leisure* and other magazines. She hikes and kayaks when she can, especially with her husband, John, and children, Katherine and Tommy.

ABOUT THE AUTHOR

YOUR TRIP

General Information: Contact the **Banff/Lake Louise Tourism Bureau** (P.O. Box 1298, Banff; ☎ 403/762-8421; www.banfflakelouise.com). When in town, go to the **Banff Information Centre** at 224 Banff Ave. (☎ 403/762-1550). The **Columbia Icefield Visitors' Center** is open daily April to September 9am to 5pm, October 10am to 5pm (P.O. Box 1140, 100 Gopher St.; ☎ 877/423-7433; www.columbiaicefield.com). **Best Lodging: Fairmont Banff Springs Hotel** offers a day spa and the best tea in town (445 Spray Ave.; ☎ 800/257-7544 or 403/762-2211; www.fairmont.com; US$247–US$665/£131–£352). The **Fairmont Chateau Lake Louise** sits right at lake's edge (111 Lake Louise Dr.; ☎ 800/257-7544 or 403/522-3511; www.fairmont.com; US$221–US$1,162/£117–£616). **Best Lodging Value: Banff Y Mountain Lodge** has cheap dorms and private rooms (102 Spray Ave., P.O. Box 520; ☎ 800/813-4138 or 403/762-3560; www.ymountainlodge.com; US$25/£13.25 and up). The **Lake Louise Hostel & Alpine Center** is owned by Hostelling International and the Alpine Clubs of Canada (203 Village Rd.; ☎ 866/762-4122 or 403/670-7580; www.hostellingintl.ca/alberta; US$20–US$95/£11–£50). **Best Restaurant:** The **Bow Valley Grill** has great breakfast and lunch buffets and equally good a la carte choices for dinner, including delicious local trout (in the Fairmont Banff Springs Hotel; ☎ 403/762-6860; main courses US$20–US$35/£11–£19). **Best Restaurant Value:** Join the local crowd at **Coyotes Deli & Grill** (206 Caribou St., Banff; ☎ 403/762-3963; main courses US$11–US$20/£6–£11).

BERINGIA, ALASKA

A region so remote & severe that few Alaskans ever come here

A person's character is formed by his environment. Being a born New Yorker, my native world consists of tall buildings and busy streets. The rhythms and nuances of vast, lonely places have no natural resonance to my eyes and ears. But we are also formed by our experiences. In summer 2004, I traveled among the islands and communities of the Bering Sea in Northwest Alaska, a region so vast, remote, and severe that few Alaskans even go there. But it was under these restless skies, amid the silence of a place unknown to most of the world, that my ideas of beauty were changed forever.

Twelve thousand years ago, during the last ice age, this was a place scientists now call Beringia, a 1,000-mile grassland steppe that stretched from Siberia to the Alaskan mainland—the "bridge" across which Siberian hunters passed, eventually settling the Americas. When the ice age ended, the rising seas flooded Beringia, making islands of volcanic peaks and turning highlands into coast. What was left was a land completely unlike the Alaska we know from pictures. Up here there are no vast stands of forest carpeting the flanks of picturesque mountains. There are, in fact, no trees at all, only a tableau of rock and tundra, sea and sky. Massive stony peaks slope up from the water, their sides stark and glacier-scoured, yet sometimes painted with thick tundra—a tiny bonsai forest to each square foot. In winter, nights can last 21 hours here, and temperatures dip to –35°F (–37°C). In summer there's enough light to read at midnight, and the tundra blooms with a profusion of wildflowers. Human occupation is sparse. Even Nome, the region's largest city, still feels like a frontier outpost, while the mostly Yu'pik, Cup'ik, Inupiat, and Aleut Native villages that dot the coast from the Arctic Circle to the Aleutians exist in their own reality, a part of America but far removed from the mainstream of American life.

Nothing is easy here, not living and not travel. On the island of Little Diomede, a rocky pyramid jutting from the northernmost reaches of the Bering Sea, a tiny Inupiat village of 160 souls rises right from the seacoast, its ramshackle homes threading up the hillside, connected by stone walkways. Ancient and modern stand side by side: For every snowmobile there's a dog sled waiting for the sea ice to form. For every satellite dish there's a pair of walrus tusks drying in the sun, waiting to be carved into art. Only 70 years ago, people here lived in semi-subterranean homes heated with seal-oil lamps. Today barges bring fuel and electric light, but in summer the men still use butterfly nets to snare birds among the rocks.

The people of Little Diomede have several times considered resettling their whole village on the Alaskan mainland, but each time it has come to a vote, none of the old people have wanted to leave, and the young have refused to vote against them. Such is life here. Though global warming is wreaking havoc with the seasonal cycles that define their traditional lifestyle, tenacity has never been an issue with these people. When you know a place, you know it in your soul.

Musk ox, Nunivak Island, Bering Sea.
© David E Myers/Getty Images

27

SPECIAL MOMENTS

1 **Experiencing Native arts.**
Though most of the villages of the Bering Sea still operate largely on a subsistence hunting and fishing economy, many supplement their income by drawing on their remarkable artistic traditions. On St. Lawrence Island, Savoonga is known for its exceptional walrus ivory carvings, a byproduct of the animals that still make up a good portion of the people's diet. On Nunivak, Native Cup'ik people from the village of Mekoryuk harvest qiviut, the cashmere-like undercoat of the musk ox, from which they produce beautiful and exceptionally warm hats, shawls, and scarves.

In various villages, including Little Diomede and Savoonga, visiting groups are often treated to programs of traditional song and dance which, though presented in abbreviated form, still capture the essence of the region's characteristic performance arts.

2 **Hiking the tundra.** Beringia's tundra ecosystem is characterized by rolling terrain and wet soil, with a layer of permafrost below and a covering of grasses and dwarf shrubs above—essentially a micro-forest of mosses, heath, and lichens that form a spongy ground cover sometimes just a few inches thick, sometimes a few feet. Either type makes for an unusual hiking experience, though you have to be careful in the thick stuff, which can hide ankle-turning holes and boot-soaking puddles.

On Nunivak Island, lucky hikers may spot one of the 500 musk oxen that roam freely around the misty hills. Though native to Alaska, every musk ox in the territory had been hunted and killed by the late 19th century. In the 1930s, 34 of the animals were brought from Greenland to Fairbanks and subsequently released on Nunivak, where they've thrived ever since. On Unga, in the Shumagin Island group (part of the Aleutian chain), hikers can scale the seaside cliffs and walk for miles through knee-deep tundra, then return along a beach dotted with petrified wood—remains of a forest buried by lava 20 million years ago, before the ice age.

3 **Crossing the border to Russia.** Only part of Beringia is in Alaska. The other half lies across the border in Russian Siberia, a place even more remote and forbidding than the Alaskan side, yet just as starkly beautiful. In villages such as Yanrakynnot and Novoye Chaplino, communities of Siberian Yu'pik and Chukchi live a lifestyle nearly identical to that of their American cousins, though their recent history has seen more upheaval. During the Soviet era, nomadic Siberian peoples and residents of small villages were collectivized into modern fox-farming operations and given subsidies by the state, but with the collapse of communism, they've returned to their ancestors' subsistence economy and are largely dependent on whale hunting.

Chaplino is a microcosm of Siberian Native life today. Located only 35 miles from the American town of Gambell on St. Lawrence Island, it's a mix of Soviet-era shacks and bright, new, single-family homes bought and paid for by Chukotka's billionaire governor, Roman Abramovich.

Beringia, Alaska

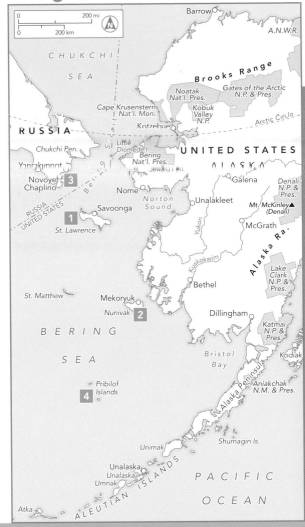

4 **Wildlife-watching in the Pribilofs.** The Pribilof Islands are so remote that populations of woolly mammoth survived here 3,500 years longer than their cousins on the mainland. Each summer, some 700,000 fur seals—the world's largest concentration—arrive here to have their pups and loll around in their seaside rookeries. Simple wooden shelters are set up on cliffs for visitors who wish to observe them.

The Pribilofs are also one of the great bird-watching sites in the world, with some 2.5 million seabirds from 254 species nesting in the seaside cliffs. The majority of the birds breed and nest on the southern island of St. George, while the human population—altogether, some 650 Aleut residents, comprising the largest remaining Aleut population on earth—lives mostly on the northern island, St. Paul. Russian Orthodox churches on both islands testify to the religion's continuing influence on Alaska Native life.

ABOUT THE AUTHOR

MATT HANNAFIN is a New York–born writer, editor, and musician now based in Portland, Oregon. Coauthor of the annual guidebooks *Frommer's Cruises* and *Cruise Vacations For Dummies*, he's also a major contributor to the new *1,000 Places to See in the USA & Canada Before You Die* and has contributed to dozens of other books, magazines, and websites, including *Gourmet* and *Travel Weekly*.

YOUR TRIP

General Information: Visit the website of the **Alaska Division of Tourism** at www.travelalaska.com. **Getting There: Alaska Air** has flights to Anchorage from many U.S. cities (☎ 800/252-7522; www.alaskaair.com). Most travelers to Beringia's remote towns and islands arrange their trip through a packager. All the islands and villages discussed are stops on an extraordinary Bering Sea voyage offered twice each summer by **Cruise West** aboard its flagship, the 114-passenger *Spirit of Oceanus* (☎ 888/851-8133; www.cruisewest.com). Carrying naturalists, biologists, and historians on board, the 13-night expeditions sail a wide, 2,500-mile semicircle between Nome and Anchorage, crossing the Arctic Circle, visiting Native villages and the Soviet city of Provideniya on the Russian side, and hopscotching from island to island down Alaska's western coast, from Little Diomede in the north to Kodiak in the south. Rates for 2007 start at $8,999 per person. For those seeking more independent travel, **Bering Air** offers air-taxi service from Nome to Savoonga, Gambell, the coastal village of Wales, and other regional Native towns (☎ 907/443-5464; www.beringair.com). Travelers can visit a different village every day, using Nome as a hub for accommodations and dining since villages lack tourist facilities. Prices vary depending on flights. For extended birding and seal-watching visits to the Pribilofs, you can book a trip through the Native-owned **St. Paul Island Tours,** which offers 3- to 8-day trips from May through mid-September (☎ 877/424-5637; www.alaskabirding.com). Prices start at $1,406, including guides, accommodations, ground transportation, and round-trip transportation from Anchorage.

◀ *Bull walruses on Round Island, Bering Sea.*
© Fred Hirschmann/Science Faction/Getty Images

BHUTAN

A land of Buddhist monasteries, remote temples & holy peaks

The captivating Kingdom of Bhutan, born in mythology and rooted in the traditions and beliefs of a fast-disappearing Himalayan Buddhist universe, opened its doors warily to the outside world only little more than a quarter-century ago. Those who trickled in soon found a place like no other. Its magnificent mountain landscapes, with holy peaks unclimbed to avoid disturbing the gods, are as pristine as its primeval forests, a naturalist's dream.

Travel can be rough here, where roads are few and precipitous, but at almost every turn there is something to see: traditional half-timbered farmhouses in sheltered valleys, arresting fortress-monasteries on hilltops, rare animals and birds—among them the agile ox-sized takin and migrating black-necked cranes—and groves of blooming trees and earthbound flowers.

Never colonized by Western powers, Bhutan remains deeply independent, the last Tibetan Buddhist monarchy not swallowed up by China or India, two powerful neighbors to the north and south. You go to Bhutan entirely on Bhutanese terms, in limited numbers, and are immersed in an encompassing Buddhism that touches everything.

This is not the Buddhism of sleek meditation cushions, matching yoga wear, and self-centered psychotherapy to be practiced in one's spare time. Bhutanese religion, the Vajrayana form of Mahayana Buddhism (further divided into several schools), is a way of life that permeates every corner of home and public space. People dressed in their *ghos* and *kiras* faithfully circumambulate even the national museum and library buildings because of the sacred objects and holy books inside.

Bhutan's monasteries and temples scattered over the hills and valleys are colorful, sometimes raucous places, suffused with the scent of butter lamps and enlivened by flocks of unruly novices, disputatious monks, and altars piled high with mundane offerings from the rural poor, who come to spin prayer wheels, finger beads, or just get advice on day-to-day problems. Monastic festivals, the *tshechus*, bring together the earthiness of local legend and the sophistication of religious philosophy in exquisitely costumed dance and drama, accompanied by otherworldly music and backdrops that are cherished temple treasures.

The contemporary world is creeping steadily into Bhutan. Television and the Internet are relatively new arrivals. Trying overzealously to cling to a unique culture, Bhutan has fallen afoul of international human rights groups for expelling ethnic Nepalis it considers non-citizens, some of them Hindus, from southern border areas. Most recently the sturdy, egalitarian Bhutanese, accustomed to welcoming adventurous travelers eye-to-eye as guests, are having to come to terms with the country's first luxury spa resorts, where more demanding visitors expect pampering, with a whiff of servitude. This development is still very much a work in progress. Hopefully, it will not spell the end of innocence.

◀ *Novice monks at the Punakha Festival.*
© Vassi Kousaftis/DanitaDelimont.com

SPECIAL MOMENTS

1 Phobjikha. It is a perfect valley designed to lift the soul and live forever in memory. The road through primeval hardwood forest hung with lichens and carpeted in magnolia and rhododendron suddenly opens into a scene of utter peace: a sunny, emerald-green bowl of land abundant in wildlife, watched over by a monastery-temple on a ridge. A few prayer flags flap, but few sounds of modernity to break the spell.

This is Phobjikha, and it is for me the essence of Bhutan.

The temple on the valley rim, and the little hamlet mostly strung along the road that leads to it, are called Gangtey. It is the largest monastery in the country for Nyingmapa Buddhists and, like many places in Bhutan, it is enveloped in legend. A monk there assured me that the paintings of the Buddhist cosmos on the 17th-century walls were, miraculously, "about 2,000 years old."

2 Thimphu's weekend market. The first time I went to Thimphu's weekend market, a sprawling affair near the Wang Chhu, I made a mental inventory of what one wizened old lady from the countryside had to offer on the table in front of her: hand-carved rustic spoons and ladles, yak-tail fly-swatters, greasy-looking medicinal brews, and a human thigh bone for use as a ceremonial horn.

A decade later the market had been updated somewhat to include flashes of red and yellow plastic, but the handiwork of rural Bhutan is still there—beautiful burled-wood bowls, Bhutanese and Tibetan-style jewelry, and woven bags and rugs. Tasty potatoes and red rice spill out of baskets and bags, next to vegetables and fruits from the small farms and orchards across two or three climate zones and many mountain miles.

For a slice of Bhutanese life at large, this bustle of farmers, monks, and herbal practitioners mixing with the urban elite is hard to beat.

3 Royalty-watching. We were hurtling along a road not far from Punakha when a large, white SUV came at us from the opposite direction. As our two vehicles passed with just a ribbon of air between us, the face in the driver's seat of the approaching car was in plain view: It was the king, Jigme Singye Wangchuck.

Monarchy in Bhutan is different. In Thailand, the whirlwind entourage of the king flies past citizens reduced to groveling at the side of the road. In Bhutan, members of the royal family pop up unannounced in daily life. Chalk it up to whatever you will—the small size of the population (fewer than a million people in a country slightly larger than Switzerland), the blessed lack of terrorist threats, the relatively modest scale of royal residences, or the royalty's frequent "meet the people" trips, where speaking out is encouraged.

The king in a neighborhood restaurant? One of four former queens browsing a handicrafts shop? A royal uncle leading a folk dance? The Bhutanese take it all in stride.

4 Bhutanese art. A visit to the National Art School in Thimphu is a

▶ *Taktsang Dzong (Tiger's Nest) in Paro Valley.*
© Keren Su/DanitaDelimont.com

lesson in the creative boundaries of traditional Buddhist culture. Here sit rows of little boys modeling identical Buddha figures from lumps of clay. Or copying mandalas with painstaking care. Or drawing exact replicas of saintly murals.

Perhaps only in Bhutan, or at least until now, art and architecture (hewing to historical national models) are expected to produce literal continuity. Self-expression and artistic liberty are not encouraged. We learn to look to other criteria to distinguish one artist from another: the excellence of execution, the natural talent of the craftsman or craftswoman.

This understanding makes choosing something to take home easier. Those *thangkas*, the hand-woven cloth or embroidered satin, the images and amulets—they are not home decor produced in colors to match walls but artifacts of an art world built around holy symbols crafted as close to perfection as human hands are able. Carry them away with respect.

BARBARA CROSSETTE, the author of *So Close to Heaven: The Vanishing Buddhist Kingdoms of the Himalayas*, was a *New York Times* correspondent in South Asia and earlier Southeast Asia, and continues to write about the region. Among her books, *The Great Hill Stations of Asia* is a ramble through colonial-era mountain resorts.

ABOUT THE AUTHOR

YOUR TRIP

General Information: See Bhutan's official website, www.tourism.gov.bt, for information about travel and entry requirements. Travelers must pay an all-inclusive minimum daily rate of $165 to $290 (£87–£153) depending on the season. Visas are required and applications must be approved before tours or transportation can be booked. Bhutan does not have an embassy or consulate in the U.S. **Getting There:** All trips must be arranged by authorized travel agents. **Geographic Expeditions,** in San Francisco, offers tours for special interests such as nature hikes, Buddhist meditation, and temple festivals (☎ 800/777-8183 or 415/922-0448; www.geoex.com). **Best Lodging:** The Bhutanese-built **Zhiwa Ling** in Paro has a spa, temple and meditation house, restaurant, and popular bar (Satsam Chorten, Paro; ☎ 975/8-271277; www.zhiwaling.com; $150/£80). **Best Lodging Value:** The **Dewachen Hotel** is a bargain at about $42 (£22) single, $55 (£29) double. More like a guesthouse, the Dewachen rooms have private bathrooms, traditional stoves, and nightly hot-water bottles (P.O. Box 236, Thimphu; ☎ 975/2-321873; www.dewachenhotel.com). **Best Restaurant:** In restaurants at Paro's most expensive luxury hotels, cuisine by foreign chefs can run as high as $75 (£40) a person for dinner. Good Bhutanese food closer to $10 (£5.30) or under is found at **Sonam Trophel** on Paro town's main thoroughfare (☎ 975/8-271287), and the **Bhutan Kitchen** on Chang Lam in Thimphu (☎ 975/2-331919). **When to Go:** Spring, when forested slopes come alive with blooming rhododendrons, azaleas, and wildflowers, and early fall. Summer rains can lead to rockslides and washouts; snow closes some passes in winter.

BIG BEND NATIONAL PARK, TEXAS

A lesser-known park as grand as Yellowstone or Yosemite

Just after sunrise, I'm sitting on a log near my tent, munching on a granola bar. A twig snaps. I realize I am not alone. A trio of tiny deer is watching me intently, apparently interested in my breakfast. I'm not about to share.

I'd backpacked to my campsite on the South Rim of the Chisos Mountains in Texas' Big Bend National Park the day before, and enjoyed a spectacular sunset before cocooning in my sleeping bag. The new day brought with it an equally sublime sunrise, and the three visitors to my campsite.

With a smile, I rise to my feet, spooking the deer away, and look at the panorama before me. The view reminds me why I love this arid patch of bleakly beautiful terrain, a diverse desert unexpectedly abundant with life. Big Bend is a lesser-known, lesser-visited gem of the national park system, home to red-rock panoramas as grand as the natural granite masterworks in California's Yosemite and a vast backcountry as rugged and wild as that of Yellowstone.

From my point of view on the South Rim (about 7,300 ft. above sea level), the forested mountains stand in stark contrast to the parched lowlands. I look out over the sharp slope down to the desert, the Rio Grande twinkling in the distance, and Mexico on the other side. Emory Peak, the park's tallest mountain, knifes high into the sky to the north, and the Sierra del Carmen Range dominates the eastern horizon. To the west, Santa Elena Canyon, carved over eons by the Rio Grande—or, as it's known south of the border, Rio Bravo—punctuates the landscape in the opposite direction: down into the earth.

Deep in West Texas, Big Bend has been dubbed "the last American frontier," and it's an apt nickname. Humans might be few and far between, but the region's wildlife population is one of the most diverse on the planet. More bird and bat species soar the skies here than in any other national park.

I get back to my car, doff my pack, and trade my hiking boots for tennis shoes. Then I drive out of the park, through Marathon and Alpine to Marfa. An artsy vibe is the strand that connects these three small desert towns.

The dinky town of Marathon is due north of the park, primarily known as the home of the landmark Gage Hotel (which I heartily recommend, if you can afford it). Alpine, known as "The Hub of the Big Bend," is the region's economic and cultural capital. Marfa is the unlikely recipient of national buzz for its avant-garde and minimalist art scene, centered on the intriguing Chinati Foundation.

Beyond the galleries and hiking trails, the other prime regional attraction is the Rio Grande itself, not only a waterway but an international border. Security reforms quashed the traditional, if unofficial, border crossings by park visitors in 2002, and the adjacent countries have in many ways grown more culturally isolated in recent years. But the stretch of the Rio Grande/Rio Bravo that takes a big bend along the southern boundary of the park—and the United States—is an ideal place to get a firsthand perspective on the border as not just an imaginary boundary but a real place.

Century plant and Chisos Mountains.
© David Muench/Corbis

35

SPECIAL MOMENTS

1 **Hike the Chisos Mountains.** Whether it's a short day hike or a multibackpacking expedition, Big Bend National Park is home to some of the best trails in the Southwest, and many of them are in the high country of the Chisos Mountains. For a short, relatively undemanding hike, I recommend the Chisos Basin Loop Trail (1.6 miles, easy), which circumnavigates the Basin and offers nice views of 7,825-foot Emory Peak and other mountains. Those with more time or hiking experience should try the Lost Mine Trail (4.8 miles round-trip, moderately difficult). This trail ascends through a forested area to overlooks perfect for gazing out over sublime mountain valleys and the sun-scorched desert below, all the way into Mexico. The trail was constructed in the early 1940s by the Civilian Conservation Corps, and evidence of their rock work can still be seen.

Keep in mind that the hottest months are May and June; the heat of July and August is usually tempered by afternoon thunderstorms. September is among the slowest times in the park, and it can be very nice then, though hot. October is a great time, still quiet and a bit cooler.

2 **Run the Rio Grande.** The 118-mile stretch of the Rio Grande (aka Rio Bravo) that makes the park's southern boundary is a great destination for raft and float trips, as is the adjacent, federally designated Wild and Scenic River that's downstream from Big Bend. While the river is relatively slow, it does have its share of white water during peak runoff season. More importantly, however, it's nice and cool, the perfect antidote to the desert heat. Numerous outfitters in the area offer raft and canoe rentals as well as guided trips ranging in length from a few hours to several days.

3 **Explore the Castolon Historic District and hot springs.** Within the boundaries of Big Bend National Park are a number of historic man-made attractions that tell an intriguing story of cultural integration and change. In the southwest quarter of the park, the Castolon Historic District includes the stabilized ruins of structures built in the early 1900s by Mexican farmers, Anglo pioneers, and U.S. Army soldiers. The oldest is the adobe Alvino House, built in 1901. On the Rio Grande west of Rio Grande Village are the remains of Langford Hot Springs, a resort that opened in the 1920s. Today the springs still fill riverside pools with soothing hot water (105°F/41°C), just the spot to soak away the fatigue from hiking the park's trails.

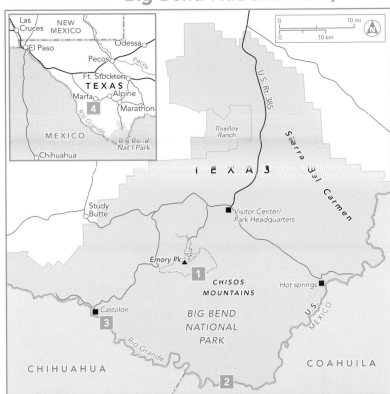

4 **Visit Marfa.** Of all of the desert towns in the Big Bend area, Marfa is the one that keeps me coming back. A 2-hour drive from the park's west entrance, this town of roughly 2,000 residents is a study in contrasts. Because Marfa is 67 miles north of the U.S.-Mexico border, the Border Patrol is the primary employer. And as the longtime home of late renegade avant-garde artist Donald Judd, Marfa is well known in contemporary arts circles coast to coast for the Chinati Foundation, a multivenue arts installation that provokes thought and defies expectations. Thirdly, being the county seat, Marfa is also home to the stunning Presidio County Courthouse, built in 1885 and brilliantly restored in 2001. After sunset, drive 9 miles east on U.S. 90 to the roadside viewing platform and scan the dark horizon for the inexplicable globs of luminance known as the Marfa Mystery Lights.

A Denver-based freelance writer, **ERIC PETERSON** has written numerous Frommer's guidebooks covering the American West, and *Ramble: A Field Guide to the U.S.A.* (www.speckpress.com). He's an avid camper and hiker, a lifelong Broncos fan, and a rock star (at least in the eyes of his nephew Mitch).

ABOUT THE AUTHOR

YOUR TRIP

General Information: Big Bend National Park (P.O. Box 129, Big Bend National Park; ☎ 432/477-2251; www.nps.gov/bibe); **Big Bend Area Travel Association** (☎ 877/244-2363; www.visitbigbend.com); **Marfa Chamber of Commerce** (P.O. Box 635, Marfa; ☎ 432/729-4942; www.marfacc.com). **Getting There: Midland International Airport** (☎ 432/560-2200; www.flymaf.com), 235 miles north; **El Paso International Airport** (☎ 915/780-4749; www.elpasointernationalairport.com), 325 miles west. **Best Lodging:** The historic **Gage Hotel** exudes peace, quiet, and desert chic (102 W. Hwy. 90, Marathon; ☎ 800/884-4243 or 432/386-4205; www.gagehotel.com; $76–$300). The **Chisos Mountains Lodge** is the only lodging within park boundaries (☎ 432/477-2291; www.chisosmountainslodge.com; $89–$105). **Best Lodging Value:** The **Chisos Mountain Mining Company Motel** offers basic lodging just outside the park's west entrance (P.O. Box 228, Terlingua; ☎ 432/371-2254; www.cmcm.cc; $50–$136). **Best Restaurant: Ocotillo,** at Lajitas, offers gourmet game at a luxury resort (HC 70, Box 400, Lajitas; ☎ 432/424-5000; www.lajitas.com; dinner specials $26–$42). **Best Budget Dining: Starlight Theatre,** in the Terlingua Ghost Town, is a funky converted theater just west of the park (P.O. Box 287, 2 Ivey Lane, Terlingua; ☎ 432/371-2326; www.starlighttheatre.com; dinners $9.95–$33). **Best Times:** Oct–Apr. Lodging and campgrounds are full around college spring break (second and third weeks in Mar), Easter and Thanksgiving weekends, and the week between Christmas and New Year's.

◀ *Paddling through Santa Elena Canyon.*
© SuperStock Inc./SuperStock

BIG ISLAND OF HAWAII

Waterfalls, fiery eruptions & black-sand beaches

God may have made the earth, but he *sculpted* the Big Island of Hawaii, the largest and youngest island in the Hawaiian chain. Molten red magma, spewing from an underwater volcano, took eons to build up from the ocean floor. Then violent blasts of wind, pounding rain, and monstrous waves pummeled, carved, and caressed the land into towering mountains crowned with snow. Verdant rainforests spread through the valleys, shrouded in mist. Beaches encircled the coast, with multicolored sand—white, gold, black, gray, and even green.

Of all the beautiful, breathtaking, awe-inspiring places I've seen on this planet, none, I think, can compare to the Big Island in drama and in what the Hawaiian call *mana* (spirituality). Where else can you experience a raging volcanic eruption of liquid fire, and, just a few miles away, discover snow-covered mountains so serene that the world's top observatories are located here? No other Hawaiian island can put you face to face with Pele, the volcano goddess, as she stirs up her caldron of lava and creates the 'āina (land). If you are looking for a mystical experience, come here to contemplate the cosmos from the top of the world's tallest mountain (yes, higher than Everest, a mere 29,028 ft. when measured from its base; Mauna Kea is an astonishing 33,476 ft. from the Pacific Ocean floor).

No trip to the Big Island is complete without exploring the Hawaii Volcanoes National Park, where the Kilauea volcano has been erupting continuously since 1983, with no sign of abating. Not only will the park rangers let you get as close as safely possible (so close that you can actually feel the heat from the lava), but you can return at night and watch the ribbon of lava slowly make its way down the mountain and into the ocean.

Because the entire Kona coast sits in the lee of two nearly 14,000-foot mountains, the waters on this side are, as we say in Hawaii, *mālie* (calm) 350 days a year—perfect for snorkeling, scuba diving, kayaking, or testing your luck in one of the world's top destinations for big-game fishing.

The Big Island is not only the largest island in the Hawaiian chain (4,038 sq. miles—about the size of Connecticut), and the youngest (800,000 years), but also the least populated (with 30 people per square mile). On the warm, sunny side of the island is Kona, a playground for visitors. On the other side is rain-soaked Hilo, the island's economic and political base, producing tropical orchids, heart-shaped anthuriums, heavenly scented ginger, and vividly hued rainbows.

The Big Island, with its stark lava fields and black-sand beaches, is not for everyone. But if you're into watersports, this is paradise. Hikers, bikers, and horseback riders can head up or down a volcano, into remote valleys, or through rainforests without seeing another soul. You can downhill ski and surf the waves in a single day. Bird-watchers are rewarded with rare sightings. Golfers can find nirvana on a wide range of courses. The coast is a kayaker's dream of caves and secluded coves. Even if your idea of heaven is doing nothing, the Big Island is the place to go.

◀ *Pu'u O'o vent in Volcanoes National Park.*
© G. Brad Lewis/Getty Images

SPECIAL MOMENTS

1 Hawaii Volcanoes National Park. I feel sorry for visitors who spend a half-hour driving through this magnificent 209,695-acre park and think they have "seen it." A 2½-hour drive from Kona or an hour from Hilo, the Volcanoes Park takes at least 2 days to explore, and that's just during the day. At night, don't miss the opportunity to see the red rivers of fire from the eruption snake down the mountain into the steaming Pacific. Yellowstone and Yosemite are spectacular, but, in my opinion, are ho-hum compared to this one. The park has the only tropical rainforest in the U.S. national park system—and it's the only park that's home to an active volcano.

2 Mauna Kea. The ancient Hawaiians thought the gods lived at the top of this 13,800-foot volcano, the world's largest mountain when measured from its base on the ocean floor. A 2-hour drive from the town of Hilo to the top (3 hr. from Kona) promises a view of the sunset that will remain with you long after your tan has faded. Bundle up in warm clothes, though. In winter you can expect several feet of snow at the top and daylight temperatures that max out at 40°F (15°C). After dark, temperatures can plunge to 25°F (–4°C), and lower. Summer days see temperatures 32° to 60°F (0°–15°C), but after dark, they can drop below freezing. On clear nights, when the last trace of color has drained from the sky, the stars are so brilliant, you feel that you can touch them. Standing alone in this immensity is a humbling but inspiring experience.

3 Kealakekua Bay. If you haven't experienced Hawaii's underwater world, you haven't seen Hawaii. My favorite snorkeling area, on an island full of the world's best snorkeling spots, lies 45 minutes south of Kona, at Kealakekua Bay. The water in this marine preserve (where, by law, no fish can be taken), is warm and calm. Oddly enough, the fish seem to know they're protected and have no qualms about swimming right up to your face mask (so close, in fact, that sometimes you have to "back pedal" to get a photo). Occasionally a Pacific green sea turtle will lumber through, and if you time your trip right (generally midmorning), you'll see the spinner dolphins charging through the bay. Just floating on your back and staring up at the 1,000-foot cliffs surrounding the bay sends even the most-stressed out,

Snorkeling off the Kona coast.
© A Witte/C Mahaney/Getty Images

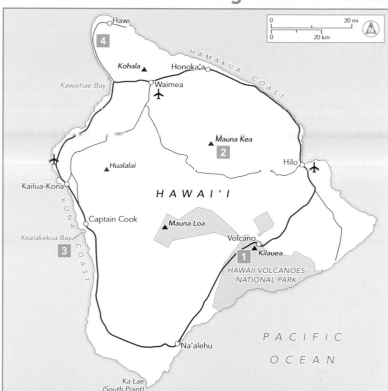

jet-lagged traveler into a state of serenity.

4 **Mo'okini Heiau.** Those who come to the Big Island with a humble heart and a keen desire to step into the spiritual realm of old Hawaii will want to head to the very northern end of the island and visit the birthplace of the king who united the Hawaiian islands. Close by sits an ancient temple, Mo'okini Heiau, once a site of human sacrifice. The Kahuna Nui (guardian priest), named Leimomi Mo'okini Lum, still personally leads noncommercial, private tours of the 150-year-old *heiau*. According to Hawaiian chants, the temple was built about A.D. 480 in just 1 night with stones passed by hand from one man to the next from a valley 14 miles away. A few hours with this incredible woman is an experience that promises to be a highlight of your trip or what we in Hawaii call a "chicken-skin" (goose bumps) experience.

JEANETTE FOSTER loves the Big Island so much, she has made it home. She is the author of more than 40 books for Frommer's including *Frommer's Hawaii, Frommer's Maui, Frommer's Kauai, Frommer's Hawaii with Kids, Frommer's Portable Big Island,* and *Frommer's Honolulu, Waikiki & Oahu.*

ABOUT THE AUTHOR

YOUR TRIP

General Information: Contact the **Big Island Visitors Bureau** (250 Keawe St., Hilo; ☎ 808/961-5797; **www.bigisland.org**). Info on **Hawaii Volcanoes National Park** is at www.nps.gov/havo or call ☎ 808/985-6000. For Mauna Kea, contact the **Onizuka Visitor Center** (☎ 808/961-2180; **www.ifa.hawaii.edu/info/vis**). My pick for exploring Kealakekua Bay is **Fairwind Snorkeling and Diving Adventures** (78-7130 Kaleiopapa St., Kailua-Kona; ☎ 800/677-9461; www.fair-wind.com). To walk the scared grounds of the Mo'okini Luakini Heiau, contact the **Mo'okini Preservation Foundation** on Oahu (near Upolu Point Airport; ☎ 808/373-8000). **Best Lodging:** The **Four Seasons Resort Hualalai** sits in the lap of luxury with oceanview villas nestled between the sea and the greens of an exclusive golf course (72-100 Ka'upulehu Dr., Ka'upulehu-Kona; ☎ 888/340-5662 or 808/325-8000; www.fourseasons.com/hualalai; $625–$925 double). **Best Lodging Value: Horizon Guest House** is a small B&B (with an uninterrupted 25-mile coastline view) with luxury accommodations, infinity pool, and hot tub (P.O. Box 268, Honaunau; ☎ 888/328-8301 or 808/328-2540; www.horizonguesthouse.com; $250 double). **Best Restaurant: Kenichi Pacific** serves Pacific Rim cuisine (Keauhou Shopping Center, Keauhou; ☎ 808/322-6400; main courses $17–$32). **Best Restaurant Value: Jackie Rey's Ohana Grill** is a neighborhood restaurant-bar with an eclectic menu, from hamburgers to gourmet fish (75-5995 Kuakini Hwy., Kailua-Kona; ☎ 808/327-0209; main courses $11–$32).

BIG SUR, CALIFORNIA

A world of bluffs & beaches, giant redwoods & miles of trails

As much as I loathe superlatives, there's just no getting around the fact that the Big Sur region of California is one of the most breathtakingly beautiful places on earth. Big Sur is more than a scenic coastal drive along plunging cliffs or a peaceful repose in a mist-shrouded forest. It's a stretch of wilderness so overwhelmingly beautiful—especially when the coastal fog glows in the moonlight—that it enchants everyone who visits.

Although there is an actual Big Sur Village 25 miles south of Carmel, "Big Sur" refers to the entire 90-mile stretch of coastline between Carmel and San Simeon, blessed on one side by the majestic Santa Lucia Range and on the other by the rocky, rugged Pacific coastline. Big Sur's tranquillity and natural beauty are ideal for hiking, picnicking, camping, and beachcombing, but it's your soul that will most appreciate this vacation. In fact, Big Sur has been a source of inspiration for philosophers, artists, and alternative thinkers since the '60s. Visiting luminaries such as Aldous Huxley, Joseph Campbell, and Jack Kerouac all frequented the healing natural hot springs of Big Sur's renowned Esalen Institute, a spiritualistic spa retreat that focuses on alternative and experiential education.

Big Sur is also home to a particular breed of nature lover who prefers their lifestyle on the rustic side. When the 1998 El Niño storms caused landslides and major road damage, cutting the area off from civilization for months, some residents fled, vowing never to return, while the remaining locals rejoiced in the temporary solitude. Such is the price paid for living amid the California wilderness where nary a Starbucks or a McDonald's will ever be allowed to spoil the scenery. One major drawback to the region's inaccessibility and anti-growth attitude is the dearth of lodging, particularly in the summer months when even the hundreds of drive-in campsites are often fully booked. Ergo, it's wise to make a reservation as far in advance as possible.

A popular lodging option is to stay in the nearby towns of Carmel or Monterey, which have a much larger selection of lodgings (and Starbucks). From Carmel it's a mere 3 miles along Highway 1 to the 1,276-acre Point Lobos State Reserve, considered the crown jewel of the state park system. Numerous hiking trails follow the shoreline and lead to hidden coves where you can spot sea otters resting in the kelp beds and—between December and May—look for migrating California gray whales offshore.

Cruising south from Point Lobos along Highway 1, you'll encounter some of Big Sur's most popular photo opportunities, such as Bixby Bridge and the Point Sur Lighthouse. More adventurous types will don their daypacks and binoculars and explore the dozens of coastal trails and crescent-shaped bays where sea lions, harbor seals, sea otters, and thousands of seabirds abound. And the truly hardy haul their heavy backpacks up the steep mountain slopes in search of the idyllic remote campsite overlooking miles of rugged coastline and deep blue sea. Me, I prefer to nourish my soul poolside with a spicy Bloody Mary at the ultra-luxurious Post Ranch Inn resort. That's why Big Sur is a dream vacation—there's something here for everyone.

◀ *Garrapata State Park Overlook, Big Sur.*
© Muench Photography Inc.

SPECIAL MOMENTS

1   **Pfeiffer Big Sur State Park.**
Big Sur has nine state parks situated along Highway 1, all of which have numerous trails, campsites, and spectacular scenery. The most popular is Pfeiffer Big Sur State Park, which offers cottage-style cabins; a family-friendly restaurant; 218 secluded campsites amid hundreds of acres of redwoods, conifers, oaks, and meadows; as well as hiking trails with panoramic views of the sea, the Big Sur River, picturesque waterfalls, and beautiful Pfeiffer Beach with its pounding surf and pristine gold-sand beach. The beach, with its wide expanse of golden sand, is open for day-use only. There's no fee, and it's the only beach accessible by car (but not motor homes). At the southern end of Big Sur is less-crowded **Julia Pfeiffer Burns State Park** (☎ 831/ 667-2315), where the highlight is the quarter-mile Waterfall Trail that leads to the 80-foot-high McWay Waterfall, one of the few falls in California that plunges directly into the sea. A trail from the parking lot at McWay Canyon leads under a highway to a bluff overlooking the falls, dropping directly into the ocean. There are miles of other trails to explore here, too. Scuba divers can apply for permits to explore the 1,680-acre underwater reserve.

2   **Bixby Bridge.** About 13 miles south of Carmel on Highway 1, you'll come to the beautiful Bixby Bridge (aka the Rainbow Bridge). Poised nearly 270 feet above Bixby Creek Canyon and 740 feet long, it's one of the world's highest single-span concrete bridges and Big Sur's most popular photo op. You can park at either end, and then walk across while admiring the canyon and ocean views from observation

▶ *The infinity pool at Post Ranch Inn.*
© Catherine Karnow/Corbis

alcoves at intervals along the bridge. For the best shooting angle, however, walk or drive a few hundred yards up the dirt Old Coast Road at the north end of the bridge.

3   **Point Sur Lighthouse.**
Towering 361 feet above the surf on a volcanic-rock promontory just south of Bixby Bridge (about 13 miles south of Carmel) is the majestic Point Sur Lighthouse, another favorite photo opportunity among tourists. The only 19th-century lighthouse open to the public in

California, it was built in 1889 when only a horse trail provided access to this part of the region. Tours, which take 2 to 3 hours and involve a steep half-mile hike each way, are scheduled on weekends year-round and Wednesday and Thursday during the summer. Moonlight tours are offered as well. About 3 miles south of the lighthouse is Andrew Molera State Park, the largest state park on the Big Sur coast. Miles of trails meander through meadows and along beaches and bluffs. I prefer it because it's much less

Big Sur, California

crowded than Pfeiffer Big Sur, and has a 2½-mile beach, sheltered from the wind by a bluff, with excellent tide pooling

4 **Post Ranch Inn.** This is one of my very favorite places to stay on the planet. Yes, it's absurdly expensive, but it's that what-the-heck, once-in-a-lifetime thing you just gotta do. Perched on 98 acres of Big Sur cliffs 1,200 feet above the Pacific, this über-romantic resort opened in 1992 and was instantly declared one of the world's finest retreats. A masterpiece of environmentally conscious design, the wood-and-glass guest cottages are built around existing trees, and some are so close to the edge of the earth that you get the impression that you've joined the clouds (imagine that from your private spa tub). Also on the premises are the best Jacuzzi I've ever encountered and an award-winning restaurant with views that will slay you.

ABOUT THE AUTHOR

MATTHEW RICHARD POOLE, a native Californian, has authored more than two dozen travel guides, including numerous Frommer's titles. He has worked as an English tutor in Prague, ski instructor in the Swiss Alps, and scuba instructor in Thailand and Maui. He currently lives in San Francisco but spends most of his time on the road.

YOUR TRIP

General Information: Contact the **Big Sur Chamber of Commerce** (P.O. Box 87, Big Sur; ☎ 831/667-2100; www.bigsurcalifornia.org) or **California State Parks** (☎ 800/777-0369; www.parks.ca.gov). **Getting There:** The entrance to Big Sur is about 30 miles south of Monterey, or 123 miles south of San Francisco, on Highway 1, which runs along the entire length of the coastline. Most of Big Sur is parkland, without major towns for reference points. **Best Lodging:** The **Post Ranch Inn** (Hwy. 1, P.O. Box 219, Big Sur; ☎ 800/527-2200, www.postranchinn.com, $550–$1,385). **Best Lodging Value:** **Treebones Resort** is a mini-resort offering yurts—sort of a cross between a tent and a cabin—perched on a secluded bluff overlooking the ocean (71895 Hwy. 1, Big Sur; ☎ 877/424-4787; www.treebonesresort.com; $135–$189). **Camping:** One of the most glorious settings is **Pfeiffer Big Sur State Park,** with 218 secluded sites amid hundreds of acres of redwoods. Call ☎ 800/444-7275 for reservations or log on to www.reserveamerica.com (Hwy. 1, 26 miles south of Carmel; ☎ 831/667-2315). **Best Restaurant:** It's certainly not the overpriced food that makes **Nepenthe** the best restaurant in Big Sur; it's the incredible view from the outdoor terrace (Hwy. 1, Big Sur; ☎ 831/667-2345; www.nepenthebigsur.com; dinner $13–$34). **Best Restaurant Value:** The **Big Sur Center Deli** sells fresh baked goods, salads, wine, sandwiches, fettuccine, calzones, enchiladas, and barbecue chicken—all made on the premises (27 miles south of Carmel, next to the Big Sur Post Office; ☎ 831/667-2225). **When to Go:** Spring or fall, when the weather is pleasant and the crowds are thin.

BORA BORA & MOOREA

Two of the world's most breathtaking tropical islands

The late James A. Michener and I never did agree on whether Bora Bora or Moorea is the world's most beautiful island.

Both are in French Polynesia, by mutual consent this planet's foremost collection of gorgeous tropical isles. I've sunned on white-sand beaches, snorkeled in clear, blue lagoons, and climbed into rugged green mountains on many islands, but only in French Polynesia have I seen these features in such dramatic combinations. Here the beach-fringed mountains literally leap from colorful lagoons enclosed by magnificent coral reefs. And these lagoons aren't shallow reef shelves more suited to wading than swimming. They are deep enough to accommodate cruise ships and oceangoing yachts, and they are so well stocked with tropical sea life that they draw snorkelers and divers from around the globe.

In *Return to Paradise*, his 1951 sequel to *Tales of the South Pacific*, Michener turned to Bora Bora, star of the Leeward Islands, northwest of Tahiti. In *Frommer's South Pacific*, I opted for Moorea, Tahiti's otherworldly sister. But it was a close call.

There wasn't much more on Bora Bora when I first arrived in 1977 than when Michener served there during World War II. My girlfriend and I pitched a pup tent beside the fabulous, lagoon-lapped beach flanking Point Matira, a flat, finger-like peninsula forming the island's southern extremity. Coconut palms primarily populated Matira back then, allowing us to cavort in total privacy on the moonlit beach.

Much has changed since then. Point Matira is now the heart of Bora Bora's throbbing tourism industry, which boasts a dozen or so super-luxurious resorts luring uninhibited honeymooners to cavort in romantic, thatch-roof bungalows standing on stilts over the sparkling lagoon. Some old-timers think tourism has turned the island into a Disneyland South Seas, but I always meet first-time visitors who are as blown away by Bora Bora as I was.

My heart still belongs to Moorea, however. I will never forget awakening on my first morning on Tahiti and espying Moorea across the Sea of the Moon, resting in the morning sun like some primordial dinosaur. I could barely wait to take the 30-minute ferry ride from Papeete, Tahiti's bustling capital city, which already was being choked by traffic.

I still have difficulty keeping my eyes on the road around Moorea, so fantastically beautiful are its jagged mountains and Cook's and Opunohu bays cutting deep into the crater of an extinct volcano. Mount Mouaroa, Moorea's oft-photographed "Shark's Tooth," dominates the thumbs and spires atop the crater's rim. And Temae Public Beach, which has all of Tahiti as the backdrop to Moorea's most colorful lagoon, is among French Polynesia's best places to swim and snorkel.

Moorea may be a bedroom community for Papeete nowadays, but it has maintained its Polynesian charm to a remarkable degree. Unhurried by tourists, its friendly residents still have time to stop and chat with inquisitive visitors, which to my mind helps turn any vacation into a dream.

◄ *A silhouette of Bora Bora from nearby Tahaa Island.*
© Jean-Pierre Pieuchot/ Getty Images

SPECIAL MOMENTS

1 Lagoon excursions. No visit to Bora Bora or Moorea is complete without a day spent swimming, snorkeling, and feeding the sharks—actually your guide hand feeds a school of reef sharks while you watch from a reasonably safe distance—and having a beachside picnic on a small, palm-studded islet atop the outer reef. You may even get to pet a stingray, although after one of these usually docile creatures caused the demise of Steve "Crocodile Hunter" Irwin, you may want to shuffle your feet when you enter the water to alert them you're around. Hotels offer all-day excursions to both islands, although I prefer Bora Bora's more picturesque lagoon. It was here that shark feeding began. Some conservationists criticize this activity, so study the issues and do what works for you. My longtime favorite outfitter is **Nono Teremoana Tours** (☎ 689/67-71-38), which locals call Nono's Tours. You spend the day going around the lagoon in a speedy outrigger canoe, stopping for a swim.

2 Dolphin- and whale-watching. The Bora Bora lagoon is famous for its resident sharks and big manta rays, but Moorea's is also populated by schools of acrobatic spinner dolphins. Pilot whales swim past all year, and giant humpback whales frolic offshore during their mating season from July to October. You can see dolphins anytime at the Moorea Dolphin Center, at the InterContinental Resort and at Spa Moorea, but I prefer to go visit them in their own habitat with Dr. Michael Poole, an American marine biologist who has lived on Moorea for many years and who helped turn French Polynesia's waters into a whale sanctuary.

3 Safari expeditions. Bora Bora and Moorea both have "safari expeditions"—guided tours in four-wheel-drive vehicles into their mountainous interiors—but I find those on Moorea to be both more informative and more scenically spectacular. I always learn something new at places such as a vanilla plantation in cliff-bounded Opunohu Valley, and I gasp at the spellbinding vista from Le Belvédère, high up on the crater wall, overlooking Cook's and Opunohu bays. To my eyes, the view of these two fingerlike bays flanking the black basaltic buttresses of Mount Rotui is the most awesome vista in the South Seas. Every hotel desk will book you on one of these adventures. **Albert Tours** (☎ 689/56-13-53) and **Moorea Explorer** (☎ 689/56-2-86) both have them. So does **Inner Island Safari Tours** (☎ 689/56-20-09). The best trips end with a drive around Moorea's south coast and a hike up to Atiraa Waterfall for a refreshing swim.

4 Tiki Theatre Village. Not only do I love these islands, I greatly admire the Polynesians who live on them. They are descended from people who sailed across the Pacific Ocean when Europeans

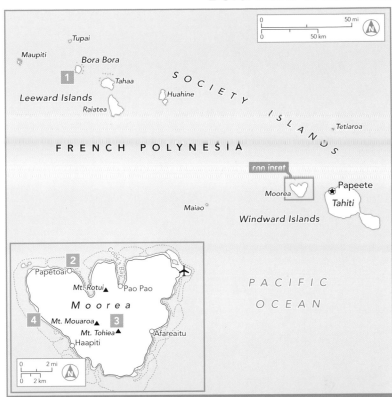

were still frightened to leave the sight of land. Their unique culture so fascinated the 18th-century European explorers who "discovered" the islands that Tahitians became known as living examples of Jean-Jacques Rousseau's theoretical Noble Savage. So I tear myself away from the beach and lagoon to visit Moorea's Tiki Theatre Village, a lovingly reconstructed Polynesian village where the staff demonstrates traditional tattooing, tapa-cloth making, painting, wood- and stone carving, cooking, and music making with nose flutes and drums. There's a "royal house" floating out in the lagoon, where you can learn about the modern art of growing black pearls. Getting married? The Village will arrange for a traditional beachside wedding. The bride is prepared with flowery *monoi* oil like a Tahitian princess, and the groom is tattooed (with wash-off ink). The authentic dance shows and feasts make nights here both entertaining and educational.

BILL GOODWIN was an award-winning political writer and Senate staffer before sailing to Tahiti in 1977 and staying in French Polynesia as long as the gendarmes would allow. His guides include *Frommer's South Pacific* and *Frommer's Tahiti & French Polynesia*. Check him out at www.billgoodwin.com.

ABOUT THE AUTHOR

YOUR TRIP

General Information: Contact **Tahiti Tourisme** (☎ 877/GO-TAHITI; www.tahiti-tourisme.com). **Dr. Michael Poole** is at **www.drmichaelpoole.com**, and **Tiki Theatre Village** is at www.tikivillage.pf. **Getting There: Air Tahiti Nui** has the most flights to and from Papeete (☎ 877/824-4846; www.airtahitinui.com); **Air Tahiti** flies domestic (☎ 689/86-42-42; www.airtahiti.pf). **Best Lodging:** Bora Bora has several over-the-top resorts, but the most charming is the venerable **Hotel Bora Bora** (Pointe Raititi, B.P. 1, Nunue; ☎ 800/421-1490; www.amanresorts.com; $675–$1,000/£358–£530). All around best on Moorea is the **InterContinental Resort** (Papetoai; ☎ 800/327-0200; www.interconti.com; $360–$807/£191–£428). **Best Lodging Value:** On Bora Bora, **Hotel Maitai Polynesia** charges least for an over-water bungalow (☎ 689/60-30-00; www.hotelmaitai.com; $242–$533/£128–£282). Moorea's **Club Bali Hai** has a phenomenal view from the over-water units (Maharepa; ☎ 689/56-13-68; www.clubbalihai.com; $185–$245/£98–£130). **Best Restaurants:** On Bora Bora, save a night for French fare at romantic **La Villa Mahana** (Povai Bay; ☎ 689/67-50-63; $32–$36/£17–£19) and another for barbecued fish at **Bloody Mary's** (Povai Bay; ☎ 689/67-72-86; $27–$32/£14–£17). On Moorea, opt for light French fare at **Le Mayflower** (Haapiti; ☎ 689/65-53-59; $17–$27/£9–£14). **Best Dining:** If you don't mind dining in a parking lot, *roulottes* are your best inexpensive bet. Check out **Roulotte Matira** near Bora Bora's southern end ($10–$15/£5.30–£8). **Roulotte Jules & Claudine** parks at the municipal market in Pao Pao village on Moorea (☎ 689/56-25-31; $8–$15/£4–£8).

◀ *Moorea.*
© Bill Ross/Corbis

BRYCE CANYON NATIONAL PARK, UTAH

Fantastic shapes & colors sculpted by an artist's hand

I've visited virtually all the major national parks and have something good to say about all of them. But my favorite—the one I keep returning to—is Bryce. I love Bryce in part because all its beauty is crowded into a relatively small, manageable amphitheater that, when time is pressing, I can easily explore in a day. I also love Bryce because it's a world of weird, fantastic shapes and colors that takes me out of my everyday life and transports me into a world of dreams. I know of no place where the forces of nature have come together with more dramatic results. Over millions of years, the power of erosion and weathering have sculpted spectacular rock formations—delicate limestone sculptures colored with an iron-rich palette of reds, oranges, pinks, and browns. If you want to escape the ordinary, Bryce is the place to go.

Few people come all the way to southern Utah to see one park. If you asked me to conjure up a dream vacation for a week or longer, I'd say, drive from Vegas or Phoenix to the South Rim of the Grand Canyon. Then drive to Bryce; take a memorable walk through one of the steep, narrow canyons of Capitol Reef National Park; visit Canyonlands and Arches; and head north to Salt Lake City and home. Or make the same trip in reverse.

The Grand Canyon, if you're willing to get down inside it, moves visitors the way religion moves fervent believers. It is not just a beautiful place but a sacred one. Half the earth's history is told in its rocks. The oldest and deepest rock layer, the Vishnu Formation, began forming 2 billion years ago before aerobic life forms even existed. The layers of sedimentary rock that piled on top speak of mountains that really did move; of oceans that poured across the land before receding; of deserts, swamps, and rivers—all where the canyon now lies.

Four hours to the northeast is Capitol Reef, where you can spend an unforgettable afternoon strolling along the floor of an ancient riverbed beneath towering granite cliffs. One of my favorite walks is along the strenuous, 3-mile (one-way) Frying Pan Trail, which provides access to the spectacular spur trail to Cassidy Arch. From Capitol Reef—one of the United States's most undervisited parks—it's on to Canyonlands, a rugged high desert of rock, with spectacular formations and gorges carved by the park's primary architects, the Colorado and Green rivers. This is a land of extremes, of vast panoramas, broad mesas, and towering red spires. Finally, it's on to Arches, which is more visitor-friendly than Canyonlands, with relatively short, well-maintained trails and a less forbidding, more accessible landscape. Arches, my second favorite park in the country, is a world of natural stone arches and fantastic rock formations sculpted as though by an artist's hand.

◄ *Sunlight on Bryce Canyon.*
© Luis Castaneda Inc./ Getty Images

SPECIAL MOMENTS

1 Grand Canyon, Bright Angel Trail. I feel sorry for visitors who see nothing more than the rim. This is the equivalent of viewing life through an attic window. Visitors go to the first overlook and ooh and aah at the vastness of it all. Then they drive to the second, and the third, peering down at what is essentially the same view, trying to capture their initial sense of awe. But the thrill is behind them. To recapture it, they need to get out of their cars and walk down into the canyon on the Bright Angel Trail—even a 15-minute hike will do. Suddenly, instead of observing nature, you're participating in it and learning what it means to feel small. On a day hike, follow the switchbacks to One-and-a-Half-Mile House or Three-Mile House, each of which has shade, an emergency phone, and seasonal drinking water. Past Three-Mile House, you begin a long descent to the picnic area near the spring at Indian Garden, where lush vegetation surrounds you and large cottonwood trees provide shade.

2 Grand Canyon, Phantom Ranch. The most joyful and intimate vacation in my life was walking down to the bottom of the Grand Canyon one February with my family (ages 9–55) and spending a night at Phantom Ranch. Why anyone would want to bounce mercilessly on the back of a donkey for hours when they can walk is beyond me. The trail is relatively wide and, contrary to expectations, safe; and the views get more spectacular with every twist and turn of the trail. The ranch, accessible only by floating down the Colorado, or by hiking or riding a mule into the Canyon, often sells out 2 years in advance (☎ 888/297-2757 or 928/638-2631), so plan ahead. Hearty meals are served family-style with new friends, so you need to carry only water and

lunch. I can tell you clean sheets never felt better, cold beer never tasted this good, and a hot shower never felt so miraculous. It's a schlep—5 hours down, 8 up—but the memories will last a lifetime.

3 Bryce Canyon. Other parks are spread out and difficult to conquer or own. But the beauty of Bryce is captured in a single, relatively flat, 2- to 3-hour walk, combining the Navajo Loop Trail and the Queen's Garden Trail. The total distance is just under 3 miles. It's best to start at the Navajo Loop trail head at Sunset Point and leave the canyon on the less steep Queen's Garden Trail, returning to the rim at Sunset Point, a half-mile north of the Navajo Loop trail head. The trails take you past the park's most fanciful creations. Be sure to go around dawn (6am), while the crowds are still slumbering and the early morning light sets the hoodoos on fire. Sunset Point is the busiest place in the park, especially in midsummer at midday. To leave the crowds behind, take a 5-minute walk south along the rim trail toward Inspiration Point. If you really want to avoid people, visit midweek in the middle of winter. The roads are plowed then.

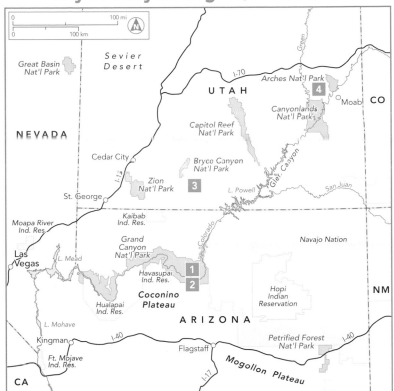

4 **Arches.** Just as soon as you've seen the most beautiful, most colorful, most gigantic stone arch you can imagine, you walk around a bend and there's another bigger, more spectacular than the last. It would take a lifetime to see them all, with more than 2,000 officially listed, and more being discovered every day. My favorite walks? The Devils Garden Trail takes you on a strenuous hike to Landscape Arch and 15 to 20 other arches. Delicate Arch has become the symbol for the state of Utah; the hike here involves a sometimes slippery 480-foot climb, but it is, for my money, the best and most scenic trail. I also like the Tower Arch Trail, because you're less likely to see other hikers. The .3-mile Balanced Rock Trail is a short, easy, wheelchair-accessible trail for visitors who want to get a close-up view of Balanced Rock. The strenuous 2-mile round-trip Furnace Trail takes you to some of the most colorful formations in the park.

MIKE SPRING is the publisher of the Frommer's travel guides. In 1963 he hitchhiked around the world on $3. In a former life, he was a contributing editor at *Condé Nast Traveler,* and a frequent contributor to *Travel + Leisure* and *Travel/Holiday.*

ABOUT THE AUTHOR

YOUR TRIP

General Information: Contact the rangers at **Grand Canyon National Park** (☎ 928/638-7888; www.nps.gov/grca); at **Bryce** (☎ 435/834-5322; www.nps.gov/brca); at **Arches National Park** (☎ 435/719-2299; www.nps.gov/arch). **Getting There:** The South Rim of the Grand Canyon is 278 miles (4½ hr.) from Las Vegas and 266 miles (3 hr. 40 min.) from Phoenix. Bryce is 293 miles (6 hr.) from the Grand Canyon. Arches is 230 miles (4 hr.) from Bryce. It's 230 miles (4¼ hr.) from Arches to Salt Lake City. **Best Lodging:** For camping reservations at all the parks, contact the **National Recreation Reservation Service** (☎ 877/444-6777; www.reserveusa.com). The most luxurious digs in the Grand Canyon is **El Tovar,** a grand hotel made of Oregon pine in 1905 (☎ 888/297-2757 or 928/638-2631; $124–$286). For camping, head to the **Kaibab Lake** (4 miles north of Williams on Hwy. 64; ☎ 928/699-1239). My favorite overnight at Bryce is the historic (1925) **Bryce Canyon Lodge** (☎ 888/297-2757; www.brycecanyonlodge.com; $110–$135). For camping in Bryce, book early for **North** or **Sunset Campground.** At Arches, your friendliest, most comfortable escape is **Sunflower Hill Luxury Inn** (185 N. 300 E., Moab, UT; ☎ 800/662-2786; www.sunflowerhill.com; $145–$215 high season). To camp in Arches, there's **Devil's Garden. Best Restaurant:** At the Grand Canyon, **El Tovar** (see above; $19–$27); at Bryce, go for the **Hungry Coyote** (199 N. Main St., Tropic; ☎ 435/679-8822; $7–$21); at Arches, there's **Buck's Grill House** (1393 N. U.S. 191; ☎ 435/259-5201; $6–$20). **When to Go:** Peak tourist season is summer, while the quietest months are December to February.

◀ *North Window, Arches National Park.*
© Gavin Hellier/Getty Images

BUCOVINA, ROMANIA

From medieval churches to Dracula's castle

Travelers have trembled before humanity's most memorable spiritual monuments, usually great buildings known for their size and austerity, and built to impress. But few know about the fantastic monastic churches of Moldavia, in a far-flung corner of Romania, east of the northern fringes of the snow-tipped Transylvanian Alps.

There, in southern Bucovina, dozens of Orthodox monasteries were built as fortresses of spiritual and military salvation during the 15th and 16th centuries, when countless battles were fought, mostly to safeguard Christianity against the ever-threatening Ottomans and Turks. Moldavia's Stephen the Great, one of Romania's most potent warriors, made a pact with God, such that he and his successors erected the churches as thanks for their fortune on the battlefield.

Although built in a climate of war and fear, and closed down during the reign of the Hapsburgs and the communists, they have survived as some of the loveliest examples of religious art in Europe. Known collectively as the "Painted Churches" of Bucovina, they are humbling for the simple brilliance of the imagery decorating their surfaces; some are covered—inside and out—with vivid tableaux recording Christian history and forewarning nonbelievers of a miserable, fiery fate.

To drive home the spiritual rhetoric of the day, Biblical myths and doctrine were translated into fierce and lively visual narratives, frescoed onto the church walls using a palette of heart-stopping colors, enriched with striking details that have survived the centuries and the elements quite miraculously. Today, you'll be transfixed by the dramatic intensity of the images—a startling reflection of the reality of a forgotten time. Best-preserved is Voronet, so magnificent it is nicknamed the "Sistine Chapel of the East," although Byzantine stylistic elements in the art and architecture make for an altogether otherworldly sensory experience.

Charmingly, the churches are situated in one of Romania's enchanting forest belts, so you can alternate your time between church-gazing and other spiritual adventures, hiking through tranquil valleys, and chancing upon romantically bucolic scenes.

Your journey through Romania can take you from brash, modern cities into remote villages barely detectable on maps. From Moldavia, head across the Carpathian Mountains to Maramureş, Romania's ultimate rural heartland. There you'll find farmers clinging to medieval ways, responding to the cycle of life as determined by the seasons, with horses for horsepower and market days serving as the social fulcrum. Maramureş seems genetically laid-back. Each day, villagers sit outside their homes, literally waiting for the cows to come home. It's a way of life that will transport you back in time.

South of Maramureş is Transylvania, where fairy tales are conjured up by the spires of Saxon villages that carve a bewitching silhouette against the sky. Amid Gothic churches and medieval towers, you can clamber through the annals of history, searching to satisfy a lust for magic and mystery. It won't take long to discover what brought you to Romania, and your discoveries will be much richer than the far-fetched legacy supposedly left by Count Dracula.

◀ *Moldoviţa Monastery, Bucovina.*
© Jon Arnold/
DanitaDelimont.com

SPECIAL MOMENTS

1 **Southern Bucovina.** A first stop on any trip to Romania should be a visit to the monastic churches of Moldavia to see the vivid colors and elaborate detail that cover their surfaces. I visited four in a day, and sighed disbelievingly at each one, starting with Voronet, where the brilliant blues of the exterior frescoes are unlike anything I have ever witnessed. At nearby Humor, I climbed the defensive tower for views of rolling farmland against a backdrop of jagged peaks—views made lovelier by a gentle rain. And then at Moldovița we handed out snacks to dear nuns who, in return, gave us outdated calendars, simple remembrances of a day spent at some of the world's most beautiful UNESCO World Heritage landmarks.

2 **Dragomirna Monastery.** Before Romania, I knew nothing of Orthodox religion, and so I was unprepared for the spiritual ascent of witnessing morning mass at the monastic church of Dragomirna, near Suceava, en route to the painted churches. The worshippers were nuns who lived and worked at the monastery, and the rite was presided over by a priest with a beautiful, resonant voice. Together they seemed to sing with the angels, invoking otherworldly rhythms as the priest presented holy icons, upon which the nuns cast an adoring gaze or placed their lips in tender devotion. Although not inclined to religion, I emerged from that intimate space with my soul gently shaken.

3 **Maramureş.** My most memorable village experience was at the Pop family homestead in Hoteni, where you can stay in Maramureş. I'd been driven through a landscape of ravishing beauty and now I could hear my own heartbeat. Minutes after I met Ion Pop, he was skillfully playing the violin, while his wife was waiting to feed me a hearty meal with honey from the farm beehive. Next day, she drove me to Săpânţa's "Merry Cemetery," where graves are marked by colorful, carved wooden gravestones bearing cheerful, comical anecdotes about the dead—it's surely one of the most unusual graveyards on earth. She also took me to the nearby anti-communism museum, an evocative former political prison where enemies of the regime were tortured and many died. Emotionally, it was an epic day.

4 **Sighişoara.** People go to Transylvania's Bran Castle believing the hype proclaiming it "Dracula's Castle." For a real taste of medievalism, head instead to the compact

citadel of Sighișoara, where there's enough cobblestone atmosphere to inspire a dozen ghostly fantasies. Sighișoara is where the "real" Count Dracula—Vlad Țepeș—was born, in a house that's now a restaurant serving the coldest beers in town. Still populated, Sighișoara's fortress sits on a hill, a tangle of colorful houses among bastion towers and sloping walls. Climbing the clock tower, you can imagine bats spiriting between the rooftops, and watch as tourists negotiate the steep approach under the archways far below. Later, climb to the Gothic "Church on the Hill" and explore the adjacent cemetery where gravestones seem to have shifted in the night. Shuddering at the necromantic possibilities, you can then head to the town square to drink beer and watch artisans peddling souvenirs and passing off ancient junk as antiques.

ABOUT THE AUTHOR

KEITH BAIN went to Romania to research a chapter for *Frommer's Eastern Europe.* His other work for Frommer's covers India, Venice, and southern Africa. In his other life, he works at a South African film school, urging students to write challenging scripts and make cinematic magic.

YOUR TRIP

General Information: Contact the **National Tourist Office** (☎ 212/545-8484; www.romaniatourism.com). For ecofriendly tours with village homestays, contact **DiscoveRomania** (☎ 40-722/74-6262; www.discoveromania.ro). Drivers and guides for the monasteries can be arranged through **Icar Tours** (☎ 40-230/52-4894; www.icar.ro). U.S.-based **Quest Tours & Adventures** has various Romania packages (☎ 800/621-8687; www.romtour.com). **Getting There:** Romania's official carrier, **Tarom** (www.tarom.ro) offers direct flights from London and other major European hubs. **Best Lodging:** The most luxurious accommodations in Bucovina, close to the painted monasteries, are **Best Western Bucovina Club de Munte** (Gura Humorului; ☎ 0230/20-7000; www.bestwesternbucovina.ro; $103–$113/£54–£60). In Sighișoara, stay in a 15th-century house that's been converted into the lovely, simple **Casa Epoca** (☎ 40-265/77-3232; www.casaepoca.ro; $58–$65/£31–£34). **Homestays:** To stay at Casa Popicu, the Pop family homestead in Maramureș, contact **DiscoveRomania** (see above). You can book village accommodation throughout Romania through the National Association of Rural, Ecological, and Cultural Tourism, which provides information about all registered guesthouses (☎ 40-21/223-7024; www.antrec.ro). **Best Restaurant:** In Sighișoara, eat at **Casa Wagner** for the best Romanian food (☎ 40-265/50-6014; www.casa-wagner.com; $4–$7/£2–£4). **Best Restaurant Value:** You'll eat hearty, home-cooked meals if you stay with a family in **Maramureș** or **Moldavia;** be sure to inform your hosts if you don't eat meat. **When to Go:** May, June, and September are best.

◀ *Veronet, Bucovina.*
© Michael Spring

BULGARIA

From sophisticated Varna to villages forgotten by time

Lounging on a large white daybed on the beach in Varna, watching scantily clad waitresses deliver cocktails to *louche* boys lolling around the bar pool, it's hard to believe that this sophisticated, Miami-style beach club is in Bulgaria, when only hours away, on roads that see more carts than cars, farmers till fields with horse-drawn ploughs. But then that is part of Bulgaria's charm: The element of surprise is never far away.

Few know, for instance, that this small eastern European country—for so long perceived as a mere vassal of the Soviet Union—has a rich and varied history. Europe's oldest state, Bulgaria recently celebrated its 1,300th birthday, but its roots reach far deeper. Five thousand years ago the mighty Thracian tribes, Europe's first civilization, settled in the region known today as the "Valley of Kings"—Bulgaria's fertile belly, surrounded by undulating mountain ranges and watered by mineral-rich rivers. Most of what we know of the Thracians was discovered by archaeologists working on their tombs, of which some 15,000 lie scattered in this region. Only a fraction of these have been excavated, but the artifacts discovered in them prove that the Thracian warriors were also the most sophisticated goldsmiths of ancient times, creating work so intricate that some examples are best viewed through a magnifying glass, and using superior alloys of gold and platinum that go as far back as 3000 B.C. Today these treasures are on display in Bulgaria's top museums. Better still, you can—with a little forward planning—visit the Thracian tombs where some of these treasures were uncovered—an exhilarating experience, given that the tombs are more than 2,000 years old and as yet untainted by tourist traffic.

But ancient history is only part of Bulgaria's appeal. Traveling along empty roads, lined with blowsy elderflowers and poppies, past men with huge moustaches and women in patterned headscarves, you'll continually want to stop and savor the bucolic scenes. Bulgaria's sparse population and lack of infrastructure has isolated its rural communities, and exploring its mountain villages is like stepping into a living museum, where meandering cobbled lanes, thick with dung and mud, are lined with 18th-century stone-and-timber homes. Village elders sun themselves against the ancient walls as their forefathers have done for hundreds of years; young lovers return from fields, hoes casually slung across their shoulders; and horse carts scatter geese and goats. It's Europe a century ago, but enjoyed with basic modern comforts and superb peasant cuisine offered by family-run guesthouses throughout the country.

Combine an itinerary that takes in a few of these villages, along with Bulgaria's dramatically situated monasteries, repositories for the country's rich iconographic art, and its two most beautiful cities—Plovdiv, where wealthy merchants bankrolled the best examples of the distinctive architectural style known as "National Revival," and Veliko Tarnovo, the medieval capital that rises precipitously from the banks of the Yantra—and you will experience the best that Bulgaria has to offer. But get here soon: Part of the appeal is experiencing it before everyone else does; and with the advent of E.U. membership in 2007, infrastructure will improve and traffic will grow.

SPECIAL MOMENTS

1 **Set scenes: Sofia City Garden.** Shaded by an old tarpaulin, a small group of worshippers stands on the concrete plinth that once carried the interred remains of communist dictator Zhivkov, their heads bowed as a tall man in a black cassock intones a sonorous prayer. Behind this makeshift church, flanked by the priest's rusty trailer, a lone bagpiper reels around, his suggestive hip movements setting off a belt of pealing bells. Near the central fountain, old-timers play cards under sweet-smelling linden trees, seemingly oblivious to the low, thumping beat emanating from an open-air bar, or the group of students passing by, all with large handmade paper hats on their heads. It is Sunday, and this surreal scene, straight out of some eastern European art flick, could only be playing out in Sofia's overgrown City Garden.

2 **Tomb raiding: Kazanluk.** Approached through a narrow, Temple of Doom–like antechamber, the burial chamber is small: no more than 2.5m (8¼ ft.) across, the frescoed dome almost close enough to touch. It should be claustrophobic, but the air is damp and cool, and the atmosphere fills you with a strange reverence, perhaps because so few humans have stepped into its narrow confines (it was opened to the public only in 2006) since the warrior portrayed on the dome was laid to rest here some 2,400 years ago. With 15,000 tombs and 400 settlements dating from the late 4th century B.C., Bulgaria is laden with ancient artifacts—comparable to those of Greece and Italy, according to archaeologists. Yet Bulgaria's treasures are unknown and virtually unvisited, so you can savor them in solitude—a rare luxury in the Age of Travel. To visit the original Kazanluk tomb, the most accessible of those excavated thus far (about 2½ hr. from Sofia, 90 min. from Plovdiv),

you'll need to call ahead (☎ 359-431/64-750 or 359-431/63-762).

3 **Bulgarian feast: Leshten.** With sublime views across the rolling, forested Rhodope foothills and the snowcapped Pirin as a backdrop, Leshten is my favorite village in Bulgaria. A small cluster of (mostly deserted) 18th-century dwellings, built onto a steep and densely vegetated hillside, the village has only one restaurant, referred to simply as *Krachma*, which means "restaurant" in Bulgarian. Heaven is sitting at a rough-hewn table under huge spreading

branches from which corks dangle (tug one, and the tinkling of bells alerts the waiter), the Pirin before you. But the best is yet to come. Order the "*Kofte*, Leshten-Style"— a single tender cut of pork—with *ljutenitza* (mashed red peppers, leeks, and spices), *kartofki* (chips), and a carafe of *cherveno vino* (red wine). Even the plain salad is delicious. All produce is "hand-reared" by Misho Marinov, who owns the restaurant and virtually the whole village, and offers 15 carefully restored houses for $39 to $78 (£21–£41) a night (☎ 359-752/552; leshten@yahoo.com).

4 **Blessing your icon: Tryavna.**
The deep, rich voice of the priest fills the Church of Archangel Michael. I stand to one side, watching as he periodically douses the icon before him with holy water. It is mine, purchased that morning from one of the masters who paint in nearby Etura, Bulgaria's charming outdoor ethnographic museum, and the best place to purchase a top-quality icon. I already love it passionately but I have been told by my guide that it will protect my home only if it is blessed by a priest. You can have this done at any church (it requires no more than a smattering of Bulgarian or a translator, and a small donation of, say, $4/£2), but the village of Tryavna, birthplace to some of Bulgaria's most talented icon painters, seems an ideal place to do so. Tryavna is 3½ hours from Sofia, but—together with Etura and Dryanovo Monastery—makes a good day trip from Veliko Tarnovo (90 min.) or Plovdiv (2½ hr.).

PIPPA DE BRUYN is an award-winning journalist and seasoned travel writer based in Cape Town. She is the author of *Frommer's South Africa*, coauthor of *Frommer's India*, and contributor to *Pauline Frommer's Italy* and *Frommer's Eastern Europe*. Her first novel is due for publication in 2008.

ABOUT THE AUTHOR

YOUR TRIP

General Information: There is no official tourism board, though a number of websites offer advice; the best is **www.discover-bulgaria.com**. The best way to get around is with a car and driver. For assistance with everything from booking accommodation to looking after your needs 24/7, contact **Svetlio** (☎ 359-088/7485174; **svelte@mail.bg**); alternatively, contact the aptly named **Rent-Cars-With-Driver** (http://rentacarsdriver.dir.bg).
Best Lodging: My favorite hotel is the **Hebros** in Plovdiv, located in a 19th-century National Revival house in the old quarter (Plovdiv, ul. "Constantine Stoilov" 51a; ☎ 359-32/260-180; www.hebros-hotel.com; $114/£60 double). Ask for no. 3 and you can stare at the same beautiful ceiling dictator Todor Zhivkov once did. **Best Lodging Value: Kapsazov's kashta** is located in Kovachevitsa, one of the most charming mountain villages, and is owned by the Kapsazovs, who entertain a mix of Sofians and foreigners with a wonderful combination of superb food, rustic peace, and utter comfort (☎ 359-099/40-3089; kapsazovs_houses@yahoo.com; $66/£35 per person, breakfast and dinner included). For the most atmospheric stay, book a bed with the monks at the **Monastery in Dryanovo**, a wonderful experience for a mere $16 (£8) a night (☎ 359/67-6238). **Best Restaurant:** For the country's most memorable fine-dining restaurant, head to **Beyond the Alley, Behind the Cupboard**, located in an Art Nouveau house in central Sofia. The decor is wonderfully eccentric, but it's what's on the plate that keeps it at the top of most Sofian foodies' lists (☎ 359/2/980 3883). **When to Go:** Visit during late May or June to early July; alternatively the fall (Sept).

◀ *A Bulgarian woman gathers roses.*
© Robb Kendrick/Aurora/Getty Images

BURGUNDY, FRANCE

Famed vineyards of the Côte d'Or, only 90 minutes from Paris

I think of Burgundy, one of the most famous wine regions in the world, as the heart of France, and a visit there as an opportunity to connect with a culture and a way of life that are deeply authentic and traditional. In Burgundy, you have the best of France—wine, food, heritage sites, magnificent countryside—in an area just 90 minutes southeast of Paris on the TGV, the high-speed train.

Burgundy during the Middle Ages was a territory separate from, and more powerful than, France itself. A large region, it used to stretch all the way north to Flanders. It has always been considered rich in agricultural products, a bounty that is well reflected in restaurants featuring scrumptious regional specialties like coq au vin made from the free-range chicken of Bresse, and beef bourguignon made from the meat of the Charolais cattle. Burgundy also has a rich spiritual tradition. My favorite religious site in Burgundy is the Cistercian Basilica of Saint Madeleine, a Romanesque masterpiece built in the 12th and 13th centuries. The basilica rests on top of a steep, cobbled hill lined with artisans' shops in the historic village of Vézelay, about an hour's drive west of Dijon, Burgundy's capital.

My dream vacation in Burgundy starts in Dijon, a handsome, historic city that is both a bustling university town and a cultural center. Dijon's must-see site is the Palais des Ducs, with its elaborate tile roof, its ornately carved tombs of the dukes of Burgundy, and one of France's oldest and best fine-arts museums.

After visiting Dijon, you'll want to wander south through the great vineyards of Burgundy's Côte d'Or, literally the "golden hillside." From north to south, the Côte d'Or, which extends about 64km (40 miles), is divided into sections: Côte de Nuits, Côte de Beaune, and Côte Chalonnaise, each known for distinct characteristics in the soil that find their way into the wine. As you travel this route, you pass through tiny villages that carry the names of world-famous wines like Gevrey-Chambertin, Chambolle-Musigny, and Nuits-Saint-Georges. Historic sites open daily and worth a visit along the route include Château du Clos de Vougeot, a Renaissance manor where Cistercian monks once made wine; and Château de Rochepot, a 13th-century fortress you won't be able to resist exploring.

A highlight of any trip to Burgundy is Beaune, the picturesque wine capital of the region. Before you reach Beaune's medieval ramparts, you can see the colorful glazed tiles of its most famous building, the Hôtel-Dieu, a fully restored medieval charity hospital now open to the public.

It can be difficult to decide how to travel in Burgundy because you have three terrific choices: rental car, bike, and barge. Though a rental car affords the most spontaneity and a barge trip is relaxing and scenic, the best option for me is biking. Whether you go on an escorted bike tour or on your own, you can ride on fairly flat roads and stop where the spirit moves you—to visit a castle, perhaps, or to sip wine at a tasting. The best part is that, after all that exercise, you get to enjoy the region's wonderful cuisine, guilt-free.

◄ *Vineyards near Bourgogne.*
© Fernand Ivaldi/
Getty Images

SPECIAL MOMENTS

1 **Biking the Côte de Nuits.** Cycling through small villages, past row after row of grapevines, is the memory that draws me back to this region time after time. My favorite route goes through the Côte de Nuits, the northern section of the famous Côte d'Or, south of Dijon, where Burgundy's most famous vineyards line the roads. I prefer the Côte de Nuits because peddling is child's play here, and the road passes through the most famous wine villages in the region. If you travel the route in September, during the 8- to 10-day period called *les vendages*, you'll see the workers actually harvesting the grapes in the fields. You can join an escorted tour and have your bags sent on ahead each night or ask an outfitter to customize a private tour for you and your family or friends. You can also go on your own with a bike rented locally, carrying your belongings in panniers or sending them ahead each day by taxi.

2 **Tastings on La Route des Grands Crus.** La Route des Grands Crus, the road of great wines, is the name given to a series of roadways (D122, N74, D1138) along the Côte d'Or. What I love about tastings, or as the French call them, *dégustations*, is that each one comes with a little lesson about wine. I remember a visit to Domaine Michel Juillot in the village of Mercurey, where I learned about *terroir*, the soil and atmosphere that give the wine its character. My favorite vineyards are Domaine Michel Juillot in Mercurey, where the owner will show you the 18th-century vaulted cellars; the 11th-century Château de Meursault, where white wines are a specialty; Morin Père et Fils, in Nuits-Sainte-Georges, for a lesson in how to taste wines; Domaine du Berceau, in the village of Chardonnay, which is devoted to traditional methods; and Andre Delorme, in Rully, which is known for the sparkling wine called *crémant*.

3 **Hôtel-Dieu des Hospices de Beaune.** You'll feel like a time traveler, transported back to the Middle Ages, when you walk for the first time into Hôtel-Dieu, which was built as a hospital for the poor in the town of Beaune. Though it looks somber and fortified from the outside, the large interior courtyard is filled with light and reflections from the bright colors of the famous roof, decorated with shiny, multicolored tiles. Rooms of the hospital have been restored and decorated with period furniture, including the pharmacy, which is set up with bottles of mysterious-looking herbal potions.

4 Vézeley. One of the must-see places to visit in Burgundy is the beautiful hillside village of Vézeley. The entire village is classified by the United Nations as a World Heritage Site. Its medieval ramparts and Romanesque buildings give you a good sense of how the town may have looked in the Middle Ages, when pilgrims set off on a month-long journey that ended in Santiago de Compostela in Spain. The highlight of a visit to Vézeley is the Cistercian Basilica of Sainte Madeleine, which is open daily sunrise to sunset. The view of the Burgundian countryside from the church's rear courtyard is unforgettable. Built in the 12th century, France's largest and most famous Romanesque church is only 9m (30 ft.) shorter than Notre-Dame. When you enter the narthex, raise your eyes to the depiction of Christ giving the apostles the Holy Spirit. Be sure to visit the Carolingian crypt, where the tomb of Mary Magdalene was said to have rested (today the crypt contains some of her relics).

LAURA M. RECKFORD is the managing editor of the *Falmouth Enterprise* newspaper on Cape Cod. She has been the author for the last 9 years of *Frommer's Cape Cod, Nantucket & Martha's Vineyard* and was a coauthor of the first edition of *France For Dummies*. She can be reached at laurareckford@hotmail.com.

ABOUT THE AUTHOR

YOUR TRIP

General Information: Contact **Comité Regional du Tourisme de Bourgogne** (☎ 33-03/80-280-280; www.burgundy-tourism.com) or the **Maison de la France,** the French Government Tourist Office (☎ 212/838-7800; www.franceguide.com). **Getting There:** The **France National Railroad** (www.sncf.com) fast trains leave from Gare de Lyon in Paris to Beaune and Dijon daily. **Bike Riders** (☎ 800/473-7040; www.bikeriderstours.com), based in the U.S., specializes in biking tours. For barge tours, contact **European Waterways** (☎ 800/394-8630; www.gobarging.com). **Getting Around:** To rent a bike, there's **Bourgogne randonnées** (☎ 33-03/80-22-06-03; www.bourgogne-randonnees.com) near the Beaune train station. The **Voie Verte** bike path is a 44km (27-mile) bike trail from Givry to Cluny, passing through a number of charming towns. **Best Lodging:** The luxurious rooms at **Château André Ziltener** stand out for their comfort and style (Chambolle-Musigny; ☎ 33-03/80-62-41-62; www.chateau-ziltener.com; 220€–380€/$264–$456). **Best Lodging Value: Château de Chorey** is a 17th-century castle and vineyard in Chorey-les-Beaune that operates as a bed-and-breakfast (Beaune; ☎ 33-03/80-22-06-05; www.chateau-de-chorey-les-beaune.fr; 160€–210€/$192–$252). **Best Restaurant: Lameloise** is one of the region's most renowned restaurants and is also an exquisite hotel (36 place d'Armes, Chagny; ☎ 33-03/85-87-65-65; www.lameloise.fr; entrees 75€/$90). **Best Restaurant Value: Le P'tit Paradis** in Beaune serves yummy food at reasonable prices (25 Rue Paradis; ☎ 33-03/80-24-91-00; 12€–20€/$14–$24). **When to Go:** Mid-Sept to mid-Oct.

◀ *Old farmhouse, Beaune.*
© Oliver Strewe/Lonely Planet Images

CAMINO DE SANTIAGO, SPAIN

A life-changing pilgrimage through Spanish art & history

Not many of us are lucky enough to find a vacation life-altering, but a surprising number of those who undertake the Camino de Santiago—an exhausting 800km (500-mile) trek across the whole of Spain—feel fundamentally changed by the experience.

The Camino (the Path of St. James), a pilgrimage to Santiago de Compostela in remote, northwestern Spain, has inspired reams of rhapsodic prose, but it's a difficult experience to capture in words. Though hugely taxing on one's legs and feet, much of the journey takes place between one's ears.

The first documented pilgrimage to visit the remains of the Apostle St. James took place in the year 950. *Codex Calixtinus*, a Latin text written by a French monk in the 12th century describing the route of the Camino, is said to be the first travel guidebook. At its apogee in the Middle Ages, more than two million spiritual pilgrims beat a path to Santiago.

More than 1,000 years later, the Camino de Santiago continues with a fervor that nearly matches its medieval heights. Modern-day pilgrims from around the globe—nearly all hikers, along with some speedy mountain bikers and a few on horseback—embark on the journey. On foot, the most traditional route takes a month, beginning in the Spanish Pyrenees of Navarra, near the French border, and finishing in misty Galicia. At the end of the road is the world's oldest hotel, established to receive pilgrims by King Ferdinand and Queen Isabella in 1499.

Today's trekkers come decked out in Polartec pullovers and Gore-Tex hiking boots; but for most, the Camino continues to be a spiritual journey. Some are devout Christians, some are drawn to the trail's legendary mysticism, while others are interested in the region's culture, history, and architecture.

They lug 25-pound backpacks, bake under the Spanish sun, and shield themselves against persistent rain. They cross ancient Roman bridges in Navarra, shuffle past 12th-century Romanesque churches and soaring cathedrals on the arid plains of Burgos and León, and trudge up and down steep goat paths in the green hills of Galicia. In villages that owe their very existence to the Camino, parish priests welcome hikers and bikers as authentic pilgrims, stamp their Camino passports, and send them on to hot showers at a hostel for the night.

Of course, not everyone has a month—or the stamina—to do the full Camino. Many *turigrinos* (tourist pilgrims) take a week and do the last leg of the journey, beginning in Villafranca del Bierzo (or Sarria, if really pressed for time). Some also choose to repair to at least an occasional upscale inn along the way.

But wherever they start or however they do the Camino, the days wear on for pilgrims. Through pine forests and over gurgling streams they walk. Eventually you get past the pain and begin to feel in sync with your surroundings; it isn't uncommon to reach a Zen-like zone. Detached from the modern world, and with ample time to live inside their heads, pilgrims reflect on the roads they've taken, and the road ahead. Their aspiration is no different from the goal of the ages: to see the spires of the Santiago cathedral emerge from the mist and signal the completion of their journey.

◀ *Salamanca Cathedral.*
© David Tomlinson/Lonely Planet Images

SPECIAL MOMENTS

1   Tripping through time. The Camino is a trail through Spanish history, art, and architecture. Many of the monuments along the road—including eight cathedrals, dozens of monasteries, and Romanesque and Gothic churches in virtually every small town—came into being because of the Camino. Two of the most spectacular cathedrals in Spain, in Burgos and León, are on the traditional "French route"; and at the Silos Monastery near Burgos, monks can be heard singing Gregorian chants. In Astorga, the bishop's palace is one of the few buildings outside Barcelona designed by Antoni Gaudí (creator of the surreal La Sagrada Familia church). After pilgrims reach the Celtic land of Galicia, the trail is lined with ancient *cruceiros,* or medieval crosses, and picturesque stone granaries.

Not all trekkers are aware that the Camino has its roots in one of the more peculiar bits of religious history. The tomb of St. James is either a stunning miracle or an elaborate hoax perpetrated by the Catholic Church, which claimed that a hermit followed a light in the sky and stumbled upon the bones of St. James—who had been beheaded by Herod 750 years earlier, thousands of miles away, near the Dead Sea.

2   Relaxing after a day's walk. Pilgrims look forward to the end of each day, and not just because of the obvious appeal of doffing their boots. Many pilgrims get together to share personal stories. The immediate camaraderie among those with a shared purpose is in itself fortifying, but for even more nourishment, head out for a meal at a local restaurant. Some trekkers seem to

exist on trail mix, but since the Camino passes right through some of Spain's finest food regions, it offers a chance for a gastronomic pilgrimage. At simple country restaurants, pilgrims gorge on local cheeses, chorizo, *morcilla* (blood sausage), and heartier fare like lamb, suckling pig, and the prized seafood of Galicia. The trail traverses classic and emerging wine regions—Navarra, Rioja, Ribera del Duero, and Bierzo; there are few better remedies after a long day's walk than sharing a good bottle of wine. As they say on the trail, *"con pan y vino se anda el camino."*

3   Arriving in Santiago de Compostela. A monumental city of stone, Santiago is an emotional place for *peregrinos.* At the cathedral, built to house the remains of St. James, pilgrims kneel at the marble column in the glorious portico and place their hands on the column under the figure of the Apostle, where a handprint has been etched into the marble over the centuries. A Mass is said, and an enormous censer called the *Botafumeiro,* which takes eight priests to hoist, is swung in dramatic arcs from the rafters, dispensing plumes of incense. Pilgrims

► *Cathedral relief, Santiago de Compostela.*
© AGE Fotostock/SuperStock Inc.

receive the *Compostela*, signifying that they, like millions of the faithful before them, have completed the Camino.

4 **A personal search for meaning.** What makes the pilgrimage to Santiago such a transcendent experience? Many, if not most, people arrive at the Camino at crossroads in their lives, searching for something. Maybe it's the shared experience of undertaking a trip that for centuries required immeasurable faith and fearlessness, or perhaps it's the meditative, hypnotic sound of one's boots trudging across the breadth of Spain. Or the colorful characters, with tales of epiphanies, encountered along the way. But the Camino rarely fails to induce soul searching and pathfinding. The author Paulo Coelho called the Camino "a contemporary quest for ancient wisdom." When villagers and fellow travelers wish you a *"Buen camino!"* they're wishing you more than just a safe journey.

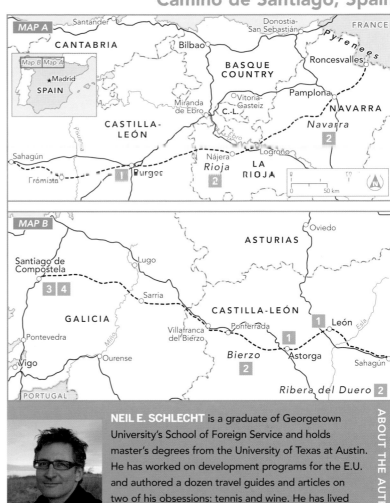

NEIL E. SCHLECHT is a graduate of Georgetown University's School of Foreign Service and holds master's degrees from the University of Texas at Austin. He has worked on development programs for the E.U. and authored a dozen travel guides and articles on two of his obsessions: tennis and wine. He has lived in Spain, Brazil, and Ecuador.

ABOUT THE AUTHOR

YOUR TRIP

General Information: Contact **Información Xacobeo** (www.xacobeo.es) or the **Oficina del Peregrino** (☎ 34-98/156-24-19). **Getting There:** Trains travel from Madrid or Barcelona to Pamplona (☎ 34-90/224-34-02; www.renfe.es); from there, **Artieda** buses go to Roncesvalles (☎ 34-94/830-02-87; www.autocaresartieda.com). **Best Lodging:** The **Parador de Santiago de Compostela** began life in 1499 as a royal hospital and refuge for pilgrims and claims to be the world's oldest hotel (Plaza Do Obradoiro 1; ☎ 34-98/158-22-00; www.parador.es; 200€/$240). **Parador de Santo Domingo de la Calzada** is a 12th-century former pilgrim's hospital in La Rioja (Plaza del Santo 3; ☎ 34-94/134-03-00; 130€–140€/$156–$169). **Best Lodging Value: Hotel La Puebla** (c/La Puebla 20, Burgos; ☎ 34-94/720-00-11; www.hotellapuebla.com; 71€–88€/$85–$106); **Casa de Tepa** (c/Santiago 2, Astorga; ☎ 34-98/760-32-99; www.casadetepa.com; 90€–100€/$108–$120). Along the Camino, there is a network of free or very inexpensive (under 10€/$12) *albergues*; the best are in Ribadiso do Baixo, Puente La Reina, and Logroño. **Best Restaurant: Casa Marcelo** (Rúa Hortas 1, Santiago de Compostela; ☎ 34-98/155-85-80; main courses 12€–28€/$14–$33). **Best Restaurant Value: Enxebre,** in the Parador de Santiago de Compostela, has tapas and *raciones* of classic Gallego dishes for 5€–15€/$6–$18. Along the route there are affordable local restaurants that cater to pilgrims. **When to Go:** Late spring and fall; avoid the heat and crowds of July and August, as well as frigid winters. During holy years, the Camino is overcrowded and *albergues* are impossible to get in. The next one is in 2010.

CAPPADOCIA, TURKEY

A landscape of sinuous stone sculpted by wind & water

The earth contorts into strange shapes in central Turkey. Stone stretches and claws the air; boulders balance on thin columns. Part Gaudí, part Dalí, the landscape of Cappadocia (Kapadokya) is one of the world's strangest—and most hauntingly beautiful—sights.

Time and space play tricks here, especially at Nevşehir Müze, an open-air museum and UNESCO World Heritage Site in Göreme. You emerge from a millennium-old church, hewn into the bedrock and painted with once-forbidden icons. Glance up its steep stairs and catapult light years forward to a scene from *Star Wars,* where George Lucas filmed the home of the Sand People.

Cappadocia is a triangular swathe of central Anatolia, between Ürgüp, Avanos, and Nevşehir. Roughly 515km (320 miles) southeast of Istanbul, the region is basically the bull's-eye on the dartboard of Turkey.

Three mighty volcanoes created this landscape of sinuous stone. The first spread delicate tufa, which was then sculpted by wind and water into ever-evolving domes, hollows, clefts, and cones—a sort of three-dimensional paisley. Later eruptions scattered harder lava. Now, as the soft underbelly erodes, huge boulders teeter upon slender tufa towers, called "fairy chimneys." The effect veers beyond PG-13; some of the formations look positively phallic. Aside from a few saucy postcards, the locals ignore this. Maybe the joke's old, since they've burrowed homes in the soft rock since the late Paleolithic era.

When marauding hordes swept across the steppes, they scratched entire secret cities into the earth. Later, Christians cowered among the caves, safeguarding sacred images and championing chastity. After a Second Crusade victory, the Selçuk Turks revived Islamic traditions, and Islamic dervishes whirled toward ecstasy. The western world lost track of this remote wonderland for centuries, until Père Guillaume de Jerphanion, a French Jesuit priest, stumbled upon these, "the most fantastic of all landscapes," in 1907.

Like Jordan's Petra, many of the monuments remain inhabited and in use. Windows glow within the troglodyte dwellings, cones pointed like the miters of Byzantine bishops. And when Cappadocians welcome guests to these unique guesthouses, their hospitality—so prized by religion and culture—is genuine.

In Istanbul, plagued by touts, I cover my fair hair and pretend not to speak English. Or any language, for that matter. Ironically, in Cappadocia—a land long hidden, designed for deception—I unfold. I barter for silver jewelry by weight. I soak in the *hamam* beside locals. I lounge on carpeted benches, sipping tea and sharing strawberry tobacco in a *nargile,* a water pipe. I discuss fresco renovation with a Turkish art student, embroidered bell-bottoms peeking beneath her *tesettür,* traditional Muslim topcoat and headscarf.

Confidence swelling, I even freely admit I'm American, despite tensions in the Middle East. The young guards shift their machine guns to shake my hand solemnly. "Over time, this land has . . .much war and much conquerors," the captain says. "But people are people. And all people are welcome here always."

◀ *Sandstone homes, Göreme Valley.*
© Jonathan Blair/Corbis

SPECIAL MOMENTS

1   **Underground cities.** A crucial crossroads between East and West, the area saw its share of invaders: Hittites, Thracians, Phrygians, Cimmerians, Scythians, and Medes. As warriors raged across the plains, the meek inhabited the earth, digging over 200 concealed cities. The oldest may date between 1,000 and 2,000 B.C.

South of Nevşehir are the most impressive constructions: Kaymakli (18km/11 miles) and Derinkuyu (26km/16 miles). In times of trouble, people dwelled in the upper levels, making wine, grinding flour, and praying in the danker areas below. Large boulders sealed the doors. Today visitors can tour the claustrophobic labyrinths, alone or with a guide.

2   **Early Christian hermitages.** Cappadocia's cultural highlight is the Open Air Museum (Nevşehir Müze). The UNESCO World Heritage Site—protecting 30 painted churches—is a 15-minute stroll from Göreme.

Early Christians settled here in the 2nd century A.D., fleeing Roman—and, later, Muslim—persecution. The twisted valleys, peaks, caves, and tunnels provided ample hiding places. Two hundred years later, Saint Basil—bishop of Kayseri, 101km (63 miles) from Nevşehir—helped build Cappadocia's first cave-churches and ignited Orthodox monasticism.

More religious refugees arrived in the 8th century, after the Byzantine Emperor Leo III forbade the worship of icons. Emboldened by the remote location, artists tackled daring themes like the Nativity, Last Supper, and Crucifixion. At Nevşehir Müze, the Buckle Church (Tokali Kilise) has Cappadocia's most sensational frescoes, followed closely by the Church with the Apple (Elmali Kilise), the Dark Church (Karanlik Kilise), and the Church of Saint Barbara. Museum visitors should pay the exorbitant parking lot fees or risk hassle from the site's guards (www.nevsehir.gov.tr).

3   **Caravansaries of the Silk Road.** In the 11th century, the Selçuk Empire renewed the area's trade ties, shuttling spices, ivory, and fine cloth from the Far East. In return, they gathered slaves in central Anatolia, trained them as soldiers, and sold them to the south.

Traveling merchants could stay at each caravansary free for 3 days, under the sultan's protection. These vast complexes included baths, mosques, stables, sleeping quarters, and marketplaces. Many now shelter carpet markets, like the splendid 13th-century Agzikarahan outside of Aksaray. Once the third-largest oasis on the Silk Road, it remains nearly intact, sprawling over 1,856 sq. m (20,000 sq. ft.). Stop in for a glass of tea, some haggling, and a glimpse of Ottoman architecture at its height.

4   **Whirling dervishes.** Three hours south of Ankara lies Konya, home to an Islamic mystic tradition. Clad in long white gowns, the dervishes dance ecstatically to droned hymns, a quarter-hour each. This ceremony (sema) dates to the 13th-century poet-philosopher Rumi's habit of spinning through the

streets. The Mevlevi philosophy eventually gained the respect of the Ottoman sultans, and Selim II, Mahmud II, and Mehmed V were among its members. The purpose of the ritual is to create a sphere of divine reality. The Mevlevi believe that purity of heart, peace with self and the universe, and the search for perfection through ritual dance bring them closer to God. The positioning of the body during the ritual has great symbolic significance: Outstretched arms with one hand facing the heavens and the other facing the earth symbolize man as a bridge between the two spheres. The white robes worn during the *sema* are symbolic of shrouds. Although this and other brotherhoods were officially outlawed by Atatürk's sweeping reforms, the order continues to exist. The Mevlevi welcome outsiders, as they believe all people are equal before God. The prime event is an early December festival; they sometimes whirl in the shopping area near the Mevlana Museum in this splendid Selçuk city.

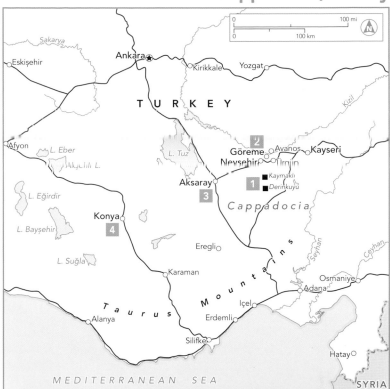

AMANDA CASTLEMAN is a freelance journalist and travel-writing instructor. For 8 years she lived in Europe, writing for the *International Herald Tribune, Frommer's, Rough Guides, Wired,* MSNBC, and the anthology *Greece, A Love Story.* Her website is www.amandacastleman.com.

ABOUT THE AUTHOR

YOUR TRIP

General Information: Research on www.tourismturkey.org and www.cappadociaonline.com. **Getting There:** Cappadocia's heart is Göreme in the Nevşehir Province. Fly into Kayseri Erkilet Airport on **Turkish Airways** (www.thy.com). The airport is 97km (60 miles) from Göreme: Hire a taxi for $18 (£9.50) or ride the **Argeus Tours** minibus (☎ 90-0384/341-4688; www.argeus.com.tr). **What to See & Do:** Ûhisar, a village outside Göreme, attracts hikers to its fortress—the region's highest peak. Trails lead to Pigeon Valley (Güvercinlik Vadisi), a canyon of rock dunes (normally a 2-hr. jaunt). **Alternatif Outdoor** offers treks, white-water rafting, and horseback-riding excursions (☎ 90-0252/417-2720; www.alternatifraft.com). **Kapadokya Balloons** lifts visitors high above the haunted landscape (☎ 90-0384/271-2442; www.kapadokyaballoons.com). **Best Lodging:** The **Ayşe Hanim Konagi Motel-Pension** has sweeping views of Ürgüp's golden cliff-houses. Join the family for dinner in the courtyard, where puppies tumble in the foliage (Dereler Mah. Sair, Mahvibaba sok 1; ☎ 90-0384/341-6949; www.aysehanimkonagi.com; double room and dinner from $72/£38). Ûhisar, famed for its sunset splendor, is home to the **Les Maisons de Cappadoce.** Spend the night in a swanky cave dwelling (Semiramis A.S., Belediye Meydani #6, BP 28; ☎ 90-0384/219-2782; www.cappadoce.com; $156–$216/£83–£114 double with breakfast). **Best Restaurant:** Push past Göreme's tourist traps to the **Orient** restaurant. This flowery bower serves hummus, tabbouleh, and samosas among trickling fountains (just past the bus station; ☎ 90-0384/271-2346; www.orientrestaurant.net; dinner for two $24/£13).

◀ *Cavusin area of Cappadocia in winter.*
© Thierry Cazabon/Getty Images

CHAMONIX, FRANCE

Off-piste skiing at the highest altitudes in Europe

People come from all over the world to ski the French Alps, the largest and most famous ski area in the world. For many of them, Chamonix, at the foot of Mont Blanc, is the ultimate destination. This historic ski town, the first to host the winter Olympics, lies at the crossroads of France, Italy, and Switzerland. Chamonix offers skiing at the highest altitudes in Europe, with extensive trails above tree line, all within view of the mythical Mont Blanc, Europe's tallest peak. Just 1 hour south of Geneva, Switzerland, the skiing near Mont Blanc is known for the best scenery and the most challenging slopes in the region. They also feature a wide range of terrain, immaculately groomed trails, and top-notch lifts and gondolas. But what may be the area's biggest draw is the off-piste, or off-the-trail, skiing. There are a number of reputable companies offering guided tours of the most challenging off-piste trails, including glacier runs. For an intermediate skier like me, this is thrilling stuff; for advanced skiers, it's a sort of mecca.

Other huge draws are the interlinked resorts and the single pass that's good for five or six excellent ski areas. This means you can ski one section, such as the groomed trails of the chic resort Megève, in the morning, take a lift up to one of the peaks of the adjacent Saint-Gervais ski area for lunch at a mountain-top restaurant, and spend the rest of the afternoon skiing the steep slopes at Saint-Gervais. With one pass, the Mont Blanc ski pass, you can ski both the Evasion–Mont Blanc and the Chamonix–Mont Blanc, with its nine separate skiing areas, and slopes for all levels.

Because Chamonix was one of the first ski resorts ever developed, there is an intriguing sense of history here that you won't find in other, more modern ski towns. It is considered the capital of the sport of mountaineering, which began here in the 19th century when climbing groups first attempted to conquer the awesome Mont Blanc and nearby peaks. Memorabilia from many early climbs are gathered in Chamonix's Alpine Museum. Though the ski resorts around Mont Blanc focus on skiing, climbing, and other outdoor sports, art enthusiasts may be surprised to know there is a mountain-top church in nearby Passy that is decorated by some of the world's most celebrated modern artists.

The ultimate activity in Chamonix is taking one of the longest cable-car rides in the world to a peak called Aiguille du Midi, literally "Needle of the South," at a height of 3,840m (12,600 ft.). This panoramic view of the Alps is unmatched. At this mountain-top way station, you have three choices. You can return down the way you came. You can walk through a rock tunnel and onto another cable car that whisks you into Italy. Or, if you're at least an intermediate skier, you can hook up with a guide and ski down the famous off-piste ski run, the Vallée Blanche, a 9-mile trip down the longest glacier in continental Europe.

◄ *Off-piste skiing on the Argentière Glacier.*
© John Norris/
PICIMPACT/Corbis

SPECIAL MOMENTS

1 **The Aiguille du Midi.** There are some opportunities in life that force you to put aside all caution and fear and step into the void. For me, one of those was the trip to the Aiguille du Midi, the thrilling and terrifying cable-car ride into the sky. This cable car, called a *téléphérique,* is not for the claustrophobic—they cram you in like sardines—but looking out the window as it makes its impossibly steep ascent can feel almost like a religious experience. Once at the top, prepare to have some altitude issues; shortness of breath and lightheadedness are the most common. But once you get used to the thin air, you can take the elevator to the rooftop observation deck where you can say bonjour to Mont Blanc

and to other peaks in Italy and Switzerland.

2 **An art-filled mountain-top church in Passy.** Exploring the Mont Blanc region has its surprises. For example, in the tiny village of Passy, about a 20-minute car ride from Chamonix, there is a trail of outdoor art along the winding mountain road. My favorite is an Alexander Calder sculpture, a black steel silhouette of the Mont Blanc range with a bright orange setting sun. Farther up the mountain, on the Plateau d'assy, is a tiny church called Eglise Notre-Dame de Toute Grâce that displays art by some of the top names of the 20th century, including a mosaic by Fernand Léger, ceramics and stained glass

by Marc Chagall, and ceramics by Henri Matisse. The church mimics the style of mountain chalets. The tall bell tower draws your eyes up to the mountains beyond.

3 **Snowshoeing in Combloux.** Vacation is a time to try new things, which is why I found myself snow-shoeing on trails at the Combloux ski resort, about 20 minutes from Chamonix. Those who have never strapped on the tennis-racket-like shoes and trudged through the snow should give it a try. It's an opportunity to take in the spectacular Alpine views at a more leisurely pace than downhill skiing allows. You can rent snowshoes and go on your own, or sign up for a guided hike on wide, groomed, and largely

flat forested trails. On a half-day group hike that might include families with children, you may be lucky enough to see a kind of snow rabbit, deer, and even the elusive chamois, a small goat-like antelope. By the end of the trip, expect to be rosy-cheeked and exhausted.

4 **The Calvary footpath in Megève.** A unique piece of history lies just on the outskirts of the trendy, chic ski village of Megève. A steep walking trail called the Calvary path begins to the east of the village (look for the sign, Le Calvaire), linking a series of 12 chapels that contain finely made wood statues in baroque and rococo styles that tell the story of the Stations of the Cross. It takes about an hour to make the round-trip journey. The trail begins at the village square. You walk up a steep portion that includes some steps, to the Mont d'Arbois plateau above the village. The breathtaking views of Megève and the surrounding mountains are your reward.

LAURA M. RECKFORD is the managing editor of the *Falmouth Enterprise* newspaper on Cape Cod. She has been the author for the last 9 years of *Frommer's Cape Cod, Nantucket & Martha's Vineyard* and was a coauthor of the first edition of *France For Dummies.* She can be reached at lawrareckford@hotmail.com.

ABOUT THE AUTHOR

YOUR TRIP

General Information: Contact the **Rhône Alps Tourist Office** at ☎ 33-4/72-59-21-59 or www.rhonealpes-tourism.us. The **Chamonix–Mont Blanc Tourist Office** is on place du Triangle-de-l'Amitié (☎ 33-4/50-53-00-24; www.chamonix.com). **Getting There:** Contact **Air France** (☎ 800/237-2747; www.airfrance.com). By rail to the Alps, **France National Railroad** (www.sncf.com) fast trains leave from Gare de Lyon in Paris to Grenoble daily; Chamonix is a 1-hour drive south. **What to See & Do:** For guided trips off-piste, including the Vallée Blanche, contact the **Compagnie des Guides** (☎ 33-4/50-47-76-55; www.guides-mont-blanc.com). For snowshoeing, there's the **Combloux-Megève Guide Company** at ☎ 33-4/50-21-55-11. They offer half-day trips for 23€ ($28). **Best Lodging: Les Fermes de Marie in Megève** offers the perfect Alpine experience: antique barns converted into luxury accommodations (chemin de Riante Colline, Megève; ☎ 33-4/50-93-03-10; www.fermesdemarie.com; 380€–454€/$456–$544). **Best Lodging Value: Hotel Gai Soleil in Megève** has a convenient location and comfortable rooms at a very good price (343 rue du Cret-du-Midi, Megève; ☎ 33-4/50-21-00-70; www.le-gai-soleil.fr; 78€–88€/$94–$106). **Best Restaurant: Restaurant Matafan** in the Hôtel Mont Blanc in Chamonix is a standout among the many restaurants in the area (BP 135–62 allée du Majestic; ☎ 04-50-53-05-64; entrees 60€/$72). **Best Restaurant Value:** When on a budget, choose pizza or an omelet at **Bartavel** in Chamonix (26 cours du Bartavel; ☎ 33-4/50-53-97-19; entrees 10€/$12). **When to Go:** Jan–Apr.

◀ *Chamonix at dusk.*
© Walter Bibikow/Getty Images

CHIANG MAI, THAILAND

From unspoiled beaches to hill-tribe villages in the north

As a travel writer, I believe that places, much like people, can be soul mates. There are destinations that have a spirit, an energy, and a pace that so perfectly mesh with your own that you feel simultaneously excited and at peace when you arrive,

I find Thailand a kindred spirit, a country whose *"mai pen rai,"* or *"no worries,"* philosophy encourages and rewards the adventurous soul, from the pristine islands of the south, to the frenetic streets of Bangkok, to the serene highlands of the North. *Mai pen rai* and the ever-present Thai smile also encourage a level of engagement with fellow travelers and locals that few other destinations do.

Nearly all international flights take you directly into Bangkok, where the glittering *chedi* of ancient temples rise amid a concrete jungle of modern skyscrapers, and where monks collect alms in the early morning as the party crowd heads home from the clubs. Though the staccato rhythm of Bangkok's controlled chaos is intoxicating, what draws me most to Thailand is the lilting pace of the islands and the northern highlands.

The south is renowned for its beaches, but overdevelopment has marred much of the landscape with high-rise hotels and hordes of foreign tourists. To truly tap into the *mai pen rai* culture, opt for the more intimate Gulf of Thailand beaches. Ko Samet, an off-the-radar island 2½ hours south of Bangkok, has been protected from overdevelopment by its status as a national park, so there is nothing to sully the silver-white sand in front of your bamboo bungalow or the gentle green hills rising up behind it.

Relaxation is the focus here, so ditch your flip-flops and prepare for a barefoot existence complete with beach massages and snorkeling. On Ko Samet, relaxation doesn't have to mean detachment; whether you're at the more upscale Paradee beach or on the younger Ao Phai, nighttime has locals and tourists sharing dinner in beachfront restaurants and dancing at small outdoor bars.

Next, take a flight via Bangkok to Chiang Mai, the northern city that combines the mellow pace of Ko Samet with the cultural liveliness of Bangkok. It's a city to get lost in, so ride a bike along the river, wander through Sunday's Walking Street market, explore Thai cuisine with a cooking class, and then prepare for the final part of your trip: a trek to visit the hill tribes of the surrounding highlands.

You may want to wait till you're in Chiang Mai to book, so you can seek advice from your hotel and other travelers. Guide companies change frequently, so it's best to get personal recommendations in order to avoid tourist traps. But the booking process is worth the hassle: There are few experiences more inspiring than perching atop an elephant on your way to a remote mountaintop village. Couple that with a candlelit dinner in a thatched hill-tribe hut, watching the sun rise over the mist-shrouded valley, and white-water rafting through raging rapids, and you have the vacation of a lifetime—one in which time, place, and people conspire to take you out of your comfort zone and reward your leap of faith with transcendent experiences.

◀ *Hill-tribe people (Meo tribe).*
© Jon Arnold Images/ Alamy

79

SPECIAL MOMENTS

1 **Ko Samet.** Within a day of arriving in Ko Samet, I felt as though I had lived there for years. It's a mere 4.8km (3 miles) long, so everything you need is within a short walk along the beach. And the slow pace allows the tiny island to quickly lull you into its restorative routine. You awaken to freshly picked pineapples and mangoes, spend days going from beach to ocean and back again, and spend evenings dining on plush pillows laid out in secluded coves. Each night, locals and tourists alike share drinks at the Silver Sand bar by the light of fire twirlers and falling stars.

2 **Cooking school.** Sure, it's often prepared on the street in makeshift carts, but don't let that informality mislead you. The complexity of Thai food—a subtle interplay of red-hot chili and fragrant lemongrass, sweet basil, and pungent ginger—is awe-inspiring. And there's no better way to explore those flavors than to take a cooking class. My favorites—Baipai Thai Cooking School in Bangkok and Pad Thai Cooking School in Chiang Mai—take visitors into the fields or local markets to learn how to select ingredients. Then it's into the kitchen, where a few hours of hard work will yield not only a spectacular feast but also the skills to recreate those gustatory experiences long after your vacation is over.

3 **Walking Street.** Shopping could be considered a national pastime in Thailand. There are day markets, night markets, weekend markets, and everything in between. Chiang Mai's Walking Street market (held on Sun on Ratchadamnoen Rd.) offers the ideal mix of local crafts, one-of-a-kind designs, and low-pressure bargaining. Walking Street starts at 3pm and continues by the light of paper lanterns till 11pm. You won't have to wade through stalls of designer knockoffs and cheap DVDs found in the city's Night Bazaar, as most of the vendors offer hand-crafted goods, from woven scarves to Laotian tapestries to wood and silver jewelry.

4 **Hill-tribe trek.** A trek through the highlands around Chiang Mai proves the travel adage that the journey is just as important as the destination. Following your guide as he machetes a path through the valley, climbing steep terrain on the back of an elephant, plunging under waterfalls—these moments are nearly as inspiring as the ultimate destination. The remoteness of the hilltop villages has enabled the tribes to maintain centuries-old traditions. You'll get a window into the lives of these Akha, Hmong, and Karen peoples as you watch them prepare traditional foods and share

rice moonshine while singing by candlelight. Be sure to request a trek that ends with a trip on a bamboo raft through the Mae Tang Valley. Floating gently down the river, mountains cradling you on either side, you realize that with such beauty in the world, there's little excuse not to live by *mai pen rai*.

Keep in mind that there are two kinds of trips—tribal village tours and jungle treks. If you join the former, you'll travel by van or coach to several villages and spend perhaps an hour in each. These villages have had decades of exposure to foreigners and have many modern conveniences—including hostels or small hotels for overnight guests. The jungle treks are more rugged, taking smaller groups (4–10) for 3 days to 2 weeks. Guests are often invited to sleep in a separate area of the headman's house, which is usually the largest in the compound, on basic straw mats and blankets.

COLLEEN CLARK made stops in England and Kenya before settling into Washington, D.C., but her best trip was through Thailand with her sister, Katie. She is a former assistant travel editor for USATODAY.com, coauthor of *Night+Day D.C.*, and a regular contributor to *DC Style* and *DC* magazine. Contact her at colleen.clark@gmail.com.

ABOUT THE AUTHOR

YOUR TRIP

General Information: The **Tourism Authority of Thailand** (**TAT**; www.tourismthailand.org) has a list of guides certified to lead hill-tribe treks. You'll book (and bargain) directly with trekking companies in Chiang Mai. Opt for a 3-day trip, which goes into areas out of reach from the tour-bus circuit. **Best Lodging: Paradee**'s private villas for luxurious seclusion in Ko Samet (☎ 66-038/64-4283; www.samedresorts.com/resort/paradee.htm; $300–$1,500/£159–£795); **Mandarin Oriental Dhara Dhevi**, in Chiang Mai, is a 24-hectare (60-acre) luxury resort with terraced rice paddies and private palace-style compounds (☎ 66-053/88-8888; www.mandarinoriental.com/chiangmai; $350–$6,000/£186–£3,180). **Best Lodging Value:** The **Silver Sand** beachfront bungalows are popular among the younger party set (Ao Pahi Beach, Ko Samet; ☎ 66-012/18-5195; $15–$40/£8–£21). Or try the more private **Ao Prao** cottages for the secluded beach and sunset views in Ko Samet (☎ 66-038/64-4100-3; www.samedresorts.com/resort/ao_prao.htm; $130–$250/£69–£132). In Chiang Mai, **Lai Tai**'s rooms filled with handcrafted furniture are a steal (☎ 66-053/27-1725; www.laithai.com; $20–$25/£11–£13). **Best Restaurant:** Dine on fresh grilled seafood under the colorful paper lanterns at **Jep's Bungalows** in Ko Samet (☎ 66-038/64-4112; www.jepbungalow.com; entrees from $4/£2). Nosh on spicy curries at **The Riverside,** a teak house on the Mae Ping River in Chiang Mai (☎ 66-053/24-3239; www.theriversidechiangmai.com; $5–$7/£3–£4). **Best Dining:** Roti—fried flatbread drizzled with condensed milk—cooked at a beach stand or mango, freshly chopped by a fruit seller.

◀ *A beach on Ko Samet Island.*
© Gavriel Jecan/Riser/Getty Images

CONNEMARA, IRELAND

A wild, windy, isolated land clinging to the "old" ways

The cutesy leprechaun-and-shillelagh tourist clichés of Ireland quickly wear thin for me—and that's when I head straight for the wild west: the untrammeled countryside of Connemara. It's just an hour northwest of lively, artsy Galway City, but it seems like another world entirely, all scrappy fishing villages, granite headlands, and wind-buffeted marshy heath. While coachfuls of tourists clog the panoramic highways of the Cliffs of Moher or the Ring of Kerry a few hours' drive south, you can meander happily for hours along Connemara's narrow roads without worrying much what you'd do if a car came from the opposite direction.

Granted, at first it may strike you as a bleak and moonlike landscape—"Where are all the trees?" you may wonder. Well, history lies heavy on this land: Those trees were hacked down a century ago by impoverished locals and turned into ship timbers and furniture for English country houses (although, if you head inland, eventually you'll see how reforestation efforts have recently blanketed the hillsides with sturdy little green conifers). In some ways, the 21st century doesn't even seem to have arrived yet in Connemara; isolated stone cottages huddle close to the roadside, perhaps with a donkey tethered in the side yard. The map pinpoints a town and, when you get there, you find nothing more than a crossroads with two pubs and a store. But that's just how I like it—I feel as if here, at last, I have found the "real" Ireland.

Cut off by abrupt mountain ranges with odd, evocative names—the Maum Turks, the Twelve Bens—this tough countryside has been sparsely populated ever since the infamous Potato Famine of the 1840s, and those stubborn survivors who remained here have clung as tenaciously as barnacles to the old ways. In this designated *Gaeltacht* (Irish-speaking area), the pubs feature traditional music, a lively scramble of fiddles and bodhrains and tin whistles; natives wear thick handmade Aran knit sweaters in the same elaborately stitched patterns their fisherman ancestors wore. (You can pick these up at bargain prices in crafts boutiques in every town, along with gift objects carved of vivid green Connemara marble and richly hued Connemara tweeds.) Even today, resourceful locals slice up the bog soil for peat, an important cheap source of fuel; look along the roadside for stacks of turf bricks, set out to air dry, and inhale deeply to detect the sweet scent of a nearby cottage burning turf in a fireplace.

Forget about waiting for fair weather; you won't get it anyway, not here in the west of Ireland, where just about every day has at least a little period when the weather is "soft." How would the land attain that astonishing shade of green if it didn't rain constantly? But Connemara is the sort of land that only gets more breathtaking when the clouds pile up in dramatic masses, with the sea boiling and crashing off the ragged coastline. The wild, lonely, land's-end feel of the place is what makes my blood race. I wouldn't have it any other way.

◀ *A pub in Connemara.*
© Paul A. Souders/Corbis

SPECIAL MOMENTS

1 **Sky Drive and Clifden.** All tourists know about the spectacular Cliffs of Moher down south in County Clare; many fewer find their way to the equally jaw-dropping views from Sky Drive, which winds along the coastal precipice north of Connemara's principal coastal town, Clifden. Come here in the late afternoon when the sun begins to lower into the glittering western sea; stand on one of the roadside pull-outs and face into the winds, and you'd swear you could see across to Boston. Just don't look down.

Clifden is a busy tourist town these days but has an enviable location at the top of picturesque Clifden Bay. It's an attractive town with tall church steeples and Victorian architecture at the edge of thick forests. With its plentiful restaurants, hotels, and pubs, it makes a handy base for exploring the area.

2 **Pony rides.** If you really want to learn the intricacies of this terrain,

get in the saddle. The landscape may *look* flat, but each twist of the track reveals hidden gorges, streams, and lakes. Horses need to be sure-footed to cross Connemara's delicate bog lands, where sudden marshy patches can plunge you fetlock-deep into water, and the native Connemara pony is sure-footed indeed. It's also known for its gentle temperament, which makes it ideal for children. Up close you see how the harsh rock-strewn land is softened by gorse and heather and wildflowers; you can feel the turf spring under your pony's hooves. Or, if splashing along the Atlantic beaches is your dream, rent a pony in a seacoast village like Cleggan, where your mount may be able to wade at low tide across the shallow channel to Omey Island. The **Cleggan Riding Centre** (www. clegganridingcentre.com) offers beach and mountain treks. Another good outfitter is **Connemara and Coast Trails** (www.connemara-trails.

com). Rides are for beginning and experienced riders alike.

3 **Cong.** From the inland town of Oughterard—considered the gateway to Connemara—cruises launch across Lough Corrib, Ireland's biggest lake, beloved of fishermen for its wealth of brown trout and salmon. After stopping at the monastery island of Inchagoill, boats proceed on to the picturesque village of Cong, which trades heavily on its role as location for the John Ford/John Wayne classic film *The Quiet Man*. I find something endearing about the rascally way the townsfolk work to profit from their brief brush with Hollywood—stroll through the village, certainly, to take a look at this stage-set perfect Irish village. But it's out on the lake that I feel most in touch with the Gaelic spirit of the film, gazing across the serene waters to the green hills of the Galway-Mayo border.

4 **Roundstone.** Another stage-set perfect village is Roundstone, on the coast south of Clifden, which bills itself, with some justification, as Connemara's most picturesque village. Don't expect Miami-style beaches in this part of the world, but Roundstone's Gurteen Beach is one of the best, its white sands made of finely ground shells rather than clumpy gray quartz. Surrounding the busy fishing harbor is a sea-front main street jam-packed with charming cafes and shops, with a local specialty in bodrans, flutes, and harps. After a day tramping, cycling, or pony trekking around the area, it's glorious to ensconce yourself by a crackling fire in a pub—Eldon's, Ryan's, take your pick—and enjoy a rousing singalong. From Roundstone you can head on to the little community of Letterfrack at the edge of the Connemara National Park, close to Kylemore Abbey. Founded by Quakers, it has a handful of pubs and B&Bs in a glorious natural setting.

HOLLY HUGHES has traveled the globe as an editor and writer—she's the former executive editor of Fodor's Travel Publications and author of *Frommer's New York City with Kids* and *Frommer's 500 Places to Take Your Kids before They Grow Up.* She also edits the annual *Best Food Writing* anthology. New York City makes a convenient jumping-off place for her travels.

ABOUT THE AUTHOR

YOUR TRIP

General Information: Contact **Ireland West Tourism** (Aras Fáilte, Foster St., Galway; ☎ 353-091/537700) or the **Oughterard Tourist Office** (Main St., Oughterard; ☎ 353-091/552808). **Getting There:** The best way to get around this region is to drive on your own. Drive northwest out of Galway City on the N29; Clifden lies about 64km (40 miles) from Galway City. From Galway City, **Bus Éireann** provides daily service to Clifden (☎ 353-091/562000; www.buseireann.ie). **Best Lodging: Ballynahinch Castle,** in a converted 16th-century manor, is the place to sleep in style after a night's fly-fishing (Recess; ☎ 353-095/31006; www.ballynahinch-castle.com; 210€–450€/$250–$540). **Ross Lake House Hotel** is a well-situated Georgian country house with a welcoming atmosphere (N29, Rosscahill, Oughterard; ☎ 353-091-550109; www.rosslakehotel.com; 130€–260€/$156–$312). **Best Lodging Value: Errisbeg Lodge** has rustic decor, ocean *and* mountain views, and a location within a short walk of fine beaches (Clifden Rd., Roundstone; ☎ 353-095/35807; www.errisbeglodge.com; 80€–96€/$96–$115). **Best Restaurant: The Station House Hotel** offers sophisticated dining in bustling downtown Clifden (N59, Clifden; ☎ 353-095/22946; 20€–45€/$24–$54). **Best Restaurant Value: O'Dowd's Seafood Restaurant,** on the harbor in Roundstone, is a homey, warm-hearted place where you can sample the bounty of the nearby sea (☎ 353-095/35809; www.odowdsrestaurant.com; 10€–25€/$12–$30). **When to Go:** The best time to visit Connemara is between May and September.

◀ *Connemara landscape.*
© Art Kowalsky/Alamy

THE COTSWOLDS, ENGLAND

A world of quaint stone villages & ancient country lanes

After a visit to the Cotswolds, 62km (100 miles) west of London, the rest of England will become a footnote.

From the 14th to the 16th centuries, fat wool merchants grew even fatter on great profits made from the heavy ringlets of fleece on their contented sheep. With all that loot, they built the finest examples of domestic architecture in England—manor houses, churches, and even entire villages made of honey-colored stone that turns golden at sunset.

The hamlets have such names as Old Sodbury (that's no joke) and Chipton-under-Witchwood. Many English families dream of owning "a little snuggery in the weal," or a cottage in the dale. Those English families include Prince Charles and the Duchess of Cornwall, Camilla, who live at Tetbury.

Since the Industrial Revolution forgot about the Cotswolds, the network of quaint villages in these limestone hills remains to delight later generations. Throw in old stone walls, rivers with such names as Windrush, streams guarded by weeping willows, ancient country lanes, and well-manicured cottage gardens, and you've got one of those photo ops for an English country calendar, the kind local merchants pass out free at Christmas.

If I've painted too rosy a picture, here's the downside. "It's inhabited mainly by geriatrics," one critic lamented. "Trampled by too many Americans who didn't buy enough souvenirs in Stratford-upon-Avon," claims another. "Overpriced, overrun, and overhyped," cries yet another. All critics, even unfair ones, have a point. But in the case of the Cotswolds, don't listen to the naysayers. These rolling hills and villages are a timeless tableau of England the way it used to be. There is authentic and rustic nostalgia here that existed long before decorators heard of the "Laura Ashley aesthetic."

The pre-Raphaelite artist and craftsman William Morris "discovered" the Cotswolds in 1871, and the world has been wearing out shoe leather "walking the Wolds" ever since. Even if at home you drive 2 blocks to where you're going, abandon your car here, as I do, and walk in the Cotswolds. From the woodlands to the grassy knolls to the russet-earth fields, there are enough panoramas to satisfy any hiker.

Wave if you see a parson and always be willing to stop for a greeting, as I recently did with a man who was young in 1910. In his croaky voice, he said, "I see you're discovering our patches of lichen and spotted antiquity." He hobbled on his way, leaving me to ponder what he'd said.

Because of its stately High Street of elegant buildings, Broadway is the most visited town. In the words of Henry James, it has "so much character that it rubs off on the visitor." Well, the great novelist never saw all of today's souvenir shops, ice-cream stands, "quaintery" tearooms, and massive traffic.

Instead of spending time here, I'd suggest visits to Chipping Campden, Moreton-in-Marsh, Bourton-on-the-Water, and Stow-on-the-Wold. These are small towns, but even more alluring are the little villages where time has stood still. My favorites are Bibury and Painswick.

◀ *Arlington Row, Bibury.*
© Charles A. Blakeslee/ AGE Fotostock, Inc.

SPECIAL MOMENTS

1 The Cotswold Way. I've walked the length and breadth of England over the years, but in all my hikes none appealed to me more than the 64km (104-mile) path called "The Cotswold Way." To traverse its length would take 7 to 8 days, but you can join it at any point, even for an afternoon.

The path begins at Chipping Campden, on the northern frontier of the Cotswolds, meandering its way to the spa city of Bath—and marked with bright yellow signs at every intersection en route. You traipse through forests and fields along rocky escarpments where views open onto medieval wool villages and farmhouses. You can always do as the English do and detour over to one of these hamlets for a pint at a time-mellowed pub.

Any tourist office will give you a map outlining the route, or else you can buy the English Ramblers' *The Cotswold Way Handbook.*

2 Bibury & Painswick. William Morris called Bibury "the most beautiful village in England," and we have no cause to dispute his 19th-century assessment. What the artist saw is still here, still intact, still awaiting a visit from you. Lying 10km (6 miles) northeast of the city of Cirencester on the B4425, Bibury opens onto the little River Coln. With its river meadow, the town has been featured on more English calendars than any other. Its highlight is Arlington Row, a group of 17th-century gabled cottages built for weavers.

Just when I fall in love and want to live forever in Bibury, Painswick beckons to my fickle soul. The sleepy stone-built Cotswold town lies 24km (5 miles) northwest of Cirencester and is almost as beautiful as Bibury. Instead of honey gold, houses here appear in a silvery gray. Painswick is a journey back to yesterday, and even Prince Charles called it the epitome of an English village.

3 Antiquing the Wolds. Let's have truth in advertising here. The days are long gone when you could arrive in Burford (one of the best centers for buying antiques) and make off with a collectible such as a piece of exquisite antique porcelain that Greta Garbo "stole" for £5 in 1966. Today, antiques dealers in the Cotswolds are serious dealers who know the price of everything from that old barometer that would look great in your study to that 19th-century cameo brooch allegedly worn by Queen Victoria when she was still a princess. Stow-on-the-Wold competes with Burford as the antiques center of the Cotswolds. Even Moreton-in-Marsh has gotten in on the act of putting up ANTIQUARIUS signs, hawking everything from 19th-century surgical instruments to Victorian miniatures. I'll let you in on a secret: Today I skip these high-priced antiques shops and search the backcountry roads and little hamlets. Almost every village has an antiques store charging prices often half of what the greedy Broadway merchants demand.

4 Sleeping around. Nothing seems more Dickensenian than to

sleep in an old stone inn deep in the heart of the Cotswolds, minus the tasseled nightcap, of course. From Georgian manors to 15th-century half-timbered houses, the Cotswolds have the classiest inns in all of England. Over the years, I have slept in most of them, including both the fancy ones and those that define themselves as country pubs with rooms upstairs. Regrettably, Cotswold bedrooms are pricey retreats but can teach you much about the art of living. Expect creaky floors, low-beamed ceilings, and, of course, a ghost or two. I once had a chat with Henry VIII's last wife, Catherine Parr, the last of his "daisy chain" of queens. Or did I merely dream that? After the hordes of day-trippers have departed from Broadway for the day, the **Lyon Arms** on High Street (☎ 44-01386/852255) is still the market leader. In business since 1532, it even sheltered Charles I. Sit in the private rear garden at twilight and listen to the sound of a nightingale.

ABOUT THE AUTHOR

DARWIN PORTER is one of the world's most prolific travel writers. His books for Frommer's include guides to the Caribbean, Italy, France, Germany, and England. A Hollywood columnist and a celebrity biographer, Porter is also a radio broadcaster; his shows on American popular culture are heard in all 50 states.

YOUR TRIP

General Information: For an overview, check with **Heart of England Tourism** (Larkhill Rd., Worcester; ☎ 44-01905/76100; www.visitheartofengland.com). The website for **Cirencester** covers the whole of the Cotswolds (www.cotswold.gov.uk). **Cotswold Walking Holidays** offers both self-guided and guided tours (Festival House, Jessop Ave.; Cheltenham; ☎ 44-01242/633680; www.cotswoldwalks.com). **Getting There:** From London, take the motorway to Oxford and from here head west along A40 to Burford, gateway to the Cotswolds, lying 122km (76 miles) northwest of London and 32km (20 miles) west of Oxford. **Best Lodging:** Luxurious digs are found at **The Cotswold House Hotel** (The Square, Chipping Campden; ☎ 44-01386/840330; www.cotswoldhouse.com; £130–£265/$234–$477 double, including English breakfast). This 1800 Regency hotel stands in a walled garden. **Best Lodging Value:** **The Pear Tree at Purton** is 13km (8 miles) southeast of Cirencester (Church End, Purton, near Swindon; ☎ 44-01793/772100; www.peartreepurton.co.uk; £110–£140/$198–$252 double). The Pear Tree is a country house with four-poster beds and a Victorian garden. **Best Restaurant:** **Le Champignon Sauvage** is the finest French cuisine in the Cotswolds, with exquisite flavors (24–26 Suffolk Rd.; Cheltenham; ☎ 44-01242/573449; four-course fixed-price dinner £55/$99). **Best Restaurant Value:** Celebrity chef Raymond Blanc operates **Le Petit Blanc**, in the Queen's Hotel, where a fixed-price French dinner costs £12/$22 (the Promenade, Cheltenham; ☎ 44-01242/266800). **When to Go:** Apr–Oct.

◀ *Cotswold village.*
© Nik Wheeler/Corbis

CRETE, GREECE

A rugged walk on an island both epic & timeless

In Crete you leap from one epic time frame to another with the greatest of ease, from the imposing harbor-side Venetian walls of Heraklion, where novelist Nikos Kazantzakis of *Zorba the Greek* fame is buried, to the profusion of needle-like Turkish minarets at Rethymnon where Ottoman pashas once ruled, to the lovingly restored Minoan ruins at Knossos, with their frescoes of fearless young girls vaulting over large bulls.

The rugged scenery is equally epic and timeless, and in the White Mountains to the west you'll find my favorite walk on earth, the 16km (10-mile) Samaria Gorge. This one-way trek, which ends at the sea, is an exciting amalgam of awesome cliffs, icy clear rock pools, tiny chapels, and magical flowers ranging from rich purple sun roses to bright gold chrysanthemums. If you're lucky, you may even spot the odd eagle circling up there in the azure, or a wild mountain chamois (or *kri kri*) perched sure-footed on a high ledge. Pliny thought it was the most magnificent canyon in the world. Who are we to argue?

Any reasonably fit person up to 70—if that doesn't sound too ageist—can manage the walk with ease in 5 hours. (Just remember to take water with you and wear strong shoes.) The weather in April can be iffy, and in July and August the gorge is a congested oven. May and October are quieter and not too hot. From November to March the gorge is a raging flood, impassable.

You can make this trip from your hotel in the Venetian-influenced former capital Chania either by tour coach or private taxi. An hour-long drive brings you to Omalos, a 1,067m (3,500-ft.) plateau so perfectly flat and circular you would think aliens had made it their base. Descend the steep winding Xylóskalo wooden steps past huge pines. Once all of western Crete was filled with such trees. An incredible 3-year fire in the Middle Ages decimated most of them. Today, maples, cypresses, and holly trees proliferate once more in the sheltered canyon.

As you continue along the bottom of the gorge, stumbling over dazzling rocks interspersed with bright pink oleanders, you'll pass numerous shrines and chapels. The highlight is the 14th-century Ossias Maria church with its gorgeous Byzantine frescoes in the old ruined village of Samaria, halfway down the gorge. Take invigorating dips in natural pools along the bed of the canyon, continually refreshed by a mountain stream: You won't stay in long.

The gorge narrows as you go on. At Sideroportes (the Iron Doors) you could lie on the stony ground with your feet touching one side and your outstretched hands the other while above you ochre cliffs soar to 549m (1,800 ft.). The gorge finally opens out onto the seashore at the hamlet of Aghia Roumeli, where you'll find a handful of tavernas, a beach of baking-hot pebbles—try not to walk on them barefoot—and the cool, deep gunmetal-blue Libyan Sea. No swim will ever feel as good. The next part of the trip is by boat eastward along the rugged coast to the village of Chora Sfakion, where allies made their retreat from the Germans down the parallel Askifou Gorge in 1943. There the bus or taxi that brought you to Omalos is waiting to take you back across the White Mountains to Chania. Kalimera!

◄ *Samaria Gorge.*
© Ute & Juergen Schimmelpfennig/Zefa/Corbis

SPECIAL MOMENTS

1 Paleochoria. Built on the site of ancient Kalamidis, beside the remains of a 13th-century Venetian fort, this coastal village of 2,000 is 24km (15 miles) west of Aghia Roumeli. You get to Paleochoria by the mountain road from Chania, a scenic trip easily managed in an hour and a half by rented car or taxi (avoid the slow local bus). The village has long been popular with backpackers looking for a place to chill out. Today it's expanded a bit but the atmosphere has hardly changed at all, having acquired a cult status among loyal regulars who wouldn't dream of holidaying anywhere else. Sophisticated it is not: You come here to escape the comforts of your hotel and delights of Chania town for the day and enjoy the basic Mediterranean pleasures of sun, sea, and sand in one of the island's most isolated settings. The village's prized mile-long beach is fringed by tavernas, rooms to let, and modest hotels, and there's a nearby wealth of Byzantine churches and archaeological sites such as Lissos, Syia, Irtakina, and Elyros to explore.

2 The ghosts of Franko-castello. Located almost on the seashore 9km (6 miles) east of Chora Sfakion, this is one of the most hauntingly memorable ruined forts you'll see anywhere. Venetian-built, with walls and towers still largely intact, it's best viewed from the sea. The Hamlet-style legend is that at dawn during late spring the ghosts of dead Sfakians can be seen parading beside the crumbling walls. They're called *droussolites*, as they appear when the dew (*drossia*) is on the ground, but spoilsport scientists say the whole thing is just a mirage caused by humid weather conditions. A tiny, nondescript escapists' resort has sprung up of late, and the whole coast is studded with caves and Byzantine remains.

3 Chania. This, for my money, is the best town in Crete, leaving tatty capital Heraklion out in the cold. Pride of place goes to the crescent-shaped Venetian harbor, miraculously well preserved after the heavy German bombardments of World War II and ringed by evocative tavernas where you can sample *oktapodi*, *lithrini*, *astakos*, and other Cretan marine delights with some chilled white Minos wine at a waterside table. As you explore the town, don't miss the Venetian-built Kastelli walls, the old Topanas quarter with

its traditional mansions, the Marseille-style central market, and the lovely public gardens.

4   Kastelli-Kissamou. The extreme northwestern corner of Crete—where two tiny peninsulas enclose the charming, laid-back port of Kastelli-Kissamou (named Kastelli after its Venetian fort and Kissamou after the surrounding subprovince)—is a secret area I treasure greatly. Even now so few people visit here that its natural beauty and character have remained largely unspoiled. Farming and agriculture continue to prevail over tourism, and the people are especially warm and welcoming (as indeed they are all over Crete). The scenery is magnificent, with long beaches, lush plains, and high purple mountains, and you can enjoy the simple pleasures of home-grown olives, sheep's cheese, and wine (try the excellent Kissamiotiko red) in a local taverna. It's like going back a few decades. Check it out when you go—but don't tell everyone.

PETER STONE is a London-born writer living in Madrid. As well as being the author of *Frommer's Madrid*, he's a Mediterranean addict who has enjoyed prolonged sojourns in Greece, Italy, and North Africa and published articles on a variety of Homeresque havens from Akrotiri to Astipaleia. Contact him at petine@teleline.es.

ABOUT THE AUTHOR

YOUR TRIP

General Information: Contact the **West Crete Tourist Office** (29 Kythonia St., Chania; ☎ 30-28210/92-000; www.west-crete.com). The official tourist office in Chania is at 40 Kriai, off 1866 Square (☎ 30-28210/92-943). **Getting There: Delta** is the only American airline with nonstop service to Athens (☎ 800/241-4141; www.delta.com). **Olympic Airlines** offers at least three flights daily from Athens in summer (www.olympicairlines.com). Contact any one of the local travel agencies in Chania for bookings to and from the Gorge. **Best Lodging:** The **Minoa Palace** is a luxury hotel on 2.4 hectares (6 acres) of beachside gardens 13km (8 miles) from Chania town (Platanias-Chania; ☎ 30-28210/93-6500; 200€–350€/$240–$420 double). **Best Lodging Value:** The **Palazzo di Pietro** is not especially cheap but still an excellent value. This marvelously converted old Venetian house in Chania has only seven rooms, so book well in advance (Aghion Deka 13, Old Harbor; ☎ 30-28210/20-410; www.palazzodipietro.com; 117€/$140 double). Another charmingly preserved hostelry is **Pension Teresa** (Angelou 2; fax 30-28210/92-798; 40€–50€/$48–$60 double). **Best Restaurant: Pigadi tou Tourkou** is a former Turkish steam bath converted into an atmospheric eating spot in the heart of the old town (K. Sarpaki 1–3; ☎ 30-28210/5-4547; 20€–25€/$24–$30). **Best Restaurant Value: Konaki Restaurant** (Georgious Theodorakis Kondilaki St. 40, Old Town; ☎ 30-28210/91-7130; 12€–15€/$14–$18). **When to Go:** May–June, Sept–Oct. The Gorge is open mid-April through mid-October.

◀ *Rethymnon harbor at dusk.*

CUBA

A visit to the finest colonial cities in the Americas

Were Cuba like any other Caribbean nation, its appeal would be predictable: miles of stunning sandy beaches lined with palm trees, charming colonial towns, a surfeit of dark rum and attractive women. But Cuba is not like any other nation.

Cuba is like no place on earth.

For nearly half a century, this complicated nation of 11 million has commanded the world stage in a manner wholly incommensurate with its small size and economic insignificance. Cuba under Castro has fiercely but painfully defied a U.S.-led trade embargo and both achieved and renounced some of its lofty ideals. It remains a fascinating living laboratory of social and political experimentation, as well as a test case for a people's perseverance.

Creaky and sputtering, Cuba remains caught in a tortuous time warp. On my very first night in Havana, in 1999, a blackout crashed the capital, and I spent the rest of the night wandering the streets of La Habana Vieja, the crumbling heart of the city. With no generators or backup systems, virtually the only illumination in the entire city came from vintage American Chevys and Cadillacs as they rumbled around corners and shined their watery headlights down dark alleyways.

While most of the planet plunges ahead at a dizzying digital pace, Cuba, a once-prosperous place, crawls along in isolated slow-motion. Many of Havana's disintegrating, formerly grand colonial buildings are little more than facades, like movie sets hiding hollow interiors. Those American jalopies from the '40s and '50s are patched together with a hodgepodge of parts. Public transportation is more a matter of prayer than policy, so roads are crowded with ordinary folks desperately hitchhiking, trying to get to work, to school, to the next town. Neighbors are forced to improvise and invent solutions for their accommodation, plumbing, and electricity needs.

Yet Cuba is exhilarating, one of the most mind-bending and sensation-tingling countries a traveler can visit. And it is a flood of indelible images, many inspiring, others heartbreaking: Groups of underemployed men wiling away the hours playing dominoes on card tables set up in the street. Sexy couples with well-oiled hips gliding across dance floors. Combative political billboards forlornly pitched along the side of empty highways. Mile-long lines for ice cream at state-owned Coppelia shops. School children—those famous "young pioneers"—in identical maroon- and mustard-colored uniforms, smiling sweetly for photographs.

And then there's the music. I marveled when I realized that during my first visit to the island I saw at least one live band—and usually several—every single day during 5 weeks in Cuba. In midafternoon or late at night, you're likely to stumble upon an open-air cafe with a smiling band of preternaturally cool musicians locked in a perfect swing groove.

Of course, Cuba cannot forever remain a land of time travel. At some point, surely, it will get reeled in by a ravenous Western world. Some, both within and beyond Cuba, pray for that day. Others plainly fear it. Intransigence lingers, but as always, Cuba soldiers on.

◀ *A man from Havana.*
© Jon Arnold/
DanitaDelimont.com

SPECIAL MOMENTS

1 **Havana.** Once the grandest colonial city in all the Americas, Havana is an intoxicating place. Decades of neglect have done little, amazingly, to destroy its grandeur. The old quarter, La Habana Vieja, is the hub of life. Gringos flock to Cathedral Square, marked by a glorious baroque church, while Hemingway's old haunts, El Floridita and La Bodeguita del Medio, are quintessential spots for a mojito. UNESCO, Canadian, and European monies have been instrumental in restoring the sheen to—and compared to the rest of the city, sanitizing—La Habana Vieja, giving birth to new cafes and hotels in handsomely renovated buildings. Beyond the old quarter are zones that offer a truer window onto Cuban life, including the dilapidated sea-front Malecón, Centro Habana, and Vedado.

2 **Colonial Trinidad.** Fetching Trinidad, founded in 1514 and one of Cuba's original seven settlements, is one of the finest colonial towns in all of the Americas. Within a few square blocks of cobblestone streets—with pastel-colored 18th- and 19th-century houses, palaces, and plazas—is a world of undisturbed beauty and quiet charm, almost jarring when juxtaposed against the decay and chaos of urban life elsewhere in Cuba. The town's setting, perched on the slope of a hill, with stunning bell-tower views of the Caribbean and thickly forested mountains, is as lovely as the town itself. The baroque, 19th-century Plaza Mayor, elaborately adorned with statuary and towering palms and enclosed by white wrought-iron fences, is one of Cuba's most beautiful. It's ringed by magnificent palaces and pastel-colored houses with red-tile roofs and wood shutters. The highlight of the Plaza Mayor, and the most evocative reminder of Trinidad's glory days, is the lovingly restored Palacio Brunet, a colonial mansion dating back to 1704. Though Trinidad has been very much discovered, and busloads of tourists wander it by day, there is no massive tourism infrastructure yet, and the city's 300-plus *casas particulares,* or private guesthouses, are the perfect place to stay.

3 **El Oriente (Santiago and Baracoa).** The *Oriente,* or East, of Cuba marches to its own Caribbean rhythms. Santiago de Cuba, Cuba's second city, is on the opposite side of the island from Havana and a world apart. Sweltering and a bit frenetic even when not engulfed in lively *carnaval* celebrations, the city has produced some of Cuba's greatest contemporary musicians as well as several of its most stalwart revolutionaries, and its strong traditions of Afro-Cuban culture and resolutely Caribbean feel distinguish it from the rest of Cuba. Small and isolated, thickly tropical Baracoa,

cradled by bays and mountains, and fed by 10 rivers, is the most picturesque spot in all of Cuba. Established by Diego Velázquez in 1511, it is the oldest colonial city in the Americas. Locals also claim that Cristóbal Colón (or Columbus, as he's known in English speaking parts) first landed at this spot in late November 1492.

4 **Cuban *son* and *casas de la trova*.** Septets of octogenarian musicians play traditional Cuban *son*, which has its roots in the 1920s and whose rhythms are largely unaffected by outside influence and changing global tastes. You can and will hear live music anywhere you go in Cuba, but the best places for authentic traditional son and salsa are Havana, Trinidad, Camagüey, Santiago, and Baracoa. The last three possess the country's best *casas de la trova*, relaxed, usually open-air bars that are thick with sultry air, slowly rotating ceiling fans, and grinning musicians plunking away on weathered guitars and stand-up basses.

NEIL E. SCHLECHT is a graduate of Georgetown University's School of Foreign Service and holds master's degrees from the University of Texas at Austin. He has worked on development programs for the E.U. and authored a dozen travel guides and articles on two of his obsessions: tennis and wine. He has lived in Spain, Brazil, and Ecuador.

ABOUT THE AUTHOR

YOUR TRIP

General Information: For Americans, traveling to Cuba is complicated, even for those with official and family reasons to travel. Other nationalities can travel freely to Cuba, and Canadian, Latin American, and European airlines fly to Havana (chartered flights depart from New York and Miami) as well as Santiago de Cuba and Varadero. Americans without explicit permission from the U.S. Treasury who choose to travel illegally (at the risk of significant fines) must go through a third country. Contact **Cuba Tourist Board Canada** (☎ 416/362-0700; www.gocuba.ca); **Cuba Tourist Board Great Britain** (☎ 44-0207/240-6655; cubatouristboard.london@virgin.net); and, in the U.S., the **Cuban Interests Section** (☎ 202/797-8518). The Cuban websites www.cubatravel.cu and www.cubaweb.cu also have useful information. **Best Lodging:** In Old Havana, **NH Parque Central,** Calle Neptuno, between Prado and Zulueta (☎ 53-7/860-6627; www.nh-hotels.com; $205–$270) or **Hotel Santa Isabel,** Calle Baratillo 9 (☎ 53-7/860-8201; $221–$269). **Best Lodging Value: Casa Meyer,** Gustavo Izquierdo 111, Trinidad (☎ 53-419/344-4 20; $25); **Hotel El Castillo,** Calle Calixto García, Loma el Paraís, Baracoa (☎ 53-21/4-2125; www.gaviota-grupo.com; $46–$58). **Best Restaurant: La Bodeguita del Medio,** Habana Vieja (☎ 53-7/867-1374; main courses $8–$30); **ZunZún,** Av. Manduley 159, Reparto Vista Alegre, Santiago de Cuba (☎ 53-22/64-1528; main courses $6–$21). **Best Restaurant Value:** *Paladar* restaurants, such as **Paladar Estela,** Trinidad (☎ 53-419/4329; $5–$10) or **La Colonial,** Martí 123, Baracoa (☎ 53-21/4-5391; $6–$9). **When to Go:** Dec–Mar, during the dry season. Hurricane season is June to October.

◀ *Trinidad street scene.*
© Bob Krist Photography

CUMBERLAND ISLAND, GEORGIA

Birds, beaches, sunsets, wild horses & a venerable inn

Off the southern coast of Georgia, Cumberland Island remained America's best-kept secret until "Prince Charming," as he was called, changed all that. The date was September 23, 1996, when *People* magazine's "sexiest man alive"—otherwise known as John F. Kennedy, Jr.—arrived by boat with a beautiful blonde. It was the chicly dressed stylist, Carolyn Bessette, who would become his bride that day, far removed from the invasions of the paparazzi.

Long before "John-John," Cumberland had been a retreat of the rich and famous. The island was a 19th-century haven for Thomas and Lucy Carnegie. Thomas was the business partner and younger brother of the legendary financier Andrew Carnegie.

A salt marsh, a river, and a sound separate Cumberland from the mainland of Georgia. The island is 18 miles long and 3 miles wide, and locals like to tell people they have a larger land mass than Manhattan.

Cumberland's 36,415 acres is real Scarlett O'Hara country, with salt-pruned live oaks dripping with Spanish moss. Once antebellum plantations flourished here, growing indigo, cotton, and sugarcane in the rich soil. But this slave economy came crashing down after the Civil War. Now maritime forests have reclaimed the former plantations.

Cumberland is the largest and southernmost of the romantic Sea Islands. In 1972, it was established as a National Seashore, protected by the government. Previously the National Park Service had singled out Cumberland and Cape Cod as the two most significant natural areas along either the Atlantic or Gulf Coast.

I never tire of looking at the chestnut-brown wild horses grazing. Thomas Carnegie set loose a train car's worth of horses on the island in the 1920s. As you make your way through cabbage palms and resurrection ferns, the whinnies of these horses can be heard floating on the breeze.

You can ride bikes along the Main Road (that's what it's called), and visit some offshoot arteries. But bikes are forbidden on the floor of the wilderness. Cars are also outlawed, even on the main roads, which are really no more than paths.

Pick up a trail map at the St. Marys Visitor Center and chart your course on the island, as hiking is the only option for seeing Cumberland. There are more than 50 miles of backcountry trails.

Instead of the heavily trod routes, I prefer the romantically named "Lost Trail," heading north to the "Roller Coaster Trail," following the old dune ridges to Lake Whitney. This will be clearly plotted on your map. Swamp rabbits will flee at the sound of your footsteps, and you'll see otter and mink.

The island exists for all seasons, and I've enjoyed every one of them, even late fall and early winter. Visit in November and December, when the insects die down and the reptiles go into seclusion. The bottle-nosed dolphin often appears at this time as the marsh grasses turn an autumnal gold. Unlike New England, the fall color season doesn't reach its peak here until the first week of December.

◀ *A wild horse on Cumberland Island.*
© Melissa Farlow/National Geographic Getty Images

SPECIAL MOMENTS

1   Beaches. I've combed the beaches of the East Coast for years, all the way from Key West, Florida, to the rocky, wave-lashed shores of Maine. The beaches of Cumberland Island get my vote as the most gorgeous along the East Coast. In 2006 the Travel Channel added these sandy shores to its list of "America's Best Beaches." There are 17 miles of hard-packed sand as blonde as the hair of the late Princess Grace. The undulating dunes open onto beaches that are nearly 1,000 feet long in some places. The good news is that you'll often have them virtually to yourself. Dozens of visitors frequent the beaches not just for sun, sand, or whatever, but for shells. Shells are particularly prevalent after storms roar in from the Northeast.

2   Greyfield Inn. Take your choice of images, "Tara by the Sea" or a Gatsby-esque inn. Whatever, the stately Greyfield Inn is reason enough to visit Cumberland Island.

Accessible by private ferry from Fernandina Beach, Florida, the tranquil inn is filled with family heirlooms and antiques. The 17-room Greyfield has been a mansion inn since Lucy R. Ferguson, one of the Carnegie daughters, converted it into a hotel in 1952. Staying here is an expensive luxury but a dreamy travel memory.

Meeting the 2-night minimum stay is no hardship. In spite of the prices, don't always expect a private bathroom. What everybody gets is an old-fashioned Southern breakfast (ever had creamy, buttery grits with red-eye gravy?), a gourmet picnic lunch, an exquisite candlelit dinner, and a natural-history jeep tour of the island. Surrounded by 200 acres of stunning beauty, the four-story plantation mansion opens onto a wide, inviting veranda. At the turn of the 20th century, it was built as a family vacation retreat for the Carnegie family.

3   Bird-watching. Nearly 300 species of birds have been identified

on Cumberland. Its maritime forests shelter one of the most diverse bird populations in America. Of course, the best times for birding are in the spring and autumn when migratory birds use Cumberland as a refueling stop. But at any time of the year I've seen a fascinating array of fowl, including songbirds like the painted bunting, which starts nesting here in May and June. In the fall you have a good chance of seeing a peregrine falcon. Almost invariably, you'll see an American bald eagle on one of your jaunts. The sandpipers, plovers, and whimbrels prefer the mud flats. Our special favorites are the green-winged teal and the American black duck. Pick up a map at the Sea Camp Ranger Station before going birding.

4   Sunsets. Long before television, Southerners used to entertain themselves by sitting out on verandas watching the sun go down. I know that sounds like some reincarnation of a Southern Gothic novel

Cumberland Island, Georgia

from the 1920s. But I like to see some elegant customs from the Old South revived before everything becomes a trailer park and a McDonald's. Every year I look forward to my return to Cumberland Island to sit out on the veranda of the Greyfield Inn, sipping a mint julep at twilight while listening to a cacophony of tree frogs. The sun, often a violent orange, sinks slowly over the alligator- and cottonmouth-filled local swamps, which are framed by live oaks and palmettos. In the distance, bottle-nosed dolphins are playing their twilight games. A deer appears almost in silhouette, getting in some final daylight, grazing beside a salt-marsh pond. And then suddenly the sun sinks like a fiery ball in a final blaze of red-orange and golden light. Only once in all the years of indulging in the sundowner ritual did I see the legendary, brilliant "green flash"—written about by Ernest Hemingway—at the exact moment the sun goes below the watery horizon.

ABOUT THE AUTHOR

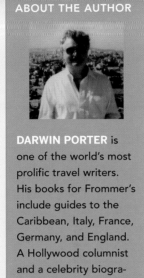

DARWIN PORTER is one of the world's most prolific travel writers. His books for Frommer's include guides to the Caribbean, Italy, France, Germany, and England. A Hollywood columnist and a celebrity biographer, Porter is also a radio broadcaster; his shows on American popular culture are heard in all 50 states.

YOUR TRIP

General Information: For advance planning, contact the **Division of Tourism, Georgia Department of Industry, Trade & Tourism,** P.O. Box 1776, Atlanta, GA 30301 (☎ 800/VISIT-GA or 404/962-4000; www.georgiaonmymind.org). Also contact **Cumberland Island National Seashore,** Coastal Road, northeast of St. Marys (☎ 912/882-4335; www.nps.gov/cuis). **Getting There:** Take Interstate 95 to Exit 2/3 and travel 10 miles east on GA 40 to St. Marys. From here, ferries operate year-round but call for a reservation (☎ 912/882-4335). In summer, book as far in advance as possible. Cumberland Island lies 7 miles northeast of St. Marys. There's an airstrip for small planes near Greyfield Inn, and air-taxi arrangements can be made from Jacksonville or St. Simons Island. Call the Inn for details. **Best Lodging:** The only lodging on the island is the **Greyfield Inn,** a historic, circa-1900, former Carnegie home now functioning as one of the most luxurious inns in the Deep South. The Inn also operates a ferry from Fernandina Beach, Florida, three times a day (☎ 904/261-6408; www.greyfieldinn.com; $350–$450 double with full board). **Best Camping: Sea Camp Beach** is the best developed, with 16 sites accommodating 60 guests with toilets, cold showers, and drinking water. Reservations needed 60 days in advance; call ☎ 888/817-3421 (Mon–Fri 10am–4pm). **Best Restaurant: Greyfield Inn Restaurant,** previously recommended, is the only restaurant. Candlelit dining room for guests of the Inn (see above) features market-fresh international and regional dishes. The price of a meal is included in hotel rate. **Best Restaurant Value:** Make your own picnic at the **Riverside Cafe** in St. Marys, across from the ferry terminal to Cumberland (☎ 912/882-3466). **When to Go:** Apr–Oct.

◀ *Live oaks covered with Spanish moss.*
© Art Wolfe/DanitaDelimont.com

DONEGAL, IRELAND

Peat fires, traditional music, Guinness, Gaelic & Irish stew

County Donegal, a rugged region in the extreme northwest of the country, is the wild west of Ireland. The people here don't hate the harshness; they embrace it. The isolation and rawness of the land have kept their culture safe for hundreds of years.

When the English first began their slow, cruel campaign to detach Ireland from its Irishness, Donegal found it easiest to resist. While fellow Irishmen were stripped of their traditional musical instruments and gradually stopped speaking in their ancient Gaelic tongue, in Donegal the fiddlers kept fiddling and the old language was kept safe.

The mothers and fathers in Ireland today were often sent to Donegal during their school holidays to learn the Irish language and ways. They would stay in small crofts with local lairds or storytellers—men with wind-burned skin, bright eyes, and a love of alcohol. They were the tramp kings of their communities. Locals would pile into their houses at night to listen to tales and songs, spoken and sung in Gaelic, until the stout ran out or the first beams of dawn began to creep across the cold flagstone floors.

Now it's not just the old men who speak Gaelic and play traditional Irish music—the young have made it a part of their identity and Gaelic can be heard in the streets and pubs. But the county remains as harsh. There is a welcome here but you have to hunt to find it. Visitors expecting things laid out especially for them will be disappointed. Travelers who like to discover a country as it is will be delighted. You had better leave your plans loose, however, as it's impossible to say where you will end up in County Donegal: The roads are hideously signposted and only occasionally in English.

It is best just to head in a direction and see where it takes you—possibly to a tiny wooden chapel towered over by dark green hills (on the way to Malin Head) or to the top of some gray, shaley cliffs, spitting their castoffs into the sparkling cobalt seas below (Slieve League Cliffs).

Undoubtedly, you will curse the ugly PVC bungalows that have been built by the natives on some of Donegal's most beautiful landscapes, and then completely forgive them when you stumble into a one-room roadside inn and are regaled with stories of characters from the local area.

Whenever you visit, it will rain. But it's the rain that keeps the place so beautiful, so don't curse it. This is a place shaped by and devoted to the elements, inspiring artists and writers and luring young adventurers. They flock to the Irish coasts every year between August and November, waiting for the American hurricanes to send waves screaming across the Atlantic and create some of the best surf in the world.

After hours spent riding waves, sometimes as big as buses, they rub their skin dry and head to the pub. Here they'll gather around a sweet-smelling peat fire, order an Irish stew and a pint of Guinness, and continue that great tradition of Donegal: telling stories.

◀ *Celtic cross in churchyard, Glencolumbkille.*
© Richard Cummins/Corbis

SPECIAL MOMENTS

1   **Malin Head.** Malin Head is the end of Ireland, the most northerly point, where even on a sunny day, the wind often howls and the temperature can be 10 degrees colder than it is a short drive south. This is a great spot for watching migrating birds in late fall. Few visitors make it up this far, but those who do are rewarded. Standing on its peak is one of those brilliant moments when you become overwhelmed by the enormity of nature—its beauty, power, and slow, majestic nobility. Nothing happens quickly up here. The space is too large. From here, there's only cold blue sea between you and the Arctic. On the steep slope down to the sea EIRE is spelled out in huge stone letters. It let World War II pilots know they were over neutral Ireland. Since then others have

added their own stone graffiti. Beyond these human proclamations, whales and dolphins swim silently by in the icy waters.

2   **Tory Island.** In the relentless waters of the Atlantic Ocean there's a small hunk of granite whose people have created their own magical kingdom and installed their own king. No, seriously, I'm not making this up. Beautiful, barren Tory Island has a population of less than 200 people. It's not an easy place to get to and can often be cut off by storms for days, or even weeks, at a time. Virtually everyone who makes it across is guaranteed a greeting by the current king, Patsy Dan Rogers, who is also an accordion player and part of Tory's acclaimed school of artists, whose work is the perfect counterbalance to the

callous pounding of the sea. There are more than a half-dozen places to stay, from friendly B&Bs to the two-star Tory Hotel. During the day you can climb some of the most spectacular bird cliffs in Ireland and wander among the kittiwakes and puffins. The **Tory Island Ferry** (www.toryislandferry.com) has seasonal service from Bunbeg and Magheroarty

3   **Letterkenny.** People will tell you not to go to Letterkenny. Don't listen to them. This is a real Irish town, untainted by tourism and on the up. If you do make it here, you must go for a drink at The Wolfe Tone. Part drinking establishment and part museum, it appears hundreds of years old but was in fact only recently created by its republican owner in 2005. What it shows is

how absolutely and fundamentally important the Irish struggle for independence has been. And to many, still is. The entire place is a shrine to all those who have fought before, from Michael Collins to the hunger striker Bobby Sands. Have a pint of Guinness and indulge your curiosity.

4 Bundoran. Drive into Bundoran and it's difficult to resist the urge to drive straight back out the other side. Don't. This is one of the country's premier surfing resorts. Not far from here lies the stunning Tullan Strand, where Atlantic rollers power onto the dune-fringed shores. Adventurers can follow the lead of the stars of the cult surf film *Litmus*, who put this place on the world surf map over a decade ago. Or indulge in the hipper sport of kite-surfing. Others can simply stroll and watch in awe.

OLIVIA EDWARD is a British writer who began specializing in travel after a couple of years spent in Shànghǎi. She's since written for *Time Out, DK*, and MTV Guides, and glossy publications for companies like American Express and Orange. Happiest when swimming in rough seas, she can be tempted onto dry land by rain, mud, and off-road motorbikes.

ABOUT THE AUTHOR

YOUR TRIP

General Information: Contact **Tourism Ireland** (☎ 800/233-6470; www.tourismireland.com). **Getting There:** To get to Tory Island, contact **Tory Island Ferries** (☎ 353-74/953-1320; www.toryislandferry.com). To go surfing, get in touch with **The Bundoran Surf Company** (☎ 353-71/984-1968; www.bundoransurfcompany.com). To find **The Wolfe Tone,** wander along the High Street (leaving the Court House, Post Office, and Library on your left) until you reach Lower Main Street and it seems as though you're heading out of town. The bar is on your left (☎ 353-74/912-4472). **Best Lodging:** Stay in **Termon House,** an 18th-century land agent's house on the seashore in Maghery near Dungloe (☎ 353-1/670-4733; www.irishlandmark.com; 790€–1,295€/$950–$1,550 per week, sleeps 6). Or try the restored Victorian home **Frewin** (☎ 353-74/915-1246; www.frewinhouse.com; 110€–160€/$132–$192). **Best Lodging Value:** The **Malin Head Hostel,** run by the rosy-cheeked Mary Reynolds, is budget paradise. Cook locally caught crab supplemented with fresh salad from Mary's organic garden (☎ 353-74/937-0309; www.hostels-ireland.com; 36€/$43). **Best Restaurant:** The decor may be a little dated but the food—Modern Irish using local ingredients—is up-to-date (☎ 353-74/913-6985; www.themillrestaurant.com; 19€–27€/$23–$32). **Best Restaurant Value:** Homemade breads and soups can be followed by gooey puddings at **The Blueberry Tearoom** (☎ 353-73/972-2933; 7€–13€/$8–$16). Find it right on the town square, The Diamond. **When to Go:** May, June, or Sept. July and August can be busy. After October, places close down and the weather closes in.

◀ *McGrory's Pub, Culdaff.*
© Stefano Amantini/Atlantide Phototravel/Corbis

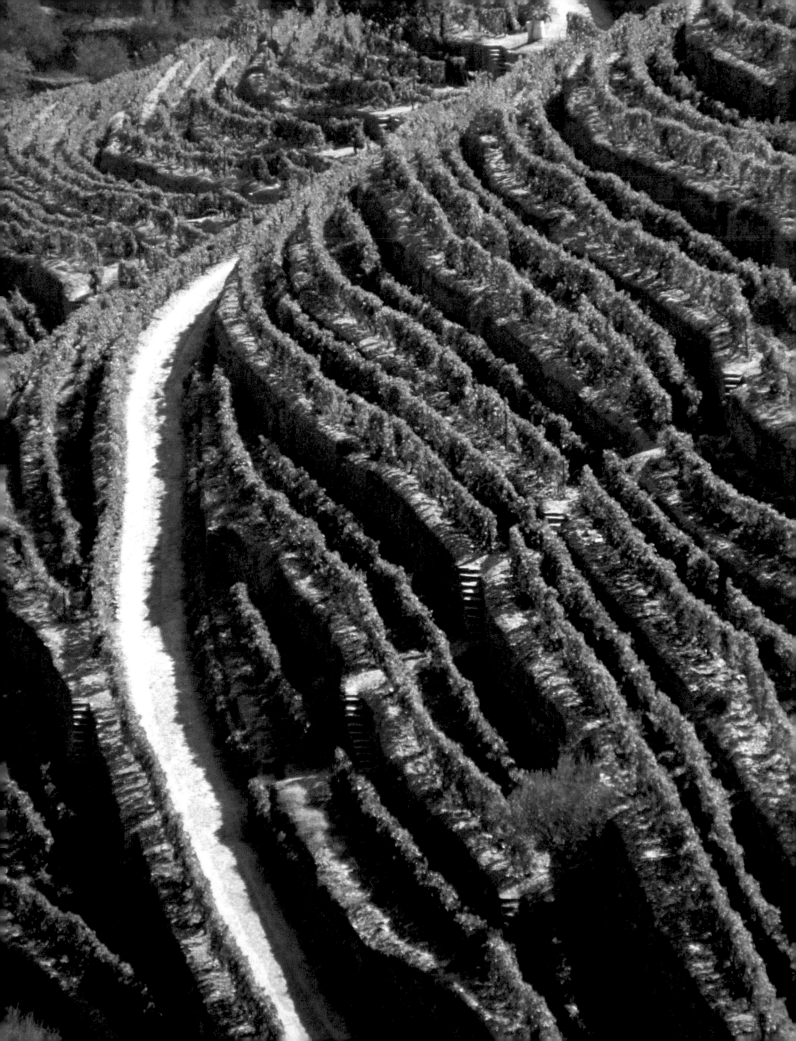

THE DOURO, PORTUGAL

A pilgrimage in search of one of the world's great wines

There are plenty of longer, more important, and more famous rivers in the world than the Douro, which begins in central Spain as the Duero, changes its name at the border, and cuts across northern Portugal before flowing through the city of Oporto and emptying into the Atlantic.

But the Douro—the "River of Gold"—has something special going for it: The river snakes its way through the steep, neatly stone-terraced vineyards that produce the grapes for port wine, the legendary dessert wine Portugal is famous for. Port—fortified by adding grape brandy, as British merchants first did back in the 17th century to protect wines over long sea voyages—is one of the world's great wines. The Douro River Valley, the world's first demarcated wine region, where wine has been produced for 2,000 years, is both gentle and harsh, but never less than stirringly beautiful.

Though it may seem as though there's little left to explore in western Europe, much of northern Portugal, the country's most conservative and devout region, seems remote by comparison. The north is filled with unexpected delights for travelers, including four UNESCO World Heritage Sites, picturesque medieval towns, splendid *solares* (manor houses), and country *quintas* (estates). Not to mention the noblest of wines.

Oporto, Portugal's second city (called Porto locally), a fascinating mercantile center that clings to a gorge at the mouth of the river, is where the cool and damp, centuries-old lodges used to store port are located. Long ago, port wine was shipped downriver in oak barrels loaded on *barcos rabelos*—magnificent wooden boats with billowing sails and long oars—and stored in Gaia, across the river from Oporto. Some 50 wine producers still have their *caves* (lodges or warehouses) there, where port wines continue to be blended and aged (even if they're now rather less romantically transported by truck).

One of the highlights of northern Portugal, not surprisingly, is a port wine-country tour. Beginning at a point about 64km (40 miles) inland from Oporto, vineyards stretch along the deep valleys and contours of the river on both sides. Some are owned by winemaking conglomerates—several maintain long-held English and Scottish surnames and ownership—though many parcels are farmed by tiny, Portuguese family-owned operations. This is not the place to see the latest, high-tech winemaking in action. The making of port wine remains largely artisanal: Grapes are hand-picked, loaded into rustic baskets, and at some small wineries, still stomped by foot in *lagares,* or giant pressing tanks, in a jubilant atmosphere accompanied by singing and guitar (and a fair bit of drinking).

The severe local conditions, including a prevalence of hard schist in the mountain soil and extremes of brutally hot, dry summers and equally cold winters, produce a unique microclimate—and intensely flavorful grapes. True port wine can be made nowhere else in the world.

A sense of history and national identity is evident throughout the unpretentious north of Portugal. And it adds even greater depth to the region's finest vintage port, which can take several decades to fully mature.

◀ *Vineyards in the Douro Valley.*
© Fausto Giaccone/ AGE Fotostock, Inc.

SPECIAL MOMENTS

1 **Oporto and the Port wine lodges.** Oporto, which means "the port," has both shipping and wine on its mind. While the city isn't the obvious charmer that Lisbon is, its old town is a delight, and the city's intriguing grittiness is complemented by a revitalized cultural scene. A red-roofed jumble of buildings creeps up the hillside to the imposing cathedral, or Sé, and the São Bento train station, whose interior is swathed in painted ceramic tiles. The colorful Ribeira neighborhood crowds the river bank, and a splendid 19th-century iron bridge traverses the Douro to Vila Nova de Gaia, where most port is blended and aged; famous names like Taylor, Cockburn, Fonseca, and Ramos Pinto are emblazoned in neon and large white signs on modest rooftops. Most winemakers' companies offer tours and tastings, perfect as a precursor to heading out along the Douro.

2 **The Minho.** Just north of Oporto is the lush, historic region of Minho, the birthplace of independent Portugal. Guimarães, the one-time capital with a 10th-century castle, cobblestone streets, and squares lined with old town houses, is something like the Bruges of Portugal. Stately Braga, famous for its Holy Week celebrations, has more than 30 churches, one of which is the nearby pilgrimage church of Bom Jesus do Monte, where the devout climb a steep, grand staircase on their knees. The Minho's cold northwest "green coast" on the Atlantic has lovely beaches, and though they're hardly the international tourist attraction that the Algarve is in the south, a pretty resort town, Viana do Castelo, with an elegant collection of Manueline buildings, is a real draw.

3 **The Port Wine Route.** To take in the dramatic scenery of the Douro River Valley, you can drive, take the train, or take an upriver cruise. From Pinhão to Pocinho, the train traces the contours of the Douro's switchbacks, with scintillating views at every turn; another pleasing route is north to Tua. Wine enthusiasts follow an established "Port Wine Route" to visit atmospheric *quintas* (vineyard estates) and sample many types of port wine (and excellent dry red table wines). It's even possible to stay at one of the quintas, which virtually all produce their own port. The prettiest towns in the area are

Amarante and Lamego, while near Vila Real is the glorious 18th-century baroque manor house Solar de Mateus (long featured on Mateus wine bottles). Other villages tucked into the craggy green hills and terraced vineyards are Alijó, São João da Pesqueira, and Sabrosa (birth place of the explorer Magellan).

4 Northern Portugal's *pousadas*. No visit to the region would be complete without experiencing a stay at a *pousada* (a network of historic luxury hotels). Several are standouts for renovation and design; you'll even find ancient religious buildings equipped with hip design interiors. My favorites are Santa Marinha, in Guimarães, housed in a hilltop 12th-century monastery; Pousada Santa Maria do Bouro in Amares, a daring modern adaptation of a former Cistercian Monastery; and Pousada Solar da Rede in Mesão Frio, a regal 18th-century manor house with orchards, a vineyard, and mesmerizing views over the River Douro.

NEIL E. SCHLECHT is a graduate of Georgetown University's School of Foreign Service and holds master's degrees from the University of Texas at Austin. He has worked on development programs for the E.U. and authored a dozen travel guides and articles on two of his obsessions: tennis and wine. He has lived in Spain, Brazil, and Ecuador.

ABOUT THE AUTHOR

YOUR TRIP

General Information: Visit the **Instituto de Turismo de Portugal** (www.visitportugal.com) or **Oporto** (www.portoturismo.pt). **Getting There:** The Portuguese airline **TAP** (www.tap-airportugal.us) and trains (☎ 351-213/185-990; www.cp.pt) travel from Lisbon to Oporto; tours of the Douro wine region are possible by boat, train, or car, but to visit many quintas, a tour group or private automobile is required. **Best Lodging: Vintage House** is a wine-themed Relais & Châteaux hotel (Lugar da Ponte, Pinhão; ☎ 800/735-2478 in the U.S. or 351-254/730-230; www.relaischateaux.com/vintage; 113€–176€/$135–$211). Or try **Pousada Solar da Rede** (Santa Cristina, Mesão Frio; ☎ 351-254/890-130; www.pousadas.pt; 165€–220€/$198–$264). **Best Lodging Value: Quinta do Paço de Calheiros** is a sumptuous rural inn (Calheiros, Ponte de Lima; ☎ 351-258/947-164; www.solaresdeportugal.pt; 110€/$132); **Castelo do Bom Jesus** is an 18th-century estate in the same family for 250 years (Braga; ☎ 571/723-6347 in U.S. or 351-253/676-566; www.armilarworldusa.com; 100€/$120). **Best Restaurant:** In Oporto, **Churrascão do Mar** (Rua João Grave 134; ☎ 351-226/096-382; main courses 20€–35€/$24–$42); **D' Tonho** (Cais da Ribeira 13-15; ☎ 351-222/004-307; main courses 13€–29€/$16–$35); in Pinhão, **Rabelo** (in Vintage House; prix-fixe menus 25€–50€/$30–$60). **Best Restaurant Value:** In Oporto, **Taverna dos Bêbobos** (Cais de Ribeira 21–25; ☎ 351-222/053-565; main courses 10€–24€/$12–$29). **When to Go:** Early autumn for harvest season or spring; avoid the intense heat of summer and bitter cold of winter, when few wineries are open to receive visitors.

◀ *Rabelo boat in Porto.*

EASTER ISLAND, CHILE

Mysterious statues on the most remote inhabited island

My travels have taken me to some unusual places on six of the seven continents and on hundreds of islands, but no place has fascinated me more than Easter Island, home of those tall, mysterious stone statues that no one can explain.

Easter Island—or Rapa Nui to its Polynesian residents, the Rapanui—was the final stop on my 25-year journey to the three corners of the Polynesian Triangle, the vast area of the Pacific Ocean whose far-flung islands were settled by the Polynesians a few millennia before anyone thought of inventing a map or a compass. Easter Island is the easternmost outpost of the triangle, which runs north of the equator to the American state of Hawaii and then far southwestward to the antipodean nation of New Zealand.

Easter Island's nearest neighbors are descendants of the H.M.S. *Bounty* mutineers who live on Pitcairn Island some 1,868km (1,160 miles) to the west. Chile, which owns Easter Island and officially calls it Isla de Pascua, is 3,623km (2,250 miles) to the east. In other words, it is the world's most remote inhabited island.

Polynesians settled it sometime between A.D. 300 and 1200. Theories abound as to what happened next, but it's certain that sooner or later they carved almost 900 huge, long-nosed statues, known as *moai,* to evoke the images of their ancestors. They stood them on platforms known as *ahu* along the shorelines of their coastal villages, their inlaid white coral eyes staring ghostlike back at the villagers.

The task required enormous resources, eventually denuding the island of its forests, eroding its soil to the point of bringing starvation and cannibalism to the islanders, and setting off tribal warfare. And then, suddenly, the Rapanui toppled all the statues.

The question of how and why this Polynesian culture accomplished such a great feat and then went so awry absolutely fascinates me, as it has numerous others for more than a century. It is with a sense of total wonderment that I walk among the *moai,* some restored to their upright stances but most still lying where they fell centuries ago.

The Museo Antropológico P. Sebastián Englert, the island's anthropological museum in its only town, Hanga Roa, is an excellent start for your visit. The museum displays wooden *rongorongo* tablets, whose hieroglyphs were unique to Easter Island and were the sole writing method developed in Polynesia before the arrival of Europeans. Here also is one of the few original *moai* eyes, for even though some have been replaced, most statues stand or lie blinded, their pupils crushed or discarded. As informative as this little museum is, however, it only deepens the mystery of how and why.

My only regret is that I had only 4 days. Next time I will stay at least a week and take advantage of Easter Island's numerous outdoor activities—hiking into the hills, climbing atop the three volcanoes that created the land, riding a horse across the central plain, and snorkeling and diving along the rocky coast.

Most of all I will wander among these blind, mute figures. Perhaps in some mystical moment they will whisper into my ear and reveal their long-held secret.

◀ *Moai statue near the Rano Raraku Volcano.*
© Walter Bibikow/
DanitaDelimont.com

SPECIAL MOMENTS

1 **Rano Kau and Orongo.** The *moai* get most of the attention, but Orongo ceremonial village atop Rano Kau blew me away—almost literally, since it was extremely windy atop this 1,932km (1,200-ft.) volcano in the island's southwestern corner, directly facing the winter-time cold fronts blasting up from Antarctica. Sitting on a narrow ridge between Rano Kau's reed-covered crater lake and a precipitous cliff dropping to the sea, Orongo consists of low stone houses entered through small, crawl-through doorways. The village was inhabited only once a year, when it was home to the island's "Bird Man" cult. A young man from each of the island's tribes would live in one of the houses before climbing down the cliff, swimming across choppy waves to one of the three rocky islets offshore, and retrieving the first egg laid by a sooty tern. The winner's image became one of Orongo's petroglyphs, and he spent the next year living in relative luxury as the Bird Man. More importantly, his tribe ruled the island for the next 12 months.

2 **Anakena Beach.** I've been to hundreds of beaches during my travels throughout Polynesia, but the one at Anakena is special to me. Easter Island's first Polynesian in-habitants apparently came ashore on this picturesque, half-moon curve of sand wedged into a small bay on the northern coast. Although Anakena is a fine place to swim and sun during the austral summer from December through March (it can get quite chilly here the rest of the year), it has no resort hotel or other tourist facility. Instead, its only per-manent residents these days are several restored *moai*, watching the beach like silent lifeguards.

3 **Rano Raraku.** *Rano* in the lo-cal language means volcano, and while Easter Island has several vol-canic mountains, Rano Raraku most piqued my imagination. I climbed to the top for a 360-degree island view and a look down into its crater lake, but its southern side drew my attention, for it was here in a quarry known as the "Nursery" that the Rapanui carved their *moai*. In vari-ous stages of completion, some 300 of them still lie in or near the quarry, including the largest at more than 20m (65 ft.) long. A few stand up-right nearby with only their heads protruding from a grassy field, just as Caribbean pirates would plant their victims on a beach so they would drown on the next incoming tide. Why the *moai* were partially

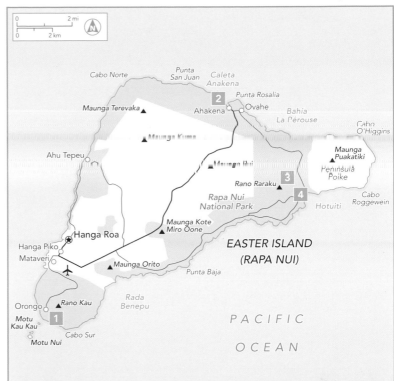

buried in that position is anyone's guess. Others were left in their tracks between the quarry and the southern coast when work suddenly stopped.

4 **Ahu Tongariki.** I saw my first *moai* in Hanga Roa shortly after debarking at the nearby airport—whose enormous runway, in a modern twist, is an emergency landing site for the space shuttle—and many more of them as I toured the island. But most impressive to me were the 15 standing at Ahu Tongariki, on the southern shore near the "Nursery" at Rano Raraku. Scattered by a tsunami that swept the island in 1960, they have since been restored to their original upright positions. The site itself is not as spectacular as others on the island, but these *moai* appear as they did when erected atop the *ahu* hundreds of years ago. Although the red obsidian head stones are missing from most *moai,* one here has its original "topknot."

ABOUT THE AUTHOR

BILL GOODWIN was an award-winning political writer and Senate staffer before sailing to Tahiti in 1977 and exploring French Polynesia, the Samoas, Tonga, and New Zealand. He has written widely about the islands including *Frommer's South Pacific* and *Frommer's Tahiti & French Polynesia*. Find him at www.billgoodwin.com.

YOUR TRIP

General Information: Contact the **Tourism Promotion Corporation of Chile** (☎ 866/YES-CHILE; www.visit-chile.org). **The Easter Island Foundation** has excellent background information at www.islandheritage.org. The **Museo Antropológico P. Sebastián Englert** is at (Spanish only) www.museorapanui.cl (☎ 56-32/255-1020). **Getting There: Lan Airlines** flies to Easter Island from Santiago, Chile (☎ 866/435-9526; www.lan.com). Several companies offer tours, including **Explora** (☎ 866/750-6699; www.explora.com). All hotels will hail taxis and arrange guided tours and rental vehicles. **Best Lodging:** Easter Island has no deluxe hotel, so adjust your expectations accordingly. However, Explora recently opened a small lodge and larger luxury hotel (see above for contact info). The **Hotel Iorana** enjoys the best sea view from a bluff on avenue Policarpo Toro, a 20-minute walk south of Hanga Roa (☎ 56-32/100-608; www.ioranahotel.cl; $86–$207/£46–£110). **Best Lodging Value: Tauraa Hotel,** on avenue Tekena in Hanga Roa, is tops among several small hotels and guesthouses (☎ 56-32/100-463; www.tauraahotel.cl; $90/£48). **Best Restaurant: La Taverna du Pêcheur,** near Hanga Roa's harbor, offers excellent French fare, especially rock lobster (☎ 56-32/100-619; entrees $15–$60/£8–£32). **Best Restaurant Value:** For a summertime lunch, inexpensive food stalls grill fresh fish at Anakena Beach. In Hanga Roa, a fine view complements fresh seafood at **Restaurant Playa Pea** (☎ 56-32/100-619; entrees $10–$15/£5–£8). **When to Go:** The island is crowded during the Tapati Rapa Nui (Easter Island Festival) in late January and early February, but it is the best time to visit.

◀ *Moai statues at Ahu Tongariki.*
© Keren Su/DanitaDelimont.com

FORMENTERA, SPAIN

The least known & developed
of the Balearic Islands

Spain's beach-filled Balearic Islands cater to a wide variety of tastes. Perennially popular Mallorca, the largest, satisfies everyone from tots to grandpops, with everything from mass-market entertainment to exclusive tranquillity. Sedate Minorca, with its tasteful, low-level tourist developments and sheltered beaches, is the family destination par excellence. Fun-loving Ibiza, whose all-night disco attractions merge with a chic post-hippie atmosphere, draws a mainly young crowd. Unspoiled, laid-back Formentera, the smallest, tends to attract well-heeled free spirits of all ages who enjoy looking after themselves and making their own entertainment.

My absolute favorite is Formentera, which I like partly for what's not there—no airport, no railway, no cinemas, no theaters, no high buildings, no monuments—but mainly for what *is* there: a pure Mediterranean landscape of olive groves, vineyards, pinewoods, and fig trees so big their branches have to be supported by wooden stilts. There are also saltpans; sand dunes; long, white-sanded beaches; small, clear-watered coves enclosed by rocky outcrops; hidden caves bored out of porous, phantasmagoric outcrops; bleached rickety shelters and ramps for fishing boats that seem to have been there forever; windmills that date back 2 centuries (Bob Dylan stayed in one in the '60s); clifftop watchtowers and lighthouses; isolated coves; Bronze Age remains; and endless panoramic sea views. If it sounds like a natural paradise, it is. And it's all packed into an area just 13km (8 miles) by 6km (4 miles).

I've been visiting the island on and off for over 30 years and the atmosphere never seems to change, though a handful of Internet centers have sprouted up recently. There are four small towns with a combined population of 5,000: Sant Francesc Javier, the capital; Sant Ferran of '60s "hippie" fame; Es Pujols, the main resort; and Sa Savina, the entry port (the absence of an airport means you come by sea from nearby Ibiza). There's also a hamlet of around 100 resident souls, El Pilar, with a small, delectable Moorish-styled white church. South coast Mitjorn is barely a hamlet but has the longest beach on the island and the best hotel. After dark, attractions are scarce outside of Es Pujols's small, late-night bar zone. Though there are plenty of eating spots, genuinely first-class restaurants like Lucius (see "Your Trip," below) are rare.

As most of Formentera is flat—apart from the 183m (600-ft.) pine-covered Talaiassa Hill—you can cycle around a lot of it easily. Low walls made of local stone border country lanes designated *vías verdes*, or "green routes." Warning: *Don't* come in winter, as many hotels, shops, and restaurants outside of Sant Francesc Javier close down and the weather can get alarmingly cold and windy, turning the usually idyllic Ibiza crossing into an ordeal.

◀ *Windmill on Formentera.*
© Mediacolor's/Alamy

SPECIAL MOMENTS

1   Arriving by sea from Ibiza.
The short trip to the tiny arrival port of Sa Savina—18km (11 sea miles) and a half-hour by fast boat from Ibiza Town—is a miniature odyssey in itself, taking you past tiny rock-bound lighthouses and exquisite unpopulated islets like Espalmador with its dazzling white beaches, and offering unexpected panoramas like the view back at the 305m (1,000-ft.) sugarloaf-shaped Es Vedrà rock just off Ibiza's southwest coast. If you're lucky, you'll see flying fish skimming above the deep blue waters.

It's an easy and relaxing day out for holidaymakers from Ibiza who, on disembarking at Sa Savina, can rent a bike or scooter in the port and tour Formentera in a few hours. Of course, you can do this in reverse,

basing yourself in Formentera and spending some down time on Ibiza. Those who appreciate the finer cultural nuances of travel should avoid Ibiza during the summer months—there are few points of interest that don't involve gin and strobe lights. But if you like to dance, look good, feel good, and ride excess like a bareback horse, Ibiza will knock your socks off. This is the biggest fire-breathing Godzilla of a party you ever saw. This is the time and place to try something that you think will make you feel good but have never had the nerve to try back home.

2   La Mola lighthouse. This imposing, weather-worn beacon, built of white masonry in 1861, stands at the eastern tip of Formentera on a barren outcrop. Look right and

there's nothing but water between you and North Africa 160km (100 miles) away. Look left and on very clear days you can see Mallorca, a smudge on the distant horizon. The setting leaves you speechless. Next to it is a small monument to Jules Verne, who is said to have been inspired by the setting when he wrote "The Lighthouse at the Edge of the World."

3   The panoramic view from Talaiassa. You're barely 183m (600 ft.) up, but you can see the whole length of the island as you gaze down through the trees from Formentera's highest point. The patchwork of yellow fields and pine crests is bordered by the sea on either side. Ahead to your left extends Cap Barbaria, a windswept

headland of gnarled pumice and rock shrubs that's the home of Formentera's other lighthouse and some Bronze Age remains. Ibiza in the near distance seems like an extension of the island till you see the ferries gliding in across the straits to Sa Savina. Best way up here is on foot via the old stone-covered Roman road, which twists and climbs through the woodlands from El Pilar.

4   Cala Saona. There are many coves on the island, but this is my particular favorite. A hotel, a restaurant, and a few inland houses are the only buildings around, plus a small bar set in the neighboring rocks. The beach is a fine crescent of bright sand and the water is azure clear. I can't think of a better place to swim (in the nude, if you prefer). Inland is a rural world in miniature of trails, stone walls, pine copses, and vineyards. Come here on foot from Sant Francesc Javier and you'll hardly know you're in the 21st century.

PETER STONE is a London-born writer living in Madrid. The author of *Frommer's Madrid,* he's a Mediterranean addict who has enjoyed prolonged sojourns in Greece, Italy, and North Africa, and has published articles on Homeresque havens from Akrotiri to Astipaleia. Contact him at petine@teleline.es

ABOUT THE AUTHOR

YOUR TRIP

General Information: Check out **Turismo de Formentera** online at www.turismoformentera.com. For information on the Balearics, try www.visitbalears.com. The **tourist office** in Formentera is at Edificio de Servicios de Puerto s/n, in Port de la Sabina (☎ 34-97/132-20-57). **Getting There:** There's a wide choice of charter flights from European cities to Ibiza. The top bargain value for budget travelers is EasyJet from the U.K. (www.easyjet.com). On arrival in the island, **Mediterránea Pitiusa** has fast boats that go from the Ibiza port to Sa Savina in Formentera starting at 7:45am (☎ 34-97/132-32-83). The trip takes a half-hour. **Umafisa Lines** has slower boats starting at 6:45am that accommodate cars and take 1 hour (☎ 34-90/216-01-80). Catch a taxi from the pier to your hotel or the beach. **Getting Around:** Rent a bike or a moto from **Moto-Rent** in La Sabina or Pujols (☎ 34-97/132-21-38). Rent a car through the **Formotor** kiosk at La Sabina (☎ 34-97/132-22-42). **Best Lodging:** Be sure to make reservations in advance. **Insotel Club Formentera Playa,** on the southern-coast Mitjorn Beach, has gardens, a pool, and modern, well-kept amenities (Playa Mitjorn; ☎ 34-97/132-80-00; 228€/$274). **Best Lodging Value: Hotel Roca Bella,** in Es Pujols, is only 20m (70 ft.) from Es Pujols beach (☎ 34-97/132-81-30; www.roca-bella.com; 90€/$108). **Best Restaurant: Restaurant Lucius,** in Es Caló (☎ 34-97/132-70-14), is the best fish restaurant on the island, so booking is essential. The wonderful lobster stew is 100€ ($120) for two. **Best Restaurant Value: Fonda Pepe** in Sant Ferran (☎ 34-971/32-80-33; paella 25€/$30). **When to Go:** May–June or Sept–Oct.

◀ *Ibiza at sunset.*
© Frank Chmura/Alamy

FUERTEVENTURA, SPAIN

An otherworldly Canary island where the beaches are your own

These days getting to the island of Fuerteventura is a breeze—it's a 3-hour nonstop flight from London or Madrid. The first time I headed this way, I arrived by hydrofoil after a stomach-churning 3-hour ride from Tenerife. There was a band on board. People clapped. I concentrated on not throwing up.

As I stepped tentatively ashore in Jandía, on the southern end of the island, I was less than impressed. The port was tiny and hectic, with cars and taxis parked along a narrow road, vying for passengers in the blinding light. I was met by a friendly young man from my hotel, in a crisp suit and perfectly knotted tie. As we drove away in his Mercedes, my stomach settled and a strange and glorious landscape unfolded.

Fuerteventura's beauty is otherworldly—its rusty-red soil makes for an extraterrestrial landscape, dotted with lunar mountains and pitted with arid valleys. This is the closest you'll get to seeing Mars without traveling 35 million miles.

It's hard to imagine anything growing in this dry, unforgiving soil, but for centuries farmers grew vegetables with water pulled up by ancient windmills. Some of these structures remain as mournful reminders of an earlier age.

Today, I always rent a car and strike out on the highway that stretches from one tip of the island to the other. It's a winding, 90-minute drive, tracing the edge of precipitous, rocky cliffs, at the foot of which windsurfers with vivid sails weave quick patterns in the water, propelled by the steady leeward winds. "Fuerteventura" means "strong winds," and windsurfers get a great ride here, especially at sunset, when the breeze picks up.

If you prefer less action on the water, head to Jandía, where a wide, smooth expanse of white sand stretches unbroken for more than 16km (10 miles). Here's where your dream of a gorgeous empty beach, all to yourself, comes true. It's a blissful place—nothing but sand, turquoise water, and an easy surf. This is a desert island, so even palm trees are rare. The only crowds you'll find are near the resort hotels, amid the beach umbrellas and folding chairs. Outside these small patches of civilization, the island is yours. Gorgeous. Undiscovered. Choose the stretch that appeals to you, park, and stroll to your own island paradise.

As you head north, the landscape changes. By the time you reach the northern region of Corralejo, massive golden sand dunes tower above your head. Crossing them requires a bit of legwork, but you're rewarded by the translucent sea, peppered with big chunks of black volcanic rock.

In the end, the thing Fuerteventura has going for it, even as its popularity grows, is that it hasn't yet *arrived*. It's overshadowed by its glitzier cousin, Gran Canaria, and its more accessible neighbor, Tenerife. What it has to offer that they don't is a preternatural beauty and space—wide open space. You can drive for miles on its winding roads without seeing another car, and stretch out on its beaches with the sand all to yourself. This is an island for those who do not believe that sunbathing is a contact sport. Its solitary beauty works for me every time.

◀ *Fuerteventura landscape.*
© Adri Berger/Getty Images

119

SPECIAL MOMENTS

1 Jandía. The peninsula at the southern end of Fuerteventura, Jandía, is home to both one of the highest points on the island—the rocky mountain known as Pico de Zarza, which rewards those adventurous enough to climb it with spectacular views of both the sea and the island—and the longest, most spectacular beach, the Playa de Sotavento. You can stop to shop, dine, or drink at the small, upscale resort enclave of Costa Calma and the more egalitarian Morro Jable, where you can stock up on T-shirts and postcards or dine on fresh seafood. Both are quite tiny and manageable, but are more utilitarian than attractive. If you prefer a bit more peace, just head off down the beach, where, as the guidebooks say, the only footsteps are your own. For people like me who love isolation, this is about as close to heaven as you can get. Jandía is more popular with Germans and Scandinavians, whose laissez-faire approach to beachwear never fails to take me by surprise. The last time I was here I saw a German couple cheerfully playing tennis stark naked on the sand, surrounded by sunbathers. Oblivious.

2 Corralejo. At the busy northern tip of the island is the town of Corralejo, where you go if you're feeling lonely. While German travelers dominate the south, in the north it's the British. The biggest resort town on the island, Corralejo is a basic, straightforward tourist town filled with British pubs, timeshares, fish and chips shops, budget hotels, and signs in English. It's not lovely. Slip a mile or two out of the busy burg, though, and find extraordinary towering sand dunes formed by sand blown from the Sahara across the 100km (62 miles) of sea that separate the island from Africa. The shifting dunes stretch for miles and lead down to a striking rocky shore, where the waves are bigger and badder than they are farther south. This entire area is a protected national park, so resort hotels will never sprawl into the dunes, interrupting their beautiful progress as they move slowly around, blown by the nonstop ocean breeze. You can climb to the top of the massive dunes and tumble down their curling, sandy lips on a soft cushion of Saharan sand. The dunes eventually give way to a beach, where volcanic boulders jut out of the water, and the surf—while beautiful—tends to be too strong for easy swimming.

3 Los Lobos. For a change of pace, buy a ticket on one of the ferries for Los Lobos, a tiny island that you can see from Corralejo, shimmering offshore. A 20-minute boat ride away, the entire island is an uninhabited nature reserve offering a glimpse of what all the Canaries must have looked like once. There's no place to buy provisions on the island, so I always pack a picnic lunch and bring along a big bottle of water. You can circumnavigate the tiny island on foot in a couple of hours, or just spend the time swimming in its emerald-green lagoons and relaxing on its sandy shores, miles from the crowds in Corralejo.

4 Pájara and Betancuria. Near the center of the island, down a scenic road that passes extinct

volcanoes and through deep ochre valleys, is the village of Pájara. I think this is the prettiest village on the island, with shady, tree-lined streets and Spanish colonial architecture. From here, look for signs pointing toward Betancuria. I highly recommend that you visit this beautifully maintained 15th-century village but be warned: The road climbs one of the tallest mountains on the island and is so narrow that, after a certain point, should you change your mind, there's no turning back. If you have no fear of heights or of heart-stopping precipices, the view from the top is breathtaking. Once you descend the far side of the mountain, you can park at the edge of Betancuria and walk its narrow streets, enjoying the simple integrity of its ancient architecture. It holds several tiny museums that are worth your time, and a tiny church that dates back to the town's earliest days. There are also a few shady, picturesque cafes where you can relax over a *café con leche* and fortify yourself for the hair-raising drive back.

CHRISTI DAUGHERTY is a London-based freelance writer and editor. Her guides include *Frommer's Ireland*, *Frommer's Paris Day by Day*, and *Frommer's MTV Europe*. She summered on Ocracoke Island for many years, and has recently replaced it with Fuerteventura, which is now closer to her home. Visit her at her website, www.christidaugherty.com.

ABOUT THE AUTHOR

YOUR TRIP

General Information: Log on to the **Tourism Institute of Spain** website at www.spain.info. The **tourism office** in Corralejo can be found at Plaza Grande de Corralejo s/n (☎ 34-92/886-62-35). **Getting There:** You can fly to Fuerteventura direct from Britain on **Excel** (www.xl.com) and from within Spain on **Iberia** (www.iberia.com). More airlines fly to Tenerife, from which you can fly to Fuerteventura on **Binter Canaria Airline,** owned by Iberia. The flight takes about 45 minutes. **Transmediterránea** operates a jetfoil from Fuerteventura to Gran Canaria, daily in the high season and several times a week in the low season. You can either book your journey online (www.transmediterranea.net) or buy your tickets directly at the ferry landing the day before you travel. **Best Lodging: Hotel Faro Jandía** is on the beachfront in Jandía. All rooms have balconies and the food in the pleasant restaurant is high quality (Av. del Saladar 17; ☎ 34-928/54-50-35; www.farojandia.com; 104€–166€/$125–$200). **Best Lodging Value:** In Corralejo, the **Lobos Bahía Club** has a great pool and restaurant (Av. Gran Canaria 2; ☎ 34-92/886-71-43; www.lobosbahiaclub.com; 33€–63€/$40–$75). **Best Restaurant: St. Andrews Restaurant,** at the Elba Palace Hotel, offers excellent Continental cuisine in Antigua, in central Fuerteventura (35610 Antigua-Fuerteventura; ☎ 34-92/816-39-22; www.slh.com; 21€–38€/$25–$45). **Best Restaurant Value: El Sombrero,** on the seafront in Corralejo, has unique local cuisine (Av. Marítima 25, Corralejo; ☎ 34-92/886-75-35, 8€–17€/$10–$20).

◄ *Fuerteventura seascape.*
© Jon Arnold/DanitaDelimont.com

GALÁPAGOS, ECUADOR

Welcome to a world of sea lions & blue-footed boobies

Flying over these bizarre and barren-looking volcanic islands 1,120km (700 miles) off the coast of Ecuador, you might look out the airplane window and think to yourself, "What kind of god-forsaken place have I dragged myself to?" Indeed, lacking the lush blanket of flora and five-star resorts that most tropical islands have, the Galápagos can look decidedly un-vacationlike from afar. But beyond the harsh veneer, the islands teem with more crowd-pleasing marine and land wildlife than you could have possibly imagined. Within a few hours, you'll have seen your first sea lions and blue-footed boobies, and you'll already be hopelessly smitten.

Let me be clear: The Galápagos is not your average island destination. Coming here is not about sitting on a palm-strewn beach, sipping rum cocktails while giant, century-old old tortoises amble by. A Galápagos vacation is an active expedition, a thrilling and intimate voyage into a largely untouched time capsule where nature thrives, unplugged and unconcerned about human beings. After a day's immersion in this remote wonderland, it hits you: These creatures really have no fear. Zero skittishness. Predators have always been few in this laboratory of adaptation, and thanks to the careful stewardship of Galápagos National Park, humans are just one more stimulus the animals have gracefully absorbed.

Sun, sand, sea, and charming local flavor will be significant elements of your Galápagos trip, but what draws most people here is the amazing opportunity to get up close and personal with all kinds of exotic species that most people never see in their lifetime, from brightly colored marine iguanas (yes, they swim in the ocean) to seabirds with feet the color of a child's wading pool (the famous blue-footed boobies). Seeing these animals' unaffected yet totally mesmerizing behavior, in their own pristine environment, is what makes visiting this extraordinary archipelago such a privilege and a soul-cleansing experience. Every day you're here, you'll spend hours with the animals, in their surf and on their turf. Every shore landing or snorkeling excursion puts you within mere feet of some of the coolest, strangest animals you'll ever meet. You return from the Galápagos recharged and refreshed, not because you've been lounging in a tropical paradise for a week, but because you've had the rare treat of living in this fascinating bubble of untainted nature.

Because the islands are quite diverse and often far apart (in all, they cover 44,000 sq. km/17,000 sq. miles of ocean), ship-based expeditions are far preferable to land-based packages for your first Galápagos trip. You'll go ashore on small rubber landing craft called *pangas*, and naturalists, who are required by law to accompany all Galápagos tours, will tell you about what you can expect to see.

The state of nature in the Galápagos is so basic and delightful that it feels almost too bizarre to be real. When Charles Darwin visited in the 19th century, he wondered, "How did this come to be?" Today, the astonishing Galápagos still conjure the same kind of grateful head-scratching in visitors. That such a place *still* exists on our abused planet is truly remarkable.

◀ *A giant tortoise—a familiar sight on the Galápagos.*
© James Martin/ Getty Images

SPECIAL MOMENTS

1 **Watching seabirds on Española Island.** Sea turtles and sea lions may be cuter, and giant tortoises and marine iguanas more exotically prehistoric-looking, but no troupe of Galápagos wildlife puts on a better variety show than the seabirds. Punta Suarez, the windblown, rocky northwestern tip of Española Island, is a three-ring circus where it's as much fun to watch what's taking place on the ground as in the air. On the inland paths, practically underfoot, blue-footed boobies perform their endearing courtship ritual: Male birds whistle and pose to attract females, and then win them over by offering a twig or pebble, or by tapping their aqua feet in a slow, deliberate "dance." Over the water beyond the cliffs, see the death-defying acrobatics of frigate birds, whose klepto-parasitic livelihood depends on their ability to steal other birds' freshly caught fish right from out of their mouths—in midair!

2 **Snorkeling off Punta Vicente Roca, Isabela Island.** The western coast of Isabela has the most dramatic topography in the archipelago, with steep walls of striated, oxide-rich volcanic rock tumbling toward the ocean. In the protected cove below Punta Vicente Roca, you can snorkel with sea turtles, sea lions, flightless cormorants, and penguins. But it's the enormous sea turtles that are the most mesmerizing. They just drift in slow motion, pumping their flippers every so often, surfacing now and then for unhurried gulps of air. As you float along, less than a yard above these gentle giants, you enter a rare and wonderful state of relaxation, and the annoying task of breathing through a snorkel somehow becomes easier.

3 **Beach time with sea lions on Gardner Bay, Española Island.** As with any tropical destination, the best beaches in the Galápagos have been discovered, and they're crowded—not with cabanas and colorful umbrellas, but with sea lions. The pristine, sugary-white beach at Gardner Bay is the top hangout spot in the archipelago for these adorable mammals. You'll encounter the playful antics of immature pups, who toss seaweed in the air like a dog's chew toy, the sassy attitude of sea-lion "teenagers" who mug for the camera as cheekily as any MySpace kid, and even an aggressive bull or two, who might decide to take possession of, and refuse to surrender, your snorkel gear. There are

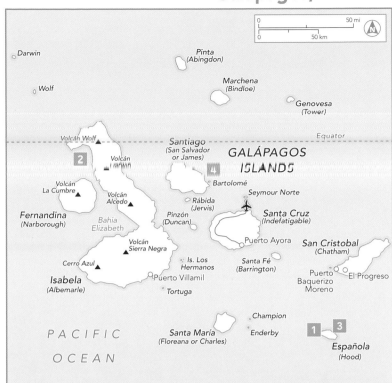

also plenty of lazy brown lumps who just want to catch some rays—you can, too.

4 **Bartolomé Island.** To use a film term, this square-mile speck of land is the unmistakable "establishing shot" of the Galápagos, a strangely gorgeous landscape that never fails to make a strong visual impression on visitors. Hike to the eastern summit, and take in the *Master and Commander* view over the otherworldly tableau of Pinnacle Rock, dense mangroves, and the twin crescent beaches whose reddish sand has turned the water a mystical shade of blue. Go for a walk on the south-facing beach and watch the surreal traffic of penguins, sea turtles, and reef sharks that swim back and forth along the shore. On the north-facing beach, swim or snorkel with more sea lions and penguins, or just hang out on the sand, with that iconic spike of Pinnacle Rock always in your peripheral vision.

ABOUT THE AUTHOR

A California native and past resident of four continents, **SYLVIE HOGG** finds every excuse she can to cross oceans, rivers, and county lines to soak up history, art, and culture—and gluttonously partake of the local food and drink. Sylvie is the author of several Frommer's guides to Rome and Italy and a frequent contributor to other travel media worldwide.

YOUR TRIP

General Information: Galápagos Conservancy has an informative website with links to tour operators (www.galapagos.org). For further information about the Galápagos, check out www.darwinfoundation.org or www.galapagospark.org. **Getting There:** Several U.S. airlines (American, Continental, and Delta) fly to Quito or Guayaquil, Ecuador. Most flights arrive in the evening, necessitating an overnight stay. From Quito or Guayaquil, you take another 2-hour flight to Baltra airport in the Galápagos. **Best Outfitters:** The best outfitter is **Lindblad Expeditions** (www.expeditions.com; ☎ 800/EXPEDITION; from $4,000/£2,120). Lindblad's naturalists are astonishingly good (many are native Galapagueños), and their cruise itineraries are carefully thought-out. **AdventureSmith** offers ship-based trips (from $2,500/£1,325 for an 11-day package) on vessels of varying size (☎ 800/728-2875; www.adventuresmithexplorations.com). Keep in mind that lower-cost outfitters often don't have English-speaking naturalists, or their snorkeling equipment may be worn out and so on. Land-based tours (including kayak tours) are less expensive than ship-based trips, but you won't experience the enormous variety of wildlife that you see on a ship-based trip. **When to Go:** The Galápagos straddle the equator, so the weather is fairly warm year-round. The warm season runs January to June; the cool season runs August to December. Depending on when you go, you'll see different animals doing different things: Sea turtle eggs hatch and sea lion pups are born in the cool season, but visitors find the warm season to be the most congenial for a first trip—and there's still plenty of wildlife to observe.

◀ *Two marine iguanas.*
© Arthur Morris/Corbis

GREAT SAND DUNES
NATIONAL PARK, COLORADO

Climbing the tallest dunes
in North America

Hiking in sand is harder than hiking on solid ground. Hiking *up* sand is harder yet.

That thought crosses my mind as I follow my friend up the tallest dunes in North America, the namesake of Great Sand Dunes National Park and Preserve in southwest Colorado, about 250 miles southwest of Denver. Rising from the foothills of the Sangre de Cristo Mountains, the dunes are among the most dramatic and unexpected sights in the world. To the west, the land levels into the vast San Luis Valley. Encircled by a crown of imposing peaks, this is the largest Alpine valley in the world—2 million acres at about 7,700 feet above sea level.

Thanks to gravity, sand cannot pile into a dune any steeper than 34 degrees. The Great Sand Dunes are no exception, but the hike up feels steeper. And because the dune-field is perpetually shifting with the wind, there are no permanent trails leading up the dunes. Every hiker blazes his or her own trail, but the elevated perspective makes it nearly impossible to get lost.

We continue onward and upward. Other hikers dot the slopes here and there. Only a few are higher than us. I've been all over the West, but I've never walked through a more unique, uncluttered, pristine environment in my life. Setting foot in this giant sandbox, for a few minutes or several hours, is like entering a different world. It reminds me of the old Buddhist tenet: All things are temporary.

The Great Sand Dunes inhabit just one peculiar corner of the San Luis Valley. Stories of crystal skulls, flying saucers, and incidents that inspired *X-Files* plotlines abound throughout the region. For thousands of years, people have believed the San Luis Valley to be an "inter-dimensional" crossroads, a nexus where otherworldly beings came and went.

In recent years, the valley has been home to another unexpected population, the reptilian denizens of Colorado's only alligator farm. I recommend visitors spend a day or two exploring the dunes and surrounding wilderness, and a day or two driving around the valley, sampling some of the other intriguing attractions.

The night before our hike up the dunes, my friend and I spent an hour on the lookout for extraterrestrial activity from the UFO Watchtower, a roadside attraction of note near the dinky hamlet of Hooper, Colorado. While we saw shooting stars, no other flying objects, identified or unidentified, lit up the night sky.

My friend takes the last of his lanky strides to the highest point in the entire dune-field, at the top of the Great Sand Dunes. A minute later, I plop down in the sand at his side. As I catch my breath, the view takes over. The soul-stirring tableau stretches for miles in every direction. I see the backside of High Dune (8,691 ft. above sea level), and the sea of waves made of sand beyond, and the flat plain of the largely agricultural valley floor beyond that. On the western horizon, I see the San Juan Mountains, at the foot of which we slept the night before, in my old family cabin. The laborious hike up is an afterthought.

◀ *Artistic patterns in the dunes.*
© Wesley Hitt/
Getty Images

SPECIAL MOMENTS

1 **Hike the dunes.** There is no way to experience the dunes like venturing into the sand. Sure, from the base they are quite a sight, but from the top of High Dune, another world is visible, encompassing the heart of the dune-field as well as the surrounding San Luis Valley. Sublime views aside, hiking in the Great Sand Dunes is a unique recreational experience, manageable for visitors of all ages, even small children. Some visitors take things a little further. I've seen sledders rocketing downhill on saucers and an especially adventurous visitor winding his way down the sandy slope on a snowboard. If you aren't up for hiking to High Dune itself, a number of trails skirt the base of the dunes and offer commanding views of these mountains of sand.

Of them, the moderate trail from Medano Creek to Castle Creek (10 miles round-trip) runs along the face of the dunes and gives hikers a lesson on how water contributes to the perpetually moving landscape.

2 **Visit Zapata Falls.** A short but somewhat steep hike from a trail head about 15 miles southeast of the Great Sand Dunes takes you to this idyllic waterfall. (Look for the ZAPATA FALLS RECREATION AREA sign off U.S. 150.) After reaching Zapata Creek, the route takes trekkers on a wade across the water and a climb up a ladder to a narrow gorge. At the end of the gorge, the 30-foot Zapata Falls comes into view, careening down the chute it has carved from the rock wall over the eons. The hike is only about a mile

round-trip, and is great for families traveling with young children. Even if you don't make it up the often slippery slope to the falls, the trail head offers sublime views of the Great Sand Dunes nestled at the foot of the Sangre de Cristo Mountains to the north.

3 **Check out Colorado gators.** The state's only alligator farm grew, not surprisingly, out of a fish farm that was looking for a way to naturally dispose of surplus fish. The farm's owners, the Young family, bought 100 baby alligators in 1987 and plunked them down in a pool warmed by natural hot springs. The reptiles not only survived, but they also thrived. Several hundred alligators now live in the 87°F (31°C) water year-round. (The reptiles are

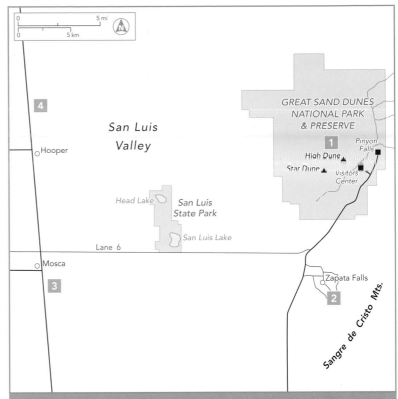

even known to climb out on the winter snow to warm up in the mid-day sun.) For those who want to get to know the gators better, visit during the annual Gatorfest in August for gator-wrestling classes and "the world's only gator rodeo."

4 **Look for flying saucers at the UFO Watchtower.** Since the 1960s, the San Luis Valley has been a hotbed of alleged extraterrestrial activity, with all sorts of mysterious happenings, according to the local rumor mill. The best spot to learn about the phenomenon and gaze at the night sky for unusual activity is the UFO Watchtower, one of my favorite roadside attractions in the West. The bare-bones facility, composed of a two-tiered metal "tower," a domed gift shop, and a primitive campground for diehards, has been the venue for over 30 UFO sightings since opening in 2000, proprietors claim. I didn't spot any when I visited, but it still made for an unforgettable night.

ABOUT THE AUTHOR

A Denver-based freelance writer, **ERIC PETERSON** has written numerous Frommer's guidebooks and *Ramble: A Field Guide to the U.S.A.* (www.speck press.com), as well as numerous travel articles. He's an avid camper and hiker, a lifelong Broncos fan, and a rock star (at least in the eyes of his nephew Mitch).

YOUR TRIP

General Information: Contact the **Great Sand Dunes National Park and Preserve** (☎ 719/378-6300; www. nps.gov/grsa). For more information on the **San Luis Valley,** check out www.slvguide.com. The **Colorado Gators** can be contacted at ☎ 719/378-2612 or www.coloradogators.com; the **UFO Watchtower,** in Hooper, can be reached at ☎ 719/378-2271 and at www.ufowatchtower.com. **Getting There:** From Alamosa, go east 14 miles on U.S. 160, then north on Colo. 150; or north 14 miles on Colo. 17 to Mosca, then east on Six Mile Lane to the junction of Colo. 150. **Best Lodging: Cottonwood Inn Bed & Breakfast and Gallery,** in Alamosa, is a historic house decorated with regional art, most of it for sale (☎ 800/955-2623; www.cottonwoodinn.com; $99–$125 high season). **Best Lodging Value: La Casita Bonita** is a delightful adobe house for six people, adjacent to a natural grocery store in Del Norte (☎ 877/673-3353; www.organicpeddler.org; $75 weekday, $95 weekend). **Best Restaurant: Trujillos, A Dining Place,** took a vintage diner and morphed it into an upscale eatery serving a diverse menu of American, Italian, and Mexican specialties such as seafood-stuffed chiles rellenos (326 Main St., Alamosa; ☎ 719/589-9801; most main courses $10–$20). **Best Restaurant Value:** In the funky New Age town of Crestone, **Desert Sage Restaurant and Bakery** has a utopian vibe and serves great breads, burgers, seafood, and a solid selection of vegetarian fare (on Camino Baca Grande, on Colorado College's Baca campus; ☎ 719/256-4402; most main courses $6–$12). **When to Go:** Apr–Oct.

◄ *The tallest dunes in North America.*
© Michael Melford/Getty Images

HERON ISLAND, AUSTRALIA

Giant turtles, seabirds & the Great Barrier Reef

When summer comes to Australia, giant green turtles swim ashore along the northern coastline and islands, lumber up the beach, dig a hole in the sand, and lay their eggs. One of their major nesting grounds is Heron Island, a tiny coral cay remarkable for its abundant birdlife and its location right on the Great Barrier Reef.

Visitors stay in a lone resort built in the dense *Pisonia grandis* forest and among the gentle sand dunes that cover the island. Heron Island Resort is a tasteful low-rise, low-key place that is renowned for giving visitors easier access to the reef than they can find anywhere else. The difference between staying on Heron and on other Great Barrier Reef resort islands is that once you're here you have no need to travel farther to explore the reef. The island lies on the Tropic of Capricorn, on the edge of the continental shelf. Step off the beach and you enter magnificent fields of coral that seem to stretch for miles—with formations as colorful and varied as any in the Reef.

Don't expect a picture-postcard island with swaying palm trees and brilliant tropical flowers. If you arrive on Heron in summer, two things will strike you—the number of birds in the air and the distinctly earthy smell that goes with them. The resort and a University of Queensland marine research station are the only buildings on the island, while the rest of it—a National Park since 1943—is covered by Pisonia forest and spiky pandanus trees, with sandy tracks crisscrossing the grassy interior. A beautiful fringe of dazzling white sand circles it.

No matter what time of year you arrive, nature is performing some kind of marvel. With one of the most diverse ecosystems on earth, Heron Island has been given World Heritage status—it's this that makes it stand out from other Great Barrier Reef resort islands. It is also one of the most important seabird nesting locations on the Great Barrier Reef.

Turtle nesting season, November to February, is my favorite time to visit. A close second is hatching time, from February to mid-April, when the baby turtles pop out of the sand, scuttle across to the water, and swim away.

Every night during the nesting season, volunteer guides are on hand; you can watch and ask questions as the researchers tag and measure the turtles before they return to the water. It's a far different scene from the 1920s, when Heron Island was the site of a turtle soup cannery.

In June the humpback whales pass by on their northern migration from Antarctica. Until September or October they are frequently sighted as they make their return journey with their calves.

At night you will hear the eerie call of the wedge-tailed shearwaters (or "mutton birds"), backed by the sound of the ocean. Thousands of black noddy terns and migratory birds such as ruddy turnstones and eastern golden plovers arrive in September, Australia's spring.

Heron Island.
© Holger Leue/
Lonely Planet Images

SPECIAL MOMENTS

1 **Turtle time.** Small hands gently pass precious cargo, one to the other. The turtle's egg is soft, warm, and about the size of a Ping-Pong ball. If you have kids with you, they will be as entranced as you are. Under strict supervision, a ranger will allow you to handle an egg, before it is replaced into the nesting chamber under the turtle. This is one of the things that makes turtle time on Heron Island one of those special experiences that stays with you for years, and that young minds never forget. The turtles are not easily disturbed once they are laying, and you can get very close. A giant green turtle sighs deeply with exertion as she lays a clutch of about 120 eggs in a pear-shaped chamber dug from the sand. A large tear rolls from her eye; this

may be astonishing, but you will soon learn from the ranger that this is not like a human tear, but her way of ridding her body of excess salt and of cleaning the sand from her eyes. The laying season runs from mid-December through February. From February through mid-April you can see the hatched babies scuttle across the sand to the water. Only one in 5,000 hatchlings will live to return in about 50 years to lay their eggs. Humpback whales pass through from June through September.

2 **Island walks.** Guided walks of the island and reef are run daily. Island walks may mean birdwatching or include a visit to the research station based on the island. For the reef walk, just borrow a pair

of sandshoes, a balance pole, and a "viewing bucket," which, when placed in the water, will magnify what's beneath it. Walks are held at low tide, when your guide will lead you out across the sand toward the sea. Stopping to investigate what's in the water and in the sand under your feet may take some time—the whole trip usually takes around 90 minutes. And a solitary stroll around the island can do wonders to blow away those city cobwebs.

3 **Discovering the reef.** In addition to exploring the reef by scuba or snorkel, you can board a semi-submersible vessel and view the ocean floor without getting wet. Heron Island's reef sites have loads to offer divers and snorkelers, from

HERON ISLAND

manta rays to turtles, moray eels, sharks, colorful reef fish, gorgonian fans, huge coral "bommies" (out-crops), gutters, and more. More than 70% of all Great Barrier Reef coral species can be found here. Of some 20 dive sites, about half are within 15 minutes by boat from the jetty.

4 **Fishing.** This is a place where even novice fishermen are almost guaranteed success. For a price, you can join small groups—usually of only about six people—on fishing expeditions to locations such as Lamont, Fitzroy, Sykes, Wistari, and Broomfields reefs. All bait and fishing gear is provided, and if you're a beginner you'll get help and instruction on how to use it all. If you land a fish—and here, they just seem to jump onto the hook—you can take it back to the resort to be cooked and served for you that night.

LEE MYLNE is a freelance writer based in Melbourne, Australia. She is the author of several travel books, including *Frommer's Portable Australia's Great Barrier Reef*, and is a passionate traveler who admits to a penchant for islands. She is a life member of the Australian Society of Travel Writers. Check out her website, www.leemylne.com.

ABOUT THE AUTHOR

YOUR TRIP

General Information: For information on the research station, go to www.marine.uq.edu.au/hirs. Day-trippers are not allowed on Heron Island. **Getting There:** Heron Island is at the southern end of the Great Barrier Reef, 72km (45 miles) northeast of Gladstone on Australia's Central Queensland coast. A courtesy coach meets flights from Brisbane (with connections from other cities) at Gladstone airport daily (except Dec 25) to take guests to Gladstone Marina for the 1-hour, 40-minute launch transfer to the island. Round-trip transfers aboard the sleek 130-seater catamaran *Heron Spirit* cost US$160 (£85) for adults, half-price for kids 3 to 14. Helicopter transfers can be arranged for US$233 (£123) adults and US$116 (£61) children one-way. **Best Lodging: Heron Island Resort** is the only place to stay; there is no camping on the island. Accommodations options are the family-style "Turtle Room" cabins (US$400/£212 double), the Reef suite (US$456/£241), or Heron Beachside suite (US$576/£305). The adults-only Wistari Suites, luxury Point Suite, and Beach House cost US$768 (£407) per double per night. Rates include all meals and many activities (☎ 61-2/8296-8010; www.heronisland.com). **Best Restaurant:** The **Shearwater Restaurant** is the only dining option on the island (although picnic hampers can be prepared on request). Lunch is buffet-style, while dinner features a three-course table d'hôte, with a seafood buffet on Saturdays and a barbecue midweek. All meals are included in the room tariff. **When to Go:** Heron Island is a year-round destination, but I think the best time to visit is November to April, which covers the laying and hatching time for the turtles.

◀ *A common sight in the Great Barrier Reef.*
© Fred Bavendam/Minden Pictures

HONG KONG, CHINA

The perfect marriage of East & West, old & new

Hong Kong wakes me up and makes my heart race. Being there is like being thrust into the busy, pulsating center of a gigantic, multicultural beehive, where the lights are never extinguished and workers never sleep. It is life in the fast lane, "life on intravenous adrenalin," and I am addicted.

Take sensational shopping; breathtaking high-rise architecture; rich cultural heritage; efficient transport systems; an endless, throbbing vein of markets; a harbor to die for; and pack them all into a total land area of just 1,091 sq. km (421 sq. miles), and you have one of most compact, exhilarating destinations in the world.

I never tire of this tight-fitting jigsaw of human existence, this complex weaving of culture, history, and state-of-the-art modernity. Chinese medicine shops selling ancient remedies butt up against mirror-glass shopping complexes teeming with phone-toting locals. Double-decker buses filled with sleepy commuters compete with old bicycles carrying fresh vegetables. Alley markets sit at the foot of some of the most expensive real estate in the world, and old sampans sway across the harbor in the company of luxury yachts and modern ferries. It is the consummate synthesis of everything I love—the perfect marriage of East and West, of comfort and challenge, of old and new.

I love to sit on the steps of Kowloon Park and watch this tangle of humanity going about its daily business. A giggling girls' brigade skips its way through suited businessmen; miniskirted Chinese girls in big-heeled shoes and knee-high stockings share the footpath with veiled teenagers heading for the local mosque. Plump tourists bob about in a daze as turbaned Sikhs ply them with the idea of a personally tailored suit; and everywhere, the darting red taxis, the flashing neon, and the sing-song syllables of Cantonese.

A Siberian fur shop, a sushi bar, a noodle house, obscene quantities of solid-gold jewelry, preserved ducks suspended in windows, high-tech electronic stores, black pearls, dried seahorses in jars, high-fashion boutiques, karaoke bars, multi-leveled shopping arcades—they're all there, jostling for space amid this ever-moving wall of mankind. This is where you can take the second-biggest escalator in the world, or wander aimlessly through the labyrinth of 150-year-old lanes. This is where you can party all night at exclusive nightclubs, or take time out in a little backstreet shrine, smelling the incense and contemplating life in one of the most densely populated places on the planet.

I like that. I like the unexpectedness of Hong Kong existence, the eye-popping juxtapositions, the staggering contrasts. When I last visited, thunder and lightning exploded through Kowloon. It was the city's first hailstorm in 3 years—a harbinger of bad luck, announced the feng shui experts. It wouldn't be good for the Hong Kong economy, they said; and as hail lashed against my 10th-floor hotel windows and colored umbrellas unfurled on the streets below, I took temporary relief from unpredictability in smooth cotton sheets. This is a city where entrepreneurs and billionaires still believe that success can hinge on the way a building faces, the way the furniture is arranged.

◀ *The view from Victoria Peak in the evening.*
© Glen Allison/ Getty Images

135

SPECIAL MOMENTS

1 **The city heart.** Kowloon and Hong Kong Island are where the city heart beats fastest, and taking the Star Ferry between the two is the quintessential Hong Kong experience. Victoria Harbor is one of the busiest in the world, and night or day I'm dazzled by unforgettable cityscapes that unfold around its edges. Hong Kong Island is home to the business hub of Central—a glittering showcase of mirrored, multimillion-dollar high-rises, as well as to the lively night scene of Wan Chai and to one of my favorites, the Western District's Hollywood Road, a browser's paradise filled with antiques stores, curio shops, galleries, and calligraphy suppliers. The south side of the island gives you Stanley, one of Hong Kong's oldest settlements; and Aberdeen, where, if you peel back the layers of modern concrete, you'll still find the sampan, the houseboats, and the floating restaurants. But it is at the top of Victoria Peak that I always draw the biggest sigh. On a clear day, standing 554m (1,817 ft.) above this dense metropolis, I have to pinch myself to fully register the fact that I am a part of one of the most dynamic cities on earth. Yet back in Kowloon, pottering about in the Bird Market, listening to caged birds sing, or squeezing through the Jade Market on Kansu Street, haggling over the price of a pair of jade fish, I delight in the more intimate human scale of the city.

2 **The new territories.** Stretching from Kowloon to the border of Mainland China, this vast territory was once entirely rural. New towns now punctuate its fields. My memories of Chuk Lam Shim Yuen Monastery, lush banana plantations, duck farms, rice fields, markets, peaceful bird sanctuaries, walled Hakka villages and Hakka women in wide-brimmed black hats, and Sam Mun Tsai fishing village are so removed from central Hong Kong I wonder if I wasn't in an entirely different country. Often called "the land between," this tapestry of wildlife reserves, hilly woodlands, and new towns dividing Hong Kong from China's Shenzhen Special Economic Zone is too often overlooked. One of my happiest Hong Kong days was spent riding the train line, getting off on a whim at the New Territories towns of Fanling, Tsuen Wan, Tai Po, and Sheung Shui, and exploring back alleys, markets, and temples.

3 **Outlying islands.** More than 235 islands—most of them uninhabited—make up the other face of Hong Kong. Most visitors head for the two best known, Lamma and Lantau, with their beaches and seafood restaurants. Lantau also has terrific walking trails and the Po Lin Monastery, with its popular vegetarian restaurant and the world's largest

▶ *Nathan Road, Kowloon, at night.*
© Jean-Marc Truchet/Getty Images

seated outdoor bronze Buddha. My preference is to leap aboard the wonky Polly Ferry at Ma Liu Shui, Sha Tin, and cruise to the unhurried fishing island of Tap Mun in Tolo Harbor. Remote, forgotten-looking, it tumbles down a rocky face to the water's edge. You can wander through the village—its temple and spartan shops—in just a few minutes, but there's something idyllic about sitting on the shore watching the old junks, the fishermen, and the houseboats puttering by.

4 Macau. The minute I set foot in old Macau—a 1-hour boat trip from Hong Kong—I knew I had found one of those special places you never forget. I fell in love with its cobbled streets and its disheveled colonial buildings complete with peeling paint, wobbly shutters, and the overpowering whiff of Portuguese history. I immersed myself in its maze of lanes, delighting in antiques stores, Chinese markets, Portuguese signs, grand stately buildings, and gushing fountains.

ADRIENNE REWI is author of *Frommer's New Zealand*, three other nonfiction titles, thousands of magazine articles, and endless fictional short stories. Her writing passion has taken her throughout Asia. When she is not planning her next trip, taking photos, or writing her next book, she is safely housed in Christchurch, New Zealand.

ABOUT THE AUTHOR

YOUR TRIP

General information: Check out the **Hong Kong Tourism Board (HKTB)** website at www.discoverhongkong.com; and the **Macau Government Tourist Office** website at www.macautourism.gov.mo. The HKTB also offers excellent tours into the New Territories if you're short on time. **Best Lodging: The Peninsula** has history, style, and perfect location on its side (Salisbury Rd., Tsim Sha Tsui, Kowloon; ☎ 852/2920-2888; www.peninsula.com; US$390–US$637/£207–£338 double, from $727/£385 suite). **Best Lodging Value:** The **Salisbury YMCA** is next door to the Peninsula (41 Salisbury Rd., Tsim Sha Tsui, Kowloon; ☎ 852/2268-7888; www.ymcahk.org.hk; US$110–US$227/£58–£120 double). Both are walking distance to the Star Ferry terminal, to get you across to Hong Kong Island. **Best Restaurant:** The choices are endless, but for avant-garde style go for the stunning Philippe Starck–designed **Felix** in The Peninsula Hotel (☎ 852/2315-3188; main courses US$30–US$45/£16–£24). But no trip to Hong Kong would be complete without trying dim sum. For a good introduction to this lunchtime tradition, try the **Shang Palace** in the Kowloon Shangri-La (64 Mody Rd., Tsim Sha Tsui E., Kowloon; ☎ 852/2733-8754; individual dim sum US$4–US$5/£2–£3). **Best Restaurant Value:** After a stroll through the **Temple Street Night Market,** you can sit down at any number of street-side restaurants serving fresh fish. Have your fill with rice and beer for a mere US$8/£4. **When to Go:** Anytime, although the summers can have uncomfortable 90% humidity.

ICELAND

A Stygian landscape of cones & craters, sand & stone

As publisher of Frommer's, I'm frequently asked about my favorite place in the world. My answer is always the same: Iceland. Most visitors see nothing but the airport gift shop en route to mainland Europe. What a crime! Even on a 3-day stopover—which Icelandair throws in for free—you can go pony-trekking, fish for trout in raging mountain streams, or hike through some of the world's most awesome scenery.

Iceland: Don't be put off by the name. It's a chilly misnomer for a country that's almost 90% ice-free, with warm summer afternoons and a winter climate warmer than New York's. The capital, Reykjavík, is as hip as it gets, with all-night dance clubs and some of the best fish restaurants on the planet. Driving along the coast takes you through a world of farms and mossy meadows, where cows, sheep, and ponies graze on velvety green pastures. Waterfalls drop from heath-covered mountains with spiked ridges and snowcapped peaks. Daylight never ends in summer, so you never have to be anywhere by dark.

Spectacular as it is, the coast is familiar terrain to me, so happiness is traveling inland to a world of shapes and colors I've never seen before, except perhaps in dreams—a world still being created. The earth here steams and bubbles. Volcanoes rise like islands in a sea of sand. The lava is cracked and cooled in thousands of grotesque shapes that seem to have eyes that follow you wherever you go. The Iceland Touring Club runs mountain chalets in the most stunning and isolated spots, some as close as 3 hours from the airport, so you can travel in relative comfort through a Stygian landscape of cones and craters, sand and stone.

The Icelandic people are as full of surprise as their land. They are 100% literate. More books get published per person than in any other country on earth. The infant mortality rate is the lowest, and the illegitimacy rate the highest in Europe. There is virtually no unemployment or poverty. The highest salaries go to airline pilots. Even farm workers address Iceland's president by his first name.

Iceland's summer weather is reminiscent of western Ireland—marble skies, heavy mists, alternating periods of rain and bright warm sunshine. Travelers addicted to sunshine should stay away—Iceland is for those romantic fools who know that only on a misty day can you see forever.

No, there are no native Eskimos on Iceland. The first permanent settlers came from Norway in 874. The country came under Danish control in 1380. Complete independence wasn't won until 1944. The official language is Icelandic, a highly inflected Germanic tongue brought to the island by early settlers. It has changed so little that the Icelanders have only minor difficulty reading 12th- and 13th-century sagas in the original.

◀ *Thorsmork.*
© PatitucciPhoto/Aurora/
Getty Images

SPECIAL MOMENTS

1 A farmstead visit. The best way to get inside the Icelandic world is to spend a few nights on a farm. The Johannson farmstead, where I stayed, was only 40 minutes north of Reykjavík, perched on the edge of a steep fjord. I spent 1 day helping the farmer load his wagon with hay, blueberrying with his granddaughter, and pony-trekking through a valley filled with saxifrage, milkwort, and daisies. After dinner, the farmer's wife led me along the shore in search of fossils and semiprecious stones. While she chipped away at the cliffs, I walked among the bones of birds and boats, balancing on shiny wet stones as smooth as gulls' eggs. We took our time.

2 Thorsmork. One of my favorite spots is Thorsmork—Thor's woods—a surprisingly isolated nature reserve only a few hours' drive from Reykjavík. I passed through a valley of gray sand surrounded on three sides by huge guardian glaciers. The icefields sent tongues of ice into this wasteland, ending in lagoons with icebergs. Groves of stunted birch grew near the end of the valley, creating an Alpine setting crisscrossed by treacherous rivers. On this relatively treeless island, hiking through the patchy woodlands of Thorsmork seemed especially magical. Behind the lodge here is a scarped mountain that the English writer and designer William Morris climbed in 1871. Morris later wrote in his journals: "Below was the flat black plain space of the valley, and all about it every kind of distortion and disruption, and the labyrinth of the furious, brimstone-laden Markarfljot [River] winding among it. Surely it was what I came to see, yet for the moment I felt cowed, as if I should never get back again; yet with that came a feeling of exaltation too, and I seemed to understand how

people should find their imaginations kindle amid such scenes."

3 Landmannalaugar. I first glimpsed the strangely colored mountains of Landmannalaugar from Thorsmork on my first trip to Iceland; I found them so haunting that years later I fulfilled a promise to myself and returned with my sons to make the 4-day trek between the two. It's the premier walk in Iceland,

on a par with the Milford Track in New Zealand and the Inca Trail in Peru. In high season it can be made by anyone in decent condition, independently or with a group. With its twisted lava and hissing sulfur craters, Landmannalaugar is unearthly, fantastic; the mountains undulate like folds of silk, with rare, mineral colors—blues, yellows, bright reds. The pools behind the touring club's lodge are bathtub

warm, perfect for skinny-dipping. If you have only 2 or 3 days for Iceland, I'd say come here; it doesn't get better than this.

4 **Asjka.** As a travel writer, I went where press trips sent me; but left on my own I rented a 4WD with my wife and crossed the Central Highlands to Asjka, the "Box of Ashes." If you want to escape the familiar, this volcanic caldera is the place to go. A 19th-century clergyman wrote, "I didn't know what fire and brimstone were until I came here." In fact, the first American astronauts trained here before going to the moon. The nearby crater Viti, formed by an eruption in 1875, still contains a hot lake, the temperature a dreamy 77°F (25°C). Swimming in these milky green waters was happiness for us, as it should be for you. It was a quarter-century ago, but I still remember stripping down and jumping in, laughing at the absurdity of where we were and what we were doing—our senses jolted awake, our hearts full to bursting.

MIKE SPRING is the publisher of the Frommer's travel guides. In 1963 he hitchhiked around the world on $3. In a former life, he was a contributing editor at *Condé Nast Traveler,* and a frequent contributor to *Travel + Leisure* and *Travel/Holiday.*

YOUR TRIP

General Information: Contact the **Iceland Tourist Board** (☎ 800/345-6555; www.icelandtouristboard.com). **Getting There:** Contact **Icelandair** for information on flights and stopovers on the way to mainland Europe (☎ 800/779-2899; www.icelandair.net); to get around once you're there, contact **Air Iceland** (☎ 354/570-3030 in Iceland; www.airiceland.is). The **Iceland Touring Club** (Ferðefélag Islands; www.fi.is) provides simple lodges along popular hiking routes throughout the country; **Icelandic Farm Holidays** organizes farmhouse stays all over the country (☎ 354/570-2700; www.farmholidays.is). **Best Lodging:** In Reykjavík, the **Radisson SAS 1919 Hotel** has boutique-hotel elegance in a restored historic building (Posthustraeti 2; ☎ 354/599-1000; www.radissonsas.com; $200–$605/£106–£320). **Hotel Ranga** is a sophisticated country resort on the southern coast (851 Hella; ☎ 354/487-5700; www.ice hotel.is; $145–$345/£77–£183). **Best Lodging Value: Hotel Edda Eiðar** on the east coast belongs to a dependable chain of simple, clean hotels (705 Eiðar; ☎ 354/444-4000; www.hoteledda.is; $94–$112/£50–£59). **Best Restaurant: Sjavarkjallarinn** serves award-winning seafood in sleek surroundings (Aðalstraeti 2, Reykjavík; ☎ 354/511-1212; www.sjavarkjallarinn.is; entrees $39–$85/£21–£45). **Best Restaurant Value: Ánæstu Grösum** serves hearty vegetarian fare that's filling and not too pricey (Laugavegur 20b, Reykjavík; ☎ 354/552-8410; $11–$40/£6–£21). **When to Go:** Plan your trip between May and September—the rest of the year there isn't sufficient light for hiking. If you want to see the Northern Lights, go in December or January.

◀ *Skogafoss Waterfall.*
© Franz Aberham/Digital Vision/Getty Images

KACHEMAK BAY, ALASKA

From kayak trips & glacial walks to full-service spas

Alaska is a huge state, and visiting can be daunting. There are so many places to discover—so many rivers to navigate, mountains to climb, valleys to explore. Having traveled in every region of the state, I'd have to recommend Kachemak Bay State Park, surrounding the scenic town of Homer, as my favorite place of all—not because it's the wildest or most remote, but because it gives you a taste of the best of everything that Alaska has to offer in a manageable package.

It doesn't matter how often I come here. Each time I crest the hill of the two-lane Sterling Highway overlooking Kachemak Bay, with the town of Homer tucked along its shore and the mountains beyond, the scene takes my breath away. Often I pull over, get out of my car, and breathe in the salty air in silence. It is a remarkable sight.

Homer prides itself on its funky personality—an oddball mix of artists, farmers, hippies, and fishermen, all of whom somehow manage to peacefully coexist. It's a friendly place, where you can walk up to anyone and ask for directions, and they might just talk your ear off. Art galleries, eclectic eateries, and outdoor outfitters abound. In the summer the streets bustle with visitors taking a break from bird-watching, tide pooling, kayaking, bear viewing, halibut fishing, and hiking.

It's a beautiful place, too, flanked by the Kenai Mountains on one side and Kachemak Bay on the other. Its lush maritime climate supports towering spruce trees, a profusion of wildflowers, and such wildlife as moose, caribou, and bears. Sea and shorebirds flock to the plentiful waters, which are home to sea otters, sea lions, whales, and other marine mammals. Come to Kachemak Bay and you needn't wonder *if* you'll see wildlife, but *how much* you'll see.

Homer's location at the western tip of the Kenai Peninsula in south-central Alaska earns it the nickname "End of the Road" because the road truly does end here, at a spit of land jutting into the bay. The 4½-mile "Spit," as locals call it, is believed to be the remains of an ancient glacial moraine, and today those who live here work hard to keep storms raging from the northwest from tearing it apart. The sliver of land, which houses the state ferry system, the harbor, and gift and art shops, is a key element to Homer's charm.

What I love most about this place, though, is Kachemak Bay and the surrounding state park, just across the water. From the Spit, water taxis will take you on day tours, and charter-boat operators will help you haul in a giant halibut and other trophies. You can have the most primitive adventure—climbing a distant, glaciated peak, say—or indulge in the relaxing cocoon of a full-service, waterfront spa. You can kayak by day and dance the night away at the local bars.

After all, this is the land of the midnight sun, where during the long, almost endless days of summer, you never have to be anywhere by dark.

A trio of American bald eagles, Kachemak Bay.
© Klaus Nigge/National Geographic Getty Images

SPECIAL MOMENTS

1 Halibut Cove. In at least one of the art galleries in this tiny, water's-edge community within Kachemak Bay State Park, you probably won't encounter the artist. Instead, you'll find an old coffee can with a sign inviting you to take what you like and leave your money behind—a reminder of a simpler, more innocent time. This is an opportunity to acquire some unique Alaskan artwork made in one of the most inspiring settings in the state.

Halibut Cove is a tiny village, a collection of houses on pilings, really, that encircles a small lagoon. From here, you can hike into the park or simply wander the carefully tended boardwalks around the lagoon and take in the scenery.

In the summer, the wooden ferry *Danny J* takes you on daily trips across Kachemak Bay, via the Gull Island rookery, to watch the seabirds and dine at Halibut Cove's sole restaurant, The Saltry.

2 Grewingk Glacier. No matter where you go in Alaska, there is likely a flight-seeing service or guide company eager to show you the state's majestic glaciers. And they are an awesome sight, brilliant blue and gleaming, spreading for tens and sometimes hundreds of miles.

Another reason why I love Kachemak Bay State Park, Alaska's first and oldest state park, is that it's also home to one of the most accessible glaciers, called Grewingk, a 13-mile-long slab of ice that literally shimmers above Kachemak Bay on sunny days. Access to the glacier is via a water taxi from Homer that will deposit you at the trail head.

Experienced hikers can go it alone for a 3- to 5-hour round-trip hike to Grewingk Glacier Lake, through stands of cottonwoods and spruce and across the glacier's outwash.

3 Hallo Bay. Watching a giant brown bear scouring a creek bed for spawning salmon is a majestic sight. At times, these bruins of the Far North look imposing and huge, but at others, they look like caricatures of people, walking awkwardly in giant brown furs.

Brown bears are indeed beautiful animals—more than 98% of the U.S. brown bear population makes its home in Alaska. Hallo Bay, a short flight from Homer in Katmai National Park, is one of the most likely bear-viewing locations in the state.

Stay overnight in a lodge at Hallo Bay and search for the bears on foot with the safety of experienced guides, or take a day flight-seeing tour to watch them from above. The choices are endless; the memories permanent.

4 **The Ring of Fire.** The rugged mountains surrounding Homer are alive with activity, and seeing these masterpieces of nature up close is an unforgettable experience. You can see four volcanoes—Redoubt, Lliamna, Augustine, and Douglas—on a short flight across the bay from Homer, but adventurous travelers will want to make a full day of it, fly right into this Ring of Fire, and land at the foot of them. As recent as 2006, Mount Augustine blew her top, and locals watched for weeks as the mountain sputtered ash and fumes miles into the air.

To the south is Mount Douglas, which, at 7,300 feet, has a turquoise lake in its crater and a superb beach at its base, which is why I like it the best for hikes. To the north is the still-active Lliamna Volcano, in Lake Clark National Park. The largest of the volcanoes, Redoubt, towers more than 10,000 feet. On a clear day it stands like a sentry over the southern Kenai Peninsula, reminding us how small we really are.

ABOUT THE AUTHOR

MELISSA DEVAUGHN is on the Outdoors staff at the *Anchorage Daily News* in Alaska and author of *The Unofficial Guide to Adventure Travel in Alaska*. She enjoys dog mushing, cycling, and running. She lives in Chugiak with her husband, two children, 12 dogs, and a cat. Reach her at devaughn@mtaonline.net.

YOUR TRIP

General Information: Contact the **Homer Chamber of Commerce** (☎ 907/235-7740; www.homeralaska.org). For trips to Halibut Cove, contact **Central Charters** (☎ 800/478-7847; www.centralcharter.com). For bear viewing at Hallo Bay, visit **Hallo Bay Bear Lodge** (☎ 888/535-2237; www.hallobay.com). For details on **Grewingk Glacier guided hikes,** go to www.thedriftwoodinn.com or call ☎ 800/478-8019. To visit the Ring of Fire, contact **Homer Air Service** (☎ 800/478-8591; www.homerair.com). **Getting There:** Homer/Kachemak Bay is 225 miles south of Anchorage. The most scenic way to arrive is by car along the Seward and Sterling highways, which are both National Scenic Byways. **Best Lodging: Tutka Bay Wilderness Lodge** is on Kachemak Bay's waterfront, on an isthmus with incredible views (☎ 800/606-3909; www.tutkabaylodge.com; $740–$820 for 2 nights). **Best Lodging Value:** The **Homer Hostel** for private rooms (304 W. Pioneer Ave.; ☎ 907/235-1463; www.homerhostel.com; $50–$73); or **The Sea Lion Cove** for self-contained apartments (☎ 907/235-3400 May–Sept, or 907/235-8767 Oct–May; www.sealiongallery.com; $125–$135). **Best Restaurant:** In Homer, **Homestead Restaurant** for fine dining (Mile 8.2, East End Rd.; ☎ 907/235-8723; www.homesteadrestaurant.net; main courses $25–$35); **Fat Olives** for casual dining (276 Olson Lane; ☎ 907/235-8488; main courses $11–$18). **Best Restaurant Value: Captain Patties Fish House** on the Spit in Homer (☎ 907/235-5135; choices under $15). **When to Go:** Early May to mid-August; late June is particularly good because of the long summer days and drier weather.

◀ *Kenai mountains and Grewingk Glacier.*
© DanitaDelimont.com

KAUAI, HAWAII

One of the most lush & vibrant tropical landscapes on earth

By the time you arrive in Kauai after a seemingly endless flight (6 hr. nonstop from L.A.), you may feel as though you've survived purgatory and arrived in paradise. From that first turn out of the airport, the sight of so many hibiscuses bursting with sweetness and color is bound to put you in a relaxed, tropical frame of mind.

Kauai is the oldest and most isolated of the major Hawaiian Islands—the most remote in the world's most remote archipelago. Compared to Maui and its throngs of tourists, Kauai feels like a private garden with abundant space for all who want to indulge in its lush and vibrant landscape. It offers an intimacy with nature rather than high-rise beach hotels or a hopping nightlife scene, like those found in Oahu. However, it's more developed, with more amenities—think spas and golf courses—than islands like Molokai, making it perfect for getting away from it all without sacrificing comfort or convenience. Kauai is a dream destination because it offers peace and tranquillity as well as a playground for active vacationers.

Thanks to Kauai's position in the Pacific, it maintains a temperate tropical climate year-round. It tends to get more rain than the other Hawaiian islands, but, thanks to its diverse ecosystems—rainforests, high desert, and white-sand beaches all share this island—the weather can be quite varied, depending on where you are. While the North Shore typically gets more rain, the South Shore's glorious beaches usually enjoy uninterrupted sunshine with only the occasional shower. If you're not in the mood for some North Shore drizzle, hop in your car and head south. The sun will probably be waiting for you.

One thing I love about Kauai is its manageable size. It's only 553 square miles, which makes it easy for you to drive just about anywhere on the island in under an hour, and take advantage of everything there is to see and do here. If you're looking for more than a tan-line, hike through some of the most lavish tropical landscapes on Earth and check out the larger-than-life flora up close. You'll be dwarfed by leaves large enough to wrap yourself in. Grab your snorkel, strap on your mask and fins, and swim out to a coral reef for first-rate snorkeling. Or venture into Waimea Canyon, where the colors of nature have never looked more spectacular. Of course, no one will feel sorry for you if all you want to do is sun yourself on one of Kauai's amazing white-sand beaches or hole up at one of its many quality resorts.

It would be a mistake to dismiss Kauai as another mass-market or cliché honeymoon destination. This utopia is not exactly a secret—you'll be among tourists here—but Kauai offers more than just a magnificent backdrop against which to sip mai tais at sunset (though worse fates could befall you). All of its colors and smells invite you to communicate with the natural world, to slow down and get back in touch, and return home renewed and restored.

◄ *Waimea Canyon.*
© Jacques Jangoux/
Workbook Stock/
Jupiter Images

SPECIAL MOMENTS

1 **A trip up the Na Pali Coast.** The dramatic Na Pali Coast has some of the most magnificent views I've ever seen. The lush, precipitous cliffs tower as high as 4,000 feet above the Pacific. Cascading waterfalls and half-hidden caves surprise you at virtually each turn. The only way to visit the coast is by water or by air; no road navigates this part of the island. (More intrepid and robust visitors may want to hike in via the spectacular Kalalau Trail.) In summer months, kayakers launch from Kee Beach and paddle their way 16 miles along the coast to Polihale Beach, a sublime spot for picnicking and camping. Helicopter tours and boat trips (in rubber zodiac boats or high-powered catamarans) also run unforgettable outings along the shore. On a springtime visit, my boat was accompanied by a pod of dolphins. Just when I thought the moment couldn't be more perfect, a whale and her calf began breeching only 20 yards from our boat.

2 **Hiking in Waimea Canyon.** It's easy to assume that the Waimea Canyon, aka the Grand Canyon of the Pacific, might be less than grand or less than a canyon. Not so. The deep gorge is stunning. The stratified layers of color—copper, green, crimson, ochre, brown—inspire serious contemplation on the passage of time. Though the views from the roadside pullouts are excellent, I highly advise you to hop out of the car and follow a trail down into the canyon. You'll spy hidden waterfalls, unusual plant life, and nimble (and feral) canyon goats. If you're at all like me, you'll be in a perpetual state of awe as you wend your way down the trail. Few people actually go beyond the lookout points, so if you descend just a few yards into the canyon you'll find yourself virtually alone. Another great option is to enjoy this natural wonder from a helicopter.

3 **Hanging out in Hanalei.** Hanalei is a picture-perfect Hawaiian town. Nestled on the North Shore, just east of where the Na Pali Coast begins, Hanalei is a haven for laidback locals and visitors. A big surfer draw, Hanalei Bay has a wide crescent beach with fantastic waves. Surfers flock here year-round. Any time of day, any time of year (waves are most formidable in winter) you'll see them paddling out and floating, waiting for the perfect wave. Join them, or just applaud their efforts from the beach. On shore, you'll be happy to while away an afternoon visiting the shops and markets in the town center, including some charming local gift stores and roadside food stands. Grab a shave-ice from

one of the several kiosks in town, or browse the local farmers' market for fresh mangoes, papayas, and other exotic local fruits.

4 **Snorkeling a reef.** Anybody can go to an aquarium and peer at exotic sea life through glass. But why not get up close and personal while you're in one of the most glorious natural settings on the planet? A snorkel, fins, and mask will outfit you perfectly for your expedition into the clear, sublime emerald waters off Kauai's shores. North Shore beaches are my favorite snorkeling spots, particularly Puu Poa, Kee, and Tunnels beaches, all of which have reefs close to the shoreline. On the South Shore, the waters off Poipu State Park have abundant marine life, which you can commune with up close. You may encounter anything from the state fish of Hawaii, the glorious yellow Humuhumunukunukuapua'a (aka a Picasso Triggerfish), to the majestic Honu (Hawaiian Green Sea Turtle).

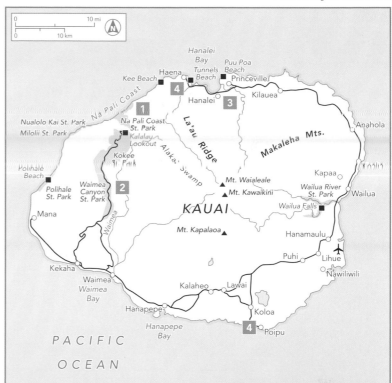

CATE LATTING is an editor at Frommer's. Her recent work includes editing the post-Katrina edition of *Frommer's New Orleans* and the first edition of *Frommer's Barcelona Day by Day*. Before working at Frommer's, she worked for nearly a decade in film and broadcast design. She lives in New York City with her husband, Eben, and their dog, Junebug.

ABOUT THE AUTHOR

YOUR TRIP

General Information: Contact the **Kauai Visitors Bureau** (☎ 800/262-1400; www.kauaidiscovery.com). Their website is thorough and informative. Another helpful resource is www.kauai-hawaii.com. **Getting There:** Most flights from the U.S. route through Los Angeles. Some airlines offer direct flights to Lihue (Kauai's airport), but most have layovers in Honolulu. **United Airlines** (☎ 800/225-5825; www.ual.com) and **American Airlines** (☎ 800/433-7300; www.aa.com) both offer daily nonstop flights to Lihue from LAX. **Aloha Airlines** (☎ 800/367-5250; www.alohaair.com) and **Hawaiian Airlines** (☎ 800/367-5320; www.hawaiianair.com) both offer inter-island flights between Lihue and Honolulu nearly every hour. **Best Lodging:** The **Princeville Resort** on Kauai's North Shore is luxurious without feeling stuffy (5-4280 Kuhio Hwy., Princeville; ☎ 800/826-4400; www.princeville.com; $465–$695 double). Even if you don't have a fat wallet, look into special rates; you might be surprised. **Best Vacation Home Rental: Na Pali Properties** offers North Shore vacation homes and apartments that cover a wide range of sizes and budgets (☎ 800/715-7273; www.napaliprop.com). **Best Restaurant:** For lunch, **Hanalei Mixed Plate** dishes out tasty pork, fish, and vegetable plates among other offerings like burgers and salads (5-5190 Kuhio Hwy., Hanalei; ☎ 800/826-7888; plate lunch $5.95–$7.95). They have lunch counter service with a few seats outside. **When to Go:** The high seasons, when hotels are completely booked, are mid-December through April and the summer months. I recommend a visit in low season in the late spring or fall.

◀ *Hiker on the Na Pali Coast trail.*
© Tyler Stableford/Aurora Outdoor Collection/Getty Images

KENYA

The last remaining mass herd migrations on earth

Kenya is seductive. It makes the heart beat faster, eyes open wider, and ears hear more clearly. It calms the mind, while the body tingles with anticipation. You wait. You watch. You drive by a lone baobab tree. White morning glories dot the earth's green canvas. And then you witness it—nature at its most spectacular. Elephants wave their trunks up and down, rhythmically splashing themselves with red mud (a natural sunblock and bug repellent). A lion and lioness cuddle in open grassland. Hippos pop their heads in and out of water. Warthogs mate. Florescent birds float above the earth. Buffaloes graze.

No doubt about it, nature reigns in Kenya.

Every year, in June, more than a million wildebeest form a single herd and move from Tanzania's Serengeti National Park toward Kenya's Masai Mara National Reserve. By September, most of the animals have arrived and spread out to graze in the Mara. They fertilize the plains before making their way south in October. This awe-inspiring phenomenon, earth's last remaining mass herd migration, lures countless tourists. If your dream is to witness throngs of wild animals moving to the soundtrack of pounding hoofs and guttural grunts erupting in unison, visit Kenya during the summer.

But if crowds, animal or human, aren't for you, go before or after the migration. In this case, it's harder to plan or promise things—not just because no one can control what wild animals you'll see on your safari, but because poor roads and oft-delayed flights tend to discourage precise timetables.

Year-round, there's a high likelihood of seeing the Big Five—elephant, lion, black rhino, buffalo, and leopard—or even the Big Nine, which includes hippopotamus, zebra, giraffe, and cheetah. On a typical weeklong safari in Kenya, you'll observe many creatures living in the wild, but it's impossible to guarantee which ones.

To get the best overview of this animal kingdom, fly into Nairobi and fly out the next day. Spend as much time as possible in two or three national parks—most notably Tsavo West National Park, Amboseli National Park, and Masai Mara National Reserve. In Masai Mara (Kenya's most well-known and popular game park), so many creatures roam the land and so many visitors spend the majority of their time here, that at times it feels surreal; it's hard to believe there aren't fences and your Land Cruiser isn't an amusement-park ride at a zoo. In Tsavo and Amboseli, the grasslands can feel eerily empty, and your eyes might scan the vast landscape for an hour without seeing any movement other than blades of grass swaying in the breeze. Eventually, and seemingly out of nowhere, a family of elephants silently strolls by, or a giraffe in the distance stands tall and still, and your sense of amazement feels as new as it did the first time you spotted an animal in the wild.

"No domestic animal can be as still as a wild animal," Karen Blixen wrote in *Out of Africa*. "The civilized people have lost the aptitude of stillness, and must take lessons in silence from the wild." Reminders like this are Kenya's most generous gifts to its visitors.

◀ *Grant's zebras.*
© Art Wolfe/Getty Images

SPECIAL MOMENTS

1 **Flying to a game park.** Don't avoid a land-transfer in Kenya; it's the best and only way to get an up-close-and-personal view of daily life in the country's small villages. But considering the country's bumpy and diesel-congested roads, not to mention the amount of time you'll spend in a car viewing game, a short flight—at least once—is worth it. My first domestic flight in Kenya was especially memorable. As our 18-seater SafariLink plane descended over Tsavo West National Park, we spotted wild animals—a group of zebras—camped out on our intended landing strip. Refusing to be deterred by the plane's proximity and its propellers' loud buzz, the zebras held their ground. After two attempts to scare them away, the game was over. Our chuckling pilot shook his head and, with a shrug, conceded the runway to the striped creatures, turning our aircraft's nose toward another clearing.

2 **Enjoying a sundowner with Mt. Kilimanjaro in the background.** After finishing an adrenalin-packed afternoon safari drive, there's no better way to relax for an hour or two before dinner than with a "sundowner" (as Kenyans call this happy hour–like experience). For the best views, try to do this when you're staying near Amboseli National Park. Your guide can drive to a picturesque spot, with Mt. Kili's peak in the distance, where you can sit on wooden stools or lean against your 4×4 and enjoy your drink of choice—often a gin and tonic, Tusker beer, or glass of wine—as you reminisce about the day's adventures. Take the time to talk with your guides. They're a wealth of knowledge about the area's wildlife, landscapes, and cultures.

▶ *Masai Mara National Reserve.*
© Anup Shah/Getty Images

3 **Visiting a Masai village.** What's as memorable as the animals and land—if not more so—are Kenya's people. Some of the most fascinating moments on a trip like this are those spent talking with locals. Many different tribes live in Kenya, making up a diverse population of approximately 30 million, but Masai are probably the best known to Westerners. With their colorful robes and reputation as long, lean, and proud warriors, they maintain many of the ancient practices of their nomadic, pastoralist lifestyle.

One of the best opportunities you'll have to interact with Masai is at your tented camp. Just talk to the staff members. But you might also want to spend some time at a local, traditional village. Villages consist of round huts, constructed from dung and covered with thatch roofs, set in a circle. Upon arrival, you might see a dance performance, listen to a song, or tour a hut. Masai warriors might demonstrate their spear-throwing skills.

4 **Sleeping in a tent on a private game conservancy.** Yes, it's a little scary to hear hyenas howling outside your tent at night. But sleeping so close to nature is one of the most exciting and unique elements of a safari.

The exteriors of the tents at each Porini camp (see "Your Trip," below) are modeled after basic ones you'd pitch yourself, but the insides are more like luxurious hotel rooms. Instead of bedding down in sleeping bags on dirt floors, guests sleep beneath high-end linens atop plush mattresses. There's an in-tent bathroom complete with a flush toilet, sink, and shower. The camps also serve top-notch meals prepared daily by a resident chef, and are equipped with modern technologies such as generators and satellite phones for emergencies.

Another benefit for guests who stay at Porini camps is the freedom to try activities that aren't allowed in national parks, such as guided walking safaris (during which you might see fresh lion prints in the mud) and night game drives (a rare and intimate experience you don't want to miss). Porini camps are set on conservancies, which means they have fewer restrictions because the land is private, leased directly from Masai communities.

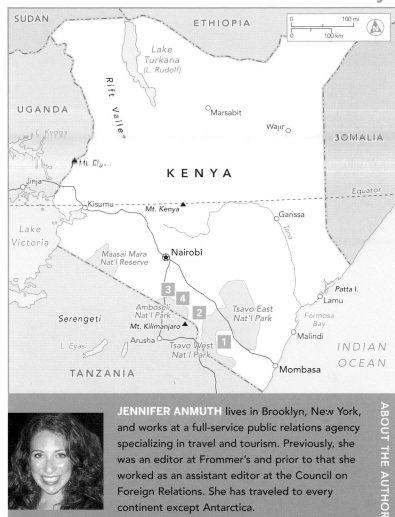

JENNIFER ANMUTH lives in Brooklyn, New York, and works at a full-service public relations agency specializing in travel and tourism. Previously, she was an editor at Frommer's and prior to that she worked as an assistant editor at the Council on Foreign Relations. She has traveled to every continent except Antarctica.

ABOUT THE AUTHOR

YOUR TRIP

General Information: Contact the **Kenya Tourist Board** on the official website, http://magicalkenya.com or call ☎ 866/44-KENYA). Pick up a copy of *Footprints Kenya*, by Lizzie Williams. For information on entry requirements, contact the **Embassy of the Republic of Kenya** in Washington, D.C. (2249 R St. NW, Washington, D.C., 20008; ☎ 202/387-6101), or a consulate in New York (866 UN Plaza, Suite 4016, New York, NY, 10017; ☎ 212/421-4741) or Los Angeles (Park Mile Plaza, Mezzanine Floor, 4801 Wilshire Blvd., Los Angeles, CA 90010; ☎ 323/939-2408). **Getting There:** Numerous airlines fly to Kenya, but none go nonstop from the U.S. If you book through a tour operator, your itinerary will include at least 1 night in Nairobi upon arrival and another one before you depart the country. **Best Outfitter:** Although it's possible to navigate Kenya on your own, we don't recommend it. Driving on the country's poor roads is extraordinarily difficult and not worth the risk of breaking down or getting lost. Exploring with a guide is much easier, more cost-efficient, and beneficial because you'll see a greater number of game—not to mention learn more about what you're looking at. We like **Gamewatchers Safaris** for its ecosensitive safaris (www.porini.com; ☎ 800/998-6634). A safari like the one above costs about $2,300 (£1,220) per person in high season and about $1,850 (£980) per person in low season. **Best Lodging:** Near the game parks, the **Porini Camps** have comfortable tent accommodations on private conservancies (www.porini.com; ☎ 254/20-712-3129 or 254/20-712-2504; $200–$390/£106–£207). **When to Go:** July–Sept for the wildebeest migration; otherwise, mid-Dec to Feb and May–June.

KYOTO, JAPAN

A glimpse of traditional Japan with its gardens & geishas

I have visited most major Asian cities, but the one that has captured my heart, the one that enthralls me, is Kyoto, the cultural capital of Japan. Nowhere have I found a more alluring, evocative place filled with such tantalizing mystery, than in this former Imperial capital.

It was raining the first day I visited, but that did nothing to dull my enthusiasm. With water glistening on a sea of multicolored umbrellas, secretive timber shutters closed to the elements, and white-faced geisha emerging from the Gion's mist-enshrouded teahouses, it was love at first sight.

Located in central Honshu, Kyoto is famous for its autumn colors, its temples and gardens, its traditional crafts, and its narrow, cobbled lanes. Its 1,600 or so Buddhist temples, 400 Shinto shrines, palaces, gardens, and old architecture were thankfully spared during World War II bombing; so, minus an architectural casualty or two since, it remains the best place to start your search for "old Japan."

Visit in autumn for jewel-like colors as the city's maples turn russet red, orange, and yellow; visit in spring and you can marvel over that quintessentially Japanese treat, the cherry-blossom party—those slightly frenzied, fun-packed family gatherings under the *sakura* (cherry blossom) trees. Nothing gives you quite the same glimpse into the enigmatic contrasts of Japanese life—the quiet, friendly etiquette loosened by *sake* makes for memorable viewing.

As modernity spreads throughout greater Kyoto—replete with hip fashion stores, stylish restaurants, and striking modern architecture—it is in the quaint little back streets, the artisan zones, that you find the unexpected delights: the kimono weavers; the umbrella, fan, and sweet makers; the paper makers; the potters; and the tofu makers—and some of the most spectacular temples you'll ever draw breath in.

I can think of nothing more pleasurable than leaving the glitz and glamour of modern Japan behind and wandering these charming "old world" lanes where the mind plays with glimpses, inferences, suggestions. You hear things, you sense things, and but for the muffled hum of traffic, you could be lost in some other more refined, veiled world where nothing is ever quite what it seems.

If I close my eyes I can still "see" the intricate screens, the louvered shutters, the willows swaying along the banks of small canals and the shop curtains (noren) blowing in a warm Kyoto breeze. It is the stuff of dreams and reveries.

And when you're done with dreaming, you can wander the exquisite traditional gardens where single rocks placed in a sea of shingle have never looked so breathtakingly lovely. Tall bamboo; still, unruffled ponds; reflected maples; and peonies, iris spears, and lotus leaves conspire to win you over.

Kyoto to me is all about the small beauties—the subtleties and the unexpected cultural juxtapositions that reach out of nowhere and make you gasp. It would be difficult to conjure a more intriguing place—a place of elegance, a place of exquisite teahouses and ancient temples. It is a place of ritual, tea ceremonies, and endless festivals—a place you will need to visit over and over again.

◀ *Yoshimine Temple in autumn, Kyoto.*
© DAJ/Getty Images

SPECIAL MOMENTS

1 The temples. I love Higashi-Honganji, the largest wooden building in Kyoto—home to hundreds of young monks, huge flocks of pigeons, exquisite *shoji* (paper screens), oh-so-smooth ancient surfaces and a bizarre coil of rope made from female human hair. Kiyomizu is a close second—memorable for its gorgeous three-story red pagoda rising from an apron of green prayer boards fluttering with wishes, its 100 stone gods, and its chubby clipped bushes. And I defy anyone to resist the tangle of cute shops that line the winding cobbled lanes below the temple. I came home with strings of prayer beads, a fat little teapot, and memories of smooth-talking rickshaw drivers.

2 Walking Kyoto. One of my favorite Kyoto memories centers on the charming Hajime Hirooka, better known as Johnny Hillwalker. His 5-hour walking tour of Kyoto is a must. Starting at the modern JR Kyoto Station, Johnny takes his 10 to 20 walkers through a maze of back streets. With 45 years of guiding experience and excellent English, he unveils treats you'd never find on your own. He talks about Buddhism, Shinto practice, geisha, history, and traditional crafts, and feeds you sushi and green tea along the way. There's "no up and down" as Johnny puts it, and by the end of the day, he'll know everyone by name. The tour ends near Kiyomizu temple, which you can see under your own steam.

3 The Gion. Nothing quite prepares you for coming face-to-face with the astonishing beauty of a geisha in full regalia. You can be wandering the narrow cobbled lanes of The Gion, wondering about life behind the closed teahouse doors, when suddenly, there she is, right in front of you—white face, petal-shaped red mouth, exquisite kimono—a butterfly, a vision from the 18th century. This is my favorite place on earth. A place riddled with romantic, enigmatic history. There are few geisha left now—around 200. They're a relic of an exotic, bygone era, and seeing them, listening to the click-clack of their wooden clogs, has left me with indelible memories. Just sit and wait—morning or early evening is best.

4 Nara. Take the Kintetsu Kyoto Limited Express (33 min.) to Nara, Japan's ancient capital, which has enough wooden monuments to make you dizzy. The jewel in the crown is Todaiji Temple. There, standing at 15m (49 ft.), is the world's largest gilded bronze Buddha, complete with serene smile and a million visitors. He's worth seeing, but you may be just as happy wandering Nara's streets, slipping into a temple here, a shrine there—always

welcomed by friendly caretakers and monks. The special moments, the human interactions, are often found in the quiet places. Make time for Kofukuji Temple and the five-story pagoda reflected in nearby Sarusawanoike Pond, and wander among the deer in Nara Park.

In early Japanese history, the nation's capital was moved to a new site each time a new emperor came to the throne. In 710, the first permanent Japanese capital was set up in Nara. After only 74 years, however, the capital was moved again, to Nagaoka and then to Kyoto, where it remained for more than 1,000 years. What's important about those 74 years is that they witnessed the birth of Japan's arts, crafts, and literature under the influence of China. Buddhism flourished, and Nara grew as the political and cultural center of the country, with numerous temples, shrines, pagodas, and palaces—many on view today. Japanese flock here to commune with ancestors. Foreigners come for a glimpse of the Japan "that was."

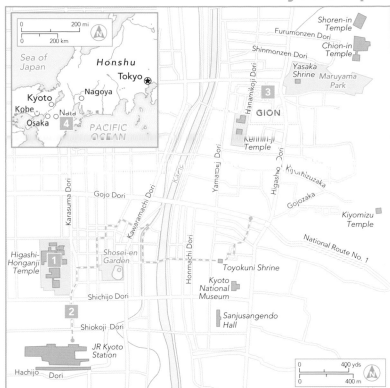

ADRIENNE REWI is author of *Frommer's New Zealand*, three other nonfiction titles, and thousands of articles and short stories. Her writing passion has taken her throughout Asia. When she is not planning her next trip, taking photos, or writing her next book, she is safely housed in Christchurch, New Zealand.

ABOUT THE AUTHOR

YOUR TRIP

General Information: Contact the **Japan National Tourist Organization (JNTO)** at www.jnto.go.jp. North American travelers can log on to www.japantravelinfo.com; British travelers can go to www.seejapan.co.uk. The **Kyoto City Tourist Information Office** is on the second floor of the Kyoto Station (☎ 81-75/343-6656). On the Web, check www.japanvisitor.com or www.kyoto-kankou.or.jp. For **Johnny Hillwalker's Kyoto Walk,** contact Hajime Hirooka (☎ 81-75/622-6803; http://web.kyoto-inet.or.jp/people/h-s-love). **Best Lodging: Hotel Granvia Kyoto** is a terrific central location in the hub of the rail system, giving you easy access to Nara (JR Kyoto Station Building; ☎ 81-75/344-8888; www.granvia-kyoto.co.jp; $220–$330/£117–£175 double). In Nara, **Kikusuiro** is 130 years old and a beautiful example of a *ryokan* (1130 Takahata-cho Bodaimachi; ☎ 0742/23-2001; $300–$381/£159–£202). **Best Lodging Value:** Kyoto has the most choices for traditional *ryokan* accommodations in Japan. **Hiraiwa Ryokan and Annex** is a reasonably priced traditional stay with the Hiraiwa family close to temples and walking distance to the station (314 Hayao-cho, Kaminoguchi, Ninomiyacho Dorei, Shimogyo-ku; ☎ 81-75/351-6748; www2.odn.ne.jp/hiraiwa; $40–$50/£21–£27). **Best Restaurant: Grace Garden** has great city views and big buffet selections (in Hotel Granvia; ☎ 81-75/342-5522; buffet dinner $38/£20). **Best Restaurant Value: Izusen,** just 1 minute's walk from the station, has tasty Japanese vegetarian fare at really reasonable prices (Surugaiya Building, second floor, Karasuma Shichijo Dori-sagaru; ☎ 81-75/343-4211; set meals $15–$33/£8–£17). **When to Go:** Apr–May and Sept–Oct.

◀ *Pathway through bamboo forest, Kyoto.*
© Art Wolfe/Photodisc Green/Getty Images

LADAKH, INDIA

An easy spirituality prevails in a remote Himalayan setting

A visit to India is a hallucinogenic, life-transforming trip. The colors seem brighter, the sounds more intense, the smells and flavors relentless. Yet of all my many cherished memories of India, it is the remote Himalayan region of Ladakh—an almost-forgotten land wedged between Tibet and the Kashmir Valley—to which my heart and soul keep returning.

For centuries at the center of important trade routes between India and central Asia, Ladakh is a sparsely populated, high-altitude region, bounded by majestic mountain ranges. The desolate landscape is strewn with Buddhist monasteries and shrines, marked by wind-blown prayer flags and whitewashed *chortens*.

Bleak and arid and unforgiving in parts, Ladakh is imbued with the type of original beauty the surrealists might have dreamed up in an outburst against reality. Along the mighty Indus River are many of its sometimes-imperceptible villages, simple and honest behind low mud walls amid a shock of green.

Up here, the India we know as a crowded confluence of humanity is replaced by vast, empty expanses and silent rock-desert terrain. Even in its tiny capital, the trade-route frontier town of Leh, life seems filled with the mystery of isolation.

Ladakh's peaceful, weather-worn inhabitants—the Changpas, Mons, and Dards—seem to tread lightly upon the earth, some of them still leading nomadic lives. Ladakh was opened to the outside world in 1974, yet today an easy spirituality still prevails, its people flirting less prolifically with modernity than in most other parts of the country.

Ladakh feels like the perfect setting for its ubiquitous Buddhist monks seeking enlightenment through the renunciation of reality. Some of them, I discovered, meditate under the warming embrace of whiskey and beer, but I still find myself imagining Ladakh as the very nirvana they're seeking.

India may be known for its spiritual virtuosity, but nowhere are the tenets of a religious belief—in this case, Buddhism—more indelibly etched into the physical landscape. For Ladakh is, at least at first glance, a barren, rock-strewn wilderness naturally predisposed toward ascetic mysticism. It's a dry, avant-garde landscape sculpted over centuries by the winds and shifting waters.

It may sound like a place where there's nothing to do, but Ladakh is imbued with great rivers, gorgeous lakes, and venerable lamaseries. Hanging out in Leh, with short walks through the surrounding landscape, will be enough adventure for some. But thrill-seekers can raft the Zanskar and Indus rivers and join challenging treks along routes once used by caravan traders. Head 5 hours north of Leh over the world's highest motorable pass and into the fertile Nubra Valley to see two-humped Bactrian camels, wildflower gardens, and hot sulfurous springs. Or take a 10-hour jeep trip south to Tso Moriri Lake, where you can spot Tibetan wild ass and exotic birdlife. You can also relax to the resonant chanting of *lamas* on a visit to a monastery, enjoy a polo match in Leh, or climb aboard a yak for the furriest ride of your life.

Enigmatic Ladakh satisfies my drifting, daydreaming imagination like few places I've visited. Or dreamed up, for that matter.

◀ *Man with wool spindle, Ladakh.*
© Michael Spring

159

SPECIAL MOMENTS

1 **The Manali-Leh Highway.** You can fly to the Ladakhi capital of Leh from Delhi, but I would choose the road journey of a lifetime. More than mere adventure, the overland trip has the practical benefit of reducing acclimatization time once you're there. I came in on a bus full of awestruck travelers cooing at one breathtaking scene after another: moonscape cliff faces, staggering peaks, and jagged avenues of Buddhist prayer flags fluttering at places said to be holy. We passed tented truck stops, ramshackle outposts, and monasteries clinging to the rock face. Sometimes, we'd stop for a pee and a prayer, or to pick up villagers walking between here and there. Midway, we joined an overnight camp and became, for a time, explorers sharing small tents under the heavens. We arrived in Leh, rattled from the drive and enchanted by all we'd seen; there was no getting around the lightheadedness that comes with altitude—our heads were literally in the clouds.

2 **Leh.** Surrounded by barley fields and mountains, Leh is a languid, dusty place, with the shifty-eyed personality of a settlement that accidentally became a town. I thought I'd landed in a traders' town straight out of *Star Wars*, with all its exotically dressed extras already on set. Your first day in Leh will be accompanied by dizzying lightheadedness as your blood adjusts to the altitude, but soon you'll be wandering the streets like an old familiar, taking comfort in a plate of freshly steamed Tibetan *momos* dumplings. On my last night, the sounds of folk dancing lured me to a local celebration where I drank a potent, pungent concoction. Beyond the festive circle of this neighborhood party, Leh was blanketed in darkness and silence.

3 **Alchi Monastery.** The drive from Leh to the 11th-century monastic complex at Alchi is scintillating. From a jeep's window you can witness the changing scenery—staggering contrasts of jagged, soaring peaks and plunging valleys carved out by the Indus River. Although inactive, Alchi is watched over by yellow-hat Gelugpa monks from Likir monastery, 30km (19 miles) away. A monk will lead you through the maze of sacred chambers, grasping a set of keys and a candle for the dim glow that allows you to gaze upon the ancient

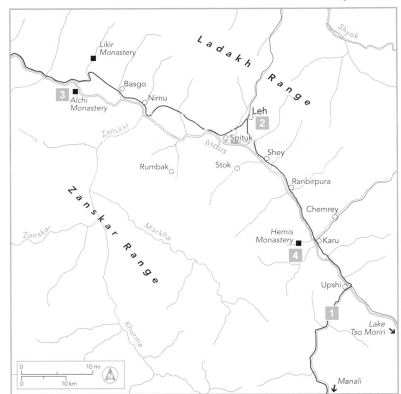

statues, posing Buddhas, and elaborate friezes sheltered here for 8 centuries. The spectacle of these cloistered spaces will be a gateway to undiscovered mysteries—and turn you into first-time explorers.

4 **Cham festivals.** You won't find discos in this half-forgotten world, but chance upon farmers in celebration, or discover the whirligig *cham* dances at monastic festivals, and your spirit will soar, fuelled by sequences designed to invoke the miracles of another world. Masked monks dancing out the dramas of the universe are a wonder in themselves, but juxtaposed against the stark Ladakhi landscape, the colorful costumes, exotic tunes, and elaborate movements are all the more thrilling and startling. You'll witness the transformation of the tranquil, holy *gompa* into the setting for a wildly spiritual party where the ethereal and mundane become one.

KEITH BAIN spent months traveling the length and breadth of India during his first assignment for Frommer's. Now he longs to return to the country that completely changed his life. He most recently traveled to Romania and Slovenia for a Frommer's guide to eastern Europe.

ABOUT THE AUTHOR

YOUR TRIP

General Information: For information on any aspect of Ladakh, visit www.reachladakh.com. India's official tourism site, www.incredibleindia.org, also has information. For adventures in Ladakh, including treks and rafting, use **Aquaterra Adventures** (☎ 91-11/2921-2641; www.treknraft.com). San Francisco's excellent **Geographic Expeditions** has all-inclusive trips into Ladakh (☎ 800/777-8183; www.geoex.com). **Getting There:** **Jet Airways** flies from Delhi to Leh each day in summer (www.jetairways.com). The cheapest way to get to Leh is on the Himachal Pradesh state "luxury" bus, which has regular trips from Manali in summer. **Best Lodging:** The **Shambha-La Hotel,** on the outskirts of Leh, provides comfortable and dignified accommodations in a flat-roofed Ladakhi-style lodge. The staff can arrange tours to the Nubra Valley, where the hotel operates a campsite (Leh; ☎ 91-1982/25-2607; www.shambhala.com; $54/£28). For the best traditional experience, stay in a Ladakhi *yurt* (a tentlike structure of canvas and bamboo) with **Ladakh Sarai** (☎ 91-11/2757-0446; www.naturesafariindia.com; $200/£102). **Best Lodging Value:** The mountains surrounding Leh provide the perfect backdrop for **Omasila,** an intimate hotel in a Ladakhi-style building (☎ 91-1982/52119; www.hotelomasila.com; $43/£22). **Best Restaurant:** The **Tibetan Kitchen** serves the best *shabalay* (a sort of Tibetan pie with broth), steamed *momos,* and Tibetan hot pot in Leh, or anywhere in Ladakh (☎ 91-1982/25-3071; $13/£7). **Best Restaurant Value:** The atmospheric **Himalaya Café** serves tasty Tibetan and Chinese dishes (☎ 91-1982/25-0144; $10/£5). **When to Go:** June–Sept.

◄ *Buddhist prayer scrolls, Ladakh.*
© Michael Spring

LHASA, TIBET

Monks, prayer wheels & a visit to Mount Everest

The circumambulations begin at dawn. Buddhist pilgrims who have come by foot from all over the high plateau begin trudging clockwise around downtown Lhasa's Jokhang Temple as incense and the smell of yak butter waft through the air. Some continue their clockwise revolutions around the temple until dusk, perhaps making hundreds of circles, while the even more devoted pause every few feet to prostrate themselves—lifting their hands in prayer, then bending at the knee and extending their bodies on the stone ground.

Witnessing the steadfast devotion that Tibetans have to their religion has captivated Western visitors for decades, from James Hilton, who wrote his novel *Lost Horizon* about Tibet's mythical Shangri-La, to the Austrian mountain climber Heinrich Harrer, whose experience was popularized in the movie *Seven Years in Tibet*. Combine the spirituality of Tibet's living temples with the high plateau's wide, blue skies and the stark, severe peaks of the Himalayas, and you have one of the most fascinating destinations in the world.

My ideal 1-week itinerary starts in Lhasa, where you should acclimate to the plateau's thinner air over several days while taking in such sights as Potala Palace and Johkang Temple, and wandering through Lhasa's crowded, intricate alleys. Stop and hang out with the monks watching soccer games on television in the town's numerous teahouses, where a sweet milk tea is served from thermoses. In Lhasa's back alleys you'll also find small, neighborhood temples staffed by eager monks wanting to befriend you.

Two of Tibet's most captivating sights are easily reached in a few hours by four-wheel-drive. North of Lhasa is Namtso Lake, a pristine, crystal-blue lake framed by snowcapped mountains. The lake has few of the trappings of a tourist destination, aside from some cabins to stay in, but the peace and serenity is stunning. South of Lhasa is Gyantse, where an ancient fort sits dramatically atop a jagged hill, like a castle from a fairy tale.

If you have more than a week to spare, I encourage you to venture farther. Many travelers continue on to Shigatse, Tibet's second-largest town, where the vast Tashilhunpo monastery is located. Only make a brief stop here, if you must, as Shigatse's charm has been ruined by bad Chinese urban development. Continue on the bumpy roads for 2 more hours and you'll be rewarded with the relatively untouristed Sakya Monastery situated in a remote Tibetan village. After overnighting in Sakya, those with a burning curiosity to see the world's tallest mountain, Mount Everest, can continue to Everest Base Camp, a day's journey on rough roads.

Tibet isn't a five-star luxury destination, but it is becoming more tourist-friendly. Several boutique guesthouses have opened in recent years, which should make your stay more than comfortable. And Tibet's increasing links with the outside world—like the frequent flights from Běijīng and the opening of a rail-line link between Lhasa and Běijīng (a captivating 48-hr. journey over China's most remote mountains and deserts)—make it more accessible than ever.

◀ *Novice monk in Ganden Monastery, Lhasa.*

SPECIAL MOMENTS

1 Potala Palace. Come here not just to watch the monks, but to see people from all strata of Tibetan society. As I rounded the Potala Palace one morning, a dignified lady with a wide-brimmed hat and white gloves trudged past me, holding a leash cuffed to a fluffy white dog. Behind her were a pair of elderly women in weather-beaten sneakers swinging prayer wheels. Along one side of the path, vendors pack their goods tightly on tables and shelves—everything from toilet paper to big yellow blocks of soap and cans of sardines. The stalls cater to ordinary Tibetans, lending the atmosphere of a bazaar to the spiritual walk. Across the path, prayer wheels squeak in submission to the hands of passing pilgrims. It's best to get to Potala as early as possible, by 7am, to get in at least one circumambulation before you set foot inside the temple, which was the Dalai Lama's residence until he was exiled.

2 Barkhor Square/Johkang Temple. At sunrise, hundreds of Tibetans—some wearing kneepads, others standing before their mats—begin prostrating themselves in front of the Johkang, a temple that has been around since the 7th century and is known as Tibet's spiritual heart. While the Potala may be more impressive in sheer size, I find the Johkang more stunning for the number of avid devotees who regularly make the trip here. Clouds of incense blow in the open air. Pilgrims inch through the temple, as rows of monks chant, sitting in neat rows in the middle of the main room, lit with yak-butter candles. Worshippers throw white sashes on Buddha statues, bow their heads, and press their foreheads against the yellow cloth adorning the Buddha. Monks push the worshippers along so they don't dawdle—there are too many people for that. In front of the temple is Barkhor Square, lined with stores selling Tibetan jewelry and cafes where monks watch soccer and drink warm cups of sweet, milky tea.

3 Namtso Lake. This famous lake is a bumpy, 5-hour, uphill journey from Lhasa; you'll want to pack some altitude-sickness pills when you go. Walking outside your very basic cabin, you'll see jagged, snowcapped mountains framing the pristine blue waters. How far you venture from your cabin depends on how winded you feel from the altitude. After spending a night here, try walking along the shore

and enjoying its unforgettable views. It's about an hour to an abandoned monastery and unusual rock formations that Tibetans have decorated with prayer flags. On an evening ramble, the only person I saw was a woman in a long wool skirt walking her yak near the water's edge. As the sun set over the mountains, I felt that this was the closest I would ever get to the stars.

4 Sakya Monastery. Nestled in a valley on a remote stretch of road between Lhasa and Katmandu is a 13th-century monastery unique for its slate-gray walls and its intricate mural paintings. I also love this monastery for its isolation—after a hard day's drive, it's a relief to approach the tiny village full of children eager to chat with outsiders. They accompanied me on a walk atop the monastery's walls, which offer a stunning vista of a nearby river and the surrounding mountains.

ABOUT THE AUTHOR

JEN LIN-LIU is a freelance writer based in Běijīng. She is currently working on a book about Chinese cooking, which will be released in 2008 by Harcourt Books. Raised in southern California and educated at Columbia University in New York, she first moved to China in 2000 on a Fulbright scholarship.

YOUR TRIP

General Information: Contact the **China International Travel Service** (CITS; ☎ 626/568-8993 or 86-10/8511-8522 in China; www.cits.com.cn). To enter Tibet, you need an **Alien's Travel Permit.** CITS can arrange a permit, which typically costs around $25 (£13). In Lhasa, the tour operator **Shigatse Travels** is highly recommended (☎ 86-891/633-0489). **Getting There:** Tibet is China's westernmost region, bordering Nepal, India, and Bhutan. It is a 3½-hour plane ride from Běijīng, China's capital. A new railroad connects Běijīng to Lhasa in 48 hours. Contact CITS (above) for more details. **Best Lodging:** In Lhasa, the **House of Shambhala** is a boutique hotel and yoga center (No. 7, Jiri Erxiang; ☎ 86-10/6402-7151; www.houseof shambhala.com; $60/£32). At Namtso Lake, the **Nàmùcuò Kèzhàn** offers basic dorm beds. The guesthouse's restaurant serves decent Sichuan fare (☎ 0891/651-1390; $6/£3). In Gyantse, the **Gyantse Hotel** is the only establishment that you should consider (Yīngxióng Nán Lù 8; ☎ 86-892/817-2222; $50/£26). In Sakya, the **Sakya Manasarovar Hotel** is the best option in town (☎ 86-892/824-2222; $20/£11). **Best Restaurants:** In Lhasa, **Mayke Ame** (Bājiǎo Jiē Dōngnán Jiǎo; ☎ 86-891/632-4455; entrees $5/£3) or **Holy Land Vegetarian Restaurant** (Línkuò Běi Lù Wàibànshāng Píngfáng 10; ☎ 86-891/636-3851; entrees $4/£2). **When to Go:** Government-imposed travel restrictions in Tibet tend to increase around the Monlam Festival (mid-Jan to mid-Feb), the Saka Dawa Festival (mid-May to mid-June), and the present Dalai Lama's birthday (July 6).

◀ *Gyantse Dzong Fortress, south of Lhasa.*
© Angelo Cavalli/Getty Images

LOIRE VALLEY, FRANCE

Elegant Renaissance castles

only 90 minutes from Paris

As a child, I loved fairy tales. That may explain why I adore the Loire Valley region in France, a place of countless stories, where Renaissance castles and gardens are set in a pastoral dreamscape crisscrossed by rivers—the Cher, the Indre, the Vienne, and, of course, the magnificent Loire, known as "the royal river." At 998km (620 miles), the Loire is France's longest river. Wide and slow-flowing, it sets the mood for the region, giving an aura of elegance and tranquillity.

The Loire region, known as the Valley of Kings, is only a 90-minute drive southwest of Paris, but coming here is a voyage back to the 15th and 16th centuries, when the region served as France's political and religious center, and the Loire Valley offered royals a strategic location, relatively mild climate, and excellent hunting.

What makes this region unique is that there are more historic sites in a smaller area than anywhere else in France, other than Paris. There are about two dozen castles within a 70-mile radius, all open daily for tours. The flatness of the valley means that you can bike effortlessly from castle to castle, hardly breaking a sweat.

When I visit the Loire Valley, I like to stay at least 1 night in Orléans, a city that served briefly as the capital of France during the Middle Ages. I settle in at the reasonably priced Hôtel d'Arc, located in a circa-1900 building with old-world charm, and plan my castle-hopping itinerary over dinner at one of the city's fine restaurants, featuring the region's famous wines—Sancerre, Vouvray, Chinon—paired with local delicacies such as marinated boar. For dessert, it's *de rigueur* to order the delicious tarte tatin, an upside-down apple tart.

The Loire Valley offers a picture window into what the French call *la douceur de vie*—the sweet life—recalling an age when the French royals took inspiration from the Italians and embraced the Renaissance style of elaborate decoration. Castles were no longer just fortresses but homes with lavish comforts. Some castles are decorated today with opulent furniture, tapestries, and murals from the period. Others are more sparsely furnished, but with towers and dungeons to explore.

My list of must-see castles begins with Château de Chenonceau, called "the ladies' castle" because of the queens and mistresses who ran it. My second pick is Château de Chambord, the castle whose grandeur causes jaws to drop. I have a special fondness for the castle at Amboise, because it's where Leonardo da Vinci, the original Renaissance man, arrived in 1515 at the invitation of François I. He brought his painting, the Mona Lisa, with him in his baggage. The town of Amboise is one of my favorite towns for an overnight stay, in part because of its convenient, central location; in part because of the elegant, 18th-century Hôtel le Manoir les Minimes, only a short walk from the castle.

My fourth and final choice is the château of Blois. You'll find here the cabinet where Catherine de Médici stored her poisons, and, just upstairs, the room where the Duke of Guise was murdered—just a hint of the many high intrigues that took place here, and throughout the always delightful Loire Valley.

Château de Sully.
© Charlie Waite/Getty Images

SPECIAL MOMENTS

1   Château de Chenonceau. For sheer romantic inspiration, nothing can quite prepare you for the seduction of the castle at Chenonceau, which is, in my opinion, the most beautiful in the Loire Valley. To arrive at the castle, you first walk through a gate guarded by a pair of sphinx and down a path lined with orange trees, past acres of formal flower gardens. As you get closer, you can see the perfect Renaissance symmetry of the castle with its two-story gallery that stretches over the Cher River above a series of graceful arches. The interior spaces of Chenonceau are elaborately decorated with fabulous murals, antiques, and tapestries. In 1547, Henry II gave Chenonceau to his mistress, Diane de Poitiers. For a time this remarkable woman was virtually queen of France, infuriating Henri's dour wife, Catherine de Médici. Diane's critics accused her of using magic to preserve her celebrated beauty. She was in her 60s when Henri died in a jousting tournament in 1559. Catherine then became regent (her eldest son was still a child) and forced Diane to return the jewelry Henri had given her and to abandon her beloved home.

2   Joan's exploits. There are so many monuments to Joan of Arc in the Loire Valley that you expect your hotel to bear the sign, "Joan was here." One year, I decided to check out a few of the sites devoted to that cross-dressing wonder and had a lot of fun doing it. Working her story backwards, I started my Joan jaunt in Orléans, where an annual Joan festival takes place in mid-May. This is where the girl with the pixie haircut (or is that just in the movies?) led a group of French soldiers against the British. Maison Jeanne-d'Arc, a replica of her home in Orléans, is a little corny but is a must-visit for any Joan-o-phile. I also recommend the Joan Museum at the Château de Chinon, which has three floors of Joan collectibles. Chinon is where young Joan inspired Charles VII to support her cause.

3   Culture in the Loire Valley. The Loire Valley castles are ideal settings for special art shows, theater pieces, festivals, parades, and concerts, which take place all summer long. Sound and light shows—called *son et lumière* in French—take place summer evenings and feature music, pageantry, and sometimes even a parade. The one not to be missed is at Chenonceau, a pageant highlighting the women who ran the castle. At Amboise every summer, short, Renaissance-style plays are

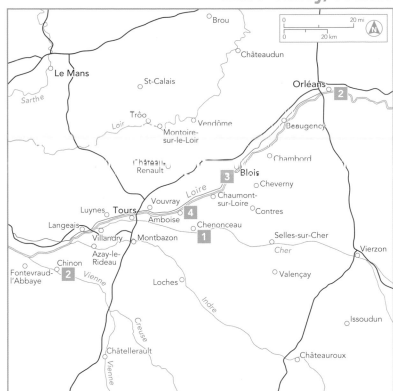

performed. At Blois, there are classical music concerts nightly in July and August in various locations in town, including the courtyard of the castle, where chairs are set up. Tourist information offices can provide details.

4   Leonardo's house, Le Clos-Lucé. When people ask me to recommend can't-miss sites in the Loire Valley, one museum always makes the list: Leonardo da Vinci's home, Le Clos-Lucé, where the great Renaissance man lived out his days. I'm fascinated by the stories of Leonardo's relationship with François I, who lived in the nearby castle at Amboise. Apparently there was an underground tunnel between the two residences for the men to use for visits. The best part of the museum is the exhibit in the basement, with 40 models based on Leonardo's drawings, from helicopters to tanks. The basement leads to the sunken garden where you can have a cup of tea in a courtyard surrounded by rosebushes.

LAURA M. RECKFORD is the managing editor of the *Falmouth Enterprise* newspaper on Cape Cod. She has been the author for the last 9 years of *Frommer's Cape Cod, Nantucket & Martha's Vineyard* and was a coauthor of the first edition of *France For Dummies*. She can be reached at laurareckford@hotmail.com.

ABOUT THE AUTHOR

YOUR TRIP

General Information: Contact the **Loire Tourism Offices** (☎ 33/02-40-48-24-20 or 33/2-38-79-95-00; www.loirevalleytourism.com). The tourist office in Orléans is located at 2 place de L'Etape. **Getting There:** Contact **Air France** (☎ 800/237-2747; www.airfrance.com). By rail, France National Railroad (www.sncf.com) trains leave from Gare d'Austerlitz in Paris to Orléans daily. Orléans is 119km (74 miles) southwest of Paris. **What to See & Do: Maison Jeanne-d'Arc** is a corny but interesting museum about the young lady's legendary heroics (3 place de Gaulle, Orléans; ☎ 33/2-38-52-99-89; www.jeannedarc.com.fr). **Le Clos-Lucé** is Leonardo da Vinci's house—a can't-miss sight (2 rue de Clos-Lucé, Amboise; ☎ 33/2-47-57-62-88; www.vinci-closluce.com). For information on **summer concerts** and other entertainment in Loire Valley towns, log on to www.loirevalleytourism.com. Rent a bike with **Amstercycles** for 13€ to 21€ ($16–$25) a day (5 rue du Rempart, Tours; ☎ 33/2-47-61-22-23). **Best Lodging: Hôtel le Manoir les Minimes,** in Amboise, is a beloved first-class option (34 quai Charles Guinot; ☎ 30/2-47-30-40-40; www.manoirlesminimes.com; 110€–170€/$132–$204). **Best Lodging Value:** The **Hôtel d'Arc** in Orléans (37 rue de la République; ☎ 33/02-38-53-10-94; www.hoteldarc.fr; 90€–124€/$108–$149). **Best Restaurant: Jean Bardet Château Belmont,** in Tours, has had a top reputation for years with two Michelin stars (57 rue Groison; ☎ 33/2-47-41-41-11; www.jeanbardet.com; 60€/$72). **Best Restaurant Value:** For crepes, look no further than **Le Viking** (233 rue de Borgogne, Orléans; ☎ 33/2-38-53-12-21; 10€/$12). **When to Go:** May–Sept.

◀ *Château de Chenonceau.*
© Jon Arnold/DanitaDelimont.com

MACHU PICCHU, PERU

The fabled lost city of the Incas, high in the Andes

Too many moments from my childhood are now frustratingly fuzzy, but I clearly remember the first time I came across Machu Picchu. I was in the first grade, and a textbook's black-and-white photograph of the ruins, dreamily cloistered in clouds amid the Andes Mountains, stopped me in my tracks. It was an epiphany of the type a six-year-old might have: I fixated on that image, determined that one day I would discover that distant, enigmatic place for myself.

When I traveled to Machu Picchu for the first time, a dozen or so years after cracking that school book, two friends and I experienced Machu Picchu virtually alone. The feeling of discovery—as though no one had ever been there before us—was overwhelming. We ran our hands over the massive, smoothly cut stones, which fit together seamlessly without mortar. We marveled at the Temple of the Sun window, perfectly aligned for winter's solstice, when the sun's rays come streaming through at dawn and set the stone at the center of the temple ablaze. We tried in vain to explain the use of the Intihuatana, a peculiar sundial our guidebook defined as a "hitching post of the sun." We scrambled to the top of Huayna Picchu for a bird's-eye, panoramic view. And we placed our suddenly less skeptical hands on a huge healing stone. But mostly, we silently imagined what this place must have meant in the Incas' worldview.

I've now been traveling to Peru and Machu Picchu for more than 20 years and have visited the ruins by foot, ramshackle local train, tourist train, and, a couple of years ago, on the luxury, white-gloved Hiram Bingham Orient Express. I keep going back, always expecting to have to accept that it has finally become overcrowded and overdone. But after remaining hidden for 400 years, Machu Picchu defiantly guards its mystique.

For me the key to Machu Picchu's allure is the powerful sense of wonder it inspires. Cleared from centuries of thick forest growth, this fabled lost city exerts a magnetic, often mystical pull even on those who know little of the Incas. A footpath through the bold Andes Mountains, today's Inca Trail, served as a highway connecting the site to Cusco, the empire's capital. Was Machu Picchu a citadel? An astronomical observatory? A ceremonial city or sacred retreat for the Inca emperor? More mysterious still, this complex city of fine architecture and masonry was constructed, inhabited, and then deliberately abandoned all in less than a century—a mere flash in the 4,000-year history of Andean Peru.

Whatever its purpose, Machu Picchu reveals itself to be the world's greatest example of landscape art. Surely the Incas chose the location for the power of its natural beauty: Encircled by rugged Andes Mountains, the ruins sit gracefully like a proud saddle between two huge *cerros*, or peaks. At daybreak, when the sun's rays creep silently over the jagged silhouette, they slowly, and with great drama, illuminate the ruins row by row and building by building. The sight provokes squeals of delight in many early-morning visitors, and it gives me goose bumps every time.

◀ *Machu Picchu at sunset.*
© Galen Rowell/ Mountain Light

SPECIAL MOMENTS

1   **Cusco walk.** The ancient capital of the Inca Empire is a feast of Inca and colonial architecture. While Spanish conquistadors razed most Inca buildings, they couldn't help but recognize the expert engineering of Inca masons. Take a walk along the streets of Cusco and you'll find, beneath monasteries and mansions, dramatic stone walls constructed of mammoth granite blocks so exquisitely carved that they fit together without cement, like jigsaw-puzzle pieces. Hatunrumiyoc is a cobblestone street lined with stunning polygonal blocks, including a famed 12-angled stone. Down an alleyway is a series of stones said to form the shape of a puma, including the head, large paws, and tail. But best of all is the Temple of the Sun/Santo Domingo, a vivid illustration of Andean culture's collision with western Europe. Today all that remains of the most sumptuous temple in the Inca Empire is fabulous stonework, tucked into the colonial church's cloister, but it is as fine as anything the Incas left behind.

2   **The Inca Trail.** The best way to experience Machu Picchu is the way the Incas did: by arriving on foot, along the ancient royal footpath that leads directly to the ruins' gates. The experience—4 days (just 2 along a less traditional path) of trekking across mountain passes—is unparalleled. The trail traverses a national park and dazzles with extraordinary natural and man-made sights: Inca ruins, exotic vegetation, and jaw-dropping mountain and cloud-forest vistas. But the most unforgettable moment is when hikers, after 3 days of trekking and rising at 4am for the last push to Machu Picchu, arrive at sunrise and see the fabled ruins emerge from the mist beneath them.

3   **Overnighting in the Sacred Valley.** Between Cusco and Machu Picchu is a serene valley, framed by towering mountains and lined with Inca stone *andenes*, or agricultural terraces. The Incas held the Urubamba Valley, and the river that ran through it, sacred. Magnificent estates, temples, and fortresses scattered throughout the Sacred Valley of the Incas are testaments to the region's ceremonial importance. It is a lovely stretch of small villages where descendents of the Incas, nearly oblivious to the tourist crush at Machu Picchu, have not abandoned traditional Quechua ways. The valley has become the focus of a wave of relaxed, upscale country hotels, which allow visitors not only an appreciation of traditional highland culture and the immense night sky, but an opportunity to adjust to the altitude in the Andes, which is 300m (1,000 ft.) lower in the valley

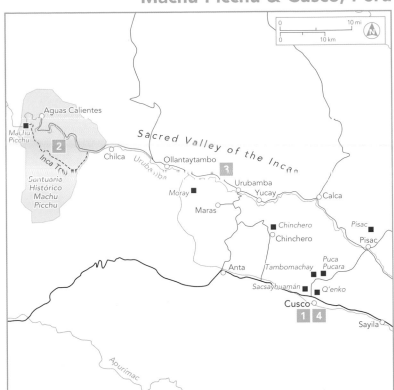

than Cusco's daunting elevation of 3,300m (11,000 ft.).

4 **Reveling in Cusco.** For all its historical significance, Cusco is the Katmandu of South America, a mecca for South American adventurers. It seems as though every other address serves the continually growing throngs of Gortex-wearing gringos who gather in the city before or immediately after a visit to Machu Picchu. Most linger, drawn to the city's vibrant expression of Amerindian and *mestizo* culture as much as Cusco's nightlife. Laid-back but lively, with an enthusiastic crowd of young people hanging out at bars, cafes, clubs, and funky restaurants, it's the ideal place to meet fellow travelers and trade tales from the Inca Trail. For all its popularity, Cusco is the rarest of places that somehow preserves its appeal despite its prominence on the international tourism radar.

ABOUT THE AUTHOR

NEIL E. SCHLECHT is a graduate of Georgetown University's School of Foreign Service and holds master's degrees from the University of Texas at Austin. He has worked on development programs for the E.U. and authored a dozen travel guides and articles on two of his addictions: tennis and wine. He has lived in Spain, Brazil, and Ecuador.

YOUR TRIP

General Information: Contact **PromPerú** at www.peru.info. **Getting There:** For trains to Machu Picchu, check the schedules and fares at **PeruRail** (☎ 51-84/238-722; www.perurail.com). Many agencies in Cusco organize treks (which must be officially sanctioned); recommended outfitters are on www.frommers.com. **Best Lodging:** In Cusco, **Hotel Monasterio** is a converted 16th-century monastery (Calle Palacios 136, Plazoleta Nazarenas; ☎ 51-84/241-777; http://monasterio.orient-express.com; $435–$1,150/£230–£586). In Aguas Calientes, **Machu Picchu Pueblo Hotel** has bungalows ensconced in gardens and cloud forest (☎ 800/442-5042; www.inkaterra.com.pe; $195–$390/£103–£207). **Best Lodging Value:** In Cusco, the **Niños Hotel** (Calle Meloc 442; ☎ 51-84/231-424; www.ninoshotel.com; $28–$34/£15–£18). The profits serve Cusco street kids. In the Sacred Valley, **Libertador Valle Sagrado Lodge** is an intimate country inn (Yanahuara-Urubamba; ☎ 51-84/251-526; www.vallesagradolodge.com; $110/£58). **Best Restaurant:** In Cusco, **Cicciolina** (Triunfo 393, second floor; ☎ 51-84/239-510; $6–$10/£3–£5.30) and **MAP Café** (Casa Cabrera, Plaza Nazarenas 231; ☎ 51-84/242-476; $10–$14/£5.30–£7). In Aguas Calientes, the **Indio Feliz** (Lloque Yupanqui 4-12; ☎ 51-84/211-090; $7–$10/£4–£5.30). **Best Restaurant Value:** In Cusco, **Greens** (Tandapata 700; ☎ 51-84/243-379; main courses $6–$9/£3–£5) and **Jack's Café Bar** (Choquechaca 509; ☎ 51-84/806-960; everything under $6/£3). **When to Go:** Late spring, early summer, and fall, avoid the rainy season (Oct–Mar) and crowded July and August. The Inca Trail is closed in February.

◀ *Inca walls, Cusco.*
© Frans Lemmens/Zefa/Corbis

MALDIVES

A sybaritic life of sun, sand & sea

I love islands, especially ones fringed by coral reefs and swaying palm trees. When I want to relax in style, however, I head to the Maldives, a clutch of low-lying islands scattered like white pearls across the equator. What makes them different from other islands around the world? Well, most are enclosed within their own coral reef, so the color of the water is exquisite, and the sand is so fine it literally squeaks when you walk on it.

Most of the 70 or so resorts in the Maldives occupy their own island and are fully geared to the hedonist within. Sun, sand, and sea are the name of the game here. At the best island resorts, accommodations are unashamedly opulent, with internationally acclaimed chefs churning out everything from sashimi to sorbets, first-rate spas, and luxurious cottages perched on poles over ravishing lagoons.

I've had some glorious times in the Maldives. I remember watching a rowboat pulling up to our villa-on-stilts with breakfast pastries and fruit, and then diving off our private terrace into a tepid lagoon darting with fish. We happily succumbed to a private sunset cruise, with the requisite champagne and caviar, followed by an intimate candlelit dinner while moored in a resort lagoon.

The lagoons, coral drop-offs, and swirling confusion of fish make the Maldives one of the best places in the world to snorkel or scuba dive. I've had unforgettable encounters with manta rays, toothy barracudas, giant groupers, and harmless sharks in water as clear as gin. And I've spent hours among psychedelic parrotfish and fusiliers, and hundreds of other species of sea creatures, shimmering in a kaleidoscope of coral.

With all this natural beauty to share, resort operators have to work hard to distinguish their island from the others. The farther away the resort is from Male, the capital, the more it relies on "remoteness" and "exclusivity" as its marketing ploy. The nearer to the airport it is, the more it claims to be within easy reach of paradise.

Words lead to actions in the Maldives, though, and blowing the opposition out of the water means being one step ahead. Here, a wine list gives way to a custom-built underground wine cellar; over-water bungalows suddenly have glass floors; and a luxury spa mutates into luxury underwater treatment rooms. Sometimes the simple things are the nicest. At a sumptuous resort called the Banyan Tree, the garden cottages are designed to reflect the spiral of a seashell. You can dine barefoot and al fresco at the beachside restaurant, before retiring with a bottle of wine to an outdoor hot tub set in your own garden under the stars.

None of this comes cheap, of course—but you get what you pay for in the Maldives. I once stayed at a cheap resort favored by mass-market package tourists, in a concrete box of a room above a noisy generator. We felt helpless and trapped—a reminder that, on any tropical island, the resort you choose can spell the difference between a disaster and the vacation of a lifetime.

◀ *Snorkeling in the Maldives.*
© Jon Arnold/
DanitaDelimont.com

SPECIAL MOMENTS

1 Swimming with baby sharks. The over-water bungalows at many resorts have a little secret that you discover only once you stand on the front porch and look down into the vibrant green lagoon. The dorsal fins, cutting through the water's surface, are unmistakable. They belong to baby reef sharks—about a foot long, and totally harmless. The sharks come into the shallow lagoons to escape predators out on the reef, such as barracuda. There are plenty of small fish for them to eat in the lagoons, so your toes are quite safe. Just jump in, and watch as they glide right by you. Other common inhabitants of the lagoons are lion fish. They have elongated dorsal-fin spines and enlarged pectoral fins, and each is colored with zebralike stripes. Lion fish are usually found hovering near crevices or caves in coral reefs, but they also like to hang out around the pylons of over-water bungalows. They can produce painful puncture wounds if provoked, but are quite docile otherwise. The lagoons are encircled by walls of coral reef, which drop down into sparkling depths filled with iridescent fish life. Here you will find angelfish with blue and yellow or orange stripes, yellow-finned surgeonfish, coral-crunching parrot fish, and inquisitive moray eels. Raise your head from the water and you might even see schools of flying fish leaping through the air, too. All in all more than 1,000 fish species call the warm seas around here their home.

2 Dining underwater. The most amazing meal I've ever eaten took place at Ithaa, the underwater restaurant at the Conrad Maldives. Ithaa means "pearl" in Dhivehi, the official language of the Maldives.

Five-lined snapper, Maldives.
© Reinhard Dirscherl/AGE Fotostock, Inc.

It's the world's first-ever all-glass undersea restaurant. Designed in New Zealand, constructed in Singapore using materials from the United States, and then shipped to the Maldives, Ithaa sits almost 5m (16 ft.) below the Indian Ocean. Diners enter the clear acrylic cave by a set of steps from the island, and I dare you not to let out a gasp when you see the colorful reef just inches from your table. The food and wine are fabulous, the service impeccable, and because the staff feed the

fish as you dine you're guaranteed a remarkable aquatic show. The restaurant holds just 14 diners, so everyone gets to see the action close up.

3 Underwater spa. If you think having a good massage is a relaxing luxury, then you'll go weak at the knees at the sight of the world's first underwater treatment room. It's located at Huvafen Fushi, a small luxury resort and spa on North Male Atoll. The resort offers 43 "naturally

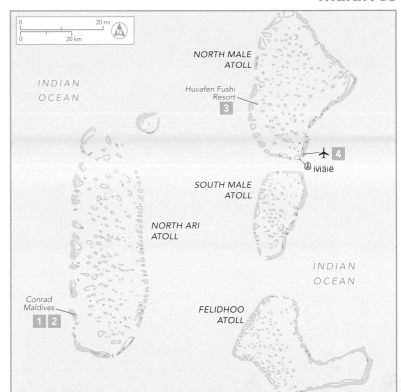

modern" bungalows, all with giant beds and their own private oasis and swimming pool. I love the yoga pavilion, outdoor floatation pool, over-water gym, and fabulous infinity swimming pool. Languidly staring into the eyes of passing fish while a masseuse massages my back with essential oils is my idea of heaven.

4 **Seaplane ride.** One of the greatest ways to see where you are in the world is from a plane, and in the Maldives that means floating above a cornflower sea streaked by sand-washed islands and lagoons the color of melon liqueur. Male International Airport sits on its own private atoll, and the seaplanes rest alongside nearby pontoons. While you can reach close-lying islands by speedboat, those farther out are best reached by air—and if you go by seaplane, getting there is definitely half the fun. Imagine yourself staring out the window at the gorgeous views below, and circling your island before swooping in to land on the sea.

Award-winning travel writer **MARC LLEWELLYN** is coauthor of Frommer's guidebooks to Australia, and the president of the Australian Society of Travel Writers. He has been traveling the globe for close to 15 years, and writes for most of Australia's travel publications. Contact him at marccom@bigpond.net.au.

ABOUT THE AUTHOR

YOUR TRIP

General Information: Look up www.visitmaldives.com. **Getting There:** For flights, contact **Singapore Airlines** (☎ 800/742-3333; www.singaporeair.com). Several companies offer cruises around the islands with overnight stays onboard or stopovers at resorts. Contact **Maldive Cruise** for details (www.maldivecruise.com). **Best Lodging:** The **Conrad Maldives Rangali Island** is perhaps the most luxurious resort in the Maldives, and it's definitely worth booking one of the over-water bungalows, in a shallow lagoon, where you really feel as if you are away from it all (☎ 800/445-8667; www.conradhotels.com; $1,065–$1,430/£564–£758). Of course, there's also the **Banyan Tree** (Vabbinfaru Island; www.banyantree.com; $780/£413). **Best Lodging Value: Vakarufalhi Resort** is on a small, round island with lovely bungalows and beaches (South Ari Atoll; ☎ 960/668-0004 in Maldives; www.vakaru.com; $215–$275/£114–£146).

Best Restaurant: Ithaa, the world's first aquarium-style undersea restaurant is at the Conrad Maldives (www.conradhotels.com; fixed-price dinner menu $220/£117). **Best Restaurant Value: Quench Restaurant,** central Male, serves local dishes such as *nasi goreng*, fish kebab, and hot and spicy Maldivian dishes (☎ 960/324-571; around $15/£8). **When to Go:** Late November to April is the dry season—a time when hotels are the most full and prices are higher. The islands get rainfall from July to August due to the southwest monsoon and from November to March due to the northeast monsoon. During these times the skies can be cloudy, humidity is higher, and rainfall is more likely, though it comes in short, often fierce bursts.

MONGOLIA

A trip to the remote Gobi desert & its nomadic tribes

If Mongolia isn't the most mysterious nation in Asia, it certainly makes the short list. It was virtually inaccessible to Westerners until 1990, when democracy peacefully took the place of communism. Landlocked between Russia and China, it's vast (more than twice the size of Texas, with a population of approximately 2.6 million), geographically diverse, and remote.

To get a feel for quintessential Mongolia in 2 weeks or less, there's only one place to go: the Gobi Desert. In the southern part of Mongolia, this vast zone of desert and desert steppe covers 30% of the country. It boasts the eternal blue sky of Genghis Khan fame, spectacular isolated sand dunes, huge red rocks, grassy plains, two-humped Bactrian camels (and, depending on the time of year, camel festivals), Mongolian horses, dinosaur fossils, and self-sufficient nomads who still live off the land. Today, the Gobi remains one of the world's last pristine destinations, unscathed by commercialism. How long this will last is uncertain, but for now a trip here is more than a dream vacation; it's out-of-this-world dreamy.

Neither McDonald's nor Starbucks has raised its flag in Mongolia yet. Beyond Ulaanbaatar, the capital city, few paved roads exist. To get to the Gobi from the capital, you can ride a train for 16 hr. or take a 2-hr. plane ride to Dalanzadgad, the Gobi's major airport. Over the past several years, occasional reports have sensationalized the government's plans to lay down some 2,575km (1,600 miles) of asphalt—best known as the Millennium Highway—but currently construction is at a standstill and estimates of the project's actual start and end dates vary. But when (or if) the pavement gets poured, Mongolia's terrain will be forever altered, and development in the countryside will likely quicken.

The issue of fencing is a more immediate threat. For centuries, Mongolia's nomadic people have lived on and moved freely across their country's land without owning pieces of it. Now, nomads who officially—through democratic means—possess portions of the land are being encouraged to erect fences to mark their borders. Not only will this hinder the movement of free-grazing herds and alter the heart of the nomads' traditional existence, it will drastically change the wide open landscape.

For the moment, though, the spellbinding Gobi remains *au naturel*—offering intrepid travelers its powerful history, its unique physical beauty, and its hospitable people whose lives are infused with a peaceful Buddhist-Shamanistic spirit.

There aren't many places this pure left on earth. And that's mainly because relatively few foreigners come to Genghis Khan's old stamping grounds. After all, getting here isn't easy. Nor is getting around. But those minor inconveniences are well worth overcoming. Visiting Mongolia is something like traveling back in time—and organizing that trip is, for most of us, best left to an expert. When planning your trip, use a reputable and ecofriendly tour operator and/or hire local drivers and translators. Mongolian guides—who can translate the language for you, navigate unfamiliar terrain, and share personal stories—are invaluable resources.

◀ *Inside a yurt tent, Arkhangai Provence.*
© Bruno Morandi/ Getty Images

SPECIAL MOMENTS

1 Exploring Ulaanbaatar. Nearly all visitors heading to the Gobi arrive in Mongolia by way of the capital city, home to a million people. Plan a day or two here to see UB's major sights. Highlights include the Museum of Natural History (exhibiting the famous fighting dinosaurs, as well as other dinosaur nests, eggs, and fossils), the Gandan Monastery (a magnificent Buddhist monastery spared during the Stalinist purges of the 1930s because it was kept as a showpiece for government officials), the outdoor Ulaanbaatar Central Market (beware of pickpockets), the State Department Store, the Soviet-era concrete buildings, throat-singing performances (music that sounds something like reverberating harmonic chanting), and traditional dance performances.

2 Sleeping in a *ger*. A *ger* (pronounced "gair" or "gurr") is a traditional Mongolian nomadic home; it's a round, tent-like dwelling, constructed of latticed wood wrapped in felt and canvas, which can be built or disassembled in about 30 minutes. Typically, a stove inside provides warmth. Sleeping inside one of these cozy gers is truly enchanting, especially at the Three Camel Lodge (see "Your Trip," below). Set in the middle of awe-inspiring Gurvansaikhan National Park, the Gobi's most luxurious and ecofriendly *ger* camp combines ancient structures and style with Western conveniences like hot water, solar-powered electricity, some en-suite bathrooms (with showers and flush toilets), and a top-notch restaurant. The lodge is also intimately involved with the local community—providing jobs for adults and hosting a conservation club for area children. There's nowhere else quite like it.

3 The Flaming Cliffs. Here, in 1922, among the breathtaking red-orange sandstone cliffs, American paleontologist Dr. Roy Chapman Andrews became the first human to find a dinosaur nest and eggs. Spend an hour or two here, climbing and searching among the visually stunning rocks.

You'll need sunscreen and patience, but if you look hard enough, you might spot some bones, nests, or eggs (just remember, it's forbidden to take them out of the country; if you find anything, tell an expert). Paleontologists on official digs often uncover remains in this fossil-rich area. Try to plan a picnic lunch overlooking the vivid scenery. For a strikingly fertile contrast to the Flaming Cliffs, spend the following day at Yol Valley National Park. The guided, safari-like drive follows a dirt path dwarfed by mountains of jagged gray rocks. With the help of good binoculars, you might see ibex, wild camels, Srgali mountain sheep, foxes, hawks, and countless other birds. Inquire in advance about taking a horseback ride here, but beware of traditional wooden Mongolian saddles. They're not so comfy.

4 Hongoryn Els. To visit these spectacular isolated dunes that run 97km (60 miles) alongside the Gobi Altai Mountain Range and reach upwards of 762m (2,500 ft.)—the

largest accumulation of sand in the Gobi Gurvansaikhan National Park—you'll need to hire a jeep from Dalanzadgad or go with an organized tour from your ger camp in the Gobi. It's about 180km (111 miles) from Dalanzadgad (and most ger camps), over some rough terrain, but every bump you hit is worth it. Camel trekking can be a highlight of a trip here, so arrange in advance to ride camels part of the way.

Not only are the dunes strikingly beautiful, the "singing sands" (as they're called) will be music to your ears as you ride toward them. When the wind blows, it makes strange, high-pitched sounds as it reshapes the dunes. If you see anyone other than your own travel companions, it will likely be a nomadic family and its personal herd of camels, cattle, or sheep. Otherwise, you'll have this magical place all to yourself. (If you have time on your way here, try to plan an hour-long visit to a nomadic family's home—another special moment in its own right.)

JENNIFER ANMUTH lives in Brooklyn, New York, and works at a full-service public relations agency specializing in travel and tourism. Previously, she was an editor at Frommer's and prior to that she worked as an assistant editor at the Council on Foreign Relations. She has traveled to every continent except Antarctica.

ABOUT THE AUTHOR

YOUR TRIP

General Information: Contact the **Mongolian Tourism Board** at www.mongoliatourism.gov.mn and pick up *Mongolia: The Bradt Travel Guide,* by Jane Blunden. **Getting There: American Airlines** (www.aa.com) flies from New York City to Tokyo, and then **Mongolian Airlines** (www.miat.com) from Tokyo to Ulaanbaatar. Other airlines offer flights that commonly include a stopover in Moscow, Seoul, or Běijīng. Note that each of these countries has different visa regulations. If you intend to tour Mongolia with a package company, the folks there will assist you with your international flight plans, and they'll certainly help set up all of your domestic flights and land transfers. **Best Outfitter: Nomadic Expeditions,** for cultural adventure and custom itineraries (☎ 800/998-6634; www.nomadicexpeditions.com). **Best Lodging:** In the Gobi, **Three Camel Lodge** is Mongolia's most sophisticated and ecofriendly *ger* camp (www.threecamels.com; ☎ 800/998-6634; $120–$350/£64–£185). **Hotel Ulaanbaatar** is a stately historic building in a prime location (Sukhbaatar Sq. 14; ☎ 976/11-320320; www.ubhotel.mn; $60–$185/£32–£98). **Best Restaurant:** Most meals in the Gobi are prepared on the road or served at *ger* camps. In Ulaanbaatar, a good bet is the **Silk Road Bar & Grill,** with rooftop views over the monastery of the Choijin Lama (☎ 976/91-91445; $5–$20/£3–£11). When you need a break from mutton there's **Taj Mahal** for Indian food (Bayangol Hotel Tower, Ulaanbaatar; ☎ 976/11-312255; $5–$20/£3–£11). **When to Go:** May to September, but even during these peak-season months the Gobi's temperature can range from about 20°F to 70°F (−7°C to 21°C). Pack lots of layers.

◀ *Gobi Desert, Khongoryn Els Dunes.*
© Bruno Morandi/Robert Harding World Imagery/Getty Images

MOROCCO

Oases, bazaars, palaces & ancient walled cities

No country I've visited is as exotic and exciting as Morocco. It's a country of extremes that overpower the senses. Morocco is oases, palmaries, and lavish gardens flooded each morning and evening with birdsong. It's also the shadowy labyrinths of walled cities, filled with dreamlike bazaars, palaces, and mosques, where you lose yourself in the distant past.

Then there are the endless spaces of Morocco's dramatic mountains and deserts, which envelop you in meditative stillness. And wherever there are people, there is music—in the south, it's the throbbing African drumbeat of Marrakesh; in the north, it's delicate Andalusian orchestrations wafting through bazaars; or the soft, trancelike Ginoua chanting from West Africa that serenades a traditional banquet in a palace restaurant deep inside Fes or Meknes. And everywhere, there's inviting, mysterious Berber music—in buses, in markets, in grand hotels and isolated villages.

Too many people encounter Morocco only as a day trip from Spain across the Straits of Gibraltar to Tangiers, a beautifully sited but seedy place filled with hawkers, touts, and cheap souvenirs. But it's the walled cities of Morocco's interior, each amazingly different, that outdo any vision from the *Arabian Nights*. The most famous—the walled cities of Marrakesh and Fes—are opposite poles of Morocco's exotic allure. Fes, in the north, is the Florence of the Islamic world, with its endless Chinese box of exquisite architecture, cuisine, music, medieval markets, crafts, and foods. Marrakesh is the brash, exciting gateway to the Sahara and Africa, its fiery, red-walled buildings rising from the desert, with Djemaa el Fna at its heart—a nightly 100-ring circus in the city's main square, filled with acrobats, fortunetellers, musicians, snake charmers, food stalls, and more.

From Fes, you can make day or overnight trips to the nearby, 17th-century imperial capital of Meknes, adorned with monumental ceremonial gates, fortifications, and palaces. Or to the rustic, magical, Rif Mountain town of Chaouen, a miraculously surviving chunk of 15th-century Andalusia transported to North Africa in 1471 by Moors and Jews fleeing the Reconquest of Spain, and hidden from Europeans until the 1920s. From Marrakesh, you can move into three different worlds. You're only 64km (40 miles) from the splendor of the High Atlas, the Alps of Africa, with marvelous walks, treks, and the chance to experience the remote world of the hospitable Berber people and to climb Mount Toubkal, North Africa's highest peak. Or you can follow the awesome Route des Kasbahs—an ancient trade route to the desert, lined with hundreds of sandcastle-like tribal fortresses (kasbahs) that guarded the turf of various clans. From there, continue into the Sahara, or to less-visited walled towns like Taroudannt. The third option, due west, takes you to Essaouira, a whitewashed, walled city on the windswept Atlantic coast, surrounded by miles of empty beaches, just 3 hours from Marrakesh. With a Greek Island atmosphere and Moroccan exoticism, it's the most easygoing place in Morocco, with charming, affordable hotels built into old courtyard mansions, and delightful restaurants and markets.

◀ *Tannery vats where leather is dyed, Fes.*
© John & Lisa Merrill/
DanitaDelimont.com

SPECIAL MOMENTS

1 **Fes.** This UNESCO World Heritage Site is the most complete walled, medieval city in the world. You'll need a guide (reasonably priced and available at hotels and the tourist office) to show you the fabulous *medersas* (study houses, which are even more intricate than the mosques) and the famous rooftop vats for dying cloth. But return on your own to explore the Tala'a Kebira and the Tala'a Seghira, the two main market thoroughfares. Both begin at the gate called the Bab Boujeloud. You can follow both as they twist gently downhill, losing yourself in a sea of olives, semolina cakes and baklavas, tribal kilims from the Middle Atlas, hand-tooled leather goods, enticing objects of old Berber silver, and mountains of spices. Take one of these routes, climb or take a taxi back to the Bab Boujeloud, and then enjoy the other.

2 **The High Atlas.** Spring is the best time to be here. The mountain hamlet of Imlil, 90 minutes south of Marrakesh, is a memorable base for walks or escorted treks with local muleteers through walnut forests and apple orchards, past dramatic gorges and cascades. Being among the disarmingly hospitable Berber people and experiencing the haunting quiet of the mountains adds to the enchantment of this powerful landscape. The climb to the top of Mount Toubkal, the highest peak in North Africa and doable for travelers in shape, can be arranged with environmental groups that provide guides, pack mules, and overnights in tent camps, in mountain huts, or with Berber families. Imlil contains a wonderful mountain-top kasbah, the Kasbah du Toubkal, now turned into a sustainable tourist hotel.

3 **The route des Kasbahs and the Sahara.** The drama of this route from Marrakesh through the passes of the Atlas Mountains and then past scores of amazing desert kasbahs (or *ksours*) that line the way is unforgettable. The crenelated towers and fretwork patterns adorning these sandcastle visions dazzle, as do the oases and palmaries of the Dades and Draa valleys that they guard. Most are eroding back into the earth, but some have been restored into desert resorts, hotels,

and tourist centers. Moroccan banquets and folkloric performances held here are touristy but always dramatic and fun. Ouarzazate is the best base for visiting the kasbahs of the Draa and Dades valleys. Among the less inhabited ksours, Ait Benhaddou, Telouet, and Skoura are the most architecturally renowned. You can take an organized tour or rent a car (and driver) and explore on your own.

4   Essaouira. No place in Morocco is as charming and fun as this walled town beside the Atlantic. Essaouira's countryside is dotted with fabled argan trees believed to have mysterious, health-giving powers; its craft shops are filled with objects made from lavishly grained, fragrant thuya trees that grow only in this region. Swim in the Gulf Stream, prowl Essaouira's markets and galleries, walk miles of beach, and sample the food in native and gourmet restaurants.

ROBERT ULLIAN is the author of *Frommer's Israel* and *Frommer's Memorable Walks in Venice*. He has also written guidebooks to Bali and Morocco. His work has appeared in such publications as *Esquire* and *Mademoiselle*. He is the recipient of a Grant for Fiction from the National Endowment for the Arts. Contact him at aramullian@yahoo.com.

ABOUT THE AUTHOR

YOUR TRIP

General Information: The **Morocco National Tourist Office** is located at 20 E. 46th St., New York, NY 10017 (☎ 212/557-2520; www.visitmorocco.org). Ask for the brochure, "The Great Trek: The Moroccan Atlas," which is helpful in planning treks and hikes. **Best Lodging:** In Marrakesh, the legendary **La Mamounia** is one of the great hotels in North Africa. The fourth-floor garden-view rooms offer a vista that Winston Churchill called, "the most beautiful in the world." (☎ 212-44/24-38-86; www.mamounia.com; $360/£191). In Fes, **Palais Jamai** is a landmark hotel in the Old City (Bab Guissa, Old City; ☎ 212-35/63-43-31; www.sofitel.com; $255–$325/£135–£172). **Best Lodging Value:** In Marrakesh, the **Hotel Sherazade** is a charming courtyard mansion hotel (Derb Djamaa 3, Riad Zeitoun Kedim; ☎ 212-44/42-93-05; www.hotelsherazade.com; $40–$60/£21–£32). In Imlil, there's the **Kasbah du Toubkal,** with dorm rooms with incredible views. It is owned by Discover Ltd. in London, which can arrange fabulous Berber ecowalks, hikes, and climbs in the High Atlas (☎ 212-44/48-56-11; www.kasbahdutoubkal.com; $180–$250/£95–£132, $40/£21 dorm bed). In Ouarzazate, a good base for exploring the kasbahs of the Dades and Draa valleys, there's **Berbere Palace Hotel** (Quartier Mansour Eddabbi; ☎ 212-44/88-31-05; www.ouarzazate.com/leberberepalace; $210–$270/£111–£143). In Essaouira, the **Riad Al Madina** is an exquisite courtyard mansion (9 rue Attarine; ☎ 212-24/47-59-07; www.riadalmadina.com; $100/£53). In Chefchaouen, try **Casa Hassan,** an especially lovely mansion (22 rue Targui, Essaouira; ☎ 212-39/98-61-53; www.casahassan.com; $90/£48).

◀ *Marrakesh.*
© Bob Krist Photography

MYSORE, INDIA

India in all its richness, sensual extravagance & mystery

You can't spend too much time in India without being struck by the feeling that you're in the most exotic and evocative land on earth. For me, this sensation becomes stronger the farther south I travel. In fact, I can't think of a better way to experience India in all its richness, sensual extravagance, and mystery than to spend time in my two favorite Indian cities, both in the south—faded but hauntingly beautiful Mysore, some 1,200km (750 miles) from Mumbai, and Cochin, a centuries-old trading post on the Arabian Sea in the southernmost Indian state of Kerala.

Mysore is far enough removed from the more clamorous north to make this quiet, old-fashioned city a bit of a backwater. Shady parks and squares invite the two best pastimes for a visitor to India: strolling and observing. You'll soon discover that Mysore's charms are not necessarily subtle. Rich hues and the heady scents of jasmine, incense, cinnamon, and coffee beans confront you on the sidewalks. Through open doorways you'll see craftsmen carving small statues of Hindu deities from sandalwood and silk weavers working at handlooms.

Remove your shoes and step into the marble-floored corridors of Mysore Palace, still the home of Wadiyar maharajas who ruled this part of India for 700 years, and you'll get an eyeful of embellishment: Every surface of every turret and minaret is carved or inlaid with mosaics. Make the short trip east to Kesava, one of the most exquisitely ornate shrines in India, where you'll be treated to the spectacle of tier after tier of stone carvings and frescoes that depict gods and goddesses and warriors from the *Mahabarata* and other legends.

Cochin, 300km (180 miles) south of Mysore, is a jumble of East and West. The delight here, an experience you won't soon forget, is to wander the narrow lanes of the old port—crossing bridges and boarding little launches that connect peninsulas and islands—and to let yourself be jolted from one culture to another. In the corridors of the Dutch Palace, portraits of Dutch burghers, looking stuffy in high white collars, hang alongside those of rajahs. The tombstone of Portuguese explorer Vasco da Gama is tucked away in a corner of St. Anthony's Church, and nearby are a Buddhist temple and one of the oldest synagogues in India, with a floor paved in Chinese tiles. The curiosity of strange structures on the shoreline will lead you to a long row of enormous Chinese fishing nets, mounted on massive poles and lowered into the water by teams of men; at night, the sound of drumming might guide you to a performance of *kathakali*, an elaborate, masked Keralan dance that dramatizes Hindu legends.

You won't want to come to this part of India without cruising on the waterways that lace through junglelike forest and coconut plantations to the north and south of Cochin. But after a day of such indolence you might feel as I always do—that it's time to step ashore again and surrender yourself to the mysteries, the little intrigues, of places like Mysore and Cochin.

◀ *Kathakali performance, Cochin.*
© Eddie Gerald/
Lonely Planet Images

SPECIAL MOMENTS

1   **Dussehra.** Mysore is always awash in color, especially during the Dussehra celebration in October, when elephants are decked out in gold and long lines of lavishly costumed dancers snake sinuously through the city. Dussehra festivities are staged throughout this part of India, but nowhere more elaborately than in Mysore, to celebrate the goddess Chamumdeswari and the promise of prosperity at the end of the monsoons. The palace—cupolas, pillars, and all—is brilliantly lit on each of the 10 nights of the festival, and often on a weekend night or two throughout the rest of the year as well. Since the lavish use of wattage sometimes throws other parts of the town into darkness, you might find that townspeople do not share your disappointment if your visit does not coincide with a time when the palace is lit.

2   **Heading south from Mysore.** The fastest and most convenient way to travel from Mysore to Cochin is to hire a car and driver. An outlay of about $30 (£16) a day helps ensure that you might arrive in one piece (few foreigners would be foolhardy enough to attempt to navigate India's roads on their own). The full-day trip across lush mountainsides planted with spice plantations and watery plains where busy country towns rise above the rice paddies is lovely and not without a little drama here and there. You'll stop more than once for cows in the road, and when you pull off to admire a view, monkeys may well swarm your car and try to steal your wallet or camera.

3   **Snake boat races.** Don't feel surprised if you shout yourself hoarse during one of Kerala's Snake Boat Races, when crews of up to 100 oarsmen propel sleek, 30m-long (100-ft.) craft across Lake Vembanad and other waterways in Kerala. Oarsmen are not only trained in boatmanship; in deeply resonant voices, they sing age-old boating songs that carry across the waters, much to the delight of thousands of spectators who line the shore. The races are held in August and September, along with many festivals and events, to celebrate Oman, the harvest season. If you are in Alleppy or another Kerala town outside of Oman, ask to see one of the snake boats, carefully stored away but shown to visitors with pride.

The oldest and most popular event is the Champakulam Moolam Boat Race, held in monsoon-soaked July, but the most famous water battle is undoubtedly the Nehru Trophy Boat Race, held on the second

Mysore, India

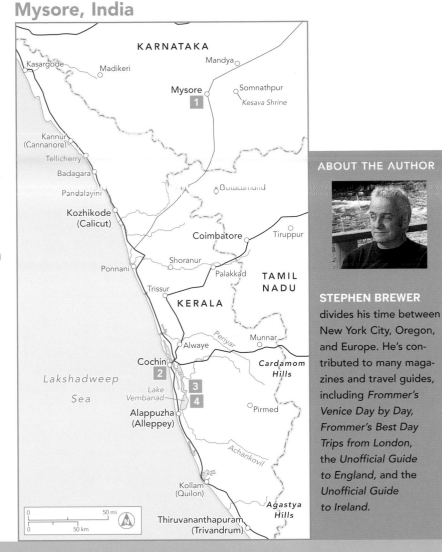

KARNATAKA

Kasargode · Madikeri · Mandya · Mysore **1** · Somnathpur · *Kesava Shrine*

Kannur (Cannanore) · Tellicherry · Badagara · Pandalayini · Ootacumund · Kozhikode (Calicut) · Coimbatore · Tiruppur · Shoranur · Ponnani · Palakkad · TAMIL NADU · Trissur · KERALA · Periyar · Munnar · Alwaye · *Cardamom Hills* · Cochin **2** · Lake Vembanad **3** **4** · *Lakshadweep Sea* · Pirmed · Alappuzha (Alleppey) · Achankovil · Kollam (Quilon) · *Agastya Hills* · Thiruvananthapuram (Trivandrum)

0 — 50 mi
0 — 50 km

Saturday of August on the Punnamada backwaters of the Alleppy in conjunction with Kerala's important Oman harvest festival.

4 **Cruising the waterways.** Thatch-roofed, junklike houseboats ply hundreds of miles of Keralan lakes and waterways. You'll spend your time on board gazing lazily into coconut groves, palm forests, and spice plantations, and catching glimpses of farmers tending their plots or tapping trees for rubber or sap that's fermented into a potent elixir. Even here on the water, though, you won't be too far removed from the colorful hue and cry of everyday Indian life—your crew will pull up at temples, Roman Catholic cathedrals, and noisy country bazaars. By the time night rolls around and you've been served a meal on deck, you'll feel positively decadent as you lie back on a bed of cushions and gaze at a canopy of stars.

ABOUT THE AUTHOR

STEPHEN BREWER divides his time between New York City, Oregon, and Europe. He's contributed to many magazines and travel guides, including *Frommer's Venice Day by Day*, *Frommer's Best Day Trips from London*, the *Unofficial Guide to England*, and the *Unofficial Guide to Ireland*.

YOUR TRIP

General Information: You can get information on Mysore from the **Karnataka State Tourism Development Corporation** (www.tourindia.com) and on Kerala from **Kerala Tourism** (www.keralatourism.org). **Best Lodging:** In Mysore, the luxurious and atmospheric **Lalitha Mahal Palace** is within the former guest quarters of the Wadiyar maharajas (☎ 91-821/247-0470; www.lalithamahalpalace.com; $170/£90 double). Ask to see the hand-cranked elevator, and beware of the monkeys who will nab your towel as you do laps in the pool; in Cochin, the **Taj Malabar**—request a room in the old colonial wing rather than the mundane seaside tower (Willingdon Island; ☎ 91-484/266-6811; www.tajhotels.com; $110/£58). **Best Lodging Value:** In Mysore, the **Lalitha Mahal Palace** (see above) charges a reasonable $70 (£37) for simple but charming doubles in the turrets; in Cochin, rooms are $70 (£37) in the 17th-century **Bolgatty Palace** (Bolgatty Island; ☎ 91-484/682-504; www.hotelskerala.com). To stay in a **houseboat,** you'll find eager skippers in every port in Kerala; expect to pay $150 (£80) a night per couple, including accommodation, meals, and crew; for more information, go to www.keralabackwaters.com. **Best Restaurant:** In Mysore, the **Lalitha Mahal Palace** (see above) serves an excellent southern Indian buffet in a cavernous, old-world dining room, for $5 (£2.65); in Cochin, the **Rice Boat,** anchored on pilings alongside the Taj Malabar, serves the best seafood in town for $15 (£8) per person (☎ 91-484/266-6811); at **Fry's Village,** on Chittoor Road, enjoy vegetarian dishes and Keralan specialties in a garden gazebo for $3 (£1.60) a meal (☎ 91-484/353-983).

◀ *Maharaja's palace at night, Mysore City.*
© Anthony Cassidy/Getty Images

NAFPLION, GREECE

One of the most beautiful towns on mainland Greece

As the ferry from Athens steamed into the harbor, the town's massive fortresses took shape atop a pine-forested hillside, above a tidy collection of tall, proud houses, tiled roofs, and ornate domes. A light haze rose off the morning sea, masking the panorama in a soft blur. The city that slowly, coyly unfolded before me seemed to say, "See, I really am the most beautiful city in Greece."

Nafplion is a mainland city on the Gulf of Argos in the Northern Peloponnese. Like all Greek cities, it is not just to be admired, but to be enjoyed; observing Greek life swirling around you is always a pleasure. So come, take a seat at one of the cafe tables that spill across marble-paved Syntagma Square. The lions of St. Mark, a legacy of the Venetians who so elegantly built much of the city, adorn the facade of the National Bank. The old mosque at one corner of the square is a reminder of the days when the Turks routed the Venetians. Another mosque, just around the corner, housed the parliament when Nafplion was the first capital of a united Greece after the war of independence in 1821. But what most captures your attention in Nafplion are the scenes that are replayed again and again on the palm-shaded squares and cool, narrow lanes—the old boys working their worry beads, widows nodding at shopkeepers and passersby, civil servants walking briskly along, in shirts a bit crisper than anyone else's.

After a coffee or two, you might be tempted to climb the 892 steps to the Palamidi, the Venetian fortress perched high above the city. Save that for later, and instead follow the cramped streets and flights of whitewashed steps through Psaromachalas, the fisherman's quarter. The sea flashes into view every once in a while as a vivid blue stripe between tall rows of red and yellow houses, then stretches before you as you stroll along the cypress-lined promenade that skirts the entire Nafplion peninsula. Squint and you might be able to make out the massive walls of the 3,000-year-old ruined city of Tiryns, on the plains to the north of the city. Of all the remains the ancient Greeks left behind in the Northern Peloponnese—and these are thick on the ground—the most impressive is the theater at Epidauros, where barely a stone has been altered in the past 6,000 years and the acoustics are still perfect, even from row 55 at the very top of the house.

Days' end is the best time to make the climb up to the Palamidi fortress. Against a backdrop of birdsong and the soughing of pine boughs, you'll watch the sun turn the old stones a golden hue, then sink into the sea. The lights of the city twinkle on at your feet, beckoning you back down to take a seat on the marble expanse of the square again, this time to sip a glass of wine from the vineyards of the nearby Nemea region. Have a couple, and you might just find yourself gesturing to the city around you and saying "Oraia, Oraia, Oraia."

◀ *Town and harbor, Nafplion.*
© Pete Saloutos/
zefa/Corbis

SPECIAL MOMENTS

1 **Epidauros.** Even when there's not an actor in sight, the world's best-preserved ancient theater works its magic and you can't help but feel you've been transported back a few thousand years. Stand on the stage, look up at the tiers of stone seats, and shout out a line or two; when you climb to the top row, you'll appreciate those on the stage below who do the same, because you'll hear every word they say. A visit is enshrined as a lifetime memory if you are able to attend the summertime Festival of Ancient Drama, when exquisite performers do justice to the Greek classics—easier to follow than you might suspect, since the actors often wear masks that depict the emotions expressed.

2 **Corinth and Olympia.** These two ancient places, both within easy reach of Nafplion, are especially evocative. From the sheer vastness of the site and the extent of the ruins, it's easy to see why Corinth was for many centuries one of the most powerful cities in the world—climb to the Acrocorinth, the natural fortress high atop the town, for endless views up and down the sea lanes and strategic land routes that lent the city its might. In Olympia, where the mountain air is zesty and pine-scented, crowds aren't a nuisance but enhance the festive mood that must have prevailed at the stadium and hippodrome during the popular games that began in 776 B.C. and continued until the Christian emperor Theodosius I banned them as "pagan" in A.D. 393.

3 **Churches.** Nafplion's inhabitants have left behind mosques, Roman Catholic churches, and Greek Orthodox basilicas. Each is imbued with a good story or two, which you'll want to pick up as you wander through the city. At St. Spyridon's basilica, on Spirdonas Square, you'll see a telltale bullet mark next to the door, left there when the Greek statesman Ioannis Kapodistrias was shot to death out front in 1831. At the church of the Virgin Mary's birth, just west of Syntagma Square, look for an olive tree near the entrance—legend has it that the tree has not borne fruit since 1655, when the Turks hanged Saint Anastasios, a Nafpliote, here after he converted to Islam under a spell, then renounced the deed, saying, "I was a Christian, I am a Christian, and I shall die a Christian." Every once in a while, walking tours depart from the tourist office, revealing these and other fascinating cultural tidbits about Nafplion's long and storied past; if your visit doesn't coincide

with one, ask for the printed hand-outs, filled with juicy details.

4 **Swimming.** A day in Greece should never pass without at least one dip in sea. One of the many pleasures of being in Nafplion is that you needn't venture far from the town center to dive into clean, warm waters. The most convivial places to swim are the seaside bars at the tip of the peninsula, just past the section of the old city wall known as the Five Brothers—some of these watering holes have created handy little swimming enclosures, so you can sip a cocktail after every few strokes. Farther along, the seaside promenade reaches Arvanitia, where you can swim off an attractive stone terrace. Karathona, about 3km (2 miles) south of the city, is a long, sandy beach backed by pines; since the water remains shallow for quite a distance, it's the best bet with families.

STEPHEN BREWER divides his time between New York City, Oregon, and Europe. He's written and contributed to many magazines and travel guides, including *Frommer's Venice Day by Day*, *Frommer's Best Day Trips from London*, the *Unofficial Guide to England*, and the *Unofficial Guide to Ireland*.

ABOUT THE AUTHOR

YOUR TRIP

General Information: The staff at **Nafplion's Municipal Tourist Office,** on Platha Maritou near the enormous OTE telephone company building, is generally quite eager to help you enjoy the city and the surrounding sites (25 Martiou; ☎ 30-27520/24-444). For information about the **Festival of Ancient Drama** and to purchase tickets, contact the **Athens and Epidauros Festival Box Office** in Athens (☎ 30-210/928-2900), in Epidauros call ☎ 30-27530/22-026, or on the Web go to www.hellenicfestival.gr. **Getting There: Delta** flies nonstop from New York to Athens (☎ 800/241-4141; www.delta.com). The **Flying Dolphin** hydrofoil from Athens makes one round-trip a day. For information on fares and the frequently changing schedules, call ☎ 30-210/419-9000 or go to www.dolphins.gr. **Best Lodging:** For a splurge, check into the **Nafplia Palace,** high atop the city with stunning views, lofty terraces, and a gorgeous pool (Akronafplia; ☎ 30-27520/70-800; www.helioshotels.gr; $300/£159 double). **Best Lodging Value: Hotel Latini,** where attractive rooms occupy the old house of a sea captain off a palm-shaded square (Othonos 47; ☎ 30-27520/96-470; from $130/£69 double). **Best Restaurant:** A tossup between two old favorites on the narrow lanes near the harbor—**Paleo Archontiko,** on Siouko (☎ 30-27520/22-449), and **Kanakarakis,** on Vasileos Olgas (☎ 30-27520/25-371); main courses at both are about $8 (£4). Many diners end the evening with a dish of ice cream at one of the cafes on Syntagma Square or along the harbor; those in the know instead head to the **Antica Gelateria di Roma,** at the corner of Farmakopoulou and Komminou streets, for gelato and sorbetto as good as or better than you're ever going to find in Italy.

◀ *Temple of Apollo, Corinth.*
© Walter Bibikow/Getty Images

NAMIB-NAUKLUFT, NAMIBIA

One of the strangest, most surreal landscapes on earth

I am not a churchgoer. Not even sure I believe in God. But when I travel through the empty expanse of the world's oldest desert, my eyes filled with the most extraordinary landscapes, I know there is a force greater than anything I can comprehend, and that *It* is an Artist.

"Surreal" is the word most often used to describe the textured landscapes of the Namib-Naukluft Park: From golden dunes that rise up from the sea to the purple gravel plains, carpeted in soft green grass after the rains, the region is one vast abstract artwork, painted with the most extraordinary palette.

At just over 50,000 square km (19,305 sq. miles), the Namib-Naukluft Park is the size of a small country—a little larger than Switzerland. But while it's touted as the biggest game park in Africa, this is certainly not the place to come if you want to see big mammals: Other than a few antelope species and the rare Hartmann's zebra, concentrated in the mountainous ridge that defines the desert's eastern boundaries, sightings of animals are rare, which is why most people combine a 4-day sojourn here with a few days in northern Namibia's Etosha National Park or—top prize—fly into the Okovango Delta in neighboring Botswana.

But wild and gorgeous as those game-rich safari destinations are, nothing clears your head of clutter like the vast open spaces of the world's fourth-largest conservation area. The best way to experience it is to drive it, with the windows open and the hot wind in your hair. Head south from Windhoek, the capital, and overnight in one of the fabulous safari camps in Namib Rand, the private reserve that adjoins the park—a 4-hour drive from Windhoek and just over an hour from the park's chief drawing card: the Sossusvlei dunes, a series of burnt-red and deep-orange pyramids that tower some 300m (984 ft.) above the white clay pan into which the Tsauchab River has its annual *petit mort* ("little death"). Time allowing, head east to the less known but equally captivating Naukluft Mountains, source of the Tsauchab's waters, where crystal streams fill jade-green rock pools; then return via the black boulders of the Kuiseb Canyon to the coastal town of Swakopmund. From here you could embark on a day trip back into the northern section of the park, visiting the Welwitschia Plains to marvel at its inauspicious fossil plants; or follow the coastal dunes south to Sandwich Harbor, teeming with flamingos and pelicans.

Aside from the geological diversity of these landscapes—said to be 80 million years in the making—it is the fearsome presence of an unconquered Nature that makes a visit to this park such a deeply humbling experience. Driving for miles and miles along gravel roads, it appears hostile and devoid of life; some find this inexplicably overwhelming and depart almost as soon as they arrive. But for most visitors, this apparently lifeless expanse forces the spirit to expand. Still not convinced? Ah, well. This is one cathedral that cares not one jot about the size of its congregation.

Dead Vlei Red dunes, Namib-Naukluft-Sossusvlei.
© Gavin Hellier/Getty Images

SPECIAL MOMENTS

1 **Aloft on the wind: Namib Rand.** The large shadow we cast spooks a small herd of long-horned oryx, which sets off across the dunes, each hoof-beat raising a puff of dust. It is eerily silent, broken only by the periodic "whoosh" of the hot-air balloon burner as we glide over the sand dunes at dawn—an essential ride for photographers wanting to shoot the dunes as the rising sun starts to cast its first brushstrokes. Where you finally land depends on the wind (be prepared for a drag across the sand), but there's always a bottle of champagne—popped with the stroke of a saber—to celebrate your safe landing. Most lodges arrange ballooning trips for guests; for more information visit **www.namibsky.com**.

2 **Dying of thirst: Dead Vlei.** A fairly gentle 1km walk from Sossusvlei takes you to its petrified twin, the Dead Vlei. An ancient pan once reached by the Tsauchab River, Dead Vlei is now a cracked clay floor surrounded by encroaching red dunes, where the blackened limbs of camel thorn trees reach their skeletal arms to the blue sky. Get here at the right time (in the early evening, when the harsh environment is slowly transformed into a soft beckoning bed, rich and saturated with color), and even the most half-baked photographer can show off images of immense beauty back home.

3 **Worshipping water: The Waterkloof Trail/Sossusvlei.** It's lip-crackingly dry: 133°F (45°C) in the shade. Having given yourself over to the mind-numbing heat, you are in a calm, even vegetative state (to keep up the metaphor).

And then suddenly you come across water. Whether this is in the crystal-clear pools of the Naukluft, or the Sossusvlei pan, it is thrilling, and makes you realize just what a privilege access to the precious stuff is. Riverbeds here are dry for at least 90% of the year; when they run, it's only for a few hours of the year, directly after a rainfall (occurring late Dec or Jan to Mar).

4 **Survival of the fittest: Namib flora and fauna.** Gazing at the tangled leaves of the Welwitschia, it's hard to imagine that this scrappy plant probably predates the European discovery of America. Or that the seemingly empty plains beyond support an amazing variety of life. Namib is not a wildlife destination per se, but all you need to do is step away from the gravel roads (preferably with a guide) and you'll

come across some of Nature's more interesting species, cleverly adapted to these hyper-arid conditions, like the rapier-horned oryx, who survives despite its body temperature reaching 113°F (45°C); or the Anchieta dune lizard, able to live on the burning sands by constantly hopping from one pair of feet to the other, "dancing" the day away. With an average annual rainfall of 63mm (2½ in.), survival is often dependent on the desert's western neighbor, the icy Atlantic, which produces a thick fog that species like the Tenebrionid beetle utilize to great effect, standing on their heads until condensation droplets form on their legs, which then run into their mouths. Similarly, the cleverly adapted leaves of the Welwitschia plant—described by Darwin as the platypus of the plant kingdom— are able to "drink" the nightly fog, enabling it to survive for hundreds, even thousands of years.

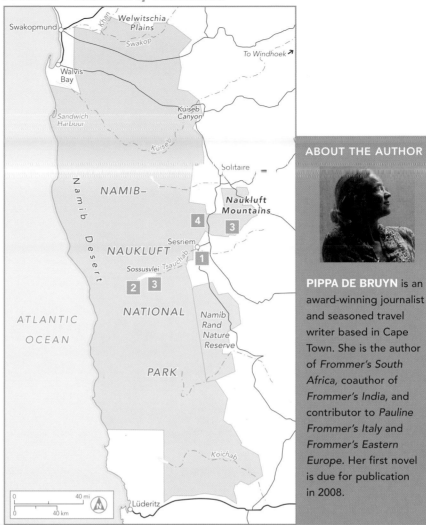

ABOUT THE AUTHOR

PIPPA DE BRUYN is an award-winning journalist and seasoned travel writer based in Cape Town. She is the author of *Frommer's South Africa*, coauthor of *Frommer's India*, and contributor to *Pauline Frommer's Italy* and *Frommer's Eastern Europe*. Her first novel is due for publication in 2008.

YOUR TRIP

General Information: Contact the **Namibia Tourism Board** (www.namibiatourism.com.na). Another useful site is **www.namibian.org**, particularly if you're interested in driving yourself (the best way to get to the park). They will help plan your route, organize your vehicle, book accommodation, obtain the necessary permits for exploring the Welwitschia plains and Naukluft mountain trails, and take the hassle out of planning. A U.S. tour operator is **African Travel, Inc.** (☎ 800/421-8907; www.africantravelinc.com). Better still, hire the services of a personal guide who will make all your arrangements, set up camp if necessary, and help you get the most out of your trip. Contact **Volker** (☎ 264-81/127-0880; turtlet@iway.na) or **Paul** (☎ 264-81/124-6362), both based out of Windhoek. **Best Lodging:** My personal favorite is **Wolwedans,** with a range of accommodations. There are two small desert camps, as well as two small, totally secluded, individual bases (☎ 264-61/230-616; www.wolwedans.com; from US$400/£212). Others are **Little Kulala,** which enjoys its own access to the park, and luxuries such as rooftop beds and private plunge pools (www.wilderness-safaris.com; from US$368/£195); or the super-lux **Sossusvlei Mountain Lodge** (www.ccafrica.com; US$315/£167). Bookings are snapped up fast, so plan well in advance. For **camping** information (you will need to camp if you want to see the Naukluft Mountains as no day-trippers are allowed), see **www.traveltonamibia.com. When to Go:** Most advise travel during the winter (June–Oct) when it's cooler, but I prefer the autumn (usually Mar–May), when you can enjoy the transformation wrought by the rains.

◄ *A dune walk in the Naukluft National Park.*
© Marc Abrahms Photography

NANTUCKET, MASSACHUSETTS

A ferry ride to a world of lonely beaches, dunes & fog

I remember the first time a friend took me out in a jeep to Great Point on Nantucket, the narrow-necked peninsula that sticks out on the island's northeast coast. Nantucket is only 14 miles long by 3½ miles wide, but on the peninsula of Coskata, it narrows to a thin spit of soft-sand dunes, with the Atlantic on one side and Nantucket Harbor on the other. It was a bumpy 5-mile ride out past wildflowers and scrub oaks and then through acres of undulating dunes. There wasn't a footprint in sight, just swooping osprey and gulls, and terns scurrying along the sand. When we reached the lighthouse, we unpacked a picnic lunch and enjoyed the sheer isolation and beauty of a vast, unspoiled beach stretching for miles. When I think of Nantucket, I think of that isolation and also of sun-drenched colors: the red-striped Sankaty Head Lighthouse against the churning blue ocean, yellow Scottish broom wildflowers on the hill in front of the old windmill with its crimson arms, and pink rosa rugosa cascading down the roof of a gray-shingled cottage in the village of 'Sconset. I also think of the fog, which creeps in and swallows you up often enough for the island to earn the nickname, the Grey Lady.

One of the great contrasts of Nantucket is that it is one of those "end-of-the-world places" where I feel like I have gotten away from it all, and yet, in the center of town on a busy summer day, it is really bustling. The Coskata conservation area, with Great Point at the tip, typifies that wild part of Nantucket for me. But Nantucket also has its civilized side. It is, after all, a place where numerous Fortune 500 CEOs go to relax. Civilized Nantucket also has its pleasures, with its fine-dining restaurants and elegant shops. Those are clustered in charming Nantucket Town, which has cobblestone streets and 18th- and 19th-century buildings, complete with picket fences and widow's walks. The island was in its heyday in the early to mid–19th century when it was one of the capitals of the whaling trade. That history is preserved at the Whaling Museum, one of Nantucket's many fascinating historic sites. Nearby is the Brotherhood of Thieves, a whaling-era vintage bar where I've overheard a salty story or two. The rarefied air on Nantucket—and all those ladies wearing pearls and cashmere—may give a hint of what makes the island so popular among the staunch Republican crowd, but it also firmly grounds it in a time and place. The island really doesn't look too much different than it did in 1950, or 1850 for that matter. Though Nantucket is just 30 miles off the coast of Cape Cod and roughly parallel to Martha's Vineyard, it feels more distinct and cohesive than either of those places. Stringent historic district laws have kept the island free of malls and chain stores. And because of the saltiness in the air and the sea breezes, I can never forget I'm only a few miles, or usually only a few blocks, from one of Nantucket's pristine white-sand beaches.

◀ *Siasconset, Nantucket.*
© Jon Arnold/
DanitaDelimont.com

SPECIAL MOMENTS

1 Four-wheeling out to Great Point. Driving off-road on Nantucket always makes me feel like a kind of pioneer, journeying out into a sand-filled wilderness. I rent a four-wheel-drive vehicle for the bumpy, exhilarating trip, just over an hour to the end of Great Point. My off-road adventure wouldn't be as much fun without a few friends along for the ride. And, of course, a set of fishing poles. We pack lunches: Big, fat sand-wiches and chocolate-chip cookies from **Something Natural,** at 50 Cliff Rd. We watch for piping plovers and terns on the way out. As we approach Great Point Lighthouse, we grow silent, moved by the remoteness. We fish and eat lunch and tell stories all afternoon. Some of us fall asleep on the trip back.

2 A hike in Sanford Farm. Off Madaket Road are almost 1,000 acres of conservation land with flat trails that are perfect for nature walks and are virtually unknown by the typical Nantucket tourist. This is my favorite place on Nantucket to get away from it all. You'll see many island locals walking their dogs on this trail, and also some mountain-bikers. The Sanford Farm trail, just over 3 miles each way, is a fine introduction to the best of the island, taking you through marshes, moors, and heath lands, then past Hummock Pond to the ocean. From here you can either collapse onto the sand and stare up at the clouds, or turn around and head back.

3 Biking to Madaket to watch the sunset. There are several ter-rific bike rides on Nantucket, but the one I enjoy most is the 6-mile trip from the center of town out to the fishing village of Madaket. The best time to go is midsummer, when it stays light late into the evening. I never tire of the view of Nantucket's moors, with wind-stunted scrub oaks and a dense groundcover of heather, bayberry, and huckleberry. I bike to the edge of Madaket's sandy beach and let my feet sink deep into the sand as I walk to the water's edge. I find a good spot on the sand and plop down for the best show in town: a Nantucket sunset.

4 Window-shopping in Nantucket Town. I always enjoy wandering around on Nantucket's cobblestoned streets, peeking through the windows at the exqui-site wares, especially the antiques

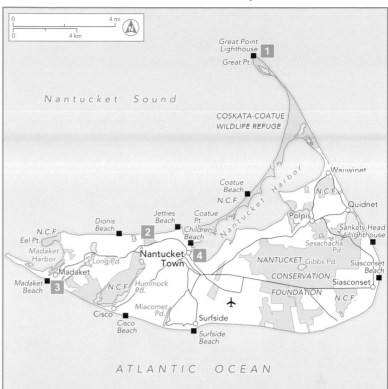

shops and arts-and-crafts galleries. You'll find quality antiques shops on Main and Centre streets, chock-full of treasures with Nantucket connections, like sea captain's chests and sailor's valentines, those wonderful shell collages. For art galleries, there's no better stroll than along Old South Wharf, which has perhaps a dozen tiny shops in converted fishing shacks. Nantucket's narrow side streets often hold unexpected delights—a custom hat shop, for instance, or a store with wooden toys. For antiques, try **Tonkin of Nantucket** (33 Main St.). The fashion of buying tomato-red cotton clothing that washes out to salmon-pink originated at **Murray's Toggery Shop** (62 Main). For elaborate hand-hooked rugs, go to **Claire Murray** (11 S. Water St.). The **Toy Boat** (41 Straight Wharf) is keen on creative, educational toys, including stackable lighthouse puzzles. For hand-fashioned furniture, from Queen Anne to Shaker, head for **Stephen Swift** (34 Main St.).

LAURA M. RECKFORD is the managing editor of the *Falmouth Enterprise* newspaper on Cape Cod. She has been the author for the last 9 years of *Frommer's Cape Cod, Nantucket & Martha's Vineyard* and was a coauthor of the first edition of *France For Dummies*. She can be reached at laurareckford@hotmail.com.

ABOUT THE AUTHOR

YOUR TRIP

General Information: Contact the **Nantucket Chamber of Commerce** (☎ 508/228-1700; www.nantucketchamber.org) or **Nantucket Visitor Services** (☎ 508/228-0925), which also has hotel availability. For ferry schedules, contact the **Steamship Authority** (☎ 508/477-8600; www.steamshipauthority.com) or **Hy-Line Cruises** (☎ 888/778-1132; www.hy-linecruises.com). For flights, there's **Cape Air** (☎ 800/352-0714; www.flycapeair.com) and **Island Air** (☎ 800/248-7779; www.islandair.net). Rent a car with **Nantucket Windmill Auto Rental** (☎ 508/228-1227). For trips out to Great Point, take the **Coskata-Coatue Wildlife Refuge Natural History Tour,** led by staff from the Trustees of the Reservations (☎ 508/228-6799). **Best Lodging:** The **Cliffside Beach Club** has the best beachfront location (46 Jefferson Ave.; ☎ 508/228-0618; www.cliffsidebeach.com; $405–$640). **Best Lodging Value:** **Anchor Inn** is an 1806 sea captain's home with loads of charm (66 Centre St.; ☎ 508/228-0072; www.anchor-inn.net; $185–$235). **Best Restaurant: Black-Eyed Susan's** has the funkiest atmosphere and the most creative menu (10 India St.; ☎ 508/325-0308; entrees $12–$29). **The Galley on Cliffside Beach** has the best setting of any restaurant (at the Cliffside Beach club, see above; ☎ 508/228-9641; $29–$39). **Best Restaurant Value:** The counter at **Congdon's Pharmacy** serves gourmet sandwiches and milkshakes at relatively cheap prices (47 Main St.; ☎ 508/228-3897). **When to Go:** You are guaranteed good beach weather in July and August. Unless you require a swim in the ocean, you'll be better off (for example, fewer people and better deals) in off season: May, June, September, or October.

Nantucket Harbor at dawn.
© Kindra Clineff/Getty Images

THE NATIVE AMERICAN TRAIL

Buttes, gaping canyons, ancient ruins & vibrant villages

I was a child when I first experienced Native American dances. Eating thin blue piki bread with mutton stew, I gazed up at people dressed in dreamy rich velvet, their limbs draped in turquoise beads. Painted warriors twirled in the dust with bison horns crowning their heads and foxtails hanging from their belts. The drum beats pulsated in my heart.

That was the beginning of my journey on what many call the Southwestern U.S. Native American Trail. Located within the region where New Mexico, Arizona, Utah, and Colorado meet, it offers the best introduction anywhere in the country to Native American life, past and present. There is no marked, single route, but the main sights are easy to find. Along the way, the trail leads around rain-carved buttes and skirts gaping canyons. The region embraces the stone cathedrals of Monument Valley, home of the Navajo, and the Sangre de Cristo Mountains, studded with pines. The fabled Rio Grande carves its way through the area, draining water from this "high desert," all of which resides above 5,000 feet. The weather ranges from hot summer days on pastel-painted dunes, to frigid winter nights on Rocky Mountain peaks, rising close to 14,000 feet. Hidden among these landscapes are ancient ruins—Mesa Verde, Keet Seel, Chaco Canyon, and Bandelier, to name a few. Home to the Ancestral Puebloans, also known as the Anasazi, these ruins, which originated around A.D. 600, reveal great architectural integrity and sophistication, and a sensitivity to nature and the stars. You can almost hear the echo of ancient voices as you follow in the footsteps of these early Americans.

The trail also takes you to vibrant, living villages, some perched high on cliffs, such as Acoma's Sky City and the Hopi villages. Others, such as Taos Pueblo and San Ildefonso, are home to towering or sprawling adobe structures. Descendants of the ancients, the people inhabiting these villages today still hold ceremonies in sacred kivas, sprinkle blue corn meal over flames before cooking, and speak in languages that are only recently taking written form. Some of them make pottery by hand, etching or painting with symbols, while others string turquoise beads onto delicate strands or cast silver into buckles and bracelets. Their dances celebrate nature—clouds, corn, deer, antelope—but the meaning of their elaborate rituals remains cryptic, even to the keenest observers.

The trail, however, is far from obscure. I'd begin by flying into Albuquerque and driving north to Santa Fe and Taos to experience Native American art and dances at their best. From here I'd head west to Monument Valley Navajo Tribal Park and then south through Gallup. Wedged between the Navajo and Zuni reservations, Gallup lives up to its self-proclaimed moniker of "Indian Capital of the World." From here, it's a short jaunt to Chaco Culture National Historic Park to see one of the largest Native American dwellings on record. I'd end the trip at the top of Acoma Pueblo's "Sky City," a village where people still live as their ancestors did over a millennium ago. It's a short drive back to the airport in Albuquerque.

◀ *Santa Fe, New Mexico.*
© Jim Zuckerman/Corbis

SPECIAL MOMENTS

1 Native American dances.
What makes the region's Native American dances so powerful is that most are authentic ceremonials—genuine acts of devotion—rather than shows put on for tourists. Some of my fondest memories in my home state of New Mexico are of dances in the open plazas of the region's pueblos. One day at Santa Ana, while dancers wearing feathers, deer skins, and moccasins performed the corn dance, monstrous thunderheads suddenly appeared on the horizon. The cloud masses marched toward us, and as the dance concluded, the sky opened, flooding the ceremony, sending dancers and observers alike racing to the pueblo's portals for shelter. Before planning your trip to the Southwest, check with the Indian Pueblo Cultural Center to see if you can align your trip with dance times. They take place most frequently in spring, summer, and fall, with some special ceremonies during the Christmas holiday. To attend most of these dances you'll want to stay in Santa Fe—a great place to browse for Native American art and eat delectable regional food.

2 Monument Valley Navajo Tribal Park. It's no wonder that Monument Valley—on the Utah/Arizona border—has been the backdrop for countless films, including *Thelma & Louise* and John Ford's classic *Stagecoach*. The valley's towering buttes set on a sea of colored sand move hearts as few other landscapes do. Waking at sunrise to view this world of giants—the Mittens, Three Sisters, Camel Butte, Elephant Butte, the Thumb, and Totem Pole—as they come alive in the pink light, may alter your view of the world. That moment is surpassed only by the experience of spending a day wandering among them. Part of the vast Navajo Nation, the park has a 17-mile self-guided loop trail that lets you see most of the major scenic attractions. You can also get a personalized tour with a Navajo guide.

3 Chaco Culture National Historic Park. A hike up the Pueblo Alto Trail at Chaco offers views across Pueblo Bonito, the largest prehistoric Southwestern Native American dwelling ever excavated. In the afternoon, in the silence of this supremely remote ruin, you can almost sense the life that once teemed here. It began in the mid-800s when the Anasazi started building this vast complex that became the economic center of the region, with some 5,000 inhabitants living in 400 settlements connected by a network of stone roads. The key ruin is Pueblo Bonito. It has some 800 rooms covering more than 3 acres. Other easily accessible ruins are Chetro Ketl, Pueblo del Arroyo, Kin Kletso, and Hungo Pavi. For details, contact the Chaco Culture National Historical Park at www.nps.gov/chcu.

4 **Acoma's Sky City.** You won't forget the memory of standing in the midst of this ancient but still vibrant village built of mud and stone, perched some 367 feet above the surrounding land, the home of 75 or so inhabitants who still speak Keresian. You'll stroll among the dwellings, shopping for pottery while eating fry bread smothered with honey. Inhabited at least since the 11th century, "Sky City" competes with the Hopi mesas for the title of the longest continuously occupied community in the United States. When Coronado visited here in 1540 he proclaimed it the "greatest stronghold in the world." Visiting today, you can stroll through the 1639 mission church of San Esteban del Rey—with its 70-foot-high ceiling, its 10-foot-thick walls, and an interior adorned with poetic devotional art—and appreciate how the Acoma still live as their ancestors once did.

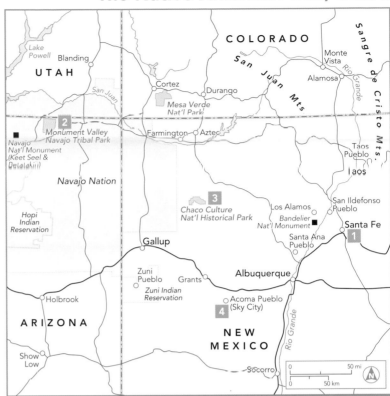

ABOUT THE AUTHOR

LESLEY S. KING grew up on a ranch in northern New Mexico. She writes for the *New York Times*, *Audubon*, and *New Mexico* magazine. She is author of *Frommer's New Mexico* and *Frommer's Albuquerque, Santa Fe & Taos*. Her newest books are *King of the Road* and the *Santa Fe Farmer's Market Cookbook*.

YOUR TRIP

General Information: Contact the **New Mexico Department of Tourism** (☎ 800/545-2070; www.newmexico.org); the **Utah Tourism Office** (☎ 800/200-1160; www.utah.com); **Arizona Office of Tourism** (☎ 866/275-5816; www.arizonaguide.com); **Monument Valley Navajo Nation Park** (☎ 435/727-5870); **Chaco Culture National Historic Park** (☎ 505/786-7014; www.nps.gov/chcu); **Acoma Pueblo** (☎ 800/747-0181; www.skycity.com); **Indian Pueblo Cultural Center** (☎ 800/855-7902; www.indianpueblo.org). **Getting There:** Santa Fe, New Mexico, is located 60 miles north of Albuquerque, New Mexico. Monument Valley is 200 miles northeast of Flagstaff, Arizona. Chaco Culture National Historic Park is southeast of Farmington, New Mexico, off U.S. 550 and C.R. 7900 or east of Gallup, New Mexico, off I-40 and N.Mex. 57. Acoma Pueblo can be reached by taking the McCarty exit off I-40 near Grants and following the signs. **Best Lodging:** In Santa Fe, book a room at the Picuris Pueblo–owned **Hotel Santa Fe,** which offers a range of rooms from standard to luxurious, and has a restaurant specializing in Native American cuisine (☎ 800/825-9876; www.hotelsantafe.com; $99–$459). **Goulding's Lodge** is the only lodge actually located in Monument Valley and is an excellent hotel. The restaurant serves Navajo and American dishes (☎ 800/874-0902; www.gouldings.com; $80–$180). Make reservations well in advance. **Best Restaurant:** Some of Santa Fe's tastiest food is served at **Santacafe** (231 Washington Ave.; ☎ 505/984-1788; www.santacafe.com; $9–$15). Those with thinner wallets will like **The Shed** (113½ E. Palace Ave.; ☎ 505/982-9030; $8–$17).

◀ *Mesa Verde National Park, Colorado.*
© David Muench Photography

NEW YORK, NEW YORK

A cool, brash city with a surprisingly tender heart

I was 13 the first time I visited New York City, and I swear I fell in love with it immediately—breathlessly in love with its cockeyed energy and back-at-ya attitude, its sheer one-of-a-kind-ness. I'd walk around staring up at the dizzyingly tall buildings, gaping at images I'd seen in countless movies and TV shows. I could picture myself on this great movie set as Marlo Thomas in *That Girl,* Audrey Hepburn in *Breakfast at Tiffany's,* Barbra Streisand in *The Way We Were* . . . or even better, as myself, starring in my own, yet-to-be-released movie.

I've lived here now for over 25 years, but I still find it impossible to be jaded about my adopted home. No other city in the world so perfectly defines the word "metropolis," from its sky-piercing towers and traffic-thronged streets to its magnificent museums, ultrachic shopping districts, and pulsing theater district. I have to admit I even love riding the subways—those graffiti-laden trains of the 1970s that so intimidated me when I first came here have been replaced with sleek, silvery cars, where New Yorkers of every persuasion grab a seat (or cling to a pole) and rock their way swiftly to their next destination, pretending—only pretending—not to notice each other.

New York is so densely packed that it's the ultimate walker's city—there's always something intriguing just ahead on the next block, and then the next. Don't spend all your cash on yellow taxis; walk whenever possible because the walk itself is bound to reveal yet more of New York's personality. And personality it has in spades—brashness, avant-garde cool, a wacky sense of humor, and a surprisingly tender heart. Don't be afraid to ask Manhattanites for directions, no matter how harried and hurried they may appear—chances are, they themselves were newcomers once (besides, there's nothing a savvy New Yorker likes better than telling other people where to go). No wonder misfits and runaways from all over the world flock here, hoping to fit in at last. In a town where so many individuals march to different drummers, everyone can find a way to blend into the overall symphony.

The whole game, of course, is not to blow your cool—*not* to look like a tourist. You must stride purposefully through Rockefeller Plaza, pausing just for a moment to drink in the titanic, gilded Prometheus reclining carelessly over the ice skaters. Tuck a folded newspaper under your arm and find a spot on the balcony of Grand Central Station to watch the stampede of commuters racing for their trains at 5pm. Plow through the shuffling crowds in Times Square as though it were no big deal, halting only at the southwest corner of 45th Street and Broadway to do a long, slow, 360-degree turn, head craned back, jaw dropped in awe. Get your bird's-eye view of Manhattan not from the tried-and-true Empire State Building but from the sleeker observation decks at the Top of the Rock in Rockefeller Center—and not in the daytime, when all the other tourists come, but at night, when the cityscape sparkles at your feet.

And whatever you do, do not take a carriage ride through Central Park. What are you, some kinda out-of-towner?

◀ *Guggenheim Museum.*
© Frank Chmura/Alamy

SPECIAL MOMENTS

1   **The Public Library.** Relive the opening scene of the 1960 movie *A Thousand Clowns* by reclining, as Jason Robards did, at 8:30am, between the lions on the grand white front steps of the New York Public Library and watch rush hour. Spend the next 1½ hours lazily sipping a coffee (in the classic blue-and-white, Greek-logo deli cardboard cup) while you watch hordes of white-collar workers marching officeward across 42nd Street and up and down Fifth Avenue. It's the defining image of The Rat Race—and kind of a riot to observe from this detached distance. Then—why not?—go inside and take a look at the breathtaking Main Reading Room on the third floor, where so many great writers have done their research. The library, designed by Carrère and Hastings in 1911, is one of the country's finest examples of Beaux Arts architecture, a glorious confection of white Vermont marble with Corinthian columns and allegorical statues. The famous lion sculptures crouching beside the front steps even have names—*Patience* (on the left) and *Fortitude* (on the right), so dubbed by former mayor Fiorello La Guardia.

2   **Central Park.** Choose one of Manhattan's two iconic museums to visit in the morning—The Metropolitan Museum of Art on Fifth Avenue at 81st Street, or the American Museum of Natural History on Central Park West at 79th Street—and then walk across Central Park to visit the other one in the afternoon. Buy a hot dog or a hot pretzel from a sidewalk cart and eat on the go, like true New Yorkers do. Take the 72nd Street crossing and in a 20-minute stroll you can see no less than six postcard sights (east to west): the Boat Pond, the Bandshell, Bethesda Terrace, Bow Bridge, Strawberry Fields, and (facing the park on W. 72nd St.) the Dakota apartment building. You'll finally understand how New Yorkers live with so much concrete surrounding them—by regularly escaping to this life-giving 840 acres of greenery, plunked down in between the apartment-crammed Upper East and Upper West sides.

3   **Greenwich Village.** Flee for the evening to Greenwich Village, once an outlying village that the city, growing northward, swallowed long ago. It still has the low-rise, leafy atmosphere appropriate to a bohemian haven; settled before the numbered Manhattan grid was imposed, it's laid out in an oddball maze of streets, where it's easy to branch off the avenues and find some intimate little bistro on a side street. Those West Village brownstones are priced well beyond the means of most artistic types these days (head to the East Village to see the last few cheap digs), but at the peaceful intersection of Bedford and Grove streets—where TV's *Friends* supposedly hung out—you can still have a time-warp moment, glimpsing The Village as it was in the

beatnik 1950s, and the avant-garde 1920s, and the prim 1880s.

4 **The Brooklyn Bridge.** The oldest, and still perhaps the most lovely, of the many bridges linking Manhattan to the other boroughs and the mainland, this landmark Gothic-towered brownstone suspension bridge arches over the East River between City Hall and Brooklyn Heights. Begun in 1867 and completed in 1883, the bridge is the best-known symbol of the building boom that transformed the city during the late 19th century. Its cables inspired such poets as Walt Whitman and Hart Crane. There's a sidewalk entrance on Park Row, just across from City Hall Park (4, 5, or 6 train to Brooklyn Bridge/City Hall). But for Manhattan skyline views, begin your walk in Brooklyn (A or C train to High St.). It's only half-a-mile to the center point of the pedestrian walkway, where you can pause to admire that iconic downtown skyline. Ah—New York, just as I pictured it.

New York, New York

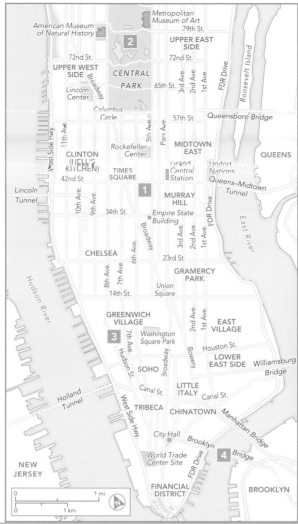

ABOUT THE AUTHOR

HOLLY HUGHES has traveled the globe as an editor and writer—she's the former executive editor of Fodor's travel publications and author of *Frommer's New York City with Kids* and *Frommer's 500 Places to Take Your Kids before They Grow Up.* She's also written fiction for middle-schoolers and edits the annual *Best Food Writing* anthology.

YOUR TRIP

General Information: Contact the **New York Convention & Visitors Bureau** (☎ 212/484-1200; www.nycvisit.com). **Getting There:** New York has three airports: JFK International, LaGuardia, and Newark Liberty International in New Jersey. Information on all three is available at www.panynj.gov. **What to See & Do:** If you'd like to tour a specific neighborhood with an expert guide, call **Big Apple Greeter** (☎ 212/669-8159; www.bigapplegreeter.org). This non-profit has specially trained volunteers who take visitors around town for a free tour of a particular neighborhood. **Best Lodging: The Carlyle** is an Upper East Side tony, elegant, and discreet choice (35 E. 76th St.; ☎ 212/744-1600; www.thecarlyle.com; $500–$3,200). **The Waldorf-Astoria** is a classic Big City hotel with Art Deco style (301 Park Ave.; ☎ 800/WALDORF or 212/355-3000; www.waldorf.com; $299–$950). **Best Lodging Value: Washington Square Inn** has a great Village location, right on Washington Square (103 Waverly Place; ☎ 800/222-0418 or 212/777-9515; www.washingtonsquarehotel.com; $230–$250). **Best Restaurant: Per Se** offers incomparable gourmet dining from renowned chef Thomas Keller (10 Columbus Circle, fourth floor; ☎ 212/823-9335; prix-fixe $210). **Café des Artistes** is a cozy-but-urbane West Side restaurant with old-world flair (1 W. 67th St.; ☎ 212/877-3500; $25–$90). **Best Restaurant Value: The Corner Bistro** is a vintage Village bar with superb burgers (331 W. 4th St.; ☎ 212/242-9502; $2.75–$5.75). **When to Go:** New York is a year-round destination. There are no low seasons in terms of availability, and the weather, while variable from season to season, doesn't really affect how much you can enjoy your trip.

◀ *Central Park Lake.*
© Mitchell Funk/Getty Images

NORTH VIETNAM

An otherworldly boat trip & a walk among ethnic hill tribes

So, you land in Hanoi, hop a $10 taxi to your hotel, and sleep like only the jet-lagged can—comatose. If you want to do it right, on Day 1 hit the town: Take in the city's central park around Hoan Kiem Lake just before dawn to watch folks do tai chi in the morning mist; walk the narrow, crowded, crooked streets of the Old Quarter; ride on the back of a motorcycle taxi through Hanoi's chaotic traffic; stop for a glimpse of a rigor-mortised Ho Chi Minh in his mausoleum; wander crowded shopping areas where hawkers pounce; go for a foot massage; dine streetside on local specialties; and cap it off with an evening show of the Thang Long Water Puppets.

What I love about traveling in Vietnam is the sensory onslaught. Everywhere there is activity: streets transformed into rivers of putt-putting motorcycles; small factory storefronts next to crowded beauty parlors; sprawling markets hung with baskets of fowl and cuts of raw meat; vendors jostling past, carrying baskets strung from bamboo poles. You'll spot oddities like snake or whole roast dog. And behind unassuming courtyard doors, you'll find ancient Buddhist temple courtyards glowing with candles and wafting with incense from huge hanging coils. There is nothing like it. If you can surrender to the minor hassles of getting around, to the chaos of the roads, and to the kindness of these resilient and welcoming people, you're in for the trip of a lifetime.

The north was once a dour communist outpost, but a visit to this stunning region today will help you unpack that old trunk of war film misconceptions about one of Asia's most enticing countries. Modern Vietnam is far too busy scampering up the rungs of globalization and building infrastructure to really notice. Modern Hanoi is home to chic expat bistros, galleries, and shops, where French influence lives in baguette sandwiches and America comes alive when local jazz musicians trade saxophone licks late into the evening.

More than half of the Vietnamese were born after 1975, and those who remember the war against the U.S. are proud of their nation's resolve in the face of a militarily superior foe. It's important to remember that the "American War" years came on the tail of a protracted struggle against French colonials and thousands of years of grinding conflict with the Chinese; Vietnam has known war for centuries and is today enjoying a long period of peace and development. The Vietnamese people welcome Western visitors, and you will rarely face ill will over politics.

The Vietnamese capital is home base for exploring the far north. Book a berth on an overnight train to the high mountains and rice terraces of Sapa, an old French colonial hill station. Use the town as a base for easy hikes through the villages of the ethnic minorities who live here, and join them in their colorful dress on market days. And don't miss Ha Long Bay, the UNESCO World Heritage Site with its towering limestone karst towers and otherworldly landscapes.

◀ *A cruise on Halong Bay.*
© Bill Hatcher/Getty Images

SPECIAL MOMENTS

1 Sapa and the far north. Reached by overnight train from Hanoi, Sapa is perched on the edge of a gaping valley of lush green terraced rice farms at the foot of Southeast Asia's highest peak, Mount Fansipan (3,143m/10,312 ft.). The old Mission Church still stands sentinel at the center of town, and the diverse ethnic hill-tribe groups still gather in town to trade goods (and sell souvenirs to the many tourists). You can day-trek to surrounding villages peopled by diverse ethnic hill tribes. On Sunday the town of Bac Ha, just 100km (62 miles) from Sapa, hosts a colorful market day, where members from hill-tribe communities gather to trade—well worth planning your trip around. And if you can't make it on Sunday, ask a guide service about the market at Coc Ly on Tuesdays—a direct drive from the train station in Lao Cai and an

off-the-beaten-track site, with far fewer tourists than Bac Ha.

Sapa is a gateway to the vast mountain regions of the far north, as far west as the border with Laos and the town of Dien Bien Phu, where the French colonial forces met their demise in 1958. Western travelers are greeted with surprise by the disparate ethnic groups that live in hidden enclaves in these hills. I traveled the region on an oil-belching Soviet-era motorcycle, but guide companies in Hanoi can arrange for jeep or minivan adventures throughout the region.

2 Ha Long Bay. This stunning UNESCO World Heritage natural wonder is no secret, really, and the bay is choked with boats, but nothing could take away from the grandeur of Ha Long Bay. Mornings begin with a sail through the misty scene of an ancient Chinese

painted scroll. The shifting light of day paints different scenes on the steep limestone towers. Not to be missed. If you can afford it, cruise on **The Emeraude** (www.emeraude-cruises.com), a copy of a French steamer that plied these waters in the early 20th century, or take a ride on one of the cool, re-outfitted junks like *The Jewel of the Bay,* run by **Buffalo Tours** (www.buffalotours.com), or *The Dragon's Pearl,* run by **Handspan** (www.handspan.com).

3 Tam Coc Grottos. If you can't make it to Ha Long Bay—or can't get enough of the scenery—try the "Ha Long Bay of the rice fields," less than 2 hours south of Hanoi. Tam Coc, or Three Grottos, is an hour ride along a narrow river through three caves. The winding waterway is surrounded by rice cultivation in and among high, arching

limestone formations similar to those in Ha Long Bay. The fun of visiting Tam Coc is sitting in a shallow draft boat and even having a go at the unique stand-up, forward-stroke rowing technique (your guide will surely let you give it a try). The area has a number of other interesting sites, including Cuc Phuong National Forest, where you can meet and greet rare gibbon species and usually shy jungle animals, and the ancient capital of Hoa Lu.

4 **Hanoi.** Among the sightseeing highlights are the Ho Chi Minh Mausoleum (be sure to get there before 11am), the National Art Museum, and the grisly Hoa Lo Prison, also known as the infamous Hanoi Hilton. Happiness is renting a *cyclo* (a three-wheeled pedicab) for a half-day, and getting on and off in the old quarter as the spirit moves you. The opportunities for shopping are endless. And don't forget to treat yourself to a foot massage from a parlor on the street.

CHARLES AGAR wrote a number of Frommer's titles on Southeast Asia, including *Frommer's Vietnam.* Born with "itchy feet," according to his grandma, he traveled and taught English in Asia before he started writing. He is currently a newspaper reporter in Aspen, Colorado. Contact him at www.charlesagar.com.

ABOUT THE AUTHOR

YOUR TRIP

General Information: The **Vietnam National Administration of Tourism** provides good background information (www.vietnamtourism.com). **Getting There:** There are direct flights now from Europe and the West Coast of the U.S., as well as from New York City to Vietnam. Fly **Vietnam Airlines** (www.vietnamairlines.com) for short domestic hops; hire cars or join tours for overland routes. **Best Lodging:** The **Sofitel Metropole Hanoi** is without rival for history and charm in the old French colonial capital—not to be missed (15 Ngo Quyen St.; ☎ 84-4/826-6919; www.sofitel.com; $190–$255/£100–£135). For transport and all arrangements in Sapa, contact Victoria Hotels' **Sapa Resort** (☎ 84-20/871-522; www.victoriahotels-asia.com; $135–$220/£71–£117). In Ha Long Bay, contact **Emeraude Cruises** (www.emeraude-cruises.com), **Buffalo Tours** (www.buffalotours.com), or **Handspan** (www.handspan.com). **Best Lodging Value:** For a no-frills choice in the heart of the Old Quarter of Hanoi, try one of the many outlets of local **Hong Ngoc Hotel** (☎ 84-4/826-7566; www.hongngochotel.com; $20–$30/£11–£16). **Best Restaurant:** In Hanoi, don't miss **Restaurant Bobby Chinn** for funky Asian fusion (1 Ba Trieu St.; ☎ 84-4/934-8577; $7–$12/£4–£6). **Best Restaurant Value:** **Cha Ca La Vong** is a real Hanoi institution serving a unique, delicious monkfish fried in oil and herbs (14 Cha Ca St.; ☎ 84-4/825-3929; $5/£3). **When to Go:** Winters are cool, as low as 14°C (60°F) in Hanoi in December and colder—even snow—in the hills around Sapa, but still the best time to beat the stifling heat and hot season (Apr–Oct) is to travel in winter months, November to April.

◀ *Market day in Coc Ly, near Sapa.*
© Michael Spring

OAXACA, MEXICO

Folklore, crafts, markets & unspoiled beaches

The State of Oaxaca is everything that's wonderful about Mexico. One of the most southern regions of the country, it's the primary center for Mexican folklore and crafts, with dramatic pre-Columbian ruins, 160km (100 miles) or so of untouched Pacific-coast beaches, and, at its heart, the city of Oaxaca itself: an exquisite, slow-paced Spanish-colonial town set in the center of a valley amid high mountain ranges, largely cut off from the rest of the country until the 20th century. Architecturally, the city is dazzling: a UNESCO World Heritage Site with 16th-century baroque basilicas dominating every neighborhood, craft galleries, small hotels, museums, and restaurants serving gourmet Oaxacan and international meals. Fascinating Indian markets and artisans' bazaars, local street musicians, purple jacarandas, and cascades of bougainvillea bring life and color to the downtown streets, many of them car-free. There's charm and enchantment at every turn.

The people of Oaxaca make it an even more compelling destination. Deeply traditional, uniquely tied to both Spanish and ancient Zapotec and Mixtec heritages, Oaxacans are known for their charm, courtesy, and artistic talent. The *zócalo*, or main plaza of the town (reputedly the most beautiful in Mexico), is shaded by linden trees and adorned with a delicate Victorian gazebo from which musicians serenade the nightly promenade of Oaxaca's citizenry. The zócalo's cafes and restaurants, sheltered beneath arcades, are great for people-watching as well as dining. Throughout the city, day and night, you encounter streets filled with mini-fiestas and religious processions. And on a hill above is the haunting remnant of Oaxaca's distant past—the mysterious ruined city of Monte Alban (dating from 500 B.C.), one of the most dramatic and ancient pre-Columbian sites in the New World. I'm always awed by the intense, almost hallucinatory sunlight and overpowering spirituality of the place.

Wild, almost impassable mountains of the Sierra Madre del Sur separate the inland Valley of Oaxaca from the Pacific Coast. Flying over them is recommended, unless you're a fan of arduous, unpredictable bus rides. The planned resort of Huatulco occupies the southern edge of Oaxaca's coastline. At a time when pristine beaches and coves the world over are being turned into resort complexes and generic tourist zones, the rest of Oaxaca's long Pacific Coast remains lost in the mellow 1950s, 1960s, and 1970s. There are just two small resort towns for 160km (100 miles). The larger, livelier Puerto Escondido (Hidden Port) has a variety of beaches, including Zicatela Beach, with the best surfing in the Western Hemisphere. The even more hidden Puerto Angel, where piglets and chickens roam the sandy streets, offers a wider range of thundering, high-surf beaches and quiet coves, each with its own character and beauty. This is the Mexican Pacific of Hemingway and Tennessee Williams. Places to stay and dine range from charming and personal to rudimentary; the sea is like flowing jade, and the beaches are dotted with Zapotec children playing in the surf, together with a smattering of tourists happily unthawing in the sun. If you're seeking a flower child's winter hideaway, this is Xanadu.

◀ *The Day of the Dead Festival, Oaxaca.*
© Richard I'Anson/
Lonely Planet Images

SPECIAL MOMENTS

1 **Craft hunting.** The markets of Oaxaca overflow with authentic handicrafts and whimsical folk art, often sold by indigenous Zapotec people who come into town wearing the traditional costumes of their villages. If you fall in love with the artisans' markets, shop windows, and galleries of downtown Oaxaca, you can visit the villages in the surrounding valley where the crafts are made—either on your own or on excellent guided craft tours—and meet the folk artists and craftspeople in their homes and workshops. Villages in the Oaxacan countryside are famous for specific crafts: pottery, woodcarving, traditional blankets, and rugs woven of rich, hand-dyed and hand-spun wools. I especially love the rug-makers' studios, with handmade wooden looms and piles of lanolin-filled wool being dyed with juniper berries, pomegranate, cactus juice, nuts, and seeds. The craft tours can take you to a weaver's home for an authentic lunch and shopping, as well as to charming towns, markets, and pre-Columbian sites in the countryside.

2 **Beaching out.** Everyone will find a beach to fall in love with. If you're a surfer, the world-famous "Mexican Pipeline" at Puerto Escondido's Zicatela Beach is guaranteed to give you the perfect wave. A quarter-mile away, it's bodyboard heaven at the gentler Playa Marinero, or you can take a simple launch to quiet coves with clear emerald water ideal for floating and snorkeling. Puerto Angel's lengthy, palapa-shaded Zipolite Beach may be the last place in Mexico that allows nude swimming and sunbathing. After a dip, you can suit up, saunter into a thatch-roof beachfront restaurant, order fresh red snapper, and swing in a shaded hammock while your meal is prepared. The surf at Zipolite is dangerous, so swim at nearby San Agustinillo and Mazunte beaches.

3 **Coastal nature reserves.** On sunrise birding excursions to the mangrove lagoons of Manialtepec, you'll cruise through labyrinths of waterways rich with tropical flora and overloaded with a tapestry of herons and egrets, falcons, wood storks, ibises, cormorants, ospreys, and parrots. A full-day tour through the larger Chacahua Lagoons glides you past fantasies of endless mangroves and birdlife, punctuated with stops at deserted, paradisiacal beaches for swimming and barbecued fish.

4 **The Night of the Radishes.** December 23 is the city of Oaxaca's quintessential night of fantastical whimsy. Hundreds of Oaxacans carve incredible sculptures of creatures, people, miniature cities, and even religious scenes, into gargantuan radishes, which are displayed in competition around the zócalo amid music, food stalls, and throngs of radish admirers. Infused with the spirit of Christmas, this is a night when Oaxaca absolutely shines!

ROBERT ULLIAN is the author of *Frommer's Israel* and *Frommer's Memorable Walks in Venice*. He has also written guidebooks on Bali and Morocco. His work has appeared in such publications as *Esquire* and *Mademoiselle*. He is the recipient of a Grant for Fiction from the National Endowment for the Arts. Contact him at aramullian@yahoo.com.

ABOUT THE AUTHOR

YOUR TRIP

General Information: Log on to the **Mexican Tourism Board**'s website at www.visitmexico.com. While in Oaxaca, visit the **State Tourist Office** at Calle Independencia 607. For more Oaxaca details, including hotels, attractions, and tours, check Travelocity's www.allaboutoaxaca.com. For Puerto Escondido details, tours, and nature excursions, go to Puerto Escondido's website: www.tomzap.com/escondio.html. When in Puerto Escondido, check in with the well-informed Gina at the main pedestrian street's Tourist Information kiosk. **Best Lodging:** The **Camino Real Oaxaca,** built as a convent in 1576, has been beautifully redesigned into Oaxaca's most atmospheric and luxurious hotel (Cinco de Mayo 300; ☎ 800/722-6466 in the U.S., or 52-951/501-6100; www.camino-real-oaxaca.com; $265–$345/£140–£183). Interior rooms have less street noise and are priced a bit higher. **Best Lodging Value:** A charming, budget choice is the **Posada Catarina** (Aldama 325; ☎ 52-951/516-4270; $60/£32 double), with quiet interior courtyard rooms. In Puerto Escondido, **Hotel Flor de María** is an architectural delight, run by a Canadian couple and filled with returnees (Playa Marineros; ☎ 52-954/582-0536; $60/£32). It's a stone's throw from a good bathing beach. In the center of Puerto Angel, the **Hotel Buena Vista,** designed and run by a Californian couple, is simple but lovely, with panoramas of the sea and sunset plus a swimming pool (Apdo. Postal 48; ☎ 52-958/584-3104; www.labuenavista.com; $45–$60/£24–£32). **Best Dining:** Nothing beats market food for a quick bite. In Oaxaca, visit **La Merced** market for tacos, quesadillas, and tamales, all for a few pesos.

◀ *Arturo García Busto's murals, Presidential Palace.*
© Russell Gordon/DanitaDelimont.com

OCRACOKE ISLAND, NORTH CAROLINA

Golden beaches & wild ponies
close to the middle of nowhere

On a map, Ocracoke is a narrow strip of white, probably thinner than your fingernail, off the southernmost tip of the Outer Banks. This is a useful reminder that there's simply not much going on here, at least in human terms—just 14 miles of soft, golden beaches, some 700 permanent residents, a handful of shaggy wild ponies, a couple of excellent restaurants, and days and days of peace and quiet.

Of course, there's a hitch. Oh yes, there's a perfectly good reason why these gorgeous beaches are often undisturbed. A reason why you can spend hours alone, lying in the sun, not listening to music somebody else thinks is good. A reason why you can watch the sun setting in a wash of red and pink, alone with someone you want to be alone with. It's much the same reason why, in centuries past, this island was a favorite hideaway for the pirate Blackbeard and other daredevil smugglers. And it's this: It's kind of hard to get to.

For ancient mariners, the lower Outer Banks was a serious no-go area, with rough seas, vicious tides, and rocky shores. These days you can reach the island only by ferry or private plane, and even the landings where you catch the ferry are miles from anywhere.

Because Ocracoke is in the middle of nowhere (unless you happen to live in coastal North Carolina), visits here usually involve serious travel. My trips used to require a 17-hour drive, culminating in an uncomfortable night in a random roadside motel outside Jacksonville, North Carolina. The next day there was a further 90-minute drive through the deepest, most spectacular marshes I've ever seen, followed by 3 hours on a ferry in a crossing that can be a bit rough.

Clearly, you don't go to Ocracoke because it's easy. But getting here can be half the fun. And it's the inaccessibility of the island that has kept it as rustic and unspoiled as it is.

Once I arrive on the island, I throw my bags in my room and head out on foot, wandering past its humble, shaded, 1940s-era bungalows, to my favorite street of all—the simply named Back Road. It lures me with its eclectic mix of art stores, book shops, eateries, and jewelry boutiques. I can happily spend an afternoon perusing the menus at its excellent restaurants, and stopping for an iced coffee or a frothy frappé in one of its bijou coffee shops, inevitably manned by one of a seemingly endless supply of sanguine local teens.

Other afternoons are spent lounging on the beach, going for long walks, taking day trips across to Cape Hatteras by ferry, or seeking out the island's shy wild ponies, now protected in fenced-off areas and thus somewhat less wild than they used to be, but still a bit hard to find.

And I relax. Almost immediately, I feel the stress slip away. Because there's no traffic, no deadline, no crowd, no headlines—nothing but golden beaches, seabirds, other intrepid regular visitors, and warm ocean breezes.

◀ *Ocracoke Lighthouse.*
© Peter Finger/Corbis

SPECIAL MOMENTS

1 **Ocracoke Lighthouse.** It's a tourist attraction—the only crowded place on Ocracoke—but you have to stop by and see this, the oldest operating lighthouse in North Carolina, and one of the oldest in the South. Built in 1823, as lighthouses go it's small—from a sturdy base it extends 75 feet up, although, through an optical illusion, it really doesn't look big enough to guide anyone in a storm. You can wander the grounds at will, but sadly you can't climb up to see how it all works, or to take in what must be an extraordinary view.

2 **Ocracoke Village.** Along with the sand and sea, Ocracoke Village is an attraction in itself. Aside from the busy harbor front, overlooking the boats on Silver Lake, this is a quiet, idyllic place, and the farther into the village you walk, the more peaceful it gets. Most of the houses are small 1940s bungalows, with deep shady porches. Many have been converted into shops. I always pop into the Secret Garden Gallery, which displays good and often affordable works by new and established North Carolina artists; Bella Fiore Pottery, with the work of talented potter Sarah Fiore; and the Sunflower Center, a combination art gallery and health-food store, which has a rudderless but pleasant mixture of covetable beauty supplies, sometimes kitsch art, and healthy goodies. Then I head to Java Books to find my holiday read and leaf through prospective purchases with a strong cup of coffee. Heaven.

3 **Hammock Hills Nature Trail.** You never doubt, wandering around the island, that this is a wild place. In the national park that stretches across most of it, nothing can, or has been, built on its undulating sea-grass-covered dunes or flat, silvery salt marshes. The flies and mosquitoes, which more or less run the place, can make your life a living hell, though, so I always strike out for the Hammock Hills Trail just north of the village with sturdy shoes, plenty of water, and bottles of super-strength bug repellent. The trail is well designed, with a wooden walkway protecting the dunes and marshes along the way. Late on a lazy afternoon, you can head through the thick forests and across waving sea grass to the shore, and, if you're lucky, get to the water just before sunset, as the water turns golden.

4 **Ocracoke Beach.** Arguably the best thing to do on Ocracoke is nothing at all. The island seems to actually encourage you to do nothing, and what better place to do it than on the beach? Wide, gold-sand beaches stretch for a solid 14 miles, and the farther you travel from the village, the quieter your bit of sand is likely to be. My secret is to park where I don't see cars anywhere, then climb one of the many wooden staircases over the protected dunes. That first view of the rough, crashing waves always takes my breath away. I'm a strong swimmer but the current and waves here are notorious, so I don't head out very far without a bodyboard for backup. But with a board for floating and a book for company in the soft sand (along with the obligatory bottle of bug repellent), this is where I want to be on a sunny day.

CHRISTI DAUGHERTY, based in London, is the author of *Frommer's Ireland* and *Frommer's Paris Day by Day*. She also co-wrote *Frommer's MTV Ireland* and *Frommer's MTV Europe*. She spent summers on Ocracoke for many years, and only recently replaced it with Fuerteventura, which is now closer to home. Contact her at www.christidaugherty.co.uk.

ABOUT THE AUTHOR

YOUR TRIP

General Information: Contact the **National Park Service Visitor Center** (☎ 252/928-4531). Virtually all of Ocracoke Island is part of Cape Hatteras National Seashore. **Getting There:** Ocracoke Island is 26 miles off the mainland coast of North Carolina. From the north, you can catch a free car ferry from Hatteras hourly—the journey takes 40 minutes. Or you catch a car ferry from Cedar Island ($15 per car). The journey takes just under 3 hours, and reservations are necessary (☎ 800/BY-FERRY; www.ncferry.org). The island itself is small, but a car is good to have if you want to head out to its most far-flung beaches; however, it's best to traverse the small village by foot. The pony pens are 7 miles north of Ocracoke Village. **Best Lodging:** The **Ocracoke Harbor Inn** is one of the most up-to-date, comfortable, and inviting inns on the island (135 Silver Lake Rd.; ☎ 888/456-1998; www.ocracokeharborinn.com; $100–$150). **Best Lodging Value: Edward's of Ocracoke** lets you choose from its bungalows, family rooms, and efficiencies with tiny kitchens (226 Old Beach Rd.; ☎ 800/254-1359; www.edwardsofocracoke.com; $48–$69). **Best Restaurant:** The **Back Porch** on Back Road offers innovative seafood and steak dishes in a purely romantic atmosphere (110 Back Rd.; ☎ 252/928-6401; $25–$50). **Best Restaurant Value: Howard's Pub and Raw Bar** is the biggest, loudest bar and restaurant on the island, cooking up fresh seafood as well as burgers, sandwiches, and pizzas in a jovial atmosphere (Hwy. 12; ☎ 252/928-4441; www.howardspub.com; $8–$15).

◀ *Ocracoke Beach.*
© Stephen Saks/Lonely Planet Images

OKAVANGO DELTA, BOTSWANA

The best place on the planet to get intimate with wildlife

If you love the wild, and want to get deep into nature, go to Africa. Better still, refine your experience with a safari in the rich, abundant floodplains of the Okavango Delta, a spectacular environment that's arguably the best place on the planet to get close to wildlife. From here, while enjoying luxurious lodges and top-end safari drives, you can get a sense of the world before mankind. Here you are literally in the midst of it all, located in such a way that you can observe an extraordinary natural spectacle, each day a majestic restaging of creation.

A peaceful, prosperous nation, Botswana has been independent for just 4 decades. It is renowned for only two things—its diamonds and its delta. The latter is a fan-shaped oasis that draws masses of animals for its life-giving waters. It is, quite literally, a place from whence life springs. Roughly the size of Texas, Botswana is 80% desert, a fact that probably accounts for its population of fewer than two million people.

Across the country's vast dry plains, herds of buffalo dawdle and drift in the thousands, their pace often determined by the whims of ever-watchful, ever-lazy lions. It's a world where edible beasts—zebras, giraffe, warthog, antelope—are forever on alert, while elephants and rhinos command their territory by brute force. Lying in wait, more elusive predators provide a tougher challenge for visitors looking for that once-in-a-lifetime opportunity to see lions, leopards, or packs of wild dogs taking down their prey. With just a few days, you should see all of these animals in action—or inaction, because sometimes they also take time out to watch the world go by.

After the summer rains, the delta is ravaged by waters from Angola in the north, transforming it into another world, soaked with life and charged with the beauty of abundance. Visitors get to watch the flood plains of the world's largest inland delta literally fill up. Waterways dotted with islands and clogged by reed beds provide a network of navigable channels where visitors are poled around in *mokoros* (dugout canoes), while hippos grunt in the near distance. Nowhere else on earth does "flood" so magically equate with "miracle."

Given enough time, you can explore Botswana's other wonders: the elephant-rich Chobe River banks, or the dry, baked-clay region of the Kalahari in the south. There, ancient baobab trees and migrating herds are complemented by a living carpet of pink, formed by some 200,000 flamingos converging on the Makgadkgadi salt pan at the end of the rainy season.

While the waters of the delta sustain life, energizing the African plains, across the border in Zimbabwe and Zambia the waters of the Zambezi enact another type of drama, plunging a spectacular 100m (328 ft.), creating the world-famous Victoria Falls. It's one of the planet's greatest natural shows, an awesome sight of such splendid magic your heart feels as though it's on the same journey, plunging into the depths of the Batoka Gorge down below, a free-falling sensory assault.

◀ *Okavango Delta.*
© Bobby Haast/National Geographic/Getty Images

SPECIAL MOMENTS

1 Moremi Game Reserve, Okavango Delta. A typical day in the delta is highlighted by early-morning and late-afternoon jeep safaris. There's no predicting what wildlife you'll encounter, but whether you prefer the gentle romance of exotic birds in flight or the vicious reality of lions tearing apart their prey, you'll be rewarded on any journey. Sometimes, within minutes, you'll have logged sightings of myriad beasts—perhaps, at first, just hoofed herbivores. But feel your excitement mount as your guide spots predator tracks and suddenly you're on the trail of leopard or wild dog. Your adrenalin will surge as you become an intrepid animal explorer, investing hours in an intimate and unforgettable relationship with a creature you may never meet, anywhere, again.

2 Duba Plains, Okavango Delta. If like me you have an inclination toward the big furry beasts, then go to Duba Plains, commonly known as "The Lion Capital of Africa." Here it's a rather everyday occurrence to pull up next to a couple of lazy lions sprawled under a tree. Locked in a dreamy stare-down, you can watch as they stretch their massive, dainty paws and preen themselves with gentle licks. Occasionally they'll let out enormous yawns, comfortable in the early-evening shade. Now here is a place where, like the lions, you can feel utterly at one with the natural world around you.

3 Baines' Camp, Okavango Delta. The delta need not be a place of early-morning game drives and the constant thrill of the chase.

Like several of the smart safari lodges in the Okavango, Baines' Camp is perched right on the edge of a watering hole where you can sip gin and tonics while watching hippos wallow in the mud below. Designers at Baines' Camp have also added a simple innovation to the luxury suites by making the beds mobile. On my last night in the delta, I wheeled my bed onto the porch, dropped the mosquito net, and slept under the stars; I awoke early to the penetrating sounds of the bush, alive with possibility and meaning. That morning, I rediscovered my lazy side and mimicked the wallowing hippos. Despite some guilt at missing a game drive, I basked like a croc next to the pool and enjoyed a self-satisfied morning, with the lodge to myself. My fellow guests returned

with spectacular tales of a morning spent trailing a leopard. I might have envied their good fortune but was too full of the thrill of being alive and in Africa.

4 Victoria Falls. After the miracle of the delta, you may not expect to be impressed by Victoria Falls, even if it's the largest waterfall on earth. But standing above the Batoka Gorge, watching the Zambezi waters cascade into the abyss below, you'll feel as though you are witnessing an apparition; no wonder the Zambians call it *Mosi-Oa-Tunya*—"the smoke that thunders." Feel free to ignore signs recommending a raincoat and walk the entire promenade opposite the Zimbabwe side of the falls. You'll be drenched in minutes by the immense back spray but pleased that you've not only seen this natural world wonder, but felt it upon your skin.

KEITH BAIN is a born-and-bred South African who went to Botswana to update a Frommer's guidebook. There, as he flew over the lush, fertile delta, he rediscovered his love of Africa. Since then, he has been writing about Venice, Romania, and Slovenia, but spends most of his time teaching future filmmakers at a private film school in Johannesburg.

ABOUT THE AUTHOR

YOUR TRIP

General Information: The **Botswana Department of Tourism** has information on the delta and Botswana (www.botswana-tourism.gov.bw). For information on the falls, visit the **Zambia National Tourist Board** (www.zambiatourism.com). For safaris in and around the falls, contact London-based **Zambezi Safari & Travel Company** (www.zambezi.com). **Getting There:** **Air Botswana** flies from Johannesburg and Cape Town to Maun, the jumping-off point for trips into the delta (☎ 800/518-7781; www.airbotswana.co.bw). From Maun, you'll be flown by light aircraft to your lodge; this should be arranged by your safari operator. **Best Lodging:** Known for its elephant safaris and the romance of its setting, as well as the wealth of game you can see, **Abu Camp** is a surefire winner (☎ 0027-11/807-1800; www.wilderness-safaris.com; $4,500/£2,300). To stay at Baines' Camp, contact **Sanctuary Lodges & Camps** (☎ 0027-11/781-1497; www.sanctuarylodges.com; $475/£252). For the best lodging near the falls, riverside exclusivity doesn't get better than what you'll find if you reserve the "Edward" suite at **The River Club**, in Zambia (☎ 0027-11/883-0747; www.wilderness-safaris.com; $690/£355). **Best Lodging Value:** You'll be in one of the finest regions of the delta on Chief's Island, despite paying bottom dollar at **Oddballs Palm Island Lodge** (☎ 866/254-1428; www.island-safari.com; $195–$395/£103–£209). Near the falls, Zimbabwe's **Ilala Lodge,** overlooking a lawn that attracts antelope and monkeys, is a 10-minute walk from the falls (☎ 888/227-8311; www.llalalodge.com; $248–$308/£127–£158). **When to Go:** June–Oct.

◀ *African elephant at a watering hole.*
© Michael Melford/Getty Images

OREGON

Waterfalls, sequoias, canyons, lakes & the spectacle of surf

Most of us think there's something special about the place where we were raised. I'm lucky that I'm a native Oregonian, because this place really is special. Some folks probably wouldn't let me get away with saying that Oregon is the most beautiful place on earth, but no one who's been here would quibble with my boast that it's certainly one of them.

Out here, we tell anyone who complains about our infamous rain just to go down the road a few miles, because the weather will be a lot different there. Well, the same goes for our scenery. Without too much moving around you'll come upon waterfalls, groves of ancient sequoias, and the spectacle of surf exploding through holes in millennia-old rock formations, and all this scenery will make you just want to gawk in appreciation for awhile.

I like to take visitors who don't get too squirmy riding in a car on a long 1-day drive from Portland through the forests and craggy, snowcapped peaks of the Cascade Mountains, a slice of high desert country, and a stretch of our 350-mile Pacific coastline. I make sure to pull over only at spots that I think show the very best sides of Oregon—like the calm surface of Trillium Lake reflecting the snowcapped peak of Mount Hood, or the rim-rock bluffs topping off Crooked River Canyon.

No matter how many times I do this drive, I never tire of the part that takes us over the McKenzie Pass through lava fields beneath the peaks of six craggy mountains, then drops into the forested valley of the white-water McKenzie River. I always feel a little pang of regret at having to tear myself and my chums away from the sight of the river waters rushing over Sahalie Falls, but a little later we're sitting on the rocks in Yachats watching the surf pound into headlands green with mossy rainforests.

Give me a few days to spare and I head to Steens Mountain, way over in empty ranch country, near the southeastern corner of the state. The mountain's flank rises through steppes covered in aspen and mountain mahogany, then comes abruptly to a precipice high above the Alvord Desert, a sheer drop of more than a mile below. Not too many people live in these parts, but those who do usually give you something to chuckle about long after you've gone home. On a recent visit I informed the woman serving dinner at the old Frenchglen Hotel that there was a rattlesnake on the lawn. "Yep. Help yourself to the potatoes." The next morning, I drove up the mountain. Even in late June a snow bank still blocked the road, so I hiked a mile or so across tundra carpeted in wildflowers and there, at my feet, spread Kiger Gorge, etched by a glacier eons ago and not marred by human interference since. A swish broke the perfect silence and I looked up to see an eagle float by chillingly close to my shoulder. Not able to contain my excitement, I told the waitress at dinner what I'd seen—an eagle, so close I could touch it! "Yep. Eat those biscuits while they're hot." Well, I guess when you live around grandeur long enough, you begin to take it for granted.

◀ *Crater Lake.*
© Muench Photography Inc.

SPECIAL MOMENTS

1   Yachats. I've yet to introduce a shore lover to this small, unspoiled string of shops and houses in the shadow of Cape Perpetua who wasn't delighted with the place. And why shouldn't they be? Surf pounds into miles of rocky shoreline; the tidal estuary of the Yachats River is riddled with tidal pools filled with starfish and other creatures, whales and sea lions swim offshore, and trails wind through old-growth forests on the surrounding headlands. The big excitement in town, and a thrill it truly is, is watching spectacular sunsets with a glass of Oregon pinot noir in hand.

2   Steens Mountain. Not too many people venture onto 9,700-foot-tall Steens Mountain, and that's one of the pleasures of being up there. If you're lucky, you'll have antelope and bighorn sheep for company, and if you're really lucky, you might find yourself looking through a cloud of dust to see a herd of wild horses galloping past. The loop road across the western flank is only 60 miles long, but the rutted track makes for slow going and you can spend the better part of a day up here gawking at the views of East Rim and Kiger Gorge and hiking into Wildhorse Lake and along the Donner und Blitzen River—so named for the thunder-and-lighting squalls, often accompanied by snow squalls, that are pretty common on the mountain, even on a fine summer's day.

3   Malheur National Wildlife Refuge. A slow drive along the 40-mile patrol road that traverses the length of this magnificent 185,000-acre refuge at the base of Steens Mountain can elicit wide-eyed rapture in even the most reluctant naturalist. Flocks of herons, egrets, and more than 320 species of birds take flight across lakes and grasslands, as deer and antelope dart through the underbrush. Come spring and fall migratory seasons, the species "binocular-toting bird-watcher" invades the refuge, but at other times the only other human presence may be the silhouette of a cowboy astride his horse in the distance.

4   Mount Hood and the McKenzie River National Recreation Trail. Oregon's tallest mountain, Mount Hood, lifts its craggy, perpetually snowcapped peak some 11,200 feet above the horizon some 50 miles southeast of Portland. Ski slopes, hiking trails, and climbing routes traverse the glaciers and forests, but on a quick

trip you might want to settle for some more easily accessible, yet memorable Alpine experiences— a stop at Timberline Lodge, hand-hewn in the late 1930s from huge timber and local stone, or a quick hike or icy dip at Trillium Lake, nestled into the forested flanks of the snowy peak.

Of all the thousands of trails that traverse the Oregon wilderness, few are as satisfying as the 26-mile-long path that follows the eddies, rapids, and deep slow-moving channels of one of our country's most scenic rivers, the McKenzie. For sheer spectacle, I recommend the 5-mile loop around Sahalie and Koosah falls; from a ledge high above these forceful, glacier-fed cataracts, the roar is deafening and you'll be gently showered in a fine mist. Head a mile or so upstream, and you'll come to the river's source in Clear Lake, where cold waters preserve a petrified forest submerged for centuries, and jumping trout send ripples across the mirrorlike reflection of the surrounding Cascade peaks.

STEPHEN BREWER divides his time between New York City, Oregon, and Europe. He's written and contributed to many magazines and travel guides, including *Frommer's Venice Day by Day*, *Frommer's Best Day Trips from London*, the *Unofficial Guide to England*, and the *Unofficial Guide to Ireland*.

ABOUT THE AUTHOR

YOUR TRIP

General Information: Contact the **Oregon Tourism Commission** (☎ 800/547-7842; www.traveloregon.com). For more information on the town of **Yachats**, call ☎ 800/929-0477 or log on to www.yachats.org; for the **Malheur National Wildlife Refuge,** call ☎ 541/493-2612 or go to www.fws.gov/malheur; for the McKenzie River, there's the **McKenzie River Ranger Station** at ☎ 541/822-3381. Keep in mind that many roads in Oregon are open only for a few months a year. The Steens Mountain loop road and McKenzie Pass are snowed under until July 4th, and impassable after mid-October. **Best Lodging:** The **Shamrock Lodgettes** accommodate guests in cozy log cabins and motel units, all with fireplaces or wood-burning stoves, at the edge of the sea, from about $79 (105 Hwy. 101S, Yachats; ☎ 800/845-5028; www.shamrocklodgettes.com). The **Frenchglen Hotel,** 60 miles south of Burns in southeastern Oregon, has eight basic, bathroomless, but atmospheric rooms in the main building and five rooms with private bathrooms in a unit in back; from $70 a night (OR 205; ☎ 541/493-2825; www.oregonstateparks.org). **Best Restaurant:** At the **Frenchglen Hotel** (see above), big ranch meals are served family style at communal tables, from about $15 for dinner. The cafe at the very rustic **Clear Lake Resort,** on the lake that forms the headwaters of the McKenzie River, makes a memorable bacon cheeseburger to be enjoyed at a waterside table (Hwy. 126, 4 miles south of Hwy. 20; ☎ 541/967-5030; www.clearlakeresort-oregon.org). A meal for two, with a can of pop or a beer, costs well under $15.

Bandon Beach, Face Rock State Park.
© Marc Muench/Muench Photography Inc.

OSA PENINSULA, COSTA RICA

Exploring the most biologically diverse land on earth

I've lived in Costa Rica for over 15 years. I've traveled the country high and low for both work and pleasure. I know most of its most isolated and interesting nooks and crannies. Yet, after all these years, there are two places I go back to—again and again—whenever I want some "me" time, or when I'm looking to share something special with someone special. At those times I head either to the Osa Peninsula or Arenal Volcano.

National Geographic famously described the Osa Peninsula as "the most biologically diverse place on earth." Most of the peninsula is protected as part of the Corcovado National Park. This is the largest single expanse of lowland tropical rainforest in Central America. What that means, in layman's terms, is big trees, fresh air, and lots of plants and animals. Jaguars and tapirs roam the forests here; four types of monkeys cavort in the trees; scarlet macaws, red-lored parrots, and Harpy eagles fly overhead; and there are big crocodiles in the rivers and lagoons. While I've never seen a live cat here, I have seen their tracks in fresh mud.

There are two main gateways to the Osa Peninsula—Drake Bay and Puerto Jiménez—and each has its charm and advantages. Drake Bay is close to Isla del Caño, where you can see ancient indigenous "stone spheres" and enjoy some of Costa Rica's best snorkeling and scuba diving. Puerto Jiménez provides easy access to the Golfo Dulce, where you can kayak through mangroves, sometimes with dolphins. Both offer you the chance to take guided hikes through Corcovado National Park, where you will be overwhelmed by the primary forest and its exuberant flora and fauna.

Whichever gateway you choose, you'll find a selection of excellent small ecolodges, all with stunning settings, simple yet luxurious accommodations, knowledgeable naturalist guides, and top-notch cuisine. You won't find televisions or even air-conditioning in most. And perhaps the most amazing part of this experience comes when you realize you need neither.

Arenal Volcano is a constantly active volcano that rises in a near perfect cone to 1,607m (5,271 ft.). It is surrounded by lush rain- and cloud forests, several spectacular waterfalls, Costa Rica's largest freshwater lake, and numerous volcanically heated hot springs. When Arenal first erupted in 1968, it wiped out its small namesake village, which was located near the site of the present-day Tabacón Hot Springs Resort. Today, the road leading out of the agricultural town of La Fortuna toward Tabacón is dotted with small hotels all oriented toward the volcano, most of them offering rooms with excellent views of the nightly volcanic show.

I like the fact that when I visit I can choose to go on exhilarating mountain bike rides or white-water rafting trips. I can take hikes to look for wildlife, or enjoy a lazy swim in the cool pool at the base of the La Fortuna Waterfall. On every visit, I'm given the chance to experience the sight, sound, and fury of an active volcano. For me, the cherry on top is always a few good hours spent soaking in one of the natural hot springs here.

◀ *Tabacón Hot Springs Resort, near Arenal Volcano.*
© Ron Niebrugge/Alamy

SPECIAL MOMENTS

1 **Arenal Volcano.** When Arenal really puts on a show, it spews molten lava high out of its crater and glowing boulders the size of small cars cascade down its steep flanks. The ground shakes. The deep rumble of its eruptions is a sound I've never heard anywhere else. Still, it's always the luck of the draw as to whether or not you'll actually see the volcano in action. The cloud and rainforests that surround it create frequent cloud cover and it does go through periods of relative calm. I like to give myself at least 2 nights, and preferably more, to ensure that I get a good nighttime view of the flowing red lava. You can also see the show while soaking in a natural hot spring and having a drink at the swim-up bar at the extensive and luxurious **Tabacón Hot Springs Resort & Spa** (www.tabacon.com). The trails in Arenal National Park take you through forests and over old lava flows, and are gorgeous and fun.

Although it's counterintuitive, the rainy season is often a better time to see the exposed cone of the volcano, especially at night. Seeing the cone, though, is never a sure thing.

2 **Tabacón Hot Springs Resort.** I never tire of the Tabacón Hot Springs. They are the most extensive, luxurious, and stunning of the hot springs found at the foot of Arenal Volcano. An abundance of sculpted pools and small waterfalls, fed by a hot river, are spread around lushly planted gardens. Find a quiet pool at the foot of one of these small waterfalls and get a free massage from the rushing water, or sign up for a spa treatment at the resort's Grand Spa. The pools get progressively hotter as you move closer to the volcano, so you can always find one where the temperature is just right. I usually head for the Pozo del Mono (Monkey's Pool), which is located near a tile pool

filled with cool water, allowing for alternating hot and cold dips.

3 **Corcovado National Park.** I often spend days at a time in Corcovado National Park. In fact, you'll need several days if you want to truly trek its trails and visit its various ranger stations. Still, a day trip out of any of the lodges here is always rewarding. This is dense primary tropical rainforest. Some of the trees tower over 61m (200 ft.) tall. The canopy is so thick that there is little ground cover. While it's bad form to guarantee anything like this, you will almost definitely see monkeys and scarlet macaws in the wild. If you get a good guide, you will see much more, and also be treated to a cooling dip in an isolated jungle pool fed by a clear rainforest creek.

Exploring Corcovado is not something to be undertaken lightly. There are no roads in the park, so once you reach one of the entrances, you'll

have to start hiking. The heat and humidity are often quite extreme, and frequent rainstorms can make the trail muddy. If you choose to hike on the beach, you'll have to plan your walk around the tides, when often there is no beach at all and some rivers are impassable. Pick up a tide table at the park headquarters in Puerto Jiménez.

4 **Isla del Caño.** Isla del Caño is a small island located 19km (12 miles) off the coast of Drake Bay. All of the lodges here offer day trips out to the island, where you'll find some of the best snorkeling and scuba diving in all of Costa Rica. I've seen manta rays here and white-tipped reef sharks. From July through early September, Humpback whales come to the waters off Isla del Caño to give birth, and whale-watching during these months is excellent. On the island, be sure to take the short hike up to a small pre-Columbian indigenous cemetery. After the hike, pick a spot on the beach and enjoy a picnic lunch.

As a teen, **ELIOT GREENSPAN** read *On the Road* and was hooked. After hitchhiking in the Americas and sailing most of the Caribbean, he went on to earn a writing degree from the Jack Kerouac School for Disembodied Poetics. Since then, he has been writing guidebooks for Frommer's.

ABOUT THE AUTHOR

YOUR TRIP

General Information: Click on www.visitcostarica.com, the official site of the **Costa Rican Tourism Institute**. **Getting There:** Arenal Volcano is located 140km (87 miles) northwest of San José. The Osa Peninsula is located 145km (90 miles) south of San José. **Nature Air** (www.natureair.com) flies to Arenal and the Osa Peninsula from San José. **Best Lodging:** At the Arenal Volcano, **Tabacón Hot Springs Resort & Spa,** the most popular place in the area, has the most extensive and luxurious hot springs (☎ 877/277-8291 in the U.S. and Canada or 506/519-1900 in Costa Rica; www.tabacon.com; $175–$290/£93–£154). On the Osa Peninsula, try **Bosque del Cabo** (☎ 506/735-5206; www.bosquedelcabo.com; $220–$330/£117–£175). **Best Lodging Value:** The **Arenal Observatory Lodge** is incredibly close to the volcano (☎ 506/290-7011; www.arenal-observatory.co.cr; $66–$144/£35–£76). On the Osa Peninsula, try **Drake Bay Wilderness Resort** (☎ 561/762-1763 in the U.S. or 506/770-8012 in Costa Rica; www.drakebay.com; $130–$250/£69–£132). **Best Restaurant:** At the Arenal Volcano, **El Novillo** has garnered a reputation as the best steakhouse in the area (☎ 506/460-6433; $5–$9/£3–£5). While on the Osa Peninsula, there's **Jade Luna** (☎ 506/735-5739; www.jadeluna.com; $4–$16/£2–£8). **When to Go:** December through mid-May is the dry season and the best time to visit. You definitely don't want to visit the Osa Peninsula between September and early November, when the rains are hardest. Oddly, though, if you are here during this period, it's a great time to actually see the Arenal Volcano in action, as it often clears up entirely after the afternoon rains.

◀ *Red-eyed tree frog.*

OXFORD, ENGLAND

A visit to one of the world's most venerable universities

There's a curious time-machine quality to the city of Oxford, England, home to one of the world's oldest universities. Its "dreaming spires" (in the words of 19th-c. poet Matthew Arnold) preside over a crenellated stone skyline, but the city below them has modern sass, grit, and energy. Automobiles rev their motors in the streets outside ivy-covered walls; inside those walls a sequestered calm prevails. You'll see an undergraduate toting a laptop in the basket of his battered bicycle, dodging in and out of traffic en route to a medieval library where ancient manuscripts are tended in high-tech, climate-control zones. Centuries-old traditions coexist with McDonald's and motor coaches; students slouch around in jeans and hooded sweatshirts, until the day they throw on a fluttering black gown to receive a diploma in a ceremony conducted in medieval Latin. Oxford's perennial rival, Cambridge University, charms with sweeping pretty vistas, but Cambridge feels to me like a stage set; the place I really imagine myself plunging into academic life is Oxford.

Technically, Oxford consists of some 40 independent colleges, sharing a common curriculum. Each Oxford student belongs to one college with its own discrete walled campus, where he or she lives, dines, and studies. While there are university-wide lectures, the heart of a student's education takes place in small (often one-on-one) tutorials in a professor's in-college living quarters. You can poke around most of these colleges during visiting hours (opening times are posted at gatehouses); the oldest and most famous, of course, are crowded together amid the town's noisy, traffic-clogged downtown. Step through their gates and you enter a timeless calm, whether it be the golden-stoned Magdalen College (pronounced "maudlin"), with its huge surrounding deer park, on High Street; stately neoclassical Queen's College, also on High Street; or prestigious Balliol College (Broad St.), where the sooty gray stone walls have a deliciously Dickensian gloom. If you don't recognize the vast front quadrangle of Christ Church College (St. Aldate's) from *Brideshead Revisited,* you'll recognize it from the Harry Potter movies, or at least you'll recognize the marvelous Gothic stone staircase leading up to its raftered dining hall. Hertford College (Catte St.) has a Venetian-style Bridge of Sighs arching over Queen's Lane, and the nearby dome of the Radcliffe Camera—centerpiece of the Bodleian Library—recalls the Duomo in Florence. Browse the rambling Blackwell's Bookshop on Broad Street (what would a university town be without its world-class bookstore?), and then stroll up St. Giles to visit the Eagle and Child pub (49 St. Giles), storied hangout of Oxford dons C. S. Lewis and J. R. R. Tolkien.

◀ *Radcliffe Camera, the reading room of the Bodleian Library.*
© Jon Arnold/DanitaDelimont.com

SPECIAL MOMENTS

1 Christ Church meadows.
Venerable Christ Church College
was founded in the days of Henry
VIII, but I like to imagine it in the
19th century, the era of mathematics
don Charles Dodgson—whose children's stories (invented to amuse the
dean's daughters) were eventually
published as *Alice in Wonderland*.
Wandering in the dreamy peace of
the Christ Church meadows, along
the Isis River (which downstream
becomes the Thames), you can just
picture Dodgson's favorite, Alice
Liddell, snoozing beneath the trees
on the riverbank with a kitten in her
lap, dreaming of white rabbits, playing cards, and a hookah-smoking
caterpillar.

Christ Church was begun in 1525
by Cardinal Wolsey as Cardinal
College. It has the largest quadrangle of any college in Oxford. Tom
Tower houses the famous 18,000-
pound bell, Great Tom, that rings at
9:05pm nightly. It peals 101 times—
once for each of the students in
residence at the time the college
was founded. Tradition dies hard in
Oxford! For hours, contact **www.
chch.ox.ac.uk**.

2 A pint at the Turf. Heading
east on Holywell Street, along a dour
stretch of the original city walls, you
duck into tiny St. Helen's Passage on
your right to follow a twisting series
of narrow passages to the Turf, a
cozy inn that has been sustaining students for centuries with real draft
ales and savory pub grub. Ensconce
yourself in a snug paneled nook or
outdoors on a stone-flagged patio.
Nestled between the back walls of
Queen's College and New College
(which, with splendid Oxford illogic,
is in fact one of the oldest colleges in
Oxford), it's definitely off the tour-bus
path, though every student and don
knows about it. The novelist Thomas
Hardy used Turf Tavern as the setting
for *Jude the Obscure*. Bill Clinton
hung out here during his college
days at Oxford. For wintertime
warmth, braziers are lighted in the
courtyard and the gardens.

**3 Punting on the Cherwell
River.** When you go punting on
Cambridge's Cam River, you pole a
flat-bottomed boat past the back
lawns of colleges where onlookers
can critique your punting style;
when you punt on the Cherwell at
Oxford, you dawdle down willow-
lined stretches of river with very few
spectators—so few, in fact, that
Oxonians may detour into hidden
inlets for a little skinny-dipping.
Tendrils trail over your boat (warn
whomever is standing in the prow
with the pole—many a puntsman
has been knocked into the river by
a low-hanging limb), and ancient
clumps of tree roots jut out from the
banks; on a lazy spring day, gliding
along the glassy Cherwell while
dragonflies buzz and birds whistle is
just about heaven on earth. You can
rent punts at Magdalen Bridge, but
I prefer to go to north Oxford and

tramp across the University Parks to the **Cherwell Boathouse** (Bardwell Rd.; ☎ 44-1865/515978)—adding a lovely meal before or after in the Boathouse's surprisingly upmarket restaurant (☎ 44-1865/552746).

4 **The cloisters at St. John's.** My candidate for the most beautiful quadrangle in Oxford would be the cloisters at the heart of St. John's. The perfect green lawn in the center is the sort of surface gardeners can only dream of achieving—a velvety smooth greensward patiently tended for half a millennium. The stone flagged pavements in the Gothic-arched arcade have been hollowed by millions of students' footsteps over the centuries; you'd almost swear the ghosts of early monks still haunt the place. The murmurous silence on a summer afternoon is so contemplative, I swear I feel smarter just walking there. It's strange to find this ivory-tower isolation just steps from the traffic scrum of St. Aldate's—but then that's the Oxford paradox.

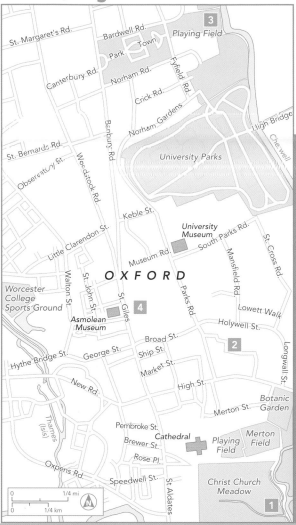

ABOUT THE AUTHOR

HOLLY HUGHES has traveled the globe as an editor and writer—she's the former executive editor of Fodor's travel publications and author of *Frommer's New York City with Kids* and *Frommer's 500 Places to Take Your Kids before They Grow Up*. She also edits the annual *Best Food Writing* anthology. New York City makes a convenient jumping-off place for her travels.

YOUR TRIP

General Information: Contact the **Tourist Information Centre** at www.visitoxford.org (15–16 Broad St., ☎ 44-1865/726871). The main business of the university is, of course, to educate. So visiting is restricted to certain hours and small groups of six or fewer. The tourist office will be happy to advise you when and where you may take in the sights. **Getting There:** Trains from Paddington Station, London, reach Oxford in 1½ hours. Five trains run every hour. Check out www.networkrail.co.uk for more information. **Best Lodging:** The **Old Parsonage Hotel** offers luxury digs in a renovated 13th-century hospital with a garden (1 Banbury Rd.; ☎ 44-1865/310210; www.oldparsonage-hotel.co.uk; £121–£223/$228–$420). **Best Lodging Value: Galaxie Private Hotel** is a tidy hotel in a converted mansion in residential North Oxford (180 Banbury Rd.; ☎ 44-1865/515688; www.galaxie.co.uk; £55–£126/$104–$238). **Best Restaurant: Le Manoir aux Quat' Saisons,** in a tiny village 19km (12 miles) southeast of town, offers superb French cuisine by Raymond Blanc (Great Milton; ☎ 44-1844/278881; £28–£32/$50–$58). **Best Restaurant Value: Brown's** is a perennially popular brasserie (5–11 Woodstock Rd.; ☎ 44-1865/511995; £8–£16/$16–$30). **The Nosebag** suits student budgets with homemade sandwiches, soups, and hotpots to eat in or take away (6–9 St. Michael's St.; ☎ 44-1865/721033; £4–£8/$7.50–$15). **When to Go:** Oxford is glorious in the summertime, but if you visit early July through early September you won't see many bona fide students (just lots of American teenagers on summer programs). Winter can be chilly and gloomy, though I like that. May is peak visiting time.

◀ *Oxford rowing crews at dawn.*
© Tony Page/Getty Images

PARIS, FRANCE

The City of Light, where living is a form of art

"We'll always have Paris," Rick and Ilse wistfully agree in *Casablanca,* and it's true. We each have our own private vision of Paris, tinged with whatever idiosyncratic romance we decide to bring to it. The challenge is not just having a glorious Parisian vacation, it's choosing *which* glorious Parisian vacation to indulge in. Maybe you want to marvel over the trove of fine art in the Louvre, or take a day trip to the exquisite royal palaces at Versailles or Fontainebleau. Perhaps you dream of loading yourself down with designer shopping bags on the rue du Faubourg St-Honoré, or picking through flea-market finds out at the Marché aux Puces de Clignancourt. You may want to treat yourself to a three-star dinner or dawdle at one of the storied cafes on the boulevard St-Germain. Me? I'm happy just to be in Paris, with no set schedule, a camera, and a good pair of walking shoes.

To me the mark of a great city is how rich its street life is, and in Paris it sometimes seems that every citizen is auditioning to be an extra in a Truffaut movie—from the chic *jeune fille* demonstrating a Frenchwoman's flair for fashion, to the middle-aged matron toting a string bag full of baguettes and cheeses, to the mustachioed workingman sucking intently on a Gauloise. Your senses are awakened by the press of cobblestones underfoot, the glitter of sunlight on the Seine as it snakes under bridges, the echo of your voice off centuries-old stone, the cacophony of traffic shifting gears as cars roar down its great avenues, even the heady mix of perfume, diesel exhaust, and cigarette smoke that hangs in the air. And the tastes of Paris—where else does butter taste so rich, pastries so flaky, meat so falling-off-the-bone savory, wine so full-bodied and intoxicating?

Should you spend your time on the Right or the Left Bank? Which of the city's 20 *arrondissements* suits your own sense of style? It almost doesn't matter; as a visitor you're free to cross the bridges arching over the Seine and wander at will, or descend into the sprawl of the Paris Metro system (some of those Art Nouveau station entrances are works of art in themselves). Don't be content just to gape at the stained glass, gargoyles, and flying buttresses of the great Cathédrale de Notre-Dame—cross the bridge behind the cathedral to the neighboring Île St-Louis, a surprisingly quiet residential area where you can wander on ancient streets unshadowed by office towers. The iconic landmarks—the Eiffel Tower's elegant upward swoosh of fretwork steel, the marble pomposity of the Arc de Triomphe—are better seen from afar. Take time to plant yourself on a bench in any of Paris's great public gardens—the Tuileries, the Jardins Luxembourg, the Jardin des Plantes—and indulge in Gallic people-watching. Don't just cruise the Seine on a touristy *bateaux-mouches* sightseeing boat—stroll along an embankment and make yourself part of the Paris scenery that the other visitors only gape at.

◀ *The Eiffel Tower.*
© John Lawrence/
Getty Images

SPECIAL MOMENTS

1 **Musée Picasso.** Paris just may be the world's great museum city, and I'll always include three or four art museums on my itinerary. But my number-one favorite is the **Musée Picasso** (5 rue de Thorigny), a sizeable town house devoted to one of the world's most complete collections spanning the Spanish painter's long and varied career—from cubism through the Blue Period into surrealism, including paintings, sculptures, collages, sketches, everything. These works, displayed in a house setting, offer not only a slice of art history but a chance to imagine the expatriate life of Picasso and his Lost Generation cronies like Ernest Hemingway, F. Scott Fitzgerald, and Gertrude Stein. Afterwards, take time to ramble around the labyrinthine medieval streets of the surrounding Marais quarter, looking for trendy boutiques and atmospheric bistros tucked away in crumbling stone buildings.

2 **Musée de Cluny.** You almost feel you're time-traveling when you visit the Musée de Cluny—an extravagant Gothic manor house built in the 15th century, when the nearby Sorbonne university was already a couple of centuries old. The gem of the collection is the beautiful and mysterious Unicorn Tapestries, a set of six medieval tapestries so richly decorated you can stand before them for half an hour each, studying the intertwined background pattern and puzzling over the elusive parables of the main tableau. Wander through the museum's jewel of a garden, with its plantings inspired by the tapestry's designs, and you can almost imagine yourself dwelling in the Middle Ages for a moment. Stepping back outside into the student scruffiness of the Latin Quarter will kick you back into the 20th century fast—the sort of mind-altering sensation that makes foreign travel worth every penny.

3 **Sacré-Coeur.** I take pride in walking the steps up the precipitous Montmartre hillside leading to the Basilique du Sacré-Coeur, though there is a funicular option for those who are less masochistic. Halfway up I often regret my decision—but when I get to the top, I feel more than rewarded. The real thrill up here is not the white Byzantine-style folly of the domed 19th-century basilica, lovely as that is—it's standing on the parapets gazing out as Paris unfolds beneath you like the world's greatest pop-up book. On a clear day you can easily pick out all the monuments. I like this view even better than the vertiginous one from the Eiffel Tower . . . and there's no line. Give your calves a rest while you sit under the dome, admiring its glittering mosaics, then pick up and wander around this pre–World War I art colony, the inspiration for Puccini's *La Bohème*. You won't find many artists living in its garrets nowadays, but get away from the souvenir stands and you'll find narrow streets with a clutter of historic architecture, a perfect stage set for your American in Paris fantasies.

4 Père-Lachaise cemetery.
Ghoulish as it may sound, one of my favorite Parisian neighborhoods to wander around is the eternal resting place of the dead in Père-Lachaise cemetery. Whether you're looking for Jim Morrison or Oscar Wilde or Marcel Proust, this vast rambling cemetery (it covers 44 hectares/110 acres) has a sort of crazy aura about it that I find enchanting. Buy a map at the newsstand across from the main entrance and wander around. You'll find Gertrude Stein and Alice B. Toklas, sharing a gravestone; Isadora Duncan tucked into a slot in the Columbarium; Chopin, Edith Piaf, Sarah Bernhardt, even the playwright Molière and the 12th-century lovers Abélard and Héloïse. For me, at least half the experience is the florid ornamentation of the 19th-century monuments, the straggling foliage, the decaying flowers laid on tombs—somehow to me it's a perfect expression of the glorious, glamorous, *outré* spirit of Paris.

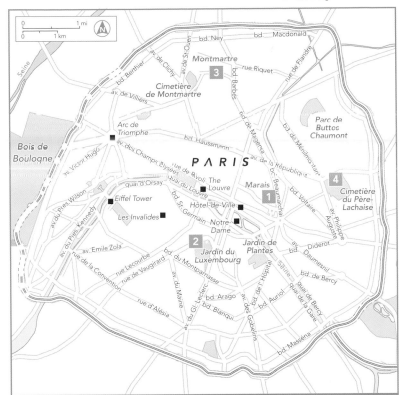

HOLLY HUGHES has traveled the globe as an editor and writer—she's the former executive editor of Fodor's Travel Publications and author of *Frommer's New York City with Kids* and *Frommer's 500 Places to Take Your Kids before They Grow Up*. She also edits the annual *Best Food Writing* anthology. New York City makes a convenient jumping-off place for her travels.

ABOUT THE AUTHOR

YOUR TRIP

General Information: The headquarters of the **Paris Convention and Visitors Bureau** is located at 25–27 rue des Pyramides, 1st arr. (☎ 33-8/92-68-30-00; www.parisinfo.com). **Getting There:** Paris has two international airports: **Charles De Gaulle** to the northeast, and **Orly** to the south. Six train stations are terminals for trains from all over Europe. **Best Lodging:** On the Right Bank, the **George V** is one of the world's great luxury hotels (31 av. George-V; ☎ 33-1/49-52-70-00; www.fourseasons.com/Paris; 712€–2,695€/$925–$3,500). On the Left Bank, **L'Hôtel** has boutique-hotel elegance (13 rue des Beaux Arts; ☎ 33-1/44-41-99-00; www.l-hotel.com; 258€–748€/$335–$972). **Best Lodging Value:** Near the Eiffel Tower, **Grand Hotel Lévêque** is on a charming pedestrian market street (29 rue Cler; ☎ 33-1/47-05-49-15; www.hotel-leveque.com; 62€–131€/$80–$170). **Best Restaurant: Laurent** wins haute cuisine accolades without feeling like a dinosaur (41 av. Gabriel; ☎ 33-1/42-25-00-39; www.le-laurent.com; 115€–212€/$150–$275). **L'Arpège** showcases the culinary genius of Alain Passard, working wonders with fresh-from-the-garden vegetables (84 rue de Varenne; ☎ 33-1/47-05-09-06; 48€–180€/$58–$216). **Best Restaurant Value:** On the Île St-Louis, **Au Gourmet de l'Île** serves French comfort food (42 rue St-Louis-en-l'Île; ☎ 33-1/43-26-79-27; 15€–31€/$20–$40). **When to Go:** Spring, when the chestnut trees blossom and the first flowers appear in the parks. Summer can be hot; Parisians vacate the city in August. I like autumn and winter best, though—Paris looks brooding and romantic under overcast skies, like a moody Atget photograph come to life.

◄ *A Paris wine and dessert shop.*
© John Lawrence/Getty Images

PETRA, JORDAN

An ancient city carved from the walls of a desert canyon

Petra is the stuff that dreams are made of. An ancient city with monumental palaces and temples carved from the walls of a secret desert canyon, accessible only through the Siq, a winding, hidden passageway, it was abandoned and lost to the world for almost 1,000 years, visited only by a handful of passing Bedouin over the centuries, while it slowly became a half-forgotten myth.

Located in the wild mountains of modern-day southern Jordan, Petra was the capital of the Nabatean Empire, which sat atop the arduous desert caravan routes between Africa, the Arabian peninsula, and the civilizations of the Mediterranean and Mesopotamia. Across Nabatean territory passed spices, gold, silk, jewels, ivory, and slaves from as far away as Yemen and East Africa. Although originally a desert people from northern Arabia, by the 3rd century B.C. the Nabateans had developed cosmopolitan tastes and over the centuries they incorporated Hellenistic and Roman design into their architecture and style of life. The fabulous facades carved into the rose sandstone cliffs of Petra are exotically Hellenistic rather than classical Greek or even Roman, and reflect the mixture of Western and Eastern, Semitic and European influences in which Nabatean civilization developed.

The Nabateans were also wizards at controlling water. At Petra and nearby, they built dams and irrigation systems to capture the flash floods and walls of water that came roaring down the canyons with the winter rains. When I walk among the dry-as-dust ruins of Petra today, I imagine the magical flowing waters, fountains, and lush gardens that once delighted travelers who were admitted to Petra's secret precincts.

As Petra was absorbed into the Roman Empire, the city's gods took on Roman attributes; in early Christian times basilicas were built. Earthquakes, floods, and the collapse of empires and trade routes after the 7th century A.D. left Petra nearly abandoned. It was briefly fortified by the crusaders, who helped keep memory of the place alive among European legends, but Petra was lost and forgotten after the crusaders were defeated, and not seen again by a Westerner until 1812, when a Swiss explorer, disguised as a Muslim trader, managed to bribe a Bedouin to take him to the uninhabited secret canyon. Only in the 1960s did a trickle of adventurous travelers begin to visit the place.

Today, Petra is a carefully maintained National Park. Dozens of hotels, some luxurious, but mostly moderate or budget, have sprung up at a distance from the Siq, that long, mysterious passageway that separates Petra from the outside world. Tourist buses arrive at Petra filled with day-trippers from Amman or from Eilat, in Israel. But Petra, "the rose-red city half again as old as time," requires time. Time to watch the carved canyon walls turn from deep red in the early morning to rose, then peach, and then bleached yellow at noon, only to reverse this slow, subtle progression of hues until twilight. At Petra you need time to explore and imagine amid the ruins, to hike to the city's sacred high places, and to enjoy the awesome natural beauty of the wild countryside that surrounds it.

◀ *Ed Deir, the largest rock-cut monument at Petra.*
© SIME s.a.s/eStock Photo

SPECIAL MOMENTS

1 **The Siq.** The three-quarter-mile journey through this towering, highly sculptural passageway is a wondrous introduction to the Petra experience: I find it prepares me spiritually for entering the lost world of Petra. You follow a fissure through the rocks created by an earthquake and shaped and widened by eons of floods as it rhythmically narrows and widens. Along the way are niches in the walls of the Siq that once held images of gods that protected the city and intimidated foreign visitors as they made their way into Petra. Suddenly, the hypnotic Siq ends in a glimpse of the "Treasury," perhaps the most exquisite of Petra's facades, and a foretaste of what awaits inside the canyon. This moment is enormous: You find yourself confronting the immensity of time, of beauty, of the melancholy loneliness of this breathtaking monument from the past. Another moment—at the end of a day in Petra, as you depart through the Siq in twilight, listen for the sound of a single owl, believed by the people of Petra to be the guardian of their city. It's always there.

2 **Inside Petra.** Maps and self-guided tours are available in the hotel zone near the entrance to Petra, but also consider hiring a Bedouin guide through the Visitor's Center. The Bedouin have camped in Petra for centuries and know its many secrets. After two generations of tourism, they've also learned English, as well as the scholarly history of the site, and are excellent, lively guides who have an intuitive feel for the place. I especially enjoy the children—even when they hawk

▶ *Al Khazneh, "the Treasury."*
© Sergio Pitamitz/Corbis

souvenirs. Once, a teenage Bedouin girl who spoke perfect English led us up to the beautiful facade of "the Monastery," overlooking Petra, and chanted into the late afternoon stillness so that the entire canyon echoed. "What does the chant mean?" we asked. "Nothing in words," she replied. "Just—it's beautiful."

3 **The Petra region.** Whether you approach Petra via Amman in the north or from Eilat in the south, you'll pass spectacular scenery and places to explore. Wadi Rum, south of Petra, is the most magnificent desertscape on earth. Desert walks, treks, and overnights in Bedouin tents can be arranged from Petra, complete with traditional music, food, and trillions of stars. A bit farther south, you can snorkel among the world-famous Red Sea coral reefs at Aquaba. Two hours' drive north of Petra, amidst rugged

Petra, Jordan

mountains, is the vast Dana Nature Reserve, administered by Jordan's Royal Society for the Conservation of Nature. Treks, both self-guided and escorted, can be arranged through these awesome, pristine mountains inhabited by the tribal Dana people. Overnight in simple Royal Society cabins or tents. Finally, farther north is the Jordanian side of the Dead Sea, with four beautiful low-rise spa hotels where you can luxuriate in endless Dead Sea health, massage, and beauty treatments, and experience super-buoyancy in the Dead Sea's dense, mineral-saturated waters. Unique and unearthly!

4 **Petra by candlelight.** Petra closes at sunset, but many nights you can return for a special candle-light tour, offered by the park authorities. Petra and moonlight are an unforgettable combination.

ABOUT THE AUTHOR

ROBERT ULLIAN is the author of *Frommer's Israel* and *Frommer's Venice Walks*. He has also written guidebooks on Bali and Morocco. His work has appeared in such publications as *Esquire* and *Mademoiselle*. He is the recipient of a Grant for Fiction from the National Endowment for the Arts. Contact him at aramullian@yahoo.com.

YOUR TRIP

General Information: Contact the **Jordan Tourist Board** for excellent maps and brochures (☎ 877/733-5673; www.visitjordan.com). At the **Petra Visitor's Center** you can get maps and guidebooks, and hire guides (☎ 962-3/215-6020). A recommended guide for Petra and Wadi Rum is Mr. Naiym Al-Nawafleh (naiym@cyberia.jo). **Getting There:** You can take a taxi to Petra from the Eilat/Aqaba border crossing between Israel and Jordan ($60/£32), or from Amman ($75/£40). Buses and shared taxis are also available for under $10 (£5). **What to See & Do:** The journey through the **Siq** can be one of the most memorable parts of the Petra experience (especially in the soft twilight as you leave Petra for the night). The **High Place of Sacrifice** is one of the most popular destinations for hikers, taking you to the great altars carved from rock far above the city. The panorama of Petra is dazzling. **Best Lodging:** Located right at the entrance to the Siq, the **Mövenpick Resort Petra,** with its atmospheric Arabesque interior, swimming pool, and seven restaurants, is the best in town (☎ 800/344-6835 in the U.S. or 962-3/215-7111; www.moevenpickhotels.com; $120–$200/£61–£101). The **Taybet Zeman Hotel and Resort** is a beautifully designed resort, created from the houses and lanes of an abandoned Bedouin village, just outside Petra (Wadi Musa; ☎ 962-3/215-0111; $100–$200/£51–£101). **Best Lodging Value:** The **Petra Guest House and Hotel** stands out for its location next to the Siq. It has clean and simple rooms and a restaurant built into an ancient Nabatean tomb (☎ 962-3/215-6246; $85/£43). **When to Go:** With the region's moderate climate, you can visit Petra year-round.

PORTOFINO, ITALY

The most glamorous village
on the Italian Riviera

Bogart and Bacall, Burton and Taylor, Bergman and Rossellini. A half-century ago the world's most glamorous couples put this tiny fishing village on the map, and it is still imbued with the chic nostalgia of *la dolce vita*. Declared a protected park in 1935, Portofino has changed little since Grace Kelly and her prince strolled along its cobblestone lanes—heads craned to admire the narrow, pastel-colored houses, with the dark green hump of Mount Portofino as a backdrop—and bumped into Perry Como at the harborside piazzetta. The only difference perhaps is that the once-humble abodes of fisher-folk are now home to Pucci and Hermès, Cartier and Louis Vuitton.

Still a favored haunt of Hollywood (if you thought that was Steven Spielberg and Denzel Washington at the table next to you last month, you were probably right), the most beautiful village on the Italian Riviera is no well-kept secret, and in high season its tiny cobblestone lanes can get choked with day-trippers. Deal with it as the locals do (if one can call the Milanese and Florentine glitterati who own weekend holiday homes here that): Pick up a couple of focaccias from Canale and clamber into a *gozzo*, the traditional Riviera fishing dinghy, and anchor off the coast in some picture-perfect cove. The next day, head out on one of the ferries that ply the coast to the Cinque Terre, and hike the trail that connects the five virtually intact medieval villages. Or explore the paths that crisscross the jutting Portofino promontory and amble over to Paraggi Beach, or to the delightful fishing village of Camogli, stopping in at San Fruttuoso, the 11th-century Benedictine abbey built above a crescent of sand, where you can swim out to view *Il Cristo degli Abissi*—the deeply moving bronze statue of Christ submerged in the bay. The tiny village of Camogli is remarkably unpretentious, given its glamorous neighbor. With a curving pedestrian promenade that follows a pebble beach lined with simple 18th-century houses, all decorated with restrained *trompe l'oeil* detailing and green shutters, Camogli is a relatively undiscovered gem, where tiny restaurants serve up what the fishing boats delivered a few hours ago.

Wherever you choose to spend your days, at about 6pm, when most day-trippers have left Portofino and the yachties are back onboard, getting ready to primp at Da Puny Ristorante or Frederica's (as U Mariu is known to the in-crowd), it's time to return home—with a generous budget, this is a suite at Portofino's aptly named Splendido, where you are king of all you survey, and treated accordingly. When the pianist starts up, take a cocktail on the terrace (mixed by barman Antonio Beccalli, who has been serving up the same to a long and illustrious guest list for more than 3 decades), then descend into the harbor to indulge in the ultimate Portofino pastime: a spot of people-watching over a steaming plate of fresh seafood.

◀ *Alfresco dining in Portofino.*
© Gary Yeowell/
Getty Images

SPECIAL MOMENTS

1   **Seaside dining: Trattoria dö Spadin.** There's nothing like having to catch a boat to get to your table, and this is the only way to get to Trattoria dö Spadin, a tiny, lone restaurant that clings to the rocks between Camogli and San Fruttuoso. It's a gorgeously unpretentious place, with tables wedged between the crashing ocean and a kitchen that wouldn't look out of place on the pages of a *cucina povera* Riviera cookbook. Order the simple seafood pasta, wash it down with a bottle of Il Monticello, then wade into the water and float around while you wait for your boat to come back in.

2   **People-watching: Portofino's Piazzetta.** If you like people-watching, Portofino's harborside piazzetta is nothing less than a human zoo. Seated at a table a few hours before the evening *passaggiata* starts up, you can bet on who will be getting back on the bus and who will be boarding the luxury boats. Through the Pucci window you may see a middle-aged woman strutting in a cat suit that wouldn't look out of place in a '70s Bond movie. While the shriveled man on the couch is clearly the Money, who is the well-dressed, good-looking young man? The son? The lover? Then she dismissively hands over the Pucci bags and you realize it's the butler. "Fifteen-love," your betting partner may smirk, but the night has only just begun.

3   **Taking pity on a statue: *Christ of the Abyss.*** Tucked away in a cove between Portofino and Camogli, San Fruttuoso's greatest treasure lies immersed 17m (56 ft.) below the surface of the water. *Il Cristo degli Abissi* is a strangely moving statue: Weighted down by a large concrete plinth, the figure of Christ stares up at a heaven he cannot see, his open arms raised up, eyes ever-imploring, while fish slowly circle, indifferent to his plight. The waters here are so translucent you can see the statue from a boat (there are plenty of water taxis in the bay), but to get a real idea of its beauty you need to dive down with goggles.

4   **The perfect day trip: Exploring the Cinque Terre Park.** The boat turns the Punta Mesco headland, and the most dramatic sight unfurls: the folded coastline of the Cinque Terre, its five tiny

medieval fishing villages dwarfed by towering cliffs, their terraced vineyards tumbling down like hooped petticoats—a unique architectural landscape that earned it UNESCO protection in 1997. With the exception of Monterosso, the villages are virtually untouched, and each has a distinct character developed during centuries of isolation, when the chief access was via mule path—still the best way to explore the Park. Having caught the first ferry to Riomaggiore, take the coastal path west via the villages of Manarola and Corniglia to Vernazza—a comfortable 3- to 4-hour walk. The only village with a safe harbor, Vernazza is historically the region's wealthiest, and still the prettiest. Reward yourself with a leisurely lunch on its dinky harbor square, then complete the last stretch to Monterosso and toast the setting sun with the Cinque Terre's own "gold," Sciacchetrà dessert wine, before catching the last ferry back to Portofino.

ABOUT THE AUTHOR

PIPPA DE BRUYN is an award-winning journalist and seasoned travel writer based in Cape Town. She is the author of *Frommer's South Africa*, coauthor of *Frommer's India*, and a contributor to *Pauline Frommer's Italy* and *Frommer's Eastern Europe*. Her first novel is due for publication in 2008.

YOUR TRIP

General Information: Contact **APT Tigullio Tourist Board** for information on Portofino (☎ 39-185/269024; www.apttigullio.liguria.it); for the Cinque Terre, visit their website: www.cinqueterre.com. **Getting Around:** The best way to get around is by ferry. Those originating from the Golfo Paradiso side offer the best value (☎ 39-185/772091; www.golfoparadiso.it); you can also hire your own boat for the day (☎ 39-185/269327; 250€/$318). **Best Lodging: Hotel Splendido,** reached by a steep and winding road from the port, provides a luxurious base from which to explore (Salita Baratta; ☎ 39-185/267801; www.hotelsplendido.com; 840€/$1,113). In the Cinque Terre, the **Luna Di Marzo,** a small hotel in Volastra, provides serene atmosphere, with jaw-dropping views—book room no. 8 (Via Montello 387c; ☎ 39-187/920530; www.albergo lunadimarzo.com; 100€/$132). **Best Lodging Value:** The cheapest bed in Portofino is at charming **Hotel Eden** (Via Dritto 18; ☎ 39-185/269091; www.hoteledenportofino.com; 140€/$180). In the Cinque Terre, try the classy simplicity of **Albergo Barbara** in Vernazza (Piazza Marconi 30; ☎ 39-187/812398; www.albergobarbara.it; 60€/$72). **Best Restaurant:** Feast on sophisticated Ligurian fare at **La Terrazza,** in the Hotel Splendido (see above; 279€/$370). **Best Restaurant Value:** At **El Portico,** dine on divine pizzas while eyeballing the clientele (Via Roma 21; ☎ 39-185-269239; 7€/$9). **When to Go:** Late May to early June; hikers arrive *en masse* in September. Whatever month you choose, try to book during the week, as crowds can become unbearable over weekends.

◀ *The town of Manarola, Cinque Terre.*
© Dennis Flaherty/Getty Images

PROVENCE, FRANCE

Olive groves & wild lavender in a soft, magical light

Gertrude Stein, who once took her lover, Alice B. Toklas, in a battered car to Provence, returned to Paris and told a young writer, Ernest Hemingway, to "go to Provence before the old way of life disappears forever." Good advice even today. Like a fast-fading tableau, scenes witnessed by Stein and Toklas are still there. Weathered old men sit on village squares shaded by plane trees. Here they play *boules* and drink *pastis*, eating a lunch of freshly baked bread and black olives. But they are a dying breed.

It's easy for the average traveler to come under the spell of Provence, the southeastern region of France, bordering Italy, with which in some instances it shares a greater identity than it does with Mother France. Its fields are filled not just with vineyards, but silver-leaved and gnarled olive trees, umbrella pines and sunflowers, fragrant meadows of wild lavender, almond groves of pink and white blossoms, and a perfumed, herb-filled air.

"We know what Matisse, Renoir, and the Fauves saw in our voluptuous Mediterranean landscape," a newspaper reporter in Toulon once told me. "But what about you? What do you find the most evocative in our country?"

"Those cypress trees," I said. "They move as if they're alive and in a lyrical dance, with a passionate intensity equaled only by lovers."

When Pope Gregory XI returned from "exile" in Avignon, bringing the papacy back to Rome in 1377, he looked around the Vatican and promptly announced his wish to return to the sensual delights of Provence. But before he could pack his bags, he dropped dead, and the popes have been living in Rome ever since.

It's easy to be like the Pope and love the wonderful things of Provence. But what separates the true native of Provence from the visiting devotee is an appreciation of the dreaded Mistral, the notorious wind that originates in the deserts of Africa and blows northward across the Mediterranean. Lasting from September to March, the Mistral is called "the scourge of Provence." Yet poets, writers, and painters have found inspiration in these winds. "You cannot love Provence until you love the Mistral," or so it is said.

Have I painted too glorious a picture of Eden? Perhaps. Here's the downside. Much of Provence is overbuilt, certainly the coastline with its dull holiday flats. The most popular resorts are high priced, densely trafficked, and touristy. The days are long gone when sex kitten Brigitte Bardot, from her seat in a harborfront cafe, ripped off her bra and shouted, "Let's wake up sleepy St-Trop!" Today, the port and its neighboring beaches are fully awake and suffering from overpopularity.

The good news is that the Provence of old, with its friendly faces, still exists. You just have to escape the most frequented spots and head for the vast, wild, hilly—and, yes, beautiful—hinterlands.

If you, like most visitors, have only 4 or 5 days for Provence, you have to make some tough decisions. After years of traveling through Provence, I drew up the following list in order of interest: (1) Avignon, (2) Arles, (3) Aix-en-Provence, (4) Nîmes, and (5) St-Rémy de Provence.

◀ *Sunflowers, Vaucluse.*
© David Noton/
Getty Images

SPECIAL MOMENTS

1 At table in Provence. The outspoken Katharine Hepburn once said, "The only reason to come to the Riviera is to taste the bouillabaisse." All savvy Provençal cooks know its secret ingredient is *rascasse* (hogfish), the ugliest creature in the world with its large, spiny head. A prick from the spikes on its dorsal fins is poisonous, but how good it is when dropped into a simmering pot of bouillabaisse. There's more: A day without aioli (garlic mayonnaise) is a day in hell. The most classic Provençal dish is *ratatouille*, the Mediterranean vegetable stew of zucchini, onions, fresh tomatoes, bell peppers, and the mandatory eggplant simmered for hours with fresh herbs in virgin olive oil.

2 The festivals. In summer, even in tiny villages, I have heard top international artists perform—ballet dancers, actors in stage plays, opera singers from Italy, and classical musicians.

The biggest, wildest, and craziest binge takes place during the Mother of all French festivals, the monthlong Festival d'Avignon in July. Actors replicating the comedies of Molière compete with Gregorian chanters, and Moroccan dancers from the Sahara appear on the stage with French rockers, all Johnny Halliday wannabes.

Another ultraclassy event is the Festival d'Aix-en-Provence, a series of operas and orchestral concerts that lasts from June to July. But it's a bit drowned out when the Zik Zac Festival, also in July, fills the night air with the sound of a ragtag group of hip-hop, rap, and reggae artists.

Beginning with the Solstice and the lighting of the Midsummer Night's fire, the weeklong Fête d'Arles celebrates gypsy and world music. Today's young Sartres flock to Arles to warm the bottoms of wicker cafe chairs while eating *saucisses d'Arles* (France's finest donkey-meat sausage) before heading out to listen to the rhythms of the Gypsy Kings or to attend a bullfight.

3 Les Baux. Visit the town of Les Baux, 80km (50 miles) north of Marseille, even if you have to skip the other villages of Provence and the Riviera.

Begin your journey along rue du Château, climbing up to the top of the Mistral-swept plateau to discover the ruins of La Cité Morte (the Dead City). I always pack a picnic to enjoy on the grounds of the old fortress, looking out onto the Val d'Enfer (Valley of Hell).

A final surprise. Les Baux is host to the grandest cuisine in Provence, which is found at such places as **Le Cabro d'Or** (☎ 33-4/90-54-33-21) and at a Relais & Châteaux, **Oustaù de Baumanière** (☎ 33-4/90-54-33-07), both rendezvous points for the savvy of the glitterati.

4 Footsteps of the painters. From Saint-Tropez in the west to Menton in the east, Provençal museums contain some of the world's greatest collections of modern art.

Paul Cézanne was drawn to the dazzling light of Aix-en-Provence in his landscape paintings. Vincent van Gogh was also attracted to the

blinding light of Provence, using it for a creative explosion that burst forth in his canvases of the mellow old streets, ancient squares, and blooming fields around Arles. For an evocative experience, walk down L'Allée des Sarcophages in a cemetery where the path is shaded by tall poplar trees and lined with tombs.

There's more: It's on to Antibes to see one of the world's greatest Picasso collections (he lived here in 1946), detouring to Biot to view the buxom nudes and the crankshafts of Fernand Léger, a treasure trove of art from 1905 until his death in 1955. Overlooking Nice at St-Paul-de-Vence stands the Fondation Maeght, one of the great modern art museums of Europe. Nearby at Vence's Chapelle du Rosaire, the great Henri Matisse, at the age of 77, decorated the chapel after "a life dedicated to the search for the truth." You can even visit Les Collettes, at Haut-de-Cagnes, where Renoir lived and worked from 1908 until his death in 1919.

ABOUT THE AUTHOR

DARWIN PORTER is one of the world's most prolific travel writers. His books for Frommer's include guides to the Caribbean, Italy, France, Germany, and England. A Hollywood columnist and a celebrity biographer, Porter is also a radio broadcaster; his shows on American popular culture are heard in all 50 states.

YOUR TRIP

General Information: All towns and cities in Provence and along the Riviera have a tourist office. In Avignon, you can get information at the **Office de Tourisme** at 41 cours Jean-Jaurès (☎ 33-4/32-74-32-74; www.ot-avignon.fr). More information on the festivals can be found at www.franceguide.com. **Getting There:** The fastest and easiest way to get here is to fly from Paris's Orly Airport to the **Aéroport Avignon-Caumont,** 8km (5 miles) southeast of Avignon. The trip takes 1 hour. Most tours of Provence begin at Avignon, which is reached by the express **TGV** train from Paris (www.sncf.com). **Getting Around:** If you'd like to explore the area by bike, in Avignon go to **Provence Bike,** which rents all sorts of bikes (52 bd. St-Roch; ☎ 33-4/90-27-92-61; 19€/$23 per day). **Best Lodging:** A pocket of posh since 1799, **Hôtel d'Europe** was created from a 16th-century palace into this bastion of graceful elegance with a Michelin-starred restaurant (12 Place Crillon, Avignon; ☎ 33-4/90-14-76-76; 141€–449€/$162–$516). **Best Lodging Value:** A three-story Art Deco structure, **Hôtel d'Angleterre** is modest and comfortable, with a most helpful staff (29 bd. Raspail, Avignon; ☎ 33-4/90-86-34-31; www.hoteldangleterre.fr; 43€–78€/$49–$89). **Best Restaurant:** With a deluxe restaurant named after himself, **Christian Étienne** elevates Provençal cuisine to giddy new heights (10 rue Mons, Avignon; ☎ 33-4/90-86-16-50; www.christian-etienne.fr; 28€–40€/$32–$46). **Best Restaurant Value:** Creative French cookery at an affordable price is found at local favorite **La Fourchette,** in Avignon (7 rue Racine; ☎ 33-4/90-85-20-93; 24€–29€/$27–$33). **When to Go:** Apr–Oct.

◀ *Lavender field, Provence, Pays de Valensole.*
© John Lawrence/Getty Images

QUEENSTOWN, NEW ZEALAND

One of the great outdoor adventure capitals of the world

The energy is almost palpable in Queenstown. No matter what time of the year you arrive, jet boats will be racing through canyons, the TSS *Earnslaw* will be steaming its way across Lake Wakatipu, bungee jumpers will be leaping from high places, and skydivers will be floating to the ground. It's madness—an addictive madness that I never tire of.

People have been flocking to Queenstown since gold was first discovered in the region in the 1860s; it's only more recently that adrenalin-addicted thrill seekers have helped brand it the world's adventure capital. It's a well-deserved reputation but free-spirited adventure is not the only reason you should come here. This tiny Alpine resort, at the edge of the lake and surrounded by the majestic peaks of the southern Alps, is just one jewel in the crown that is the southern lakes region.

From pristine lakes and primeval forests to rugged mountains and wild, deserted coastlines, this is one of the most spectacular stretches of geography in the world. Compelling, spiritual, diverse, and physically challenging, it never fails to inspire me. The color palette is astounding—deep emerald-green forests; azure-blue skies; golden, tussock-covered hillsides; military lines of bright green grapevines; white, snowy peaks—it's awe-inspiring contrast at its best. Little wonder that filmmaker Peter Jackson sought it out for so many *Lord of the Rings* locations.

My favorite times to visit the region are autumn and full summer. Each of the seasons is pronounced and distinct, but autumn is mellow and relaxed, the temperature perfect and the trees a blaze of color. Summer is hot and dry, the land burnt brown and gold and the skies impossibly blue.

The beating heart of it all is Queenstown—a fast-pumping package that delivers more variety, more excitement per square inch than just about anywhere. Where else can you find one small, compact town so close to thousands of hectares of untouched World Heritage areas and national parks, to some of the best multiday treks in the world, to four premier ski fields, to top golf courses, heritage villages, world-recognized wineries, and more chances to scare yourself silly than any sane person needs? Factor in more clubs, bars, and restaurants per capita than is good for you and is it any wonder the place is awash with happy holidaymakers and thrill seekers pushing themselves to the limits?

Queenstown is all about indulging your passions whether they center on fine food and wine, soaking up the best of natural New Zealand, or lurching from one crazy pursuit to another—sky diving, jet boating, bungee jumping, white-water rafting, skiing, snowboarding, ballooning, hang gliding, mountain biking, and canyoning are all just a scream away.

If I could afford a slice of what is now New Zealand's most expensive real estate, I would set myself up here and spend my time marveling at the way so many miracles have been dropped into one small corner of the earth. It is a powerful, elemental place where I can happily sit for hours on a tussocky hilltop watching the skies change across jagged horizons. I come away feeling enlivened, exhilarated—and conscious of how small and insignificant I really am in the greater scheme of things.

◀ *Fiordland National Park.*

SPECIAL MOMENTS

1 Milford Sound. I can never fathom why everyone wants fine weather for their trip to Milford Sound. Milford offers so much more in torrential rain, when it turns into the mysterious, almost prehistoric world I adore. Sheer, towering rock faces erupt with hundreds of temporary waterfalls plunging over 1,000m (3,280 ft.), showering the world below in eerie mist and woven rainbows. It's a 5-hour drive by car from Queenstown, passing through unspoiled mountain landscapes, moss-carpeted rainforest canyons, and the Homer Tunnel; or you can take the more dramatic helicopter approach. The sound is the final destination of the world-famous 54km (28 miles) Milford Track, and an iconic boat trip to see dolphins, seals, and penguins is a must. Kayaking may be the most popular activity here after the cruises. Your best bet is **Rosco's Milford Sound Sea Kayaks** (www.kayakmilford.co.nz). You don't have to be super-fit or have prior kayaking experience. Most popular is the Sunriser Wildlife 'n' Waterfall trips, which depart at 7:30am.

2 Cromwell. I'm a fruit lover, so Cromwell is my kind of paradise. Imagine a hot summer day, blue skies, fresh air, purple thyme, schist tors, bare brown hills, the Clutha River, fertile valleys, and a big box of fresh, succulent cherries. That's my idea of bliss. Peaches, apples, apricots, and nectarines are also grown in abundance, and now wine connoisseurs have reason to celebrate. As New Zealand's fastest-growing wine region, it boasts more than 50 scenic vineyards and some of the finest pinot noirs in the world. From Queenstown through the Gibbston Valley to Bannockburn and Cromwell—a 40- to 50-minute drive through the dramatic Kawarau River Gorge—it's one long tablecloth spread of leafy green grapevines.

3 Arrowtown. This quaint old gold-mining town, 20km (12 miles) from Queenstown, was recognized as one of the richest sources of alluvial gold in the world back in the 1860s. I've tried my hand at gold panning here, had no luck whatsoever, and retired to drown my sorrows in one of the village's growing number of excellent cafes and restaurants. Every day seems to be a lazy one in Arrowtown. As a place to admire charming historic buildings, browse boutique stores, and, in autumn, swoon over magnificent deciduous displays, it's less frenetic than Queenstown. I'm rather enamored of the nearby countryside, too, with its interwoven roads, big hawthorn hedges, and fancy country houses, all set against the backdrop of Coronet Peak.

4 Glenorchy. I've traveled the length and breadth of New Zealand and one of my favorite drives is the 45km (28-mile) stretch from Queenstown to Glenorchy—a pinhead-size village nestled into the northern tip of Lake Wakatipu, surrounded by mountains, glacier-fed rivers, and moody beech forests. As I

wind around the lake, I stop often to admire breathtaking views. There's always something new about the way clouds slumber over peaks and hanging valleys, about the way sun light dances across the dazzling blue of Wakatipu. Past Glenorchy lies the even tinier, aptly named settlement of Paradise—the gateway to a forgotten world of lichen-encrusted beech forests that make up the famous Routeburn, Greenstone, Caples, Rees, and Dart valley walking tracks. For hiking information, contact the **Glenorchy Visitor Information Centre** at www.glenorchyinfocentre.co.nz. **Dart River Safaris** (www.dartriver.co.nz) provides one of the best jet-boat experiences in New Zealand. The trip combines jet boating with walks in ancient forests and visits to *Lord of the Rings* sites in Paradise. Another option is horseback riding with **Dart Stables** (www.dartstables.com). They have exclusive rights to trek through Department of Conservation areas. Trips last from 2 hours to overnight.

ADRIENNE REWI is author of *Frommer's New Zealand*, three other nonfiction titles, and thousands of magazine articles and short stories. When she is not planning her next trip, taking photographs, or writing her next book, she is safely housed in Christchurch, New Zealand.

ABOUT THE AUTHOR

YOUR TRIP

General Information: Contact **Destination Queenstown** (www.queenstown-nz.co.nz). **Getting There:** Queenstown is 486km (290 miles) south of Christchurch, around 6 hours by car. **Air New Zealand National** and **Air New Zealand Link** (www.airnewzealand.com) make regular 1-hour trips from Christchurch. **Getting Around:** Queenstown is a compact town, with most shops, restaurants, and amenities within easy walking distance. **What to See & Do:** For helicopter flights to Milford Sound, contact **Over The Top** (☎ 64-3/442-2233; www.flynz.co.nz). For great walks information, contact the **Department of Conservation** (☎ 64-3/249-8514; www.doc.govt.nz). **Best Lodging: Eichardt's Private Hotel** is the epitome of style; rooms have great views and big sky-lit bathrooms (Marine Parade; ☎ 64-3/441-0450; www.eichardtshotel.co.nz; US$965–US$1,139/£511–£604). **Best Lodging Value: Garden Court Suites & Apartments** has great-value two-bedroom suites and studios (41 Frankton Rd.; ☎ 64-3/442-9713; www.gardencourt.co.nz; US$118–US$220/£63–£117). **Best Restaurant:** Fresh seafood and oysters are the focus at **Wai Waterfront Restaurant** (Steamer Wharf, Beach St.; ☎ 64-3/442-5969; US$20–US$30/£11–£16). Thai duck and lemon-grass curry are highlights at **Saffron,** one of the most serious fine-food places in the region (Arrowtown; ☎ 64-3/442-0131; US$20–US$30/£11–£16). **Best Restaurant Value:** Sit up at the counter while you wait for a strong espresso, bacon and bun, panini, or burger at **Joe's Garage** (Camp St.; ☎ 64-3/442-5282; US$13/£7). **When to Go:** Queenstown is a year-round destination, February to April has the best weather.

◀ *Milford Sound and Mitre Peak.*
© Wilfried Krecichwost/Getty Images

RAJASTHAN, INDIA

Castles, palaces, forts, posh hotels & Bengal tigers

Rajputana—literally, "land of princes"—is for many the very essence of India: a fantastical landscape in which crenulated castles rise shimmering from dusty plains, placid lakes reflect ethereal white palaces, and tall, turbaned men seem to embody tales of valor and honor before death.

Still very much a feudal society, the country's second-largest state is inextricably entwined with the history of its self-proclaimed aristocracy. A warrior clan that emerged around A.D. 600, the Rajputs remained invincible for more than 1,200 years, succumbing only to the British and their cunning diplomacy in the late 19th century. As the Rajputs were allowed to keep the taxes they extorted from travelers plying the Thar desert trade routes, their coffers—no longer emptied to fund internecine wars—swelled unchecked, and the maharajas embarked on a frenzied spending spree, gilding and refurbishing old forts and building new palaces, like the Umaid Bhawan Palace in Jodphur, then the largest private residence in the world.

The party ended in 1972, when Indira Gandhi stripped the Rajputs of both stipends and titles. Unable to maintain their sprawling properties, enterprising aristocrats threw open their doors to anyone with the means to pay. Today there are almost 80 of these heritage properties—castles, palaces, forts, and ornate mansions—many still home to India's monarchy, and quite possibly the world's most exotic hotels. For where else can you be hosted by an aristocrat whose forebears built—and quite often died—for the castle walls that surround you, then find yourself bedding down in their jewel-encrusted royal quarters?

But Rajasthan is also home to an altogether more elusive aristocrat: In the lotus-filled lakes and forests of Ranthambore National Park, the Bengal tiger stalks sambar deer, its barking call alerting trackers to the presence of the jungle king. Said to be the best place in the world to see a tiger in the wild, Ranthambore is an essential stop, and the perfect jumping-off point to visit tiny Keoladeo "Ghana" National Park, which boasts the largest concentration and variety of bird life in Asia; or the medieval village of Bundi, renowned for its school of miniature paintings and far enough off the beaten track to be mercifully free of pushy touts. Northwest lies tiny Pushkar, where Hindu pilgrims wade into the sacred lake to perform *puja* while scattering marigolds into its holy waters. And who could miss Jodphur, the "Blue City," where the walls of the mighty Mehrangarh Fort rise like sheer cliffs above the tangled streets below; or a sunrise over the "City of Lakes," as the state's most romantic destination, Udaipur, is known; or the far-flung Golden Fort of Jaisalmer, its sandstone ramparts inhabited since 1156, making it one of the oldest living fortified cities in the world. By the time you board your plane, weighed down by souvenirs picked up in the "Pink City" of Jaipur, state capital and shopaholic heaven, you may be relieved to escape the chaos and the heat of India's desert state. But be warned: India is addictive, and you'll be back.

◀ *Roadside merchant, Rajasthan.*
© Marc Abrahms Photography

SPECIAL MOMENTS

1 Counting time: Dargah Sharif, Ajmer. Leaving your shoes at the entrance, you enter through imposing gates, passing mosques built by the great Mugal emperors Akbar and his grandson Shah Jahan (creator of the Taj) to reach the tomb of the great Sufi saint Khwaja Moin-ud-Din Chisti, Protector of the Poor, the most sacred Islamic site in India. Enclosed by marble, lattice-like screens, the tomb is—by Indian standards—insignificant, but it is the devotees who make this experience. The voices of the *qawwali* singers, repeating the same haunting melodies that have been sung here for 800 years, wash over the suppli-cants, who lie with hands spread wide on the floor, or fervently clasped together, eyes closed, while others tie prayers to the screens. To one side sits a long line of men, mouths moving silently as they sift through mounds of beads— counting time, or so I'm told. It's a scene unchanged since the 13th century, and an honor to behold.

2 Humbled by a tout: Eklingji Temples, Udaipur. "Just say what is in your heart," the boy instructs me, before thrusting me into the melee at the Eklingji temple. Like a child told to make a wish, I am touched by the desire to abase my-self to a higher force, and try to lose myself in the chanting, but suspicion of the boy's motives keeps me self-conscious. He watches me keenly, and then asks, when it's all over, if I did indeed pray. I shake my head, embarrassed, and then offer him money for the unsolicited tour he provided of the temple complex. He declines the money and slips away, and I am left, ashamed, with a handful of rupees. India is nothing if not unpredictable—daily life pul-sates with ritual and ceremony, yet spiritual lessons come when—and how—you least expect them. The intimate Eklingji complex embraces 108 sandstone and marble temples, some dating as far back as A.D. 734, and houses almost the entire pan-theon of Hindu gods, but is pre-dominantly dedicated to Lord Shiva, guardian deity of the regents of Mewar, which is why you will often see the Maharaja of Udaipur joining his subjects here on Mondays.

3 Washing away sin: Pushkar. As the sun sets behind the low-slung Aravalli hills, temple bells accompany the pilgrims as they wade into the sacred lake, entirely surrounded by white temples and palaces. Reflections shimmer in the holy waters as they set candles, flowers, and prayers adrift. When they emerge from this ritual bath, they have cleansed their souls of sin. If you don't have time to visit Varanasi, Pushkar is just the place to experience the Hindu faith, particu-larly during the full moon in late October/November, when the tiny village population is swollen by an

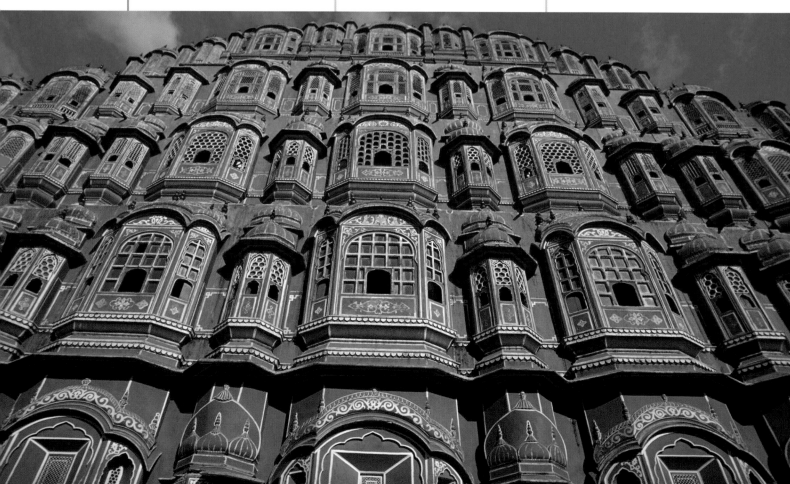

estimated 200,000 red-turbaned Rabari and Bhil tribal folk, religious pilgrims, and tourists, there to watch the races and auctions of the largest camel *mela* (fair) in Asia.

4 Meeting a maharaja: Umaid Bawan, Jodphur.

We are spread out on the lawns of the Umaid Bawan Palace, home to the maharaja of Jodphur and the largest heritage hotel in India. From here we have a magnificent view of Mehrangarh Fort, its impenetrable walls rising steeply from the rocky outcrop on which it was built. It is Diwali, Festival of Lights, when the Goddess of Prosperity and Wealth, Laxmi, is invited into homes. And where better to find her than here, at the maharaja's annual celebration. Indira Gandhi may have outlawed the monarchy, but in Rajasthan it is not a title that confers royalty, but blood. Other heritage hotels where you are likely to meet up with its aristocrat owners include Deogarh Mahal, Dungarpur and Nilambagh palaces, and Castle Mandawa.

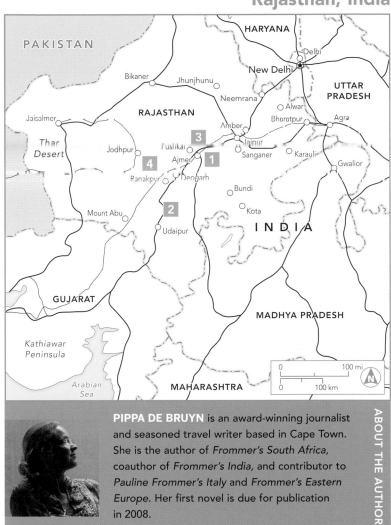

Rajasthan, India

PIPPA DE BRUYN is an award-winning journalist and seasoned travel writer based in Cape Town. She is the author of *Frommer's South Africa*, coauthor of *Frommer's India*, and contributor to *Pauline Frommer's Italy* and *Frommer's Eastern Europe*. Her first novel is due for publication in 2008.

ABOUT THE AUTHOR

YOUR TRIP

General Information: For your travel needs, contact the **Rajasthan Tourist Development Corporation** official state website at **www.rajasthantourism.gov.in**. For information on India, try **www.tourisminindia.com** or **www.tourindia.com**. **Getting Around:** To hire a car and driver, contact **Rajasthan Tourist Development Corporation** (☎ 91-141/220-0778; cro@rajasthantourism.gov.in or rtdcpr@sancharnet.in). **Best Lodging:** In Jaipur, immerse yourself in the princely style of living at **Rajvilas** (Goner Rd.; ☎ 800/5-OBEROI; www.oberoihotels.com; $530/£270). In Ranthambore, stay in one of the stylish, spacious white tents at **Aman-i-Khás,** where you can relish its Aman touches of discreet luxury (☎ 91-7462/252-052; www.amanresorts.com; $700/£357). **Best Lodging Value: The Kankarwa,** in Udaipur, is an elegant, family-run guesthouse in an ancient haveli, on the shores of Lake Pichola (☎ 91-294/241-1457; $28–$38/£15–£19). **Rawla Narlai** is an affordable stopover between Udaipur and Jodhpur (☎ 91-291/251-0410; reservations@ajitbhawan.com; $86/£44). **Best Restaurant:** The most romantic fine-dining evening, with superb food and atmosphere (huge burning braziers; beautiful dancing women), is to be had at Rajvilas's **Surya Mahal** (in Rajvilas, see above; $11–$24/£6–£12). **Best Restaurant Value: Trio** has no walls to obscure views of the maharaja's palace in Jaisalmer, while it serves great variations on signature Rajasthani dishes (☎ 91-2992/25-2733; $1–$5/50p–£3). **When to Go:** Sept–Nov, particularly late Oct to early Nov, when both Diwali and the Pushkar *mela* take place.

◄ *Palace of the Winds (Hawa Mahal), Jaipur.*
© Bob Krist Photography

RAJASTHAN, INDIA 261

REDWOOD NATIONAL PARK, CALIFORNIA

A walk among the tallest living things on earth

It's difficult to explain the feeling you get walking through the misty old-growth forests of Redwood National and State parks without citing *Alice in Wonderland*. Like a verdant jungle, a coastal redwood forest is a multistoried affair, and its trees—the tallest living things in the world—are just the top layer. *Everything* here seems immense and mysterious, as if from a prehistoric age: Giant mushrooms and colorful mosses cover the ground, 10-foot-tall ferns line the creeks, the ground is soft and eerily springy, and the smells are rich and musty. It's so outsized and primeval that you half expect to turn the corner and see a dinosaur munching on giant huckleberry bushes.

When Archibald Menzies first noted the botanical existence of the coastal redwood in 1794, more than 2 million acres of redwood forest carpeted the coasts of California and Oregon. By 1965, heavy logging had reduced that to 300,000 acres, and it was obvious something had to be done if any were to survive. The state had created several parks around individual groves in the 1920s, and in 1968 the federal government created Redwood National Park. Then in May 1994, the National Park Service and the California Department of Parks and Recreation signed an agreement to manage these conservation areas cooperatively.

I admit that getting here isn't easy. There are no convenient airports, and the drive from San Francisco will take at least 5 hours. But I promise you it's well worth the hassle—once you step out of your car and into these ancient forests, you will be awestruck at the size and grandeur of these mighty redwoods. The statistics are almost incomprehensible: trees as tall as a 35-story skyscraper, with trunks more than 20 feet thick and life spans of up to 2,000 years. And chances are good you'll marvel at the solitude as well, as this is one of the least-visited parks in California due to its isolated location.

It's also one of the most accessible parks in America, providing scenic byways and wheelchair-accessible trails for elderly and disabled visitors. Most of the National Park highlights are right off the road and open year-round, and parking is never a problem. But my favorite places to see involve a bit of hiking, such as the trail through Fern Canyon and the descent into Tall Trees Grove. You'll also encounter numerous types of wildlife such as Roosevelt elk, bald eagles, river otters, black-tailed deer, and perhaps even gray whales migrating along the spectacularly rugged coast.

It's all so incredibly beautiful and spiritually moving that one can see why people are willing to chain themselves to trees to protect what little remains of this natural wonder of the world. Although logging of old-growth redwoods in the region is still a major bone of contention among the government, private landowners, and environmentalists, it's auspicious that contention even exists—a sign that perhaps we have all learned to see the forest *and* the trees for what they are: the monarchs of all living things, a link to the age of the dinosaurs, and a humble reminder that mankind is but a hiccup in time compared to the ancestral *Sequoia sempervirens*.

◀ *Del Norte Redwoods State Park.*
© Muench Photography Inc.

SPECIAL MOMENTS

1 **Tall Trees Trail.** A short hike leads to one of the world's tallest trees—365 feet tall, 14 feet in diameter, and more than 600 years old. It was once touted as the world's tallest tree, but new candidates keep popping up nearby, and this proud giant has lost a couple of feet to time. It's still worth it to see the contender, particularly in the fall when the giant maples' blazing orange and yellow leaves—the size of dinner plates—provide spectacular contrast to the mossy forest floor. Bring a blanket and picnic basket because you'll want to spend all day here exploring the grove, relaxing under the sun-streaked canopy, and watching river otters play in the emerald-green river (I do it every year).

2 **Fern Canyon Trail.** This incredibly scenic trail is the most popular destination in the park. Flat and relatively short, the winding trail leads deep into a lush grotto of ferns—lady, deer, chain, sword, five-finger, and maidenhair—clinging to 30-foot-high vertical walls divided by a brook (bring the camera for this one). It's only about a 1.5-mile walk, but be prepared to scramble across the creek several times on your way via small footbridges. Visit the canyon in the morning, then spend the day relaxing on Gold Bluffs Beach (bring drinks and lunch).

3 **Howland Hill Road.** The most amazing car-friendly trail I've ever encountered is this hidden, well-maintained dirt road that winds for 10 miles through Jedediah Smith Redwoods State Park along the south fork of the crystal-clear Smith River. It's an unforgettable journey through spectacular old-growth redwoods, with numerous places to park and explore misty, fern-filled groves teeming with plants and critters under a towering canopy of awe-inspiring giants. Few visitors know about this road, so chances are good you'll have the forest to yourself. One of my favorite picnic spots on the California coast is at the Crescent Beach Overlook, along Enderts Road (off U.S. 101, about 4 miles south of Crescent City). Pack a picnic lunch from Good Harvest Café in Crescent City, park at the overlook, lay your

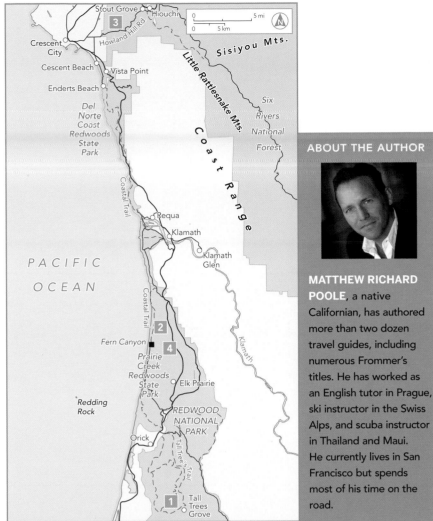

Redwood National Park, California

blanket on the grass, and admire the view from your own 500-foot bluff.

4 Prairie Creek Redwood State Park. A trip to the redwood forest wouldn't be complete without visiting the locals: A 200- to 300-strong herd of Roosevelt elk that inhabit the appropriately named Elk Prairie at Prairie Creek Redwood State Park. These beasts can weigh 1,000 pounds, and the bulls carry huge antlers from spring to fall. You can also spot the elk at the park's Gold Bluffs Beach—it's a rush to come upon them out of the fog or after a turn in the trail. For added excitement, visit during the fall rutting season, when the bulls claim their harem of cows by charging at anything that stands in their way. Nearly 100 black bears also call the park home, but they're seldom seen. Bikers should know that this park has a 19-mile mountain-bike trail through dense forest, elk-filled meadows, and glorious mud holes. Parts of it are difficult, though, so beginners should sit this out.

ABOUT THE AUTHOR

MATTHEW RICHARD POOLE, a native Californian, has authored more than two dozen travel guides, including numerous Frommer's titles. He has worked as an English tutor in Prague, ski instructor in the Swiss Alps, and scuba instructor in Thailand and Maui. He currently lives in San Francisco but spends most of his time on the road.

YOUR TRIP

General Information: Contact **Redwood Information Center** (☎ 707/464-6101; www.nps.gov/redw), the **Prairie Creek Visitor Center** (☎ 707/464-6101), the **Redwood National and State Parks Headquarters and Information Center** (☎ 707/464-6101), or the **Jedediah Smith Visitor Center** (☎ 707/464-6101). **Getting There:** The town of Orick, 40 miles north of Eureka and 336 miles north of San Francisco via Highway 101, is the southern gateway to the Redwood National and State Parks. The northern gateway to the park is Crescent City, near the Oregon border, also along Highway 101 and your best bet for gas, groceries, and outdoor supplies. **Best Lodging:** The **Lost Whale Bed & Breakfast Inn** in Trinidad is a modern Cape Cod–style house on 4 acres of forested oceanfront with a private beach (3452 Patrick's Point Dr.; ☎ 800/677-7859; www.lostwhaleinn.com; $225–$250). **Best Lodging Value:** The **Curly Redwood Lodge,** in Crescent City, was built in 1957 from a single ancient redwood and is across the highway from the beach (701 Redwood Hwy. S.; ☎ 707/464-2137; www.curlyredwoodlodge.com; $62–$87). The **park camping** fee is $20 per night for drive-in sites; walk-in sites are free. **Best Restaurant:** The mesquite-barbecue Cornish game hen is the draw at Trinidad's **Larrupin Café,** a beautifully decorated restaurant with a wood-burning fireplace (1658 Patrick's Point Dr.; ☎ 707/677-0230; $15–$22). **Best Restaurant Value:** The **Seascape Restaurant,** a pier-side cafe, serves local seafood and great breakfasts (Trinidad Bay Pier; ☎ 707/677-3762; $10–$22). **When to Go:** Fall, for its colorful foliage. As it's a temperate rainforest, you'll get rain and chilly weather year-round.

◀ *Roosevelt elk in motion, Redwood National Park.*
© Ron Sanford/Corbis

RÉUNION, FRANCE

French food & culture on a spectacular tropical island

I love France—the culture, the cafe life, the food. But I also love islands in the tropical sun; surf rolling onto pristine beaches; warm, star-filled nights; lush vegetation along rugged coastlines; and days spent outdoors—mountain biking, kayaking, snorkeling, and hiking.

Île de la Réunion (Réunion Island), nestled in the Indian Ocean, about 684km (425 miles) southwest of Madagascar, offers both worlds—call it "French culture on a tropical beach." It seems inaccessible but is fairly easy to get to: Air France has seven direct flights a week from Paris, and Air Mauritius offers flights from nearly every major European city, first stopping in nearby Mauritius.

For island collectors like me, the small, nearly round Réunion, 65km (40 miles) long by 50km (30 miles) wide, promises endless miles of sun-kissed beaches as beautiful as those on Maui; lush, tropical flora as breathtaking as on Bora Bora; and a fuming, active volcano, sometimes as dramatic as Kilauea on the Big Island of Hawaii. The interior of the island features two volcanic peaks, one of which is still erupting; verdant valleys; thundering waterfalls; spectacular ravines; and breathtaking vistas. For the visitor, this translates into a wide range of outdoor adventures.

What makes Réunion particularly unique is the blending of Creole, African, Indian, and French influences, which translates into a range of ethnic and French foods. The restaurants may not be as upscale as those in Paris, or as crowded as those in Nice, but restaurants in Réunion will offer you a selection of ethnic cuisines found nowhere else.

The island also is the world's largest producer of vanilla, which is liberally used in everything from sauces to coffee drinks. When you've had enough sun, you can spend a couple of hours touring the plantation and factory of La Maison de la Vanille, in St-Andre, and pick up a range of vanilla products.

When the French came to the island in the 17th century, they brought along vine stock to ensure that they would have wine. For years Réunion wines were not much to brag about (syrupy, sweet whites). In the late 1970s, however, wine growers upgraded their varietal stock and today they are producing very palatable (dry) whites, reds, and rosés. One of the best guided tours and tastings is at Maison des Vins, in Cilaos, where you can buy a few bottles (most in the 7€/$10 range) to give to friends back home.

Great food and drink and an exquisite landscape are powerful temptations to visit Réunion, but the people themselves are another major draw. Some three of every four islanders are *metis*—of mixed ethnic background. The result is racial tolerance: Ask the Réunionnais their ethnic background, and they tell you proudly, "French." This blending is evident in Réunion's Creole-French culture, which has its own music, dance, architecture, theater, and art. Plan to spend time mingling with the locals, seeing a play, going to a museum, chatting. The people of Réunion are unfailingly polite and, if approached with a warm smile and a hearty *"Bonjour,"* they respond in kind.

◀ *Life is a beach on Réunion, one of the Mascarene Islands.*
© Jean-Noel Reichel/ Getty Images.

SPECIAL MOMENTS

1 **Cirque de Cilaos.** The road from sea level up to this remote, 1,220m (4,003-ft.) mountain town will either be a thrilling zigzag of a ride or a white-knuckled, torturous trip with some 262 hairpin turns. Cirque de Cilaos is one of three collapsed calderas of the extinct volcano, Piton des Neiges. Along the way you'll pass precipitous gorges, rumbling waterfalls, and fertile valleys. Cilaos is known for some of the country's most magnificent hiking trails, hot-spring spas, wines, intricate embroidery, mountain biking, rock climbing, and the new sport of canyoning, where adventurers rappel down steep, narrow canyons and swim in waters below.

2 **Piton de la Fournaise.** Frequently shrouded in misty clouds, Piton de la Fournaise, Réunion's most famous landmark, simply should not be missed. It's one of the world's most active volcanoes (153 eruptions since 1690). Most visitors drive to the 2,630m (8,630-ft.), occasionally fuming volcano, then set out for a long hike around the rim of the smoldering crater, which takes about 3 hours (early morning is the best time). Others will prefer a helicopter tour of the volcano. This will give you both a view of the eruption and a chance to see the inaccessible interior regions of the island, with vertical canyons and waterfalls that you would otherwise miss.

3 **St-Denis.** Skip the modern, coastal highway circling the island, and take the slower, scenic upper road with its picturesque views as you drive into St-Denis (pronounced san-de-*nee*). The capital, this city of 146,000, is the "Paris of Réunion," but with a Creole twist. Plan to spend at least 1 day strolling down rue de Paris, where the grand old Creole houses are located. At the southern end of the street lies Jardin de l'État, a botanical garden with a terrific orchid collection, and the Musée d'Histoire Naturelle. Sprinkled throughout the city are plenty of cafes and *patisseries* where you can sample the local cuisine.

4 **The West Side beaches.**
White-sand beaches stretch along the coast; watersports abound; a string of restaurants, cafes, bars, and shops line the street—it's the vacation center of Réunion: the West Side beaches. The most famous, dubbed "Saint Tropez of the Indian Ocean," is St-Gilles-les-Bains, which is enjoyed best during the week when the crowds are gone. In addition to the chic (and pricey) restaurants and the trendy shops, this is the spot to indulge in a range of ocean activities, from scuba diving to sport fishing. Also worth your time are helicopter tours of the island (not to be missed), the Aquarium de Réunion, Le Jardin D'Eden botanical garden, and plenty of bars and discos when the sun goes down. P. S.: The best-kept secret is the town next door, L'Hermitage-les-Bains, which has an uncrowded beach and terrific snorkeling (plus great hotels and restaurants). Please: Don't tell anyone about it.

ABOUT THE AUTHOR

JEANETTE FOSTER is a collector of the world's best islands. She lives in Hawaii and writes for travel, sports, and adventure magazines, and is the editor of *Zagat's Survey: Hawaii*, the author of the Hawaii chapter in *1,000 Places to See in the USA & Canada Before You Die*, and the author of more than 40 books for Frommer's.

YOUR TRIP

General Information: For everything you want to know about Réunion, including which airlines fly there, contact the **Comité du Tourisme de la Réunion** (☎ 262-26/221-0041; www.la-Reunion-tourisme.com). **What to See & Do:** **Helilagon Helicopter Tours** gives 45-minute tours of the island (☎ 262-26/255-5555; www.helilagon.com). Spend an afternoon tasting the wines of **Maison des Vins** (34 rue des Glycines, Cilaos; ☎ 262-26/231-7969). **Best Lodging:** Immerse yourself in the lap of luxury on a quiet beach at **Les Villas du Lagoon** (28 rue du Lagoon, L'Hermitage-Les-Bains; ☎ 262-26/270-0000; www.villas-du-lagon.com; 128€–182€/$172–$242). **Best Lodging Value:** Some of the best views of the scenic mountain town Cilaos unfold from the rooms upstairs at the Creole-style **Hôtel Tsilaosa** (rue du Père Boiteau; ☎ 262-26/237-3939; www.tsilaosa.com; 75€/$100). **Best Restaurant:** Try the tapas from the eclectic menu at **Coco Beach**, a garden cafe along the beach, which serves everything from salads to curry (bd. Leconte de Lisle, St-Gilles-Les-Bains; ☎ 262-26/233-8143; 15€–28€/$20–$38). **Best Restaurant Value:** If you're looking for a great place to people-watch, join the office workers, shoppers, and tourists for lunch at **Cyclone Café**, one of the capital's trendiest cafes, serving Creole curry, quiche, salads, and daily specials. At night, the bar belongs to the 20-something crowd from the university (24 rue Jean Chatel, St-Denis; ☎ 262-26/220-0023; 10€–18€/$14–$25). **When to Go:** Réunion has two seasons: hot and rainy from December to April, and cool and dry from May to November.

◀ *The Trou de Fer chasm, surrounded by rainforest.*
© Atlantide Phototravel/Corbis

RIVIERA MAYA, MEXICO

Magnificent ruins, underground rivers & pearl-white beaches

I'm like you; I've schlepped around the world—toured the most important museums and ruins, climbed cultural icons like the Eiffel Tower, attended the opera in Helsinki and white-water rafted in Costa Rica. But when it's time to go on a *vacation* vacation—to leave the working world behind—there's a special place I go: Yucatán's Riviera Maya.

"Riviera Maya" is a term coined by the Mexico Tourism folks so North Americans will associate that exotic European coast with the Yucatán peninsula's Caribbean shore. Anyone who's ever been to both knows the difference. The Riviera Maya's beaches, from Cancún to Tulum, boast powdery sand that doesn't burn your feet no matter how strong the sun, and warm ocean waters that shimmer in turquoise and aquamarine. Palms sway in the breeze and, if you're lucky, the temperature hovers around perfect.

If you're into resort tourism, Cancún offers everything—all-inclusive hotels, an abundance of great restaurants, sizzling nightlife, and organized tours with lots of things to do. But to fill my time with nothing, to get a taste of laid-back living without a care in the world, I head down to Tulum.

Tulum is different things to different people. It's a bohemian village along the highway; a Maya city in ruin, high above the sea on a bluff; and it's a string of pearl-white beaches along the Boca Paila Road leading into the protected nature preserve of Sian Ka'an Biosphere. Each year, a gazillion people visit the archaeologically minor ruins because of their breathtakingly beautiful vista. But few tourists, in their "what's next?" rush, realize that just down the coast from where they stand, there's nothing. Or more precisely, nothing but secluded beachfront accommodations that range in size and appeal from a few rustic, sand-floor palapa huts to intimate, luxury villas.

Who can say no to a routine of an early morning swim in the warm water followed by a tropical-fruit breakfast, a long walk on the beach, and a dip in a cool pool? Then later, lunch, followed by a good book and a siesta in a breezy hammock, a cold beer, and fresh fish dinner? They turn the electricity off at 11pm on the Boca Paila Road, so drinks are served at candlelit bars; on clear nights the moon and a million stars light your way.

A Riviera Maya vacation, like a Seinfeld episode, can be about nothing. Yet when I'm tired of the lay-about lifestyle, there are a ton of fascinating diversions nearby: magnificent ruins of lost Mayan cities such as Chichén Itzá, Ek Balam, and Uxmal; natural *cenotes*, underground rivers that rise to the surface to form spectacular caverns such as the ones at X'keken and Aktun Chen; canyons of colorful coral reefs offshore; bird-watching and ecotourism in the Sian Ka'an Biosphere, and towns that combine pre-Columbian splendor with colonial buildings from the time of the Conquest of the Americas.

Yucatán's forest spirits, known to the Maya as *Aluxes*, have bewitched me. No matter how many idyllic places I visit, when it's time to unwind and decompress, that's Tulum time.

◀ *A tranquil beach on the Riviera Maya.*
© Mark Lewis/
Getty Images

271

SPECIAL MOMENTS

1 **Tulum.** The boutique hotels strung along the white-sand beach south from the ruins of Tulum are mostly small, romantic places that were their owner's dream. To go native, there are still a few spots where you can sleep in a hammock in a thatched-roof *palapa* hut. Then there's also the high end—intimate hotels with bathrooms of Talavera tile, and windows and balconies with sweeping views of the sea.

To the north, the post-Classic ruin of Tulum, known to the Maya as Zama (City of Dawn), perches high on a bluff with spectacular views of the turquoise sea below.

As development creeps down the coastline from Cancún, Tulum's Boca Paila Road is one of the last refuges from all-inclusive buffet tables, crowded beaches, faux culture, and organized everything. So get there before the charm is gone.

2 **Chichén Itzá.** The first time I stood on the apex of El Castillo, a giant pyramid rising 25m (82 ft.) above the expansive ceremonial plain at Chichén Itzá, it took my breath away. The sheer size and

scope of the ruined structures scattered around the 1,000-year-old city boggled my mind.

Known as the Temple of Kukulcán, the pyramid that towers above the jungle is also a complicated calendar, engineered so that the shadow of its terraces during the spring and fall equinoxes form the shape of an undulating serpent. There are 364 steps to the top, with a platform to equal the 365 days of the year. Although you can no longer climb to the top, you can admire the architectural feat from the ground. Clap your hands at the base of the steps and the echo imitates the revered quetzal bird.

The ancient Maya built a civilization as advanced as any in the Old World; they developed the mathematical concept of zero, used a calendar more accurate than our own, and aligned massive, ornate stone buildings to the sun and stars—all without beasts of burden, the wheel, or the telescope. What makes these ruins even more mysterious is that the Maya inexplicably abandoned the city, at the height of its splendor, leaving it to be swallowed by the jungle.

3 **Isla Mujeres.** At the northernmost part of the Riviera Maya is a sliver of a sandy island, just a few kilometers off the coast of Cancún. Wooden clapboard houses, painted a rainbow of Caribbean colors, recall a time when fishing was the only source of income and pirates sheltered in Isla's peaceful harbor.

The people-ferry that crosses the water from Puerto Juarez to the island offers a chance to get into a Mexico mood, one's that's slower and more carefree. Only the three-story-tall lighthouse stands higher than a royal palm. Narrow cobblestone streets offer a diverse mix of mom-and-pop gift shops, jewelry stores, eclectic eateries, and quaint hotels. Unlike Cancún's Hotel Zone, this is a community where people live and work.

The island offers visitors a comfortable place to hang out, good snorkeling in the warm waters of the bay, some excellent restaurants, and El Garrafón, a popular family water park near the island's dramatic southeast tip. But a fun day trip off the island is to Isla Contoy, a bird and wildlife sanctuary to the north. I like getting there on the sailboat

Estrella del Norte, the last wooden-hulled boat built on the island.

4   Sian Ka'an Biosphere. I'm a big advocate of ecotourism, a term coined to define low-environmental-impact tourism. This day trip into a unique, protected, 500,000-hectare (1.3-million-acre) wilderness of forest, savannas, salt marshes, beaches, and three large lagoons represents ecotourism at its best.

Waiting to take us into the wide lagoon are two long launches. Once again we get an object lesson in nature when I step into the water and a big stingray rises and flaps away.

Sian Ka'an is a great place to bird-watch; we see spoonbills and herons, storks and kingfishers, cormorants and vultures, but not many other of the 1,200 species of animals that call the Biosphere home. No matter, I return for a second tour; this time, an unforgettable nighttime adventure with crocodiles. If it's small enough, the croc is pulled on board and our boatman checks for identifying notches in the spiny skin of its tail. Very exciting!

BRUCE CONORD is the coauthor, with his wife, of six Latin America travel guides, one of which garnered three national travel-writing awards. On one research trip, he overstayed his welcome photographing inside a bullring, so they released the bull. It added a new meaning to "quick getaway." He lives in Mexico part time.

ABOUT THE AUTHOR

YOUR TRIP

General Information: Get travel information from the **Mexico Tourist Board** (☎ 800/446-3942; www.visitmexico.com). For information on Cancún and area sites, go to www.cancun.info and www.gocancun.com. Playa del Carmen and the Riviera Maya share the website www.rivieramaya.com. To visit Sian Ka'an Biosphere, contact **Ecocolors** (☎ 52-998/884-3667; www.ecotravelmexico.com). For Chichén Itzá, try **Halach-Winik** (☎ 52-998/892-8234; www.halach-winik.com). **Getting There:** Numerous major airlines fly to Cancún's International Airport, including **American** (☎ 800/433-7300; www.aa.com) and **Northwest** (☎ 800/447-4747; www.nwa.com). Both **AeroMexico** (☎ 800/237-6639; www.aeromexico.com) and **Mexicana** (☎ 800/531-7921; www.mexicana.com.mx) offer nonstop flights. Scheduled charters include **Spirit** (☎ 800/772-7117; www.spiritair.com) and **USA3000** (☎ 877/872-3000; www.usa3000.com). **Best Lodging: Zamas** has a get-away-from-it-all ambience to add to its excellent reputation (Boca Paila Rd., Tulum; ☎ 415/387-9806 in the U.S.; www.zamas.com; $110–$180/£58–£95). **Best Lodging Value: Tita Tulum** offers eight cabañas on a gorgeous stretch of beach (☎ 52-984/877-8513; www.titatulum.com; $125/£66). **Best Restaurant: John Gray's** serves outstanding international and fresh seafood cuisine (Av. Niños Héroes, Puerto Morelos; ☎ 52-998/871-0665; $15–$30/£8–£16). **Best Restaurant Value: Tycoz** serves up authentic crispy French baguette sandwiches and excellent coffee (Av. Tulum, opposite the bus station, Cancún; ☎ 52-998/884-6050; $3/£1.60). **When to Go:** Dec–Apr.

◀ *Cenote Dzitnup (an underground lake), near Valladolid.*

ROME, ITALY

The monumental city
of emperors & popes

A visit to Rome is an unrivalled aesthetic and historic encounter that makes jaded eyes widen and nostalgic hearts swell. No city impresses itself more sublimely on the senses.

Rome's legendary hills are home to a captivating collision of inherited splendor and provincial rusticity—a mix of crumbling brick and marble ruins, triumphant ranks of umbrella pines, and the odd grazing sheep or goat. The compact historic center is a colorful and vibrant web of rambling alleys with ochre-washed walls that open up to sun-drenched, theatrical squares, where the sinuous forms of Rome's signature architecture—the baroque—bow and flex like the heaving bosom of a diva. There are fountains everywhere. And in Rome, fountains aren't prissy jets and orderly sprays—they're exuberant masterpieces of sculpture that happen to incorporate a fabulously inviting aquatic element.

What is perhaps most bewitching about Rome, and what sets it apart from other visually endowed cities, is its breathtaking amplitude—in a matter of steps, you go from urban grit to some of the most soaring art and architecture ever created. One minute you're standing on a graffiti-covered corner, and the next, you've got some ancient behemoth, like the Colosseum or the Pantheon, looming before you. Oh, and did I mention that the Vatican is here, too?

If this magnificent city of the emperors and the popes were a static diorama, you might call Rome the world's greatest open-air museum. Instead, it's a throbbing metropolis of three million, an intensely animated stage, paved with a fishnet of black cobblestones, where locals far outnumber tourists. While 21st-century Rome is proud of its illustrious heritage, there's little of that overbearing, cloying protection of the past that makes other cities feel like historical theme parks. Modern Roman life flows around, and in some cases runs roughshod over, imposing vestiges of civilizations in graceful decay. Softened by centuries of basking in the Mediterranean sun, or scarred by the abuses of marble looters, the legacies of Rome's glory days still stand in high, formidable relief. Rome wears her weathered opulence with a welcoming smile: Her physical assets are imposing but rough around the edges, which makes them romantic and accessible, not imperious or forbidding. Almost none of Rome's masterpieces are barricaded, which makes the city's artistic mother lode intimate and remarkably lived-in—something that's missing in other Italian cities. The temperate climate, sunny color of the buildings, and passionate demeanor of the locals only add to Rome's irresistible warmth.

In Rome (as in the rest of Italy), eating and drinking well is more of a right than a privilege, which means that you'll have easy access to good food and wine at affordable prices. Rome's best culinary and social asset is its casual dining scene; some of your most memorable nights out will be at informal, family-run trattorie or at boisterous, dirt-cheap pizzerias. Rome is also the world champion of al fresco dining, so grab a rickety table out on the cobblestones, and observe the spectacle of Roman life, lit by the peach-colored glow of the ochre-washed walls.

◀ *Emperor Constantine, Capitoline Museum.*
© Peter Adams Photography/Alamy Images

SPECIAL MOMENTS

1 **The heart of Ancient Rome.** The green, undulating sweep of the archaeological park that includes the Roman Forum, the Colosseum, the Palatine Hill, the Circus Maximus, and the Capitoline Hill, is where you'll find the most spellbinding reminders of Rome's epic past. This is Rome at its most cinematic, where sweeping panoramas are easy to populate, using just a bit of imagination, with all the bustle and ceremony (and brutality) of ancient Roman daily life. Begin your nostalgic journey at the grassy hollow of the Circus Maximus, where chariots once raced in front of 300,000 spectators. Down the street are the travertine arches of the Colosseum, a splendid work of imperial architecture that also happened to be an arena of slaughter for 400 years. The Roman Forum is less intact, but this was the beating heart of the Western World in antiquity, and there's still a powerful sense of history here. Most people visit Rome's archaeological sites during the day, but I recommend coming back at night: Floodlit, the ruins of ancient Rome are an even more rapturous sight.

2 **St. Peter's Basilica, Vatican City.** Many visitors rush to view the Sistine Chapel, ignoring its next-door neighbor, the absurdly immense St. Peter's Basilica. What a shame! I'm not talking about the view from the square in front—an image plastered on every tourist handout—but the interior of the church. When you take your first step over the threshold and begin to contemplate the enormous scale and incalculable riches of St. Peter's, it's hard to remain unmoved. Virtually every inch is covered in marble, gold, and bronze. The dome crowns the Roman skyline like a papal tiara. A giddy trove of Italian art is housed in a museum that charges no admission, where centuries of popes have stashed away treasures like Michelangelo's *Pietà* and Bernini's bronze *Baldacchino*. End your visit by ascending the dome—halfway to the top there's a snack bar that serves coffee and beer!

3 **The Pantheon.** The tight quarters of Rome's *centro storico* hold many surprises, but there's nothing like emerging from a narrow side street and catching sight of the Pantheon's rotund bulk for the first time. This pagan temple is the most magnificent union of architectural elegance and engineering genius ever achieved by the Romans. Thanks in part to its eventual conversion into a church, it's also the best-preserved ancient building in the world—almost all of it is original to the 2nd century A.D. Even if you know nothing about construction, the Pantheon's existence seems baffling. Marvel at the front porch, a formidable forest of 16 monolithic granite columns, and then walk through the 1,900-year-old bronze doors (admission is free) to experience the real magic of the Pantheon. Above your head, a 44m-wide (143-ft.) hemispherical

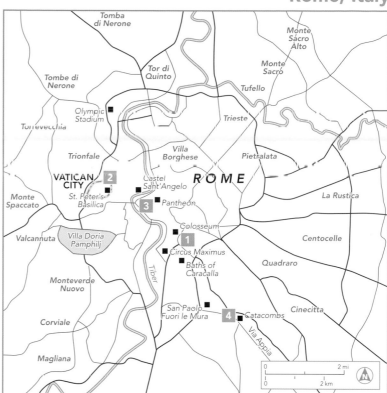

dome—poured in concrete and pierced by a single, round oculus at its apex—hangs as ethereally as the vault of the heavens.

4 Via Appia Antica (Appian Way). It's only a few miles south of the Colosseum, but the rural setting of ancient Rome's "queen of roads"—the Via Appia Antica—is a world away from the chaos of the city. Most people come here for an underground attraction—the catacombs—but it's the open-air sights that make the Appian Way so evocative of ancient times. Wheel ruts from centuries of cart traffic are still visible on the basalt paving slabs, and the grassy shoulders of the road are strewn with the sun-baked ruins of country estates and tombs of ancient Roman A-listers. As though planted here by Central Casting, shepherds still drive flocks of sheep across the Via Appia, and peasants sell homemade cheese in a park nearby. Even the air out here—slightly spicy, with the scent of pine needles and burnt leaves—seems steeped in antiquity.

A California native and past resident of four continents, **SYLVIE HOGG** finds every excuse she can to cross oceans, rivers, and county lines to soak up history, art, and culture—and gluttonously partake of the local food and drink. Sylvie is the author of several Frommer's guides to Rome and Italy and a frequent contributor to other travel media worldwide.

ABOUT THE AUTHOR

YOUR TRIP

General Information: The **Rome Tourism Board** is bright and user-friendly, with comprehensive information on monuments and museums, and an exhaustive accommodations directory (Via Parigi 11; www.romaturismo.com). Try the guided tours offered by **Context Rome** (☎ 888/467-1987 in the U.S., or 39-06/482-0911 in Italy; www.contextrome.com). **Getting There:** Rome's Leonardo Da Vinci Airport, also known as Roma-Fiumicino (FCO), is served by nearly every major airline. **Best Lodging:** The **Hassler,** gloriously situated at the top of the Spanish Steps, has the kind of old-world sophistication and polished, bright service that screams Roman holiday (Piazza Trinità dei Monti 6; ☎ 39-06/699-340; www.hotelhassler.com; 440€–790€/$536–$963). **Best Lodging Value:** If you can forgo most amenities and just want a great location and Roman charm, **Albergo Sole al Biscione,** near Campo de' Fiori, occupies a rambling, ochre-washed 16th-century building with delightful communal garden terraces (Via del Biscione 76; ☎ 39-06/6880-6873; www.solealbiscione.it; 65€–160€/$79–$195). **Best Restaurant:** There's no phone, and they don't take reservations, but for classic, affordable *cucina romana* in a homey yet hip atmosphere, you can't do much better than **Fiaschetteria Beltramme** (Via della Croce 39; 9€–15€/$11–$20). **Best Restaurant Value:** For the best pizza in the city, head for lively **Dar Poeta** in Trastevere—go early, or expect a wait (Vicolo del Bologna 45–46, ☎ 39-06/588-0516; 7€–12€/$9–$15). **When to Go:** Magnificent light and mild-to-warm weather make May and late September through early October the most enjoyable times to visit Rome.

◄ *The Colosseum at night.*
© Joseph Squillante/Photonica/Getty Images

ROTORUA, NEW ZEALAND

A world of geysers, mud pools, volcanoes & Maori culture

My childhood memories of Rotorua involve fanciful angry dragons, fire-breathing monsters, and bad smells. I still suspect there might be something unearthly and dissatisfied lurking beneath the streets of this steamy city. I was captivated then; I'm captivated still.

From the time of the famous Pink and White Terraces (destroyed by the 1886 Mount Tarawera eruption), Rotorua has been a cultural and thermal mecca—a place of geysers, hot springs, volcanoes, mud pools, Maori, and myth. This is where the earth's powerful forces burst through a thin crust, bubbling, belching, hissing, and casting that unmistakable smell of sulfur into the air—rotten eggs, we called it as children.

Every time I return to this vibrant, explosive place I am delighted afresh by the unexpected threads of steam that puff out of pavements, parks, and roadsides. I never tire of watching scalding mud plop-plopping in slippery gray pools; and I am silenced by the imagined horrors of the Buried Village, Te Wairoa, that disappeared under volcanic ash when Mount Tarawera blew a fuse and split itself in two.

When I'm satisfied that everything is still as it used to be—that the earth's core is still performing for my benefit—I like nothing better than taking a scenic drive around some of the trout-filled lakes. The city itself sits on the edge of Lake Rotorua, the largest of 11 main lakes in the area—many of them extinct volcanoes—and if time is short, this is a good place to feed the ducks, go for a walk, or take a boat ride.

My favorite lake is Lake Rotokakahi (Green Lake), which is sacred (tapu) to Maori. As a result it is invariably deserted. No one ventures onto its emerald-green waters, and the surrounding lush native bush draws you into an eerie, contemplative silence. Nearby, Lake Tikitapu (Blue Lake) is enveloped in a thick blanket of native ferns and forest, and there is an easy 5km (3-mile) bush walk around its circumference that takes about 90 minutes.

Most of Rotorua's stunning attractions are within a 30-minute drive out of the city center. The Redwood Grove in Whakarewarewa Forest is just 10 minutes from the shops—a heavenly glade of 60m (197 ft.) Coastal Californian Redwoods that always leaves me humbled. Sitting under them, drawing in the mossy scent of the undergrowth and listening to native birds, is one of my greatest pleasures. The forest as a whole boasts some of the finest walking and mountain-biking trails in New Zealand, and I never miss a chance to go there.

And if thermal activity, tall trees, and a wealth of Maori culture aren't thrilling enough, it's a comfort for many to discover that Rotorua is second only to Queenstown when it comes to iconic New Zealand adventure activities like jet-boating, kayaking, fishing, skydiving, rafting, and—inexplicably—leaping from high and dangerous places. We New Zealanders are a crazy bunch and we like nothing better than encouraging others to try our adrenalin-pumping tricks.

Me? I'd much rather retreat to hot mineral pools for a succession of those life-affirming spa treatments that every good, well-meaning citizen deserves.

◄ *Champagne Pool, Wai-O-Tapu Thermal Wonderland.*
© Jon Arnold/ DanitaDelimont.com

SPECIAL MOMENTS

1 **Wai-O-Tapu thermal wonderland.** Located a 20-minute drive south of the city, Wai-O-Tapu is the most colorful and intense of Rotorua's volcanic areas. I'm spellbound as I wander among its multi-hued pools, lakes, craters, steaming fumaroles, and mineral terraces. The Champagne Pool—a .2-hectare (half acre) of bubbling, hissing blue-green water with a vibrant ochre-colored petrified edge—is the most spectacular, but the boardwalk across the Artist's Palette is a close second. I get a childish thrill from watching the Lady Knox Geyser erupt 20m (66 ft.) into the air (every morning at 10:15am), and peering into huge fizzing geothermal craters is surely a glimpse into hell. At

Waimangu Volcanic Valley, 10 minutes north on the return trip, the Frying Pan Lake begs inspection. It's the world's largest hot-water spring.

2 **Te Puia.** Rotorua has been home to the Te Arawa Maori people for 600 years, and Te Puia, once a pallisaded Maori fortress that sits above the magnificent Whakarewarewa Geothermal Valley, presents cultural experiences that will enliven your senses. Even as a New Zealander, my spine tingles in the face of *Kapa Haka* song and dance performances. Whether its *poi* or stick games, perfectly sung harmonies or a rousing *haka* (war dance), you'll be bewitched. The Mia Ora evening event will

introduce you to the traditional *hangi*, a feast cooked on hot rocks in the earth. Carving, basket weaving, and jewelry are all featured; and with another 500 pools and the famous Pohutu and Prince of Wales geysers to view in the valley, you'll need half a day at least.

3 **Mount Tarawera.** I have yet to find an experience that compares to standing on the edge of the now-dormant Mount Tarawera volcanic crater, 24km (15 miles) southeast of Rotorua. Its deceptively pretty pink inner slopes belie the fury it exhibited when it split asunder in 1886, killing 150 people. I adore helicopters, and that's by far the best way of seeing Rotorua's geothermal treats

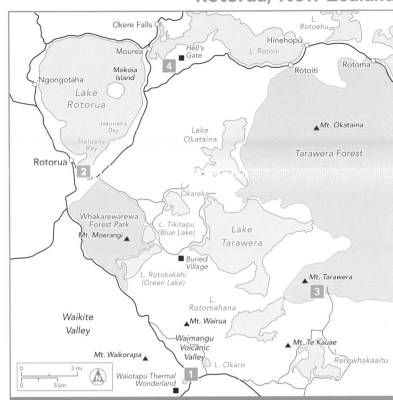

in one spectacular, indulgent serving. Include the Tarawera landing and test your nerves with a tumble into its scree belly. An excellent adjunct to your volcano spotting is a visit to the Buried Village, where buildings excavated from the volcanic ash are a sober reminder of the earth's power.

4 **Hell's Gate.** Quite apart from its geothermal excesses—the myriad volcanic lakes, the steaming cliffs, and the Southern Hemisphere's largest hot waterfall—this place gives a whole new meaning to the phrase "happier than a pig in mud." If you've never experienced the soothing powers of mineral pools and warm mud, this is your best chance. Home to Wai Ora Spa, it dispenses the earthy delights in a way that left me weak at the knees. I lay there, hidden away in a private mud bath (you can go public), feeling eternally grateful that the earth beneath Rotorua is in perpetual upheaval. I came away from the experience silky smooth, blush pink, with skin as fresh as a baby's.

ADRIENNE REWI is author of *Frommer's New Zealand*, three other nonfiction titles, and thousands of magazine articles and short stories. When she is not planning her next trip, taking photos, or writing her next book, she is safely housed in Christchurch, New Zealand.

ABOUT THE AUTHOR

YOUR TRIP

General Information: Contact **Destination Rotorua** for your travel needs (☎ 64-7/348-5179; www.rotoruaNZ.com). **Getting There:** Rotorua is 221km (137 miles; 3 hr. by car) southeast of Auckland. **Air New Zealand National** provides daily service to the area (www.airnewzealand.com). **Getting Around:** The center of town is not large. Tutanekai Street is the main shopping street; City Focus, the plaza under the sail-like structure, is in the middle of it all. City and suburban buses run approximately every hour on weekdays, less frequently on weekends. You'll find taxis at the visitor center and on Fenton Street. **What to See & Do:** If your time is short, the four must-see/must-do attractions are the Buried Village; Rotorua Museum; either of the geothermal reserves, Waiotapu or Waimangu; and a scenic flight over Mount Tarawera. **Best Lodging:** Savor the valley or lake vistas from your suite at **Treetops Lodge & Estate,** a luxurious spot set in lush native forest 30 minutes from the city (351 Kearoa Rd.; ☎ 64-7/333-2066; www.treetops.co.nz; US$1,283–US$1,518/£680–£804). **Best Lodging Value:** The **Royal Lakeside Novotel,** in the heart of the city, spoils you with amenities at affordable prices (lake end of Tutanekai St.; ☎ 64-7/346-3888; www.accorhotels.com; US$114/£60). **Best Restaurant: Lime Caffeteria** turns out a delectable range of lunch options, such as duck and shiitake wonton soup; and blue brie, fig, and pine-nut phyllo parcels (1096 Whakaue St.; ☎ 64-7/350-2033; US$15–US$25/£8–£13). **Best Restaurant Value:** Tasty vegetable bakes, lasagnas, bagels, and salads highlight the menu at **Fat Dog Café** (1161 Arawa St.; ☎ 64-7/347-7586; US$10–US$20/£5–£11). **When to Go:** Feb–Apr.

◀ *Tutea's Falls, Okere River, near Rotorua.*
© David Wall/DanitaDelimont.com

SAINT-TROPEZ, FRANCE

A Riviera resort where the only sin is the absence of a tan

I was 12 years old the first time I visited Saint-Tropez. My wealthy aunt invited me to go along with her on a private boat. We left from the Carlton Hotel pier in Cannes, boarding our leased vintage Chris-Craft and speeding along the shimmering azure coast. Our nonchalant French skipper expertly weaved around slow sailboats, windsurfers, and water-skiers, and in less than an hour we arrived at Ramatuelle, the beach area adjacent to Saint-Tropez. Arriving by speedboat enhanced the feeling that I had landed in a fairy-tale place of decadence and frivolity. My young self peered out at the myriad yachts bobbing up and down in the clear blue Mediterranean—their privileged inhabitants, tanned and beautiful, sipping cocktails on the decks.

And they are there still—almost held in time—every summer when I return to Saint-Tropez. I still land on a spectacular beach filled with sun worshippers wearing nothing. The restaurants are full of people eating and drinking and being merry. Year after year, I still feel that wonderment at how an entire stretch of beach—lined with fantastic restaurants and perfectly lined mattresses with colorful umbrellas—can be so perfect a setting for escapist happiness.

What makes Saint-Tropez especially dreamy is its isolation. It's almost like an island, inaccessible except by boat, helicopter, or a terribly congested and winding two-lane road. It is truly a place where you leave everything behind and bask in the feeling of a true escape. It is my ultimate dream vacation, a place I return to, even though I have traveled the world since that first visit when I was 12. Although I have found many beautiful beaches, nothing compares to the flair and glamour of Saint-Tropez. Not only are the people, the beaches, and the cuisine exquisite—but activities such as watersports are so easily accessible. Sailboards, kayaks, and pedal boats line the beaches ready for rent. Speedboats stand idly by, waiting for water-skiers. The charge is by the minute. Money buys everything in Saint-Tropez.

There is not much culture to this vacation. That much is true. You come here to escape reality. You come here to fall in love. You come here to do nothing. A sample day in Saint-Tropez: After a leisurely breakfast on a sun-washed terrace, everybody drives out to Ramatuelle, to the beautiful sandy beaches. After a refreshing swim, and perhaps some windsurfing, you settle in for a long lunch on the sand with a bone-dry rosé (you can dine in the nude and nobody will flinch). After an afternoon nap on your *matelas* (mattress) by the gentle lapping waves of the Mediterranean, you may go into town for a spot of shopping. At night, everybody dresses up. Late. After 9pm, you saunter down from your room, ready for dinner. By midnight, you can hit a club or two—if only to gawk at the glitzy and glamorous crowd.

Tomorrow, you will start again.

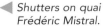

Shutters on quai Frédéric Mistral.
© Barbara Van Zanten/
Lonely Planet Images/
Getty Images

SPECIAL MOMENTS

1 Saint-Tropez fish market. There is a light in the south of France that has inspired artists from Bonnard and Signac to Matisse and Picasso, and nowhere is it softer and more translucent than in Saint-Tropez, especially in the morning in the old town, along the harbor. Alluring. I love to wake up early, while the glitterati are still dreaming of the night before, to walk the ancient cobblestone streets and watch the fishermen bring in their morning's catch at the historic fish market, teeming with energy. With a croissant and a café au lait, I feel ready to begin my day in Saint-Tropez.

2 Ferme la Douceur. The "farm of tenderness" is a 20-minute drive from Saint-Tropez, tucked away in the verdant hills. It sits in the midst of a vineyard, with its inn and lovely restaurant. An evening here is enchanting. Magical. I always ask for a table close to the vines (in late summer, you can reach out and touch the plump grapes). You sit by candlelight. There are no menus. You are served what the farm's chef has whipped up that day. There is no wine list. The wine comes from barrels, from grapes picked here, and is placed on your table in carafes. If you're lucky, the moon will be out and will splash your table with romantic light. It's a dreamy place, and I'm never disappointed. I hate hyperbole, but it's really one of my favorite places on earth.

3 Saint-Paul-de-Vence. The beautiful hilltop town of Saint-Paul-de-Vence is the unofficial center for the arts in the south of France. It's a 90-minute drive east of Saint-Tropez. Its ramparts overlook a peaceful setting of flowers and olive and orange trees. The walls remain somewhat as they were when they were built from 1537 to 1547 by François I. One of the best collections of contemporary art to be found in Europe is right here on this hillside. The Fondation Maeght is worth at least an afternoon's visit. I return again and again and never tire of the lovely gardens filled with Giacometti sculptures, the mural mosaics by Chagall, and stained-glass windows by Miró. The town is

also known for its olive-wood work; when you put your nose to a salad bowl carved by hand here, you can smell the sweet olive oil.

4 **Eze.** One of my favorite villages in the world is Eze, with its fortified feudal core high in the hills overlooking the Provençal coast. A 2-hour drive from Saint-Tropez, Eze clings to the hillside, seemingly hanging 390m (1,300 ft.) above the Mediterranean. Its medieval center contains art galleries, boutiques, and artisans' shops that have been restored. No cars are allowed, and you must walk up tiny cobblestone alleyways to reach the village. It's worth every step. Every time I go back, I'm stunned by the beauty of the buildings and the grand, sweeping views. At the top of this medieval rock is the Jardin Exotique, a densely planted garden that offers a magnificent vista for a moment of contemplation.

HAAS MROUE has authored or coauthored over 25 travel guidebooks and has written for *National Geographic*, Encyclopaedia Britannica, and *Forbes*. His most recent publications include *Frommer's Memorable Walks in Paris* and *Frommer's Amsterdam Day by Day*.

ABOUT THE AUTHOR

YOUR TRIP

General Information: For travel needs before you go, contact the **French Government Tourist Office** (www.franceguide.com). **Getting There:** Saint-Tropez is 874km (543 miles) south of Paris; 76km (47 miles) southwest of Cannes. The nearest rail station is in Saint-Raphaël, a neighboring resort. At Saint-Raphaël's Vieux Port, boats leave the **Gare Maritime de Saint-Raphaël** for Saint-Tropez four or five times a day from April to October (☎ 33-4/94-95-17-46). Buses run directly to Saint-Tropez from Toulon and Hyères and from the nearest airport, at Toulon-Hyères, 56km (35 miles) away. You can also take a helicopter from Nice airport (☎ 33-4/94-55-59-99; www.helicopter-saint-tropez.com). If you drive, note that parking in Saint-Tropez is very difficult, especially in summer. **Best Lodging: Residence de la Pinede** is a Relais & Châteaux property and the only hotel in Saint-Tropez with a private beach (Plage de la Bouillabaisse; ☎ 33-4/94-55-91-00; www.residencepinede.com; 255€–820€/$311–$1,000). **Best Lodging Value: Lou Troupelen** has basic but charming rooms and a private parking lot and is just a few minutes' walk from the old town (chemin des Vendanges; ☎ 33-4/94-97-44-88; Troupelen@aol.com; 83€–129€/$109–$169). **Best Restaurant: La Ponche** is close to the fish market and serves the best seafood in town (place du Revelin; ☎ 33-4/94-97-02-53; 18€–32€/$24–$43). **Best Restaurant Value:** Lively **Chez Maggi** serves such continental creations as brochettes of sea bass with lemon sauce and chicken curry with coconut milk (7 rue Sybille; ☎ 33-4/94-97-16-12; 14€–28€/$18–$36). **When to Go:** May–Sept, when it's the warmest and driest.

◀ *The magical light of Provence, reflected in the harbor.*
© Jochem D. Wijnands/Getty Images

SANTORINI, GREECE

The star of the Cycladic isles & countless promotional posters

My donkey clatters up the switchbacks from the sea to the ancient volcano's lip. Pedestrians flatten against the marble cliff, leap onto boulders, and cringe as the 20 beasts thunder past. *"Ela, Ela,"* shouts the guide. "Come!"

This elderly Greek is straight from Central Casting with his snaggle-toothed grin, fisherman's cap, and Zorba mischievousness. He whips the last burro's flanks. The mass of horseflesh and panicked tourists surges higher up the crater's rind.

We're not ascending a mere mountain, though. We're stampeding on Santorini, an Aegean island that exploded in the late Bronze Age.

The blast—one of the most powerful in human history—detonated with the strength of 150 hydrogen bombs. Ash scattered over the globe, frightening royal scribes in Egypt with 9 days of darkness, drifting over China, inhibiting pine growth in California. Three-quarters of Santorini vanished, leaving only a crescent rim around a 6km-wide (3¾-mile) bowl of blue, known as the *caldera*.

The deep, clear sea sparkles sapphire, emerald, and turquoise: the startling hues of a gem shop, a peacock's tail. On the ocean floor lie Minoan ruins, submerged around 1650 B.C. by the mighty eruption.

Today Santorini—officially known as "Thira"—is the star of the Cycladic islands and countless Greek promotional posters, which peddle the whitewashed walls, azure church domes, and sheer volcanic cliffs, cut away like a child's diorama, revealing the Aegean's geological secrets.

Its images are clichés, yet visitors still gape, stepping off the ferry or hydrofoil. From below, villages frost the top like snow. Flights service the petite airport here, but don't inspire the same awe: Santorini is most stunning from the waterline.

As Lawrence Durrell commented in his classic 1978 travelogue *The Greek Islands*: "Perhaps only in the fanciful reaches of science fiction will you find anything quite like this extinct volcano of white marble, which blew its head off at some moment in the Bronze Age."

Was the lost settlement of Akrotiri, in fact, the sunken city of legend: Atlantis? Many romantics, including the philosopher Plato, have believed so. I'm unsure, meditating on the surviving frescoes—their ochre and smoke tones still so vivid, their style so accomplished—in the island's Museum of Prehistoric Thira. Ancient Santorini certainly reached a cosmopolitan peak, one perhaps not even matched today, as disco beats chip at the island's bedrock.

Is this paradise regained, here among the kebab shops and boutiques peddling linen shifts, hand-thrown pottery, and packets of overpriced fava, the local legume delicacy? Some questions, I decide, are best left unanswered. And so, in the best tradition of the Greek islands, I surrender to the moment, so filled with sun and sky and sea.

At a harbor-side taverna in Amoudi, I watch a fisherman heave a sloshing bucket from his boat to the dock. Octopus tentacles twine around his flexed forearms. Minutes later, the smoke from the animal's grilled flesh perfumes the terrace. The smell reminds me of burnt offerings, the sacrifices made to the ancient Greek gods.

◀ *A typical house with walls reflecting the sky.*
© Gavin Hellier/
Getty Images

SPECIAL MOMENTS

1 **Soak in the Caldera's hot spring.** Boat excursions explore the flooded crater, home to four satellite islands. The sea's so clear and deep—300 to 600m (984–1,968 ft.)—it can inspire vertigo. But at Palea Kameni (Old Burnt Island), it turns the color of tomato soup, as volcanic hot springs pump iron and other minerals into the bay. Visitors cannonball off ships and swim toward shore, shrieking as their feet, even their hands, disappear into the muck. Yet most continue, drawn to the scarlet center of the cove. And it's worth the mineral stink, the shins scraped on hidden rocks, the pink tint ruining bathing suits. Black cliffs encircle the rust-colored bay and a white chapel gleams on a spit. Palea Kameni is a scene of extraordinary, otherworldly beauty. Generously, it bestows beauty too, as enterprising tourists fashion mud masks from the shoreline's orange clay. Tours depart from the docks beneath Oia: Options range from a cheap-and-cheerful half-day jaunt to a sunset sail on a replica 19th-century schooner, to private moonlit jaunts, fully catered with champagne, salmon, and strawberries. Taxi boats also are available from the northern ports of Amoudi and Athinios.

2 **Stand on the volcano's snout.** Nea Kameni (New Burnt Island) is the youngest land in Greece. An underwater vent—dubbed "George I" by locals—spewed lava above the waves a few centuries back. The last red-hot ribbons cooled about 50 years ago. The terrain has a barren, blasted beauty: shattered heaps of slag and cinders, spikes of black basalt, gullies belching foul steam, devoid of life, save scrims of algae and graffiti. Peter Jackson could have saved considerable

▶ *The village of Oia.*
© Christopher Groenhout/
Lonely Planet Images/Getty Images

animation effort by filming the *Lord of the Rings* Mordor scenes here.

3 **Sunset in Oia.** Oia, the main island's northernmost village, is a marble labyrinth: a clutter of white-washed buildings and turquoise domes on a sea cliff. Its refurbished cave houses and mansions are more refined than those of tawdry Thira town. The boutiques here reflect this genteel and independent attitude. Almost every evening, hundreds gather here at twilight. Designer sandals skid on polished stone as chic crowds jostle at the Aegean's most coveted viewpoint. Below the 13th-century Venetian fortress lies a series of terraces and some 300 stairs to the harbor (spectacular panoramas make the steep trail worthwhile, even for visitors with cars). The lower village, Amoudi, has some excellent coves for swimming and a handful of tavernas, which serve seafood fresh off the boats.

4 **Wander the lost city.** The island's ancient inhabitants

abandoned their city after severe earthquakes in the late Bronze Age. Blasted by the eruption and swamped by seawater, many of the ruins lie on the floor of the *caldera*. Yet the acropolis survived, as did some of its superb wall paintings—visible at the archaeological site and the Thira museum. These sophisticated Minoan artifacts encourage much speculation that Akrotiri was Atlantis. The Museum of Pre-Historic Thira (behind the Orthodox Cathedral) is home to frescoes and other finds from ancient Akrotiri, as well as objects from ancient Crete and the northern Aegean islands. Try to visit this museum and the archaeological site at Ancient Akrotiri on the same day. Views from the site are incredible, with cliffs dropping precipitously to the sea on three sides and dramatic views of Santorini. Dorians lived here as early as the 9th century B.C., though most buildings date from the Hellenistic era. You can reach the site by taxi, on foot, or by excursion bus.

AMANDA CASTLEMAN is a freelance journalist and travel-writing instructor. She lived in the Mediterranean for 3 years—split between Italy, Greece, Cyprus, and Turkey—and has contributed to *The Athens News*, *Time Out Athens*, and the anthology *Greece, A Love Story*. Her website is www.amandacastleman.com.

ABOUT THE AUTHOR

YOUR TRIP

General Information: Before you go, visit **Wonderful Greece** (www.gnto.gr), or the websites www.santorini.net and www.santorini.com. **Getting There:** Santorini is 101km (63 miles) north of Crete in the Aegean Sea. **Delta** is the only American airline with nonstop service to Athens (☎ 800/241-4141; www.delta.com). Both **Olympic Airways** (www.olympic-airways.com) and **Aegean Air** (www.aegeanair.com) service the island; in summer, shuttles link to Mykonos, Rhodes, Crete, and Thessaloniki. Flights are about 40 minutes. A slow ferry takes 7½ hours from Athens to Santorini (www.ferries.gr). **What to See & Do:** Wander the ruined pathways of "ancient Atlantis" at **Akrotiri Archaeological Site.** The acropolis lies atop Mesa Vouno, near the excellent Kamari and Perissa beaches. Examine its vibrant frescos at the **Archaeological Museum** in Thira. **Best Lodging:** Splurge on a sunset suite in **Oia Castle Hotel,** with striking views of the *caldera*, the Aegean Sea, and the sunset (☎ 30-22860/71831; www.artmaisons.gr; 240€–360€/$314–$471). **Best Lodging Value:** Flower-wreathed **Casa Francesca** provides a peaceful setting, off the main road and near the *caldera* (☎ 30-22860/71507; www.santorinitours.com; 53€–69€/$69–$90). **Best Restaurant:** Oia's showpiece is the nouvelle **1800 Restaurant,** where you can dine on Continental cuisine inside a sea captain's mansion (☎ 30-22860/71485; www.1800.gr; 15€–30€/$20–$39). **Best Restaurant Value:** Savor *foungato* (zucchini fritters) and pine-kernel pastries on **Skala**'s gracious terrace, while gazing over the jumble of pastel-domed houses and turquoise pools honeycombing the cliff's curve (☎ 30-22860/71362; 8€–15€/$10–$20). **When to Go:** Apr to mid-June.

THE SCOTTISH HIGHLANDS

A legendary landscape of peaks, ancient ruins & lonely moors

Slate-colored skies can be the norm on a visit to this moodiest of places, but the Scottish Highlands strike a deep chord that resonates with the history, legends, and isolation that have shaped the land and its people.

Venture away from the cities and villages and you will encounter a haunting and almost primeval landscape of rugged mountains; wild, windswept moors; and gnarled and twisted trees. Much of it is desolate and melancholic, but it is also savagely beautiful. Eagles and osprey swoop and soar overhead, black-faced sheep graze among stone ruins, and shaggy Highland cattle dot the fields.

The Highlands cover northwest Scotland: Imagine a line drawn roughly between Dumbarton in the west and Aberdeen in the east, including the islands of the Hebrides, and stretching to the tip of Britain at John O'Groats.

Driving is the way to see the best of the Highlands in a short time. Start in Inverness, the "capital of the Highlands," perched between the Moray Firth on the eastern coast and Loch Ness to the south. It's a bustling, friendly town of narrow streets, divided by the River Ness and watched over by a modest castle. Its central location makes it a good base for touring.

Across the breadth of the Highlands, follow any road and it will reward you with unexpected delights. As you roam, you may be seduced from your route by a sweep of beach, a mist-shrouded mountain, a track across the heather, a whitewashed village. As the weather changes, so do the moods and colors of the countryside.

To the north of Inverness, on the east coast, is The Royal Burgh of Dornoch, a pretty town of glowing sandstone buildings set back from a wide sweep of sandy beach. It is famous for its golf course, the third oldest in the world, founded in 1616.

To the southeast, 48km (30 miles) from Inverness, is the Spey Valley, a region of lochs, mountains, and villages dominated by the snowcapped Cairngorms. Highlights for me are the beautiful Cille Choirille Church near Roy Bridge, its churchyard adorned with Celtic crosses; the dramatic hilltop ruins of the Ruthven barracks near Kingussie, abandoned by the Jacobites in 1746; and, at Carrbridge, the elegant high arch of Scotland's oldest stone bridge, built in 1717.

Head west from Inverness on the A832 to Gairloch, a seaside village that has been the heartland of the MacKenzie clan for more than 500 years. On the way, you will pass through some of Scotland's most magnificent—if austere—landscapes, including Glen Docherty, a vast sweep of valley with Loch Maree at the bottom. Gairloch has views to the Isle of Skye and the Torridon Mountains. At the Free Church you can attend services in Gaelic, the ancient language now undergoing a revival in these parts.

Farther north, from Ullapool, cross to the Isle of Lewis, the largest and most populated island of the Outer Hebrides. Drive or cycle across its flat, treeless landscape to discover ancient archaeological sites, including my favorites, the Neolithic Standing Stones of Callanish, which predate the Egyptian pyramids, and the Pictish broch (roundhouse) at Carloway.

◀ *Glencoe.*
© Charlie Waite/Getty Images

SPECIAL MOMENTS

1 **Culloden.** The bloody Battle of Culloden, between Bonnie Prince Charlie's Jacobites and the British Army in 1746, is central to the history and psyche of Highlanders. Waged on Culloden Moor, just outside Inverness, the battle saw the Jacobite forces crushed and ended hopes of restoring the exiled Stuarts to the throne, effectively ending a distinctive Highland way of life and resulting in the diaspora of Scottish clansmen around the world. In recent years, archaeologists have worked to re-create the moor as it would have been at the time of the battle, and a visit to the battlefield, which has a fascinating interpretive center alongside it, can do much to enhance your understanding of this emotive story from the history of the Highlands.

2 **Gairloch.** Guest rooms at the **Old Inn,** a traditional coaching inn, overlook Gairloch's narrow Flowerdale River, which snakes in from the sea and under an old stone footbridge. Founded by Scandinavian traders in the late 13th century, today Gairloch is a fishing port made up of several small settlements and is a popular summer holiday spot. A short, easy walk along the dappled, winding path beside the river will take you into a landscape little changed over the past 5 centuries, passing Flowerdale House, the seat of the MacKenzie clan, then leading to the old barn with its coat of arms, and around a curve in the river to a waterfall.

3 **Rua Reidh Lighthouse.** A cliff-top walk is one of the delights of a stay at this lighthouse, one of 97 built around the Scottish coast by "the lighthouse Stevensons," the family of writer Robert Louis Stevenson. Hike across the heather to the north, past the old stone jetty used until 1962, when road access came to the lighthouse. The coastline is dotted with spectacular "stac" rock formations, pounded by crashing seas. Rua Reidh (pronounced "roo ray," and Gaelic for "smooth point") is about 16km (10 miles) from Gairloch in Wester Ross. Built in 1912, the lighthouse still operates, but since it was automated the keeper's house has been a guesthouse where you can share home-cooked meals and fireside stories, and watch the sweep of the beacon across the inky darkness.

4 **Isle of Lewis.** Stoop through the low doorway of the Arnol Blackhouse into a dimly lit passageway and you'll soon discover why

Historic Scotland has given this modest place the same rating as Edinburgh Castle. Built in the crofting village of Arnol in 1885 and occupied until 1964, the black house is a rare surviving example of the traditional stone cottage of the Hebrides. Another of the treasures of Lewis is the eerie Standing Stones of Callanish, an ancient circle of stones beside Loch Ceann Hulavig. A wide avenue draws you irresistibly into the heart of the circle of 13 tall, slender stones where a single stone reaches 5m (16 ft.). If you're alone, you may find it, as I did, a spine-tingling moment.

Lewis is the most northerly of the Outer Hebrides, easily reached by ferry from Ullapool. Lewis and Harris form part of the same island, stretching for 153km (95 miles). Filled with marshy peat bogs, Lewis's landscape is relatively treeless. There are more than 600 weavers on the island, and one of the fun attractions in the town of Stornoway is visiting a mill shop or weaver's cottage.

ABOUT THE AUTHOR

LEE MYLNE is a descendant of a Scot who left the Highlands in 1818 as part of a "dual migration" to Nova Scotia and New Zealand. Now living in Melbourne, Australia, she is the author of several travel guides and narratives, and a Life Member of the Australian Society of Travel Writers. Check out her website: www.leemylne.com.

YOUR TRIP

General Information: Check out www.visitscotland.com, www.visitbritain.com, or www.travelbritain.org for your travel needs. When in London, stop in at the **Scottish Tourist Board** before heading north (19 Cockspur St., London SW1 Y5BL; ☎ 44-020/7930-8661). For information on the Isle of Lewis, contact the **Stornoway Tourist Information Centre** (☎ 44-1851/703088; www.visithebrides.com). **Getting There:** Daily flights from **London's Gatwick Airport** service Inverness; the flight takes about 2 hours. Or take a train from Glasgow or Edinburgh for £32 ($60). **Caledonian MacBrayne Ferry Service** runs a car and passenger ferry from Ullapool to Stornoway on the Isle of Lewis twice a day (www.calmac.co.uk). The crossing takes a little under 3 hours. **Best Lodging:** The isolated **Culloden House Hotel,** a Georgian mansion near Inverness, is the most elegant country retreat in the area (Culloden; ☎ 44-1463/790461; www.cullodenhouse.co.uk; £240–£325/$466–$631). In the Spey Valley, **The Boat Hotel,** in Boat-on-Garten, is an elegant, family-run hotel (Inverness-shire; ☎ 44-1479/831258; www.boathotel.co.uk; £129–£180/$250–$349). **Best Lodging Value:** With a get-away-from-it-all spirit, the **Rua Reidh Lighthouse** offers sweeping seascape views and comfy rooms (Melvaig, Gairloch; ☎ 44-1445 771 263; www.ruareidh.co.uk; £28–£38/$54–$73). **Best Restaurant:** Dine on traditional Scottish and French fare at **The Mustard Seed,** set in a former church overlooking the River Ness (16 Fraser St., Inverness; ☎ 44-1463/220220; £10–£14/$19–$27). **When to Go:** May–Sept, with May and June being the sunnier, drier months.

◄ *Eilean Donan Castle and Loch Aish, near Dornie.*
© David Noton/Getty Images

SEYCHELLES

A tropical getaway with some of the best beaches on the planet

When I announced to friends long ago that I was off to the Seychelles—one of the world's very last frontiers—their first response was, "Just where in the hell are they?" Good question. The 115-island archipelago lies 1,600km (994 miles) off the east coast of Africa, just south of the equator and north of Madagascar and the Tropic of Capricorn.

Unlike many islands that shouldn't bill themselves as a "tropical paradise," the Seychelles actually are. After touring the world, I concluded that this archipelago is the most idyllic of all getaways with the greatest beaches. The pristine waters offshore contain more shades of blue and green than I ever knew existed.

The world's largest coral atolls attract divers from as far away as Canada. The Seychelles are also home to some of the world's rarest endemic birds—the Seychelles bush warbler, the bare-legged scops owl, the magpie robin, and the only remaining Indian Ocean flightless bird, the white-throated rail on Aldabra Island. Eleven species are found only in these islands.

Uninhabited until the 1700s, the Seychelles were first occupied by that "yo-ho-ho and a bottle of rum" crowd, a gang of carnivorous pirates called "the wickedest corsairs who ever sailed the Indian Ocean." The British and French navies eventually captured them and strung them up before doing battle with each other. The French named the islands for French finance minister Viscount Jean Moreau de Séychelles in 1756, a bureaucrat who didn't deserve the honor.

The French hung out for 44 years, but the Seychelles became "Rule Britannia" in 1812. The French had imported slaves to work the plantations, but the Brits emancipated them in 1839. The British held onto the islands for 164 years, including tenures during two world wars, before independence came in June of 1976.

Today, the Seychelles, like the United States, is a melting pot, with small colonies of Chinese and Indians, some expats from France and Britain, but mainly Malagasy (Indonesians and former African slaves from Madagascar).

English is widely spoken, though Creole, a French patois, is the most common language. Some 90% of the 85,000 islanders who live in the Seychelles reside on Mahé, the main island, most of them enjoying their place in the sun around the small capital city of Victoria, named after a queen who ruled from London but never visited. A third of the population is under the age of 18.

The three major islands, and the ones you'll want to include on any itinerary, are Mahé, Praslin, and La Digue, all granite terra firma. This trio, along with 38 other inner islands, constitute the oldest mid-ocean granite islands on earth. The others, most of which are uninhabited, are low-lying coral atolls and reef islets.

Even though islanders are mostly Catholic, the Seychelles aren't great believers in marriage—nearly three-quarters of the natives are born out of wedlock. The song "Changing Partners" describes their freewheeling lifestyle.

On a visit to the Seychelles in 1940, the English author J. A. Mockford wrote: "Out there in the Seychelles, love, like the climate, is hot!" And so it remains to this day.

◀ *Hawksbill turtle, off Poivre Island.*
© Peter Oxford/ Naturepl.com

SPECIAL MOMENTS

1 Mahé. No matter where your flight originates—London, Paris, Rome—you'll land on Mahé, the largest of the Seychelles, 27km (17 miles) long by 3km (1¾ miles) to 8km (5 miles) wide. Mahé is the most developed of all the islands, yet it remains largely unspoiled. Most islanders live in or around Victoria, one of the world's smallest capital cities. What Mahé promises is virgin forests, incredible strips of powdery white sands, lush vegetation, plantations of coconut palms and cinnamon, pristine coral reefs, native craft markets, vibrant green jungles, colonial mansions, old plantation houses, tea factories, national parks, spice gardens, and the best hotels, restaurants, and watersports facilities in the Seychelles.

2 Praslin. When the British general Charles Gordon in 1881 stumbled upon an enchanted, primeval palm grove in a rainforest in the middle of Praslin, he claimed he'd discovered the original Garden of Eden. Actually, it was today's Vallée de Mai, with its strange coco de mer palm, which Gordon thought was the "Tree of Knowledge." Maybe he had a point. In all my travels, I've never seen a forest as exquisitely beautiful as this one. The coco de mer is called "the love nut" because of its suggestive, erotic shape. Today the forest is a protected World Heritage Site.

Although Mahé is glorious, I like Praslin even better, with its laid-back lifestyle and unspoiled beauty. It's reached by a 3-hour boat ride or a 15-minute flight on a small plane.

All other tropical islands could well turn to Praslin for a universal blueprint. Filled with luxuriant growth and animal life, it is enveloped by coral reefs teeming with nearly 1,000 different species of fish.

We don't want to argue with the late Noël Coward about what is the world's best beach. But I found one even better than Mahé's celebrated Beau Vallon. It's Anse Lazio, on the northwest tip of Praslin, where you'll find sand used in hourglasses and the world's bluest water. Don't just take my word for it: A number of international travel magazines agree that Anse Lazio is the best beach in the world.

3 La Digue. Upon my first arrival here, when an ox cart came to fetch my luggage, I knew that I had gone back in time. Sure, there are a few cars on island, but your choice of a "vehicle" will likely be a bike or your own trusty feet. The only paved road runs along part of the west coast. Otherwise expect sandy tracks.

I've walked the entire island, no big feat as it measures only 5km (3 miles) from north to south. Lying only 5km (3 miles) east of Praslin, it is reached in 30 minutes by a schooner ferry service.

This volcanic island is one of pristine beauty, rivaling both Mahé and Praslin. Both day-trippers and overnighters head for the glorious white sandy beach of Anse Source d'Argent along the southwest coast. This dazzling beach is said to be the most photographed in the world.

Some bird-watchers come from around the world to see the endangered black paradise flycatcher in its native habitat. Locals call the male of the species *veuve* (widow) because its long black tail evokes "widow's weeds." These rare birds

can be seen at the Veuve Nature Reserve off the west central coast.

4 **Silhouette.** All of us share Robinson Crusoe fantasies about escaping to a tropical island that time forgot. On the island of Silhouette, the third largest in the Seychelles, you can indulge that fantasy.

This is our favorite island hideaway in the Seychelles. There are no paved roads here, only trails cut through the interior or sandy tracks along the coast. A few farmers and fishermen inhabit the island along with hotel workers brought in to tend to guests at the newly opened 116-room, five-star hotel, **Labriz Silhouette** (☎ 248/225005; www.slh.com/labrizsilhouette).

Except for this pocket of posh, this island remains virtually untouched, a living museum of natural history, with rare trees, such as the amazing incense tree, and animals, including giant tortoises, the survivors of the granite island species thought extinct until they were rediscovered in the 1990s.

DARWIN PORTER is one of the world's most prolific travel writers. His books for Frommer's include guides to the Caribbean, Italy, France, Germany, and England. A Hollywood columnist and a celebrity biographer, Porter is also a radio broadcaster; his shows on American popular culture are heard in all 50 states.

ABOUT THE AUTHOR

YOUR TRIP

General Information: Contact **Seychelles Tourism Board** before you go (Victoria, Mahé; ☎ 248-671300; www.seychelles.com). **Getting There:** For flights, contact **Air Seychelles** (☎ 310/670-7302 in the U.S. or 44-1293/596-656 in the U.K.; www.airseychelles.net). The airline's major gateways are London, Rome, Paris, Munich, Singapore, and Johannesburg. **Air France** also flies from Paris (☎ 800/237-2747; www.airfrance.com). There are no nonstop flights to the Seychelles from the United States. **Best Lodging:** Former hideaway for Ian Fleming and W. Somerset Maugham, **Hilton Seychelles Northolme & Spa,** the oldest hotel in the Seychelles, still offers grand comfort in private villas and a healthy dose of nostalgic charm (Beau Vallon, Mahé; ☎ 248/299000; www.hiltonworld resorts.com; $732–$906/£388–£480). **Best Lodging Value:** Twenty modern, air-conditioned rooms nestle around a pool at **Sun Properties & Resort** (Beau Vallon; ☎ 248/285555; www.seychelles.net/sun; $128–$153/£67–£81). **Best Restaurant:** On the St. Louis Road leading to Beau Vallon in Mahé, **Marie-Antoinette** serves fabulous Creole cookery in a refurbished plantation house just outside Victoria (St. Louis; ☎ 248/266222; prix-fixe menu $22/£12). **Best Restaurant Value:** *The* watering hole of the Seychelles, **The Pirates Arms** serves fresh, well-prepared casual fare, from breakfast to dinner. Try the catch of the day (Independence Ave., Victoria, Mahé; ☎ 248/225-001; $14–$19/£7–£10). **When to Go:** Apr–Oct. As it's near the equator, the Seychelles are hot year-round. November to March is monsoon season.

◀ *La Digue Island.*
© Jeremy Walker/Getty Images

SICILY, ITALY

Orchards, medieval towns, vineyards & Greek temples

In Sicily, momentous sights constantly fill the eye. The walled mountaintop town of Erice has some of the most fantastic views in the Mediterranean, while Taormina—its easterly rival in the picturesque stakes—clings ornately to a coastal hillside in the shadow of Etna's still-living volcano. The offshore, cave-dotted Egadi islands of Favignana, Lévanzo, and Marétimmo vie with the windy volcanic Aeolian archipelago formed by Vulcano, Lipari, and Stromboli (where Roberto Rossellini shot a 1950s Ingrid Bergman movie) in their claims to have the clearest waters. The stark inland mountain ranges sweep dramatically from Messina to Marsala and from Caltanissetta to Catania, their isolated hamlets mysterious and faintly menacing as befits the land of Don Corleone, while the lush valleys below them are filled with citrus orchards, olive groves, wheat fields, and vineyards.

Culturally, Sicily is equally varied. Romans, Greeks, Byzantines, Arabs, French, and Spanish have all come and gone, leaving in their wake a powerful overlap of impressions. The Doric columns at Segesta, the Valley of the Temples at Agrigento, the ancient Hellenic amphitheater at Siracusa, and the mosaics at Piazza Armerina's Villa Imperiale all stun the eye. The island's cathedrals, convents, and palaces reflect an eclectic variety of styles ranging from Romanesque and Gothic to baroque and rococo. The local language—don't even think of calling it a dialect in the presence of a Sicilian—blends Greek, Latin, Aragonese, and Norman vocabulary (though you're more likely to hear it spoken in the countryside than in the cities).

All this can prove a mite rich for the blood, which is perhaps why my favorite place on the island is laid-back Trapani, up in the northwest corner. You won't find it on the travel itinerary of most visitors who—deterred by the sight of its sprawling modern outskirts—tend to pass it by on their way to neighboring Erice. That's a pity, as they're seriously missing out. The historic center houses architectural masterpieces such as the medieval Santa Maria del Gesú Church and the 16th-century Spanish Plateresque-style Palazzo della Giudecca. The location is fascinating—like Cádiz in Southern Spain, the city is enclosed by the sea on three sides. Some say Homer wrote the Odyssey here in the days when it was known as Drepanon ("sickle" in Greek, owing to the city's shape). Its salt pans have been a source of livelihood for centuries, and its colorful market is redolent with fresh sardines and octopus. In spring the *mattanza* of tuna fish in the nearby Egadi archipelago is one of the great regional events (see "Special Moments," below). In the evenings, locals still walk the *passeggiata*, dressed to the nines, genteelly appraising each other as they've done for centuries and serenely containing the emotions that rumble just below the surface.

◀ *Agrigento, Temple of Concordia.*
© Robin Hill/Digital Vision/ Getty Images

SPECIAL MOMENTS

1 **Erice.** Perched some 610m (2,001 ft.) above Trapani, on a crest known in ancient times as Mount Eryx, Erice demands superlatives. For a start, it has the best-preserved Cyclopean (Phoenician-built) walls anywhere and the finest coastal views of all the many I've seen in the Mediterranean. They even take in distant Africa to the south on clear days. Medieval towers rise above these great walls, and behind them, immaculate cobbled lanes shelter mansions with Gothic, Renaissance, and baroque portals and secret hidden courtyards. A castle dominates the town's highest point and a 14th-century church with a campanile–cum–lookout tower stands beside the main town entrance. Though Erice could be a showplace, it manages to combine its latent open-air-museum appeal with a genuine aura of the past. Access is by road or funicular, both of which provide constantly changing vistas.

2 **Egadi Islands.** Just a short boat or hydrofoil trip from Trapani, this trio of peaceful volcanic islands, with their traditional white cubist houses, is among the most picturesque in the Mediterranean. It's also the setting for the less-than-peaceful tuna fish *mattanza* (ritual killing), which has been carried out in the same traditional Arabic way for centuries. Butterfly-shaped Favignana, the largest, has medieval castles and pellucid waters that are a skin diver's dream. Levanzo, my favorite, is the tiniest and most beautiful: a place to lose yourself amid the peace and gentle winds. Its perfect little bay, Cala Dogana, and famed Grotta del Genovese (Genovese Grotto), with its unique 10,000-year-old Paleolithic engravings, are unforgettable. Marettimo, farthest from the mainland, has two scenic ports, Scala Vecchio and Scala Nuovo, on opposite coasts, as well as countless caves and evocative archaeological remains.

3 **Palermo.** Like all great Mediterranean cities, the Sicilian capital offers a magical palimpsest of cultures. Previous occupants—from Phoenicians and Carthaginians to Normans and Aragonese—have all left their mark. Its setting on a crescent bay backed by mountains is magnificent, and the array of churches, palaces, theaters, fountains, sculptures, and piazzas is positively daunting. Santa Teresa alla Kalsa represents Sicilian baroque, and the Palazzo dei Normani is an eternal reminder of Sicily's medieval French occupants. The 12th-century cathedral and Palatine Chapel are among the other star attractions, as is the

religious "festino" in July. On a more down-to-earth level, side streets and colorful markets radiate life filled with ebullient shouts and laughter.

4 Siracusa. Siracusa rivaled Athens as the most powerful city in the world, until its golden age (roughly 5th–3rd c. B.C., when tyrants like Gerone and Dionysos ruled) was broken by the Romans in 212 B.C. Today, Siracusa is a lot more modest and provincial, and most relics of those times—apart from rare surviving exceptions like the original Greek theater and Dionysos' Euricalo Castle with its subterranean tunnel network—were destroyed by a devastating 17th-century earthquake. The rebuilt city countered by producing exquisite Sicilian baroque buildings such as the Duomo cathedral, San Giovanni Church (parts of which date from the 6th c.), Palazzo Bellomo, and Arethusa Fountain. Look for them in the old narrow-laned Ortygia head-land, which is linked to the modern section of the town by a causeway.

PETER STONE is a London-born writer living in Madrid. As well as being the author of *Frommer's Madrid,* he's a Mediterranean addict who has enjoyed prolonged sojourns in Greece, Italy, and North Africa, and published articles on Homeresque havens from Akrotiri to Astipaleia. Contact him at petine@teleline.es.

ABOUT THE AUTHOR

YOUR TRIP

General Information: For information before you go, contact the **Italian Tourist Board** (☎ 39-800/117700 in Sicily; www.italiantourism.com). Other helpful websites include www.travel-italy.com and www.regione.sicilia.it. **Getting There:** There are no nonstop flights to Sicily from the U.S. Most visitors fly first to Milan or Rome, then take a connecting flight to Sicily, most often using Palermo as their gateway to the island. Check **Alitalia** for flights to Sicily (☎ 800/223-5730; www.alitaliausa.com). **Getting Around:** Unless you're heading for remote towns and villages, riding the rails is the best way to traverse the island without a private rental car. Check out www.trenitalia.com for more information. And where the train doesn't go, a bus will. **Best Lodging:** In the heart of Trapani's old town, **Alle Due Badie Residence** provides an atmosphere of elegance and comfort (Via Badia Nuova 33; ☎ 39-0923/24054; www.duebadie.it; 100€–175€/$130–$228). **Best Lodging Value:** Set on the waterfront road, a short distance from the center of Trapani, **Hotel Vittoria** is exceedingly comfortable (Via Francesco Crispi 4; ☎ 0923-873044; 89€/$116). **Best Restaurant:** Flavorful dishes, such as roast lamb in a citrus sauce and seafood pasta with shrimp and calamari, highlight the menu at **Ai Lumi Tavernetta,** in the ground floor of a 17th-century palace (Corso Vittorio Emanuele 75, Trapani; ☎ 39-0923/872418 or 39-347/8566570; www.ailumi.it; 7€–15€/$9–$19). **Best Restaurant Value:** At **Il Ciclope,** the food is fairly simple but the ingredients are fresh and the dishes well prepared (Corso Umberto I, Taormina; ☎ 39-0942/23263; 6€–13€/$7–$17). **When to Go:** May–June or Sept–Oct.

◄ *Lipari, Aeolian Islands.*
© Nicholas DeVore/Getty Images

SILK ROAD, CHINA

An unforgettable train journey along an ancient trade route

I am eating at a late-night street stall in front of the train station in a tiny town on the Silk Road when I notice something startling about the Asian woman who is serving me noodles: Her skin is a smooth yellow, her hair jet-black, and her eyes a piercing blue. The unusual features illustrate the unique path that led from China's ancient capital of Xī'ān to the West. The trade routes—used from the 1st century B.C. to the 10th century A.D.—brought not just silk, gold, and wool, but a mixing of cultures and religions. Today, Gansu and Xinjiang, the province and autonomous region through which the Silk Road passes, is home to a largely Muslim population growing up in a rising, modern China.

There are train trips more famous than the journey along the Silk Road, but none is more stunning. Unlike the views from the Trans-Siberian Railway to the north, the changes of scenery are frequent: Crowded, skyscraper-dotted cities like Xī'ān give way to dry desert plateaus which later turn to stunning, purple mountains capped with snow. Unlike an Amtrak trip that takes you from one end of continental America to another, the Silk Road journey whisks you from one culture, one world to another. You start in the Far East but end up 10 days later in what feels like the Middle East, in dusty, mosque-filled towns where donkeys and camels are the prime mode of transportation.

The train voyage can be made in 3 days of continuous travel. But that would defeat the point of the trip; many of the stops offer unique sights. Take 10 days if you can. Begin in Xī'ān with a visit to the Terra Cotta Warriors. Between Xī'ān and Kashgar are several great stopping points, either as day trips or overnights. At Jiāyù Guān, you'll want to walk the walls of Jiāyù Guān Fort, which marks the official end of China's Great Wall. Next is Dūnhuáng, with its fantastic Buddhist caves and sand dunes. Once you cross into Xinjiang province, the famous desert basin of Turpan will lure you to the well-preserved ancient town of Gāochāng. Farther west is the provincial capital of Ürümqi, which is in striking distance of beautiful Heavenly Lake, surrounded by pine forests. The end of the line is Kashgar, known as a trading center for Pakistanis, Chinese, and Central Asians, and for its colorful Sunday market. For an even livelier, less touristed Sunday bazaar, take a 5-hour drive from Kashgar to Khotan.

One disclaimer for the independent traveler: An antiquated reservation system keeps you from booking your tickets more than 10 days in advance. You may want to book through hotels and travel agents, or join a tour group. I wholeheartedly recommend, however, that you travel independently, immersing yourself in the local culture and making friends with other passengers. Everything else about your train trip should be a breeze. Chinese trains are clean. They run often and are usually on schedule. First- and second-class sleeper compartments, called soft and hard sleepers, are both comfortable and inexpensive. In a pinch, you can hop on a plane, with flights between most of the points mentioned above. But that, of course, would be cheating!

◀ *Taklamakan desert, Gansu Province.*

© Keren Su/
DanitaDelimont.com

303

SPECIAL MOMENTS

1 Terra-Cotta Warriors near Xī'ān. Start your journey on the Silk Road in Xī'ān, with a visit to the Terra Cotta Warriors, one of the most thrilling sights in the world. The view of thousands of clay soldiers lined up in the space of a covered football field is awe-inspiring. The figures were created for Emperor Qín Shǐ Huáng's mausoleum to see him into the afterlife, some 2,200 years ago. You'll want to spend time studying the nuances of each figure, and the unique facial expressions that reveal personality and character, from the tilt of a head to a serene grin. Amazingly, the warriors are just one part of the emperor's attempt to reconstruct his empire for his afterlife. The tomb to the west is still to be fully excavated, and is said to include a full reconstruction of the ancient capital, complete with rivers and lakes of mercury. Over 700,000 workers were said to be drafted for the project. In Pit I, there are over 6,000 infantrymen in battle formation, stretching 182m (600 ft.). Originally painted in bright colors, they were constructed from interchangeable parts. Because the heads were hand-molded, no two appear the same. The average height of the warriors is 1.8m (5 ft., 11 in.); senior officers are taller. Don't miss the small hall to the right of Pit I with its display of two magnificent bronze chariots, reconstructed from nearly 3,500 pieces.

2 Mògāo Buddhist Caves near Dūnhuáng. The stunning collection of Buddhist murals and cave temples traces the influence of India on China's landscape and people. The caves are also a rare example of a Chinese tourist site done well—you'll be impressed with the university-educated tour guides who tote flashlights into the caves that were first dug in the 4th century. They pause to explain the significance of the colorful frescoes that illustrate flying celestial beings, animals, and traditional Chinese landscapes. The statues, particularly a 15m (50-ft.) reclining Buddha on the main altar, are among the finest in the world. Sadly, many were damaged by looting in the early 20th century.

3 Heavenly Lake near Ürümqi. In addition to being steeped in history, the Silk Road offers sights of extreme natural beauty. In the heart of Xinjiang, better known for its deserts, is a small range of mountains covered with Alpine trees and a lovely lake that reminds me of Lake Tahoe. Disembark the train at

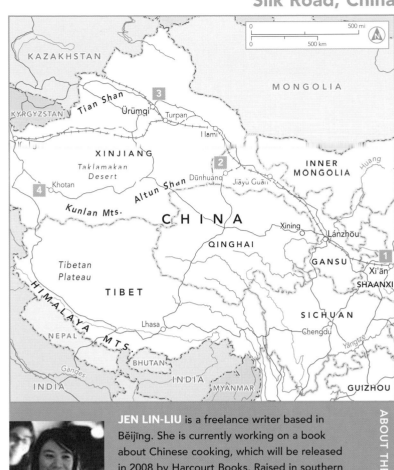

Ürümqi and transfer by taxi or bus to Heavenly Lake, a 2-hour drive from the station. The entrance to the lake may be crowded with tourists, but you can walk to the far end, where a Kazak family has set up several yurts (traditional tents) that they rent out for just a few dollars a night. With any luck, you'll get to spend an evening underneath a yak-skin tent listening to a Kazak playing his guitar.

4   Sunday market in Khotan. The last leg of the journey, between the ancient trade cities of Kashgar and Khotan, must be made on bumpy roads by car, but it's worth it. Try to arrive in Khotan in time for the Sunday Bazaar, one of the largest markets in Central Asia, with a carnival-like atmosphere where buyers and sellers haggle over live camels, silk carpets, and tomatoes by the cartload. Bearded men in Muslim skullcaps throw canvas bags full of wares over their shoulders, while outdoor barbers offer shaves for less than 50¢.

JEN LIN-LIU is a freelance writer based in Běijīng. She is currently working on a book about Chinese cooking, which will be released in 2008 by Harcourt Books. Raised in southern California and educated at Columbia University in New York, she first moved to China in 2000 on a Fulbright scholarship.

ABOUT THE AUTHOR

YOUR TRIP

General Information: When planning your trip, contact **China International Travel Service** (☎ 626/568-8993 in the U.S., 86-10/8511-8522 in China; www.cits.com.cn). **Getting There:** The Silk Road begins in the ancient capital of **Xī'ān,** located in central China, and extends west through **Xinjiang,** China's northwestern autonomous zone. Numerous direct flights connect Xianyang Airport with all major cities in China, including Běijīng, Shànghǎi, Chóngqìng, Chéngdū, Kūnmíng, Ürümqi, Lhasa, and Hong Kong. **What to See & Do:** Seeing the **Terra-Cotta Warriors** is essential. The tomb to the west is not fully excavated, and is said to include a full reconstruction of the ancient capital. The **Mògāo Caves** are the biggest, best-preserved, and most significant site of Buddhist statuary in all of China. **Best Lodging:** In Xī'ān, the **Shangri-La Golden Flower** is highly recommended for impeccable service and fine rooms (8 Chang Le Rd. W.; ☎ 86-29/8323-2981; www.shangri-la.com; $230/£122). The most luxurious digs in Dūnhuáng is the **Silk Road Dūnhuáng Hotel** (Dūnyuè; ☎ 86-937/888-2088; www.dunhuangresort.com; $100/£53). In Ürümqi, stay at the stylish **Taipei Suites Hotel** (8 N. Xinhua Rd.; ☎ 86-991/887-8888; $66–$161/£33–£82). **Best Lodging Value:** A good value in Khotan is the **Zhèjiāng Hotel** (Běijīng Xī Lù 9; ☎ 86-903/202-9999; $56–$96/£30–£51). **Best Restaurants:** In Xī'ān, lively **Dé Fā Chāng** raises dumplings to a high art form (Zhōnglóu Guǎngchǎng; ☎ 86-29/8721-4060; $15/£8) In Dūnhuáng, the restaurants in the **Silk Road Hotel** serve local and regional delicacies (see above; $20/£11). **When to Go:** Peak season is early May, and mid-July to mid-October.

◀ *Terra-Cotta Warriors, Xī'ān.*
© Jon Arnold/DanitaDelimont.com

SOMERSET, ENGLAND

Galleries, festivals, farmland, UFOs & Iron Age forts

Somerset is so fantastic because it lies just beyond the Home Counties where commuters from London live and just before the prime holiday destinations of Devon and Cornwall. So it escapes the dull, comfortable creep of suburbia emanating from London and hasn't yet been colonized by second-home buyers and grannies looking for a place by the sea.

Instead it is left real. And somewhat untamed. You can feel this as soon as you cross over the border from Wiltshire and climb up one of its Iron Age forts dating from centuries before anyone really thought to write anything down. From the top, the ancient land spreads out alluringly before you and the patchwork of small, raggedy fields lies below you like a sea.

From here you could spot a U.F.O. It's the second-most successful place in the U.K. for this activity. More likely, you'll hear the disturbing cry of the peacocks patrolling the nearby Elizabethan manor of Longleat, presided over by the eccentric Marquis of Bath and his wifelets.

Down below, you might see some strange bright lights moving across the cut corn. Don't get too excited; it's not a spacecraft wheeling out a crop circle. It's the locals out lamping rabbits, catching the creatures in the hypnotic glare of their Land Rover's headlights before shooting them dead.

It might seem harsh, but this is farming country. Always known for its agriculture—especially the strong cider made from Somerset apples—it's now nurturing a reputation for rare breeds and organic produce. This is a county where the butchers will spend an hour discussing the merits of a certain cut of meat. And agricultural fairs stick first-prize rosettes on oversized leeks and perfectly formed runner beans.

But it is also a county with a personality in flux. The old industries associated with the land no longer require so many hands, leaving many places and people poor. But the artists of England quickly sniff out a bargain. In the past decades their sensitive noses have led them to Frome, a gorgeous non-twee Somerset town with more English Heritage buildings than anywhere else in the county.

The big chains haven't yet sucked the character from Frome, and the shops are still individual and quirky, selling everything from vintage clothing to wild-boar sausages. Philosophers, writers, musicians, and other artists mix in with the racer boys waiting for the drinking-fest that is Saturday night in Somerset. But for 2 weeks in July they claim the town for their own and put on the most astounding festival.

After a day on the streets, if it's sunny, I'd head to the fab veggie eatery, The Garden Café. The name's not a tease; out back is the most glorious walled courtyard garden. And then it's on to The Griffin, the most local "local," which brews its own beer. If you're lucky they'll be hosting a jamming session or a public debate in the beer garden.

And you haven't even really got started. There are the art galleries, contemporary theater, mysterious underground tunnels, and so much more. You might find you fall so in love with the place you have to move here. I did.

◀ *Somerset countryside, late afternoon.*
© Charles Bowman/ Robert Harding World Imagery/Getty Images

SPECIAL MOMENTS

1 **Berrow.** Just beyond the fish and chip shops and out-of-town supermarkets, it's a treat to stumble upon Berrow church. And just when you thought you were going to have to eat a gas-station sandwich for lunch, it's even more exciting to find the church hall is serving up homemade scones smothered with clotted cream and strawberry jam made from fruits picked that week from one of the gardens. Afterwards, you can pick your way across the dunes to the beach. It's one of the longest in Europe, and although the sea is usually too far out to even see, you might catch Wales lurking in the mist on the other side of the Bristol Channel.

Head right from Berrow, along the dunes to Brean, and you'll wander past the bones of a ship beached on the sand. It's the wreck of the SS *Nornen*, a Norwegian boat dragged onto the mud flats during a stormy night in the spring of 1897. Happily all the crew—and even their dog—survived and were shipped to safety by the local lifeboat rescue service. But the vessel itself, despite attempts at a rescue, was eventually left to be claimed by the waves.

2 **Mells.** "Why," you wonder to yourself as you're wandering around Mells, "is there nobody else here?" There's some astounding architecture: a Tudor manor house sporting dog-topped gate posts designed by Edward Lutyens, a Grade I 14th-century church, a medieval lockup, a model street from the same period, and endless oh-so-cute cottages. The whole place looks as though it has been whisked straight from a film set. And yet it's practically a secret. In the distance you might hear some cricket being played in the summer or see a couple of people cycling through the village. Follow them and you'll probably end up at the Talbot, a 15th-century coaching inn where the locals play darts or spill out onto the flower-ridden courtyard in the summer.

3 **Frome and Wells.** Shopping in Frome is a series of special moments. If you're here on the right day you may be able to pick up some bison burgers from the farmers market, or some ripe cheese at Sagebury Cheese for lunch. Or come just to see the sweet open stream running down the center of the street from the old medieval spring. On other days there may be bargains in the auction house. If not, there's bound to be something you like in Poot, the vintage

clothing shop on Catherine Hill, a fab collection of shops all perched on a gorgeous historical hill. The whole place is a shopper's delight. From here it's a short hop to Wells, a medieval gem of a town with a 12th-century cathedral famous for its scissor arch.

4 Glastonbury. Myth has it that Jesus was bought over to Glastonbury by his uncle Joseph of Arimathea when he was a child, and then popped back later with the Holy Grail. At the time, much of the surrounding land was under water, so the old man arrived by boat. When he got here, he's supposed to have stuck his staff in the ground and been surprised to see a holy bush spring up. Glastonbury still has a strange feeling in the air, perhaps because it's built on a point where several ley lines collide. My favorite activity is to climb the tor. There are usually a couple of hippies up on top, and if you're lucky you might encounter some modern-day druids.

OLIVIA EDWARD is a British writer who began specializing in travel after living in Shànghǎi. She's since written for *Time Out*, DK, and MTV Guides, and glossy publications for companies like American Express. Happiest when swimming in rough seas, she can be tempted onto dry land by rain, mud, and off-road motorbikes.

ABOUT THE AUTHOR

YOUR TRIP

General Information: When planning your trip, take a look at www.visitbritain.com, where you can search for information by region. For information on Somerset, visit www.celebratingsomerset.co.uk; for Frome, try www.frometouristinfo.co.uk; for Glastonbury, visit www.glastonbury.co.uk. To find a full list of the best shops in Frome, go to www.catherinehill.info. **Getting There:** A car is the best way to explore the region; however, you can also reach the area by bus or train. For bus travel, visit www.nationalexpress.com; for rail travel, visit www.networkrail.co.uk. Trips from London take anywhere from 2 to 3 hours, depending on your mode of transportation. **Best Lodging:** Stay where celebrities partake in some luxurious country living at **Babington House** (Babington, near Frome; ☎ 44-01373/812266; www.babingtonhouse.co.uk; £225–£395/ $428–$750). **Best Lodging Value:** You can have the whole house to yourself in the middle of Frome with a stay at the **Lazy Dog Cottage** (Paul St.; ☎ 44-01373/855275; www.lazydogcottage.co.uk; £95–£110/$180–$209). **Best Restaurant:** The **Mulberry Restaurant** at Charlton House creates exciting three-course meals using the best local ingredients (Shepton Mallet; ☎ 44-01749/342008; www.charltonhouse.com; £50/$95). **Best Restaurant Value:** Sandwiches and breakfasts highlight the all-organic fare at the **Garden Café** (16 Stony St., Frome; ☎ 44-01373/454178; www.gardencafefrome.co.uk; £5–£8/$10–$15). **When to Go:** June to September are the warmest months, November to March are the coldest.

◀ *Wells Cathedral.*

TASMANIA, AUSTRALIA

Wild peaks & gorges, tulip farms, ruins & secret beaches

It doesn't matter where you go in Tasmania; you won't be going far. This quirky, oddball little island is all of 68,000 sq. km (26,255 sq. miles)—easily circumnavigated in one of the best 7-day road trips I've ever taken. I can't understand why it's so often overlooked, or why it's the butt of so many cruel jokes—poorly disguised envy, perhaps?

Simply put, Tazzie, as the locals call it, is a magic place. Colored by a rich convict history and a pioneering spirit that distinguishes island inhabitants the world over, it boasts spectacular and diverse landscapes, friendly people, a pleasant temperate climate, and great wine and food. What more could you want?

I can't remember the last time I had more surprises and cleaner air in one 7-day period. I passed through rain-swept temperate forests of the southwest; World Heritage areas, where ancient peaks rose like creatures from a Jurassic landscape; wild, isolated gorges; cute, rustic towns; and the haunting ruins of old penal colonies.

In the north, I made a pig of myself on Australia's favorite King Island cheeses and gasped at the perfume of lavender and tulip fields (they do export to Holland). On the east coast, I roamed through olive groves and vineyards, contemplating the legal (and heavily protected) opium poppies grown for the world pharmaceutical market. And on the Freycinet Peninsula I found heaven—"secret" pristine white-sand beaches and The Hazards, a granite wonderland where pink, white, and gray domes plunge into the unforgiving southern ocean. Once you've rested here, marveling at the crystal-clear, midnight-blue water, you'll never think of a beach the same way again.

This is where two of Australia's native wallabies hang out—the small, cuddly Bennetts wallaby and the ridiculously cute pademelon. If you're lucky, you'll see that other chubby marsupial, the wombat; and cunning brush-tail possums will descend from the trees at night to devour anything you haven't strapped down. I swear they know how to undo zippers! If you're very lucky you might see the ferocious, wee eastern quoll (native cat, but not really a cat at all), or, even rarer, the legendary Tasmanian Devil, best described as a giant jaw with four legs. The Aussies really know how to put on a show when it comes to wildlife.

My memories of good times in Tasmania wouldn't be complete without reference to iconic attractions like the Overland Track—an 80km (50-mile) walking trail that links Cradle Mountain with Lake St. Clair, threading its way through a glacier-carved landscape punctuated by tannin-stained lakes. It's hard to forget the mossy waterfalls and the general feeling that you've entered some primeval place the rest of the world has forgotten.

◀ *Tree ferns in the Tahune Forest Reserve.*
© Michael & Patricia Fogden/ Minden Pictures

SPECIAL MOMENTS

1 Hobart. I'm fascinated by ports, and Hobart is one of the best. My favorite spot is the 19th-century waterfront warehouses that once bustled with whalers, soldiers, and tradesmen and now house cafes, artists' studios, shops, and superb seafood restaurants. There's nothing more invigorating than breathing in the salty air as you wander among visiting yachts, cruise ships, catamarans, ferries, naval vessels, bulk carriers, and endless fishing boats. For what it's worth, sailors from the U.S. Navy vote Hobart one of their favorite Australian stops, and oceangoing yachties with tanned-leather skin always have a grateful look on their faces—as though arriving in Hobart has been their personal salvation. I can relate to that.

2 Freycinet National Park. Two hours east of Hobart on good roads (or a lovely 3-hr. coastal ramble south from Launceston) is Freycinet Peninsula (via the fishing town of Coles Bay), dishing up sensational seascapes, complete with seafood and overhanging crags and cliffs. The granite boulder Hazards are an imposing barrier to Wine Glass Bay. It's a vigorous 40- to 60-minute walk to their summit and exceptional views of one of the best beaches in the world. Most people turn back here; I wouldn't. I'd take the 40-minute stroll down—you're likely to find yourself the only person on an idyllic, sickle-shaped stretch of sand. No shops, no deck chairs, no locals—just palpable, intoxicating isolation.

3 Cradle Mountain. Cradle Mountain is the iconic image of the Tasmanian wilderness—easily accessible with a network of walking tracks for the brave and the lazy. You need to be fit and agile to get to the summit (with wet-weather gear, even on a fine day), but after an 8-hour return hike, I felt like I'd conquered Everest. The 1- to 2-hour walk around Dove Lake (on boarded paths) is much easier and takes you through deciduous beech forests and the famous Ball Room, an ancient enclave of rare King Billy pines. A vigorous 5 hours' return to

▶ *Australian Brushtail Possum.*
© Ted Mead/Getty Images

Marion's Lookout tempts with great views of Dove and Crater lakes and Cradle Mountain itself. It's a sublime, powerful landscape, and the ways to experience it are many and varied.

4 Strahan. Pronounced "strawn," this sweet little fishing village is the gateway to wild, ancient landscapes. If you're not convinced, head straight for Sarah Island in Macquarie Harbour. It was Tasmania's most brutal penal colony, and if it doesn't send shivers down your spine, nothing will. Join the top-notch Gordon River Cruise to get here and feel the haunting atmosphere of the Wild Rivers National Park/Tasmanian World Heritage Area. In complete contrast, Ocean Beach, 6km (4 miles) west of Strahan, is all about open-air freedom. It's Tasmania's longest beach (33km/21 miles) and the scene of my most childish moment—leaping down the enormous Henty Sand Dunes and staring, goggle-eyed, at a platypus playing in one of the creeks that run onto the beach.

ADRIENNE REWI is author of *Frommer's New Zealand*, three other nonfiction titles, and thousands of magazine articles and short stories. Her writing passion has taken her throughout Asia. When she is not taking photos or writing her next book, she is safely housed in Christchurch, New Zealand.

ABOUT THE AUTHOR

YOUR TRIP

General Information: Contact www.discovertasmania.com.au or the **Hobart Visitor Information Centre** (20 Davey St.; ☎ 61-3/6230-8233). **Cradle Mountain Visitor Centre** offers the best information on walks and treks (☎ 61-3/6492-1110). **Getting There:** **Qantas** (www.qantas.com) and **Virgin Blue** (www.virginblue.com.au) fly from Melbourne to Hobart and Launceston. The **TT-Line** runs ferries from Melbourne to Tasmania (☎ 61-3/9206-6211; www.spiritoftasmania.com.au). **Best Outfitters:** **Gordon River Cruises** gives a half-day trip and a full-day trip out of Strahan (☎ 61-3/6471-4300; www.strahanvillage.com.au). For an 8-day overland guided trip, contact **Tasmanian Expeditions** (☎ 61-3/6339-3999 or 61-3/6334-3477; www.tas-ex.com). **Best Lodging:** **Hotel Grand Chancellor,** in Hobart, overlooks fishing boats in Victoria Dock (1 Davey St.; ☎ 61-3/6235-4535; www.ghihotels.com; US$208–US$292/£110–155). If you like luxury with your rainforests, then **Cradle Mountain Lodge** is the place for you (☎ 61-3/6492-1303; www.cradlemountainlodge.com.au; US$184–US$288/£98–£153). **Best Lodging Value:** A warm, cozy room awaits you at **Wellington Lodge,** a Victorian-style town house just 10 minutes' walk from the Hobart town center (7 Scott St.; ☎ 61-3/6231-0614; US$88–US$104/£47–£55). **Best Restaurant:** Smoked blue-eyed cod highlights the Australian cuisine at **Mit Zitrone** (333 Elizabeth St., Hobart; ☎ 61-3/6234-8113; US$14/£7). **Best Restaurant Value:** You can find a range of entrees, from Thai beef curry to eggs on toast, at **Cumquat on Criterion** (10 Criterion St., Hobart; ☎ 61-3/6234-5858; US$6–US$17/£3–£9). **When to Go:** Oct–Apr.

TEOTIHUACÁN, MEXICO

Mexico's most prized ruins, only an hour from Mexico City

Mexico is filled with great monuments heralding its Indian heritage. In Yucatán province, the truncated pyramids of Uxmal and Chichén Itzá, prime mementoes of the Mayan empire, tower above a lush green jungle. On Monte Albán, near the central city of Oaxaca, where Indian women still weave traditional multicolored garments, you'll find the excavated remains of palaces, statues, and tombs built by the Zapotecs in the 3rd century. At church-filled Cholula, 75km (47 miles) from Mexico City, magnificent Toltec frescoes nestle beside the long corridors that burrow into the huge adobe Tepanapa pyramid, half buried under the earth and in the process of excavation.

All impressive stuff, but the place that really knocks me out is Teotihuacán, 2,286m (7,500 ft.) up on a sunny plateau just an hour's drive north of downtown Mexico City. Larger, better-preserved, and more stunningly picturesque than any of the above (justly vaunted) trio, it also evokes—for me—a much stronger impression of a past world. My leisurely day wandering around here was the most rewarding I ever spent in Mexico. Like some cerebral time traveler, I could almost visualize the once-flourishing metropolis of a quarter-million (estimated) inhabitants that stood on this very spot and whose period of glory (from A.D. 300) uncannily paralleled that of ancient Rome.

Teotihuacán is dissected by the awesomely long and wide Avenue of the Dead, where multitudes of citizens walked and went about their business. At its northern end looms the Pyramid of the Moon, where priests conducted services, and on its eastern side—twice as large—towers the massive 248-step-high Pyramid of the Sun, from whose summit you feel you could rule the world (see "Special Moments" on p. 316). At its southern extremity is the large sunken Ciudadela housing the Temple of Quetzalcoatl (the legendary Plumed Serpent), where fanciful murals depict the paradise of Tlaloc, the Rain God, in which people dance, fish, pick flowers, and chase butterflies.

Wander off the Avenue of the Dead, along narrower lanes that take you past statues of coiled serpents, and you'll find other pictorial evocations of the past, such as the Palace of Quetzalpapalotl, with its obsidian figures of the eponymous mythical bird-butterfly. Just behind that is the labyrinthine Temple of the Jaguars where vivid murals and painted pillars depict large black predatory felines, while in the Temple of Feathered Shells more genteel motifs of parrots and seashells cover the walls. All are haunting reminders of a once-rich and powerful world, throbbing with life and color.

Yet unlike those Mayan, Zapotecan, and Toltec sites, Teotihuacán is an enigma. There are no records of where the inhabitants came from or what language they spoke. Or why they left. Conflicting theories speculate they were driven out by attacking armies, by fire, by drought, by devastating plague. But no one knows for sure. The Aztecs who discovered the deserted city refused to settle here. Why? Superstition? Fear? For me the mystery adds to its awesome attraction.

◀ *Plaza of the Moon, Pyramid of the Sun.*
© Dallas and John Heaton/
Jupiter Images

SPECIAL MOMENTS

1 Pyramid of the Sun. Built of adobe bricks with fragments of tools, pottery, and figurines embedded inside, this 2,000-year-old pyramid is second in size only to Cheops just outside Cairo and the high point of any visit to Teotihuacán. In 1908, a cavalier archaeologist somehow failed to destroy it when he dynamited its south face in an attempt to examine its interior more closely. As I stumbled up a crudely tiered slope so steep that even the group of schoolboys alongside (too many tacos?) were panting with the effort, I could see small pebbles embedded in mortar in rough attempts at reconstruction. At the summit, wheezing in the rarified air, I peered past the array of Panama hats and denim shirts around me at the stunning 360-degree view. Even the kids were silenced for a moment.

2 The place where the flowers grow. Xochimilco—whose Aztec name means "the place where the flowers grow"—is a 40-minute taxi ride south of Mexico City's main Zócalo plaza. Built on a lake and linked by causeways, it's the last surviving reminder of the old pre-Cortés capital Tenochtitlán. At its main *embarcadero* (landing jetty) you can hire your own private gondola, steered by an eager young ferryman. He'll take you on an idyllic hour-long trip past houses whose flower-filled gardens come right down to the water's edge. Guitar-playing troubadours in big sombreros, tight fitting *chalecos* (waistcoats), and sequined, pale-gray suits serenade newlyweds in larger passing gondolas.

3 To the volcanoes. The twin volcanoes of Popocatéptl ("the smoking mountain") and Iztaccihuatl ("the sleeping woman") rise to 5,452m (17,886 ft.) and 5,286m (17,342 ft.), respectively, behind the attractive market town of Amecameca, 89km (55 miles) and a 90-minute drive southeast of Mexico City. From here their towering crags—often hidden behind swirling clouds—take on a Wagnerian splendor. To get a closer look, follow the Puebla highway into the forested Izta-Popo National Park, where the gleaming, snowy summits peek though the pines. Go suitably equipped if you intend to make the climb to the top of Popocatéptl (strictly for experienced mountaineers!). You'll need to stay overnight at the basic hostel at Tlamacas (3,950m/12,959 ft.) and accompany one of the organized climbing trips that leaves from here the following morning. It's a 9- to 12-hour upward hike that involves some rock climbing, but for those who actually reach the top—where there is a refuge hut for another overnight stay—the sensational views are something you'll never forget. Clearest days are usually during fall and winter. These climbs depend entirely on the volcanic activity situation, which is notoriously unstable. Contact the **Club de Exploraciones de México,** Mexico City (☎ 52-55/ 5740-8032), for the latest update.

4 City of Eternal Spring. You drop 600m (2,000 ft.) on the hour-long ride from Mexico City to Cuernavaca and exchange harsh plateau for lush woodlands and a

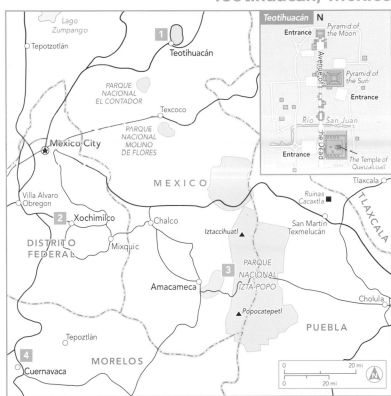

perennially springlike climate. Small wonder it's been a popular retreat since the time of Moctezuma. My favorite spot here is Hernán Cortés' highly atmospheric, 16th-century, two-story mansion, now converted into the **Museo de Cuauhnahuac.** Everything from early man to Emiliano Zapata is covered. Diego Rivera's first-floor mural of the Conquest of Mexico emphasizes the repression by *caciques* of the victimized Indian. One can imagine the middle-aged Cortés living here with his second wife, no longer governor, his days of glory past, temporarily gaining breath before embarking on final ventures to Baja California and Algiers. Cuernavaca, which can easily be visited in a day, is well worth exploring. Museum apart, it's an enchanting blend of hidden *plazas,* gardens, and imposing colonial houses. Don't miss the extraordinary 16th-century La Asunción church with its skull-and-crossbones sign over the entrance and bizarre interior frescoes of Christian missionaries being persecuted in Japan.

PETER STONE is a London-born writer living in Madrid. As well as being the author of *Frommer's Madrid,* he's a Mediterranean addict who has previously enjoyed prolonged sojourns in Greece, Italy, and North Africa, and published articles on Homeresque havens from Akrotiri to Astipaleia. Contact him at petine@teleline.es.

ABOUT THE AUTHOR

YOUR TRIP

General Information: Log on to the website of the **Secretaría del Turismo** of Mexico City, Distrito Federal (DF), at www.mexicocity.gob.mx. Or try the **Mexico Tourist Board** (www.visitmexico.com). **Getting There:** Many international airlines operate scheduled flights from major U.S. cities direct to Mexico DF. The national airlines are **Mexicana** (☎ 800/531-7921; www.mexicana.com) and **AeroMexico** (☎ 800/237-6639; www.aeromexico.com). For Teotihuacán, buses leave daily every half-hour from the Terminal Central de Autobuses del Norte. For Cuernavaca, buses depart from Mexico City Airport. **Best Lodging:** The **Best Western Hotel De Cortes,** with its colonial architecture and genial service, is located right in the old quarter of the city (Av. Hidalgo 85, Mexico City; ☎ 52-55/5518-2184; www.bestwestern.com; $140–$300/£74–£159). In Cuernavaca, **Misión del Sol** is an exceptional value (Av. General Diego Díaz González 31; ☎ 01-800/999-9100 in Mexico; www.misiondelsol.com.mx; $232–$571/£123–£302). **Best Lodging Value: Hotel Mallorca,** in Mexico City (Serapio Rendón 119; ☎ 52-55/566-6677; $45/£24). **Best Restaurant:** In Mexico City, **Antigua Hacienda de Tlalpan** is a traditional eating spot in a 17th-century mansion (Calzada de Tlalpan; ☎ 52-55/655-7315; www.antiguahacienda tlalpan.com.mx; $80/£42). **Best Restaurant Value: Café Bar Tacuba** is a popular, historic colonial-style 1912 restaurant near the Zócalo in Mexico City (Tacuba 28; ☎ 52-55/5512-8482; $9–$17/£5–£9). **When to Go:** The temperate winter is a good time to avoid the northern cold, though summer is more economical if you don't mind the higher temperatures.

◀ *Pyramid of the Sun.*
© Pictures Colour Library/Alamy

TIKAL, GUATEMALA

Breathtaking ruins nestled

in a dense tropical rainforest

The first time I visited Tikal, I was hitchhiking in from Belize. By chance, I was picked up by one of the archaeologists working at the site. I spent the next 4 days exploring the ruins, and the next 5 nights sleeping in a hammock under a mosquito net in an open-air hut at the archaeologists' camp. I had the run of the joint, and in a further gift of chance, the moon was nearly full during my stay. Standing atop Temple IV at Tikal around midnight peering over the illuminated rainforest canopy with the full moon overhead and the roar of howler monkeys remains one of my most treasured moments after decades of traveling.

I've visited most of the major Mayan archaeological sites in Mesoamerica and Tikal is by far my favorite. I've been back time and again, and Tikal never ceases to amaze me. At its peak, Tikal supported a population of more than 100,000 Maya and covered an area of 25 square miles (65 sq. km). Today, several main plazas and towering temples have been meticulously excavated and restored. These are just a fraction of the more than 3,000 structures that have been so far identified by archaeologists. Even so, the broad plazas and cleared causeways that have been excavated give a true sense of what Tikal must have been like in its heyday, sometime between A.D. 600 and 900.

Tikal is nestled in an area of dense tropical rainforest. This forest is home to a vibrant range of flora and fauna, and any visit to Tikal—with a good naturalist guide—is apt to produce sightings of howler monkeys, toucans, coatimundis, and a host of other unique plants and animals. As you walk the shady trails between the various plazas and temples, you're struck by the discovery that the forest-covered hills and mounds all around you are in truth the ruins of ancient Mayan buildings.

Tikal was inhabited and built over a period of more than 1,000 years beginning around 300 B.C. and lasting until around A.D. 900. It fought wars with neighboring cities like Caracol, in Belize. Some of its history is carved in the stones you can see as you tour the site.

As impressive as the archaeological site at Tikal is, the area around Tikal holds other abundant riches also worth exploring. Not the least of these are other satellite cities and Mayan ruins, which include Nakum, El Mirador, Uaxactún, and Yaxhá—where the famous reality show *Survivor* was filmed. While none of these are as large or extensively excavated as Tikal, they are must-visits for Mayaphiles.

There is no modern town or village at Tikal. The nearest major settlement is the twin-city complex of Flores and Santa Elena. While I love the picturesque little island city of Flores, I prefer to stay at one of the hotels located on the shores of Lake Petén Itzá, or—since I've lost my contact with the archaeologists—at one of the three select little hotels set on the grounds just outside the archaeological ruins.

◀ *Tikal.*
© Alison Wright/Corbis

SPECIAL MOMENTS

1 **Before and after hours.** The best way to enjoy Tikal is to get off of the cattle-car circuit and explore the site before and after all the tour buses fill the joint. Sunrises and sunsets are particularly rewarding. The most popular spot to catch either of these solar phenomena is from the top of the Great Pyramid, located in the area known as El Mundo Perdido, or The Lost World. If you're staying at one of the hotels near the entrance to the archaeological site, you can stay in the park until 8pm. If you're lucky to be around when the moon is bright, and the guards are feeling generous (or you've been generous to them), you may be allowed to explore the park by moonlight, even better.

2 **Temple IV.** Located at the western end of the current archaeological site, and rising to 64m (212 ft.), Temple IV is the tallest structure at Tikal. In fact, this was the tallest man-made structure in all of the Americas until the late 19th century. The climb is not for the acrophobic. But if you've got the nerve and stamina, the view from the top is amazing. The highest platform is actually above the forest canopy. From here all you see for miles in any direction is a carpet of green, broken in just a few places by the other tall temples of Tikal. And the only sound you hear should be the piercing cries of howler monkeys.

3 **Flores.** The small island city of Flores has been described as the Venice of Guatemala. While that description is stretching it, I love walking the streets of this tiny city, where you are never more than a few blocks from the shores of Lake Petén Itzá, which, like the lagoon of Venice, is actually rising. The city is teeming with little souvenir shops,

▶ *Painted ceramic figure.*
© Macduff Everton/Corbis

good restaurants, and a handful of fine little budget hotels. I like to grab a table at one of the lakeside cafes or bars here around sunset for a relaxing time watching the lake change colors in the dimming light of late afternoon.

4 **Lake Petén Itzá.** Whenever I'm in Tikal, I'm sure to spend some time on Lake Petén Itzá. This long, broad inland lake is surrounded by rainforest on most sides, with a few islands and lakeshore communities spread around. Boats, canoes, and kayaks can be hired all around the shores of Flores and at the small village of El Remate. I'm usually just happy to be on the water, but I often try to make a stop at El Mirador, a small lakeside pyramid at the ruins of Tayasal, which offers great views of Flores. The ARCAS animal rehabilitation center and small Pentencito Zoo are also worthwhile stops best reached by boat.

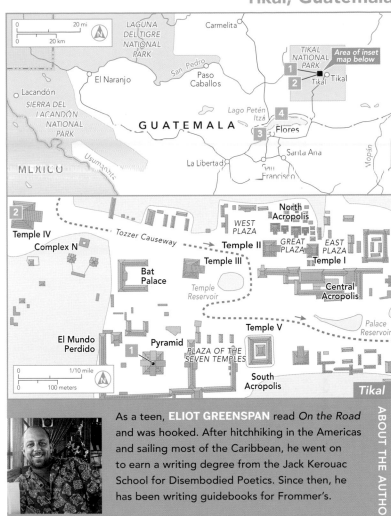

As a teen, **ELIOT GREENSPAN** read *On the Road* and was hooked. After hitchhiking in the Americas and sailing most of the Caribbean, he went on to earn a writing degree from the Jack Kerouac School for Disembodied Poetics. Since then, he has been writing guidebooks for Frommer's.

ABOUT THE AUTHOR

YOUR TRIP

General Information: For more information, click on **www.visitguatemala.com**, run by the Guatemalan Tourism Institute. **Getting There:** Tikal is located 548km (340 miles) northeast of Guatemala City. **TACA Regional Airline** has two daily flights to Flores Airport (FRS) from La Aurora International Airport in Guatemala City (☎ 502/2279-5821 or 502/2470-8222; www.taca.com). To organize a trip while in Guatemala City, call **Maya Vacations** (☎ 502/2339-4638; www.mayavacations.com), **Clark Tours** (☎ 502/2412-4700; www.clarktours.com.gt), or **Gray Line Guatemala** (☎ 502/2383-8600; www.graylineguatemala.com). **Best Lodging:** La Lancha Resort, where the main lodge has a commanding view of the lake, and features a soaring thatch roof oriented toward the view (Lago Petén Itzá; ☎ 800/746-3743 in the U.S., or 502/7928-8331 in Guatemala; www.lalanchavillage.com; $135–$210/£71–£111). **Best Lodging Value:** If you're looking to snag a lakefront room at an affordable price, **Hotel Santana** is a great choice (Calle 30 de Junio, Flores; ☎ 502/7926-0262; www.santanapeten.com; $40–$50/£21–£27). **La Mansión del Pájaro Serpiente,** set off the main road to Tikal on a hillside overlooking the lake, has both standard and deluxe bungalows, beautiful gardens, and a friendly atmosphere (El Remate; ☎ 502/7926-4246; $80/£42). **Best Restaurant:** Most folks who stay near the ruins in Tikal eat all their meals at their hotel. The hip little **La Luna** restaurant is the most creative and refined option in Flores (Calle 30 de Junio, across from La Casona de la Isla; ☎ 502/7926-3346; $6–$16/£3–£8). **When to Go:** Dec–June.

TORRES DEL PAINE, CHILE

Plunging valleys, vast cirques & three monstrous granite towers

In 1998, I took a sabbatical from magazine publishing to work as an outdoor guide in Torres del Paine National Park. It wasn't my first trip to South America, but it met every romantic fantasy I held of rugged, unfettered adventure in the remote reaches of the earth. Nearly a decade and many visits later, it is still the only place that truly jolts me awake from the inertia of the day-to-day.

Torres del Paine is Chile's prized jewel, and the park's centerpiece is the Paine Massif, a cluster of peaks that shoot up from lowland pampa as if out of nowhere, like nature's kingdom of Oz. The Massif is a solidified ball of magma that was uplifted, compressed, and sculpted for 3 million years by tempestuous weather, geological force, and glaciation, leaving behind a dazzling labyrinth of spires, plunging valleys, vast cirques, and three monstrous granite towers that soar 2,700m (9,000 ft.) high. I cannot imagine a place that better illustrates the elemental power of Mother Nature than Torres del Paine.

Paine is the Tehuelchue word for blue, and the park's rivers and lakes are strikingly unreal shades of periwinkle, robin's egg, celestial, and ultramarine. Glaciers hang in thick slabs from peaks, and fat glacial tongues lap the edges of the park. Have you heard a glacier calve? It's like the roar of giants: loud and furious. When I catch the face of Glacier Grey splintering in a thundering kerplunk, I feel like the park is showing off just for me.

With its network of well-maintained trails, Torres del Paine is heaven on earth for hikers and backpackers, and there are options for all comfort and ability levels. Adventurers will find their mecca, yet the less agile never feel left out. I like that. And unusual wildlife, such as guanacos, condors, and rheas, are always close to the park's gravely road.

The weather in Torres del Paine is capricious and intense. From November to April, the wind doesn't just blow, it *screams* through the park, punctuated by fire-hose-force gusts. It uproots tents and snaps poles like twigs. Trees grow horizontally. Hikers cower with their packs or tumble over. Some crawl. At the day's end, you can't help but feel a little shell-shocked, sporting scraped knees and a spooky hairdo, yet you also can't deny feeling internally electrified by the raw, primal power of Torres del Paine. Inclement weather here is part of the fun. You can wake to a flawless, radiantly sunny day and end it in a downpour. To expect only the unexpected liberates me from an agenda-driven day.

There is a gentle side to Torres del Paine, too. In the spring, delicate orchids poke out from the undergrowth and downy *chulengos* (newborn guanacos) prance about the steppe. In autumn, beech trees melt into shades of crimson and gold. I love that the park's rough *baquedanos*, or Patagonian cowboys, can cook and sew, and compete to knit the best *boina*, their trademark beret. But what I especially love is the casual camaraderie that bonds the park's travelers at night, as they exchange their dramatic (and often funny) tales of adventure, feeling very in the moment, and very alive.

◀ *The granite peaks of Torres del Paine.*
© Galen Rowell/ Mountain Light

SPECIAL MOMENTS

1 **The Towers.** The four most common words heard on the last stretch of this famous trail are "Is it worth it?" The 4-hour hike up to the park's eponymous attraction is difficult no matter what shape you're in, but it's the last 45-minute climb up a tumble of granite boulders when doubt and fatigue set in, the reason why this hike has been dubbed "the Towers of Pain." The trail passes through a lovely valley forded by a fast-flowing river, and through tall stands of beech forest, but you can't actually see the towers until you've arrived. It's the thought of the "prize" that keeps you going, and what a prize: three elegant pink-gray granite monoliths fronted by a hanging glacier and a milky-green glacial lake. But reconsider on a rainy day—you might do all that work only to find the towers shrouded in clouds.

2 **Glacier Grey.** From any perspective—above, in front, or on top—Glacier Grey is an awesome sight and the park's definitive crowd pleaser. It's also easy to get to. The park's largest glacier flows like a frozen river of blueberry frappé from the Southern Ice Field to its terminus, where its face stretches 5km (3 miles) across Lago Grey. Hop aboard a ferry for a relaxing ride past icebergs and up to the yawning face of the glacier, or stretch your legs on a moderate-to-difficult 9-hour round-trip hike from Refugio Pehoé to Refugio Grey. My favorite way to see the glacier is to slip on a pair of crampons and trek across it with Bigfoot Adventures, so that I can peer into the glacier's fairyland of blue crevasses and ice tunnels.

3 **The Circuit.** It takes nearly a week—but what a week. The Circuit is a "classic" trail, but really few do it, considering the hordes of hikers that stick to the easier, and shorter, "W" trail (which you can include as part of the Circuit trail). Bring a heavy dose of stamina, a sense of adventure, and quality waterproof gear—this often-punishing trail is not for the faint of heart. The reward for all your hard work is ever-changing views of otherworldly beauty: flower-flecked meadows, hanging glaciers, sheer granite walls, craggy peaks, towering primary forest, and the unforgettable view of Glacier Grey

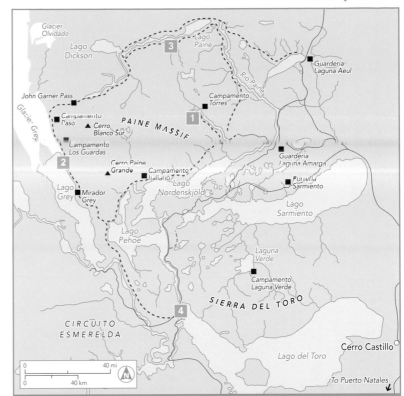

at the crest of the John Gardner Pass. I've never seen anything more humbling than the sheer dimension of this glacier and the Southern Ice Field beyond it. For the best views and an easy break into the trail, walk counterclockwise.

4 **Horseback riding, Patagonia-style.** I'll confess that I'm crazy for horseback riding, but really anyone with minimal experience can still indulge in the fantasy of riding across the pampa like a true gaucho, or *baquedano*, with an easy half-day ride. There's just something fitting about gazing out at the Paine Massif from a sheepskin saddle, and a full-day romp that takes you into territory full of vibrant landscapes with nary another soul in sight. Book a day ride at the stables next to the park's administration center, or book a stay at the Cerro Guido Lodge for a full-blown *estancia* experience, something akin to a Patagonian dude ranch.

KRISTINA SCHRECK is the author of *Frommer's Chile, Frommer's South America,* and the first edition of *Frommer's Panama.* She is also the former managing editor of *Adventure Journal* magazine. She has spent the past 9 years in Chile, dedicating herself to writing and promoting skiing in the Andes. Reach her at kristinaschreck@gmail.com.

ABOUT THE AUTHOR

YOUR TRIP

General Information: For general information, check www.torresdelpaine.com, or the **Corporación de Promoción** (CPT–Chile's Tourism Board) site at www.visitchile.org. Or, call the CPT U.S. office for more information (☎ 866/YES-CHILE). For ice hiking on Glacier Grey, contact **Bigfoot Adventures** (www.bigfootpatagonia.com; 56-61/413-247). **Getting There:** Torres del Paine is 125km (78 miles) from Puerto Natales. **Best Lodging:** The most luxurious lodging is **Hotel Salto Chico,** run by Explora, a chic, package-based ecolodge that boasts one of the world's most magnificent views (☎ 866/750-6699 in the U.S.; www.explora.com; $2,170–$3,110/£1,150–£1,648 4 nights, all-inclusive). **Best Lodging Value:** Lodging in the park is expensive, but **Hostería Las Torres** has simple rooms, a hostel with shared bunkrooms, and campground facilities with fire pits (Sarmiento 846; ☎ 56-61/360-360; www.lastorres.com; $167–$267/£89–£141, $35/£19 hostel). They're also known for their hearty nightly buffet. The **Cerro Guido Lodge** is 30 minutes from the park entrance, but I love its *estancia*-style ambience (Comuna de Torres del Paine; ☎ 56-2/196-4807; www.lodgecerroguido.cl; $120–$200/£64–£106). For lodging in the park, try the **Lodge Paine Grande,** a clean, modern hostel with shared rooms, and access to several trail heads (☎ 56-61/412-742; www.verticepatagonia.cl; $35/£19). **Best Restaurant:** There are no "restaurants" in the park; travelers dine at their hotel. **When to Go:** The only predictable thing about the weather here is its unpredictability. Summer is the worst time to come, especially from late December to mid-February, when the wind blows at full fury and crowds descend upon the park.

◀ *Guanacos in Torres del Paine National Park.*
© Galen Rowell/Corbis

TROGIR, CROATIA

One of the best-preserved towns in central Europe

Dubrovnik is the showpiece of Dalmatia, but its port is crowded with cruise ships. Split is home to Diocletian's palace, but the city is a vast spaghetti bowl of highway junctions and industrial estates. The popular island of Hvar is worth a visit, too, but is too "Italian" for my taste. The lesser-known town of Trogir, dense with history and culture, is just right—a Croatian cameo.

On arrival, I accidentally drove across—and off—the island in the space of five breaths, traffic notwithstanding. But then I spent days clopping through its narrow, crooked alleys. The stone buildings loomed tall and ornate on every side, each worthy of a grand boulevard. Yet Trogir crowds together the brie-colored gates, towers, palaces, and churches, creating the best-preserved Romanesque-Gothic complex in all of central Europe.

Summer is the glorious time here, as trendsetters hedonise on the Dalmatian beaches and nearby islands. Pine and olive groves shade trattorie, scented with sizzling calamari and wood-fired pizza. Yachts bob in the kingfisher-blue water. The sea is clean, clear, and warm, even more so than along Italy's eastern coast (balmy currents sweep past here first, and then circulate down "the boot").

The intimacy of spring is even better. Mist hangs low, shrouding the street lamps. The creamy-gray cobblestones slicken underfoot. The locals' smiles are still fresh, unsullied by a season peddling crucifixes, sea sponges, and postcards of topless babes and spotted dogs. A *dolce vita* glamour infuses Trogir. Its bars, with their mirrors, polished marble, and elaborate liqueurs, mimic Rome's. Gelato shops brim with pastel sorbets and ice creams. Women in Sophia Loren sunglasses lounge under cafe umbrellas, watching the promenaders along the waterfront.

Not that it's all champagne cocktails and frilly Corinthian columns; the micropolis has some edge, too. The dark, smoke-stained Cathedral of Saint Lovro flattens visitors with its sheer weight of woes. Even the most exuberant tourists collapse into pews, muted. What atrocities have these stones seen?

In the last 2 decades, Yugoslavia shredded itself into six Slavic nations: Croatia, Macedonia, Montenegro, Serbia, Slovenia, and Bosnia and Herzegovina. Violence and ethnic cleansing swept these shores, which U.N. peacekeepers finally left in 1998. Thus the area has that calm-after-the-storm atmosphere: Think post–Cold War Prague or the Paris of the Belle Epoque. Still gritty around the edges, it's the sort of place where hotel clerks offer black-market cellphone chips with a wink. Travelers savor wormwood wine and cabbage-pickle-beet salads, while waiting for a wood fire to char their sausages. The "holiday experience" isn't predictable and prepackaged yet.

All of Croatia is poised on the edge of rediscovery, as eastern Europe grows hip again. The young country is enjoying a moment of grace, balanced between antiquity, bloodstained headlines, and the thumping disco of charter tours. I worry that Trogir could be Balkan Disneyland by the time I return. Somehow I doubt it, though. The Slavs have too much sense and integrity. But I light a fat candle in the Cathedral of Saint Lovro, anyway, because this island gem deserves safety of every sort.

◄ *The town of Rovinj.*
© Connie Coleman/ Getty Images

SPECIAL MOMENTS

1 Mist in Plitvička Jezera. Croatia's largest natural attraction is the Plitvička Jezera National Park, which was once memorably described as "Niagara Falls diced and sprinkled over a heavily forested Grand Canyon." A chain of 16 lakes stretches 8km (5 miles), like a long turquoise necklace. Fed by numerous rivers and streams, the water descends through stepped pools before Lake Kozjak—northernmost and largest—empties dramatically into Korana Gorge.

Park Entrance One lies near this mesmerizing sight. Boardwalks snake over the water, dodging trills and rapids, skirting sheer drop-offs. A 10-minute stroll brings you to another highlight, the Veliki Slap (Big Waterfall), a 70m (230-ft.) cascade. From here, most visitors hike several miles, then catch a pontoon boat south to the Upper Lakes and the free shuttle back to their vehicles.

Though occupied by Serb forces from 1991 to 1995, the park remains fairly unspoiled. Among its caves and virgin forests live bears, wolves, wildcats, wild boar, and more than 160 bird species, including heron and eagles. The UNESCO World Heritage Site is 209km (130 miles) north of Trogir, about a 4-hour drive, given road conditions (Plitvička Jezera; ☎ 385-53/75-10-14; www.np-plitvicka-jezera.hr).

2 Dusk in Hvar. Statistically, Hvar is Croatia's sunniest spot. But the island's true charm emerges in the smudgy dusk, as lights dot Hvar Town's coastal promenade. The stone buildings reflect the amber glow, piling up the hillside toward the illuminated citadel. Shadows darken the pines and poppies— the turquoise water, too—but in the early evening, this chic Croatian resort takes a breather from the tourist bustle. Then its architecture and quiet character truly shine. Wander the cobbled, pedestrian alleys, past the convent, the monastery, the palaces, and the spindly campanile of the 16th-century cathedral. Once a haven for medieval pirates, Hvar Town has grown elegant and earned its UNESCO World Heritage chops. Its hotels no longer offer a money-back guarantee if the temperature drops below zero, but it's still worth a visit for the soft springtime dusk and lazy Adriatic beauty.

3 White nights in Dubrovnik. The poet Byron dubbed Dubrovnik the "pearl of the Adriatic," but George Bernard Shaw went one better: "Paradise on earth," the playwright declared. Either way, the walled, white-marbled city has become a magnet for independent travelers and cruise-ship passengers alike. Damaged by Yugoslavian shelling in 1991, the medieval Old Town was cleverly—almost seamlessly—restored to its World-Heritage-Site glory. Dubrovnik is

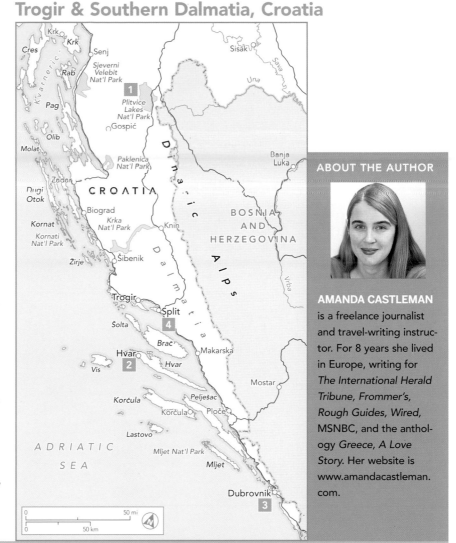

one of Europe's most romantic and venerable small cities, its churches, public buildings, and green-shuttered stone houses seemingly untouched by the 21st century.

4 Roman glory in Split.

About 161km (100 miles) north of Dubrovnik is Split, the region's transportation hub. The Emperor Diocletian—local-boy-made-good—built his retirement home here in 305. Medieval houses encrust the ancient Roman floor plan like barnacles. A 15 B.C. black-granite sphinx guards the octagonal mausoleum, now the Cathedral of Saint Domnius. Museums and palaces and modern sculpture crowd the site, which resembles a small eclectic city more than a fortified castle. Approach this architectural mélange from the Riva, the cafe-crowded waterfront that snapshots the city's soul. The palace is more accessible than the sprawling, overgrown site of Solin (Salona), just outside the city.

ABOUT THE AUTHOR

AMANDA CASTLEMAN is a freelance journalist and travel-writing instructor. For 8 years she lived in Europe, writing for *The International Herald Tribune, Frommer's, Rough Guides, Wired,* MSNBC, and the anthology *Greece, A Love Story.* Her website is www.amandacastleman.com.

YOUR TRIP

General Information: Do your research on www.croatia.hr and www.dalmatia.hr. **Getting There:** Trogir lies on the Adriatic coast in Dalmatia, 16km (10 miles) from Split, Croatia. The nearest airport is the petite one in Split (www.split-airport.hr), served by **British Airways** (www.ba.com), **Croatian Airways** (www.croatiaairlines.hr), **Malév** (www.malev.hu), **Adria** (www.adria-airways.com), and **CSA** (www.csa.cz). Or fly into Zagreb on **Wizz,** a no-frills carrier from London Luton (http://wizzair.com). **Easycar** offers good deals on rentals (www.easycar.com). Trogir requires no transportation, and buses link it to coastal cities like Zadar, Split, and Dubrovnik. **What to See & Do:** Trogir itself is a "town museum," a cameo of culture and architecture. Its highlight is the 1240 cathedral portal, depicting Adam and Eve (proudly billed as "the oldest nude in Dalmatia"). The best local beaches are Mali Drvenik and Veli Drvenik, 12km (7 miles) away by ferry. **Best Lodging:** Wood beams and wi-fi grace the **Hotel Pašike** in Trogir's center (Sinjska bb; ☎ 385-21/88-51-85; www.hotelpasike.com; $92–$202/£49–£107). This boutique hotel has just seven rooms, plus an apartment with a hydromassage tub. Its casual elegance and class don't extend to the breakfast buffet, but otherwise the Pašike is terrific value for the money. **Best Restaurant:** The owners of **Top Baloon** [sic] goofed the English-grammar test, but who cares? They're peddling the finest Italian cuisine east of Venice. Pizzas bake in a proper brick oven and the wild-rice risotto remains firm and flavorful, not a gooey mess (Obrov 7, Trogir; ☎ 385-21/88-48-69; $6.50–$17/£3–£9).

◀ *An evening stroll along the Placa in Dubrovnik.*

TUNISIA

From the souks of Tunis to a camel ride in the Sahara

North African countries have long intrigued the Western world. The imperial cities of Morocco and the pyramids of Egypt hold a perennial fascination for visitors. Far less known are the kaleidoscopic attractions of my personal favorite, Tunisia, which nestles between this famed duo. Let me say modestly, without trumpetings, that it offers something for everyone.

For culture lovers, the most well-known spot is probably Carthage—where faded Phoenician ruins overlook the sea—though the Roman temples at Dougga and the coliseum at El Djem are for me far more compelling. So too are the Arabic treasures, which include the great 9th-century Sidi Oqba mosque at Kairouan, former capital of the country, and the huge labyrinthine medina of Tunis (where I defy you to not get lost while browsing among its souks for jewelry and carpets). Down south the cave homes of villages bordering the desert reflect the simplicity of Berber life.

For hedonists there's the enticing world of tourism, in which bougainvillea and wisteria fill your hotel gardens, jasmine exotically scents the night air, and beaches of fine white sand line the Mediterranean coast, extending as far as the idyllic lotus eater's island of Djerba, which Ulysses found so difficult to leave. Add to this a mouth-watering Arabic-Gallic fusion of cuisines that range from couscous to steak tartare—duly accompanied by excellent local wines from vineyards first planted by the French a century ago—and you have a sybaritic blend fit to satisfy the most jaded taste.

The landscape is another knockout. It changes with such distinct clarity over such a relatively short distance as you head from north to south, you could draw horizontal lines across the country and paint the spaces between them different colors—green, orange, ochre, white, and yellow—as on a child's map, to show their geographical differences. First come the pine woods around Bizerta and cork forests at Ain Draham (favored for centuries by the wealthy and privileged as a place to hunt wild boar). Then the rich citrus orchards, olive groves, and vineyards of Hammamet and Nabeul that extend into the lush gardenlike peninsula of Cap Bon. Then the Sahel, a dry stony, scrubland whose western fringe touches the huge salt lake of Chott el Djerid. Then the vast leafy and water-filled oasis of Gabes, said to be the biggest on earth, which takes you an hour to ride around in a horse-driven *calèche* (or carriage).

But it's the last leg south that for me really is the icing on the cake. From the sun-bleached little market town of Douz you can organize a day trip (or longer) into the desert, initially by four-wheel-drive truck and then by camel. That first experience of swaying atop an undulating Arabic dromedary across what looks like a giant inland beach is one I'll never forget. The air is startlingly pure. There is no dirt, no vegetation. The distant horizon shimmers under a pastel sky. From Douz you can also arrange for a four-wheel-drive vehicle to take you on a 4-hour ride (60km/37 miles) southeast to Pansea Douar Ksar Ghilane (☎ 216-75/900506; **www.pansea.com**), where you stay in comfortable air-conditioned tents beside a pool and tiny oasis—the very essence of a soft adventure.

◀ *Footprints in the sand in Douz, the "gateway to the Sahara."*
© Jon Arnold/
DanitaDelimont.com

SPECIAL MOMENTS

1 **Sidi Bou Said.** This gem of a village, whose cube-shaped white houses with their light-blue doors and wooden trim shutters perch on a hillside overlooking the Bay of Tunis, is undoubtedly one of the most beautiful spots in the Mediterranean. Artists such as Paul Klee have been setting up their easels here for decades, entranced by the setting. Today you can sit over a *café* or mint tea in French-style cafes; shop for carpets, pottery, and blue-and-white birdcages in trendy little shops; and wander up and down the cobbled lanes. Tunis City, with its great medina and Bardo museum—home of the best-preserved Roman mosaics outside Europe—is just a half-hour away by taxi or train.

2 **El Djem.** The sight is so incongruous and unexpected amid the flat Sahel landscape of parched scrubland and endless olive trees that you can't quite believe it. Yet there it is at the end of the arrow-straight road north of Sfax, its unmistakable silhouette growing larger and clearer with every moment: a huge amphitheater, second in size only to Rome's great Colosseum. In its 300 B.C. heyday, 30,000 spectators would watch the circus games and gladiator fights, 10 times the population of the small town that today nestles beside it, where locals sell their tiny amphora and trinkets. The ancient monument's arches and buttresses that enclose the arena are remarkably intact, and underground you can still see the cells where both competitors and lions were kept.

3 **Matmata.** Here's another sight in a million: A genuine troglodyte burg midway between Gabes oasis and the desert, whose mainly Berber population live in cave houses set in craters in an ochre sandstone moonscape where some scenes from the early *Star Wars* movies were shot. The interiors are spotless, refreshingly cool in summer, and comfortingly warm in winter. There are a half-dozen accommodation choices

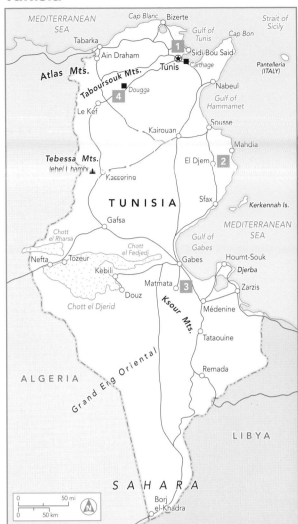

in and around the old town, ranging from underground hostels with shared amenities like the Sidi Driss—which was used as the location for Luke Skywalker's home—to modern hotels like the Matmata (see "Your Trip," below).

4 **Dougga.** Forget famous coastal Carthage—which in spite of its magnificent setting tends to disappoint visitors with its paucity of remains. Dougga (formerly Thugga) is the historic site that really takes my breath away. Nestling like a time capsule amid the haunting, mauve-gray hills of Western Tunisia, it's a remarkably intact "township" of Greek and Roman remains, whose clearly delineated streets and house foundations stand alongside a Punic mausoleum, unique in this corner of the world, as well as a variety of forums and temples intact enough for you to imagine ceremonies worshipping Minerva and Jupiter still being performed.

ABOUT THE AUTHOR

PETER STONE is a London-born writer living in Madrid. The author of *Frommer's Madrid*, he's a Mediterranean addict who has enjoyed prolonged sojourns in Greece, Italy, and North Africa, and has published articles on Homeresque havens from Akrotiri to Astipaleia. Contact him at petine@teleline.es.

YOUR TRIP

General Information: Contact the **Tunisia Tourist Office** online at www.tourismtunisia.com. More news can be found on www.cometotunisia.co.uk. **Getting There:** Flights from European cities operate to Tunis, Monastir, and Djerba. The national airline is **Tunisair** (www.tunisair.com). **Best Lodging: Hotel Dar Said** has a prime hillside location in a converted 19th-century house with bougainvillea-covered white walls and flower-filled gardens (rue Toumi, Sidi Bou Said; ☎ 216-71/729666; www.darsaid.com.tn; $200/£106). **Best Lodging Value: Hotel Matmata,** built in traditional troglodyte style and located on the very edge of the desert, is a modern, well-equipped hotel with camel- and horse-riding facilities; it even has a pool and air-conditioned rooms (Matmata; ☎ 216-75/230066; $50/£27). In Douz, try **El Mouradi** ☎ 216-75/470303; www.elmouradi.com; $60/£32). **Best Restaurant:** At **Dar Zarrouk** specialties include couscous and seafood (rue Hedi Zarrouk, Sidi Bou Said; ☎ 216-71/740591; $25–$35/£13–£19). **Best Restaurant Value:** *Brik* is a triangular crust of thin pastry fried in olive oil and with an egg inside. Hold the pastry carefully as you eat it if you don't want to get the yolk all over your clothes! *Mechoui*, Tunisia's answer to the French *ratatouille*, is a tasty oil-cooked blend of tomatoes, onions, olives, peppers, and capers usually sprinkled with tuna. Douz has a fair-sized choice of really low-priced eating locales, offering traditional Tunisian dishes like *brik* and *mechoui* at around $2.50 to $3 (£1–£1.60) a meal. **Ali Baba,** on the Kebili Road, is a big favorite. Other bargain nosheries are **La Rosa** (av. 7 Nov 1987) and **Les Palmiers** (av. Taieb Mehri).

◀ *Ksar Ouled Soltane, Tataouine.*
© Frans Lemmens/Iconica/Getty Images

TUSCANY, ITALY

Hill towns, cypress-studded landscapes & pecorino cheese

Surprisingly, I've talked to travelers who claimed they preferred the countryside of Tuscany to urban Florence and the glories of the Renaissance. Michelangelo, Leonardo da Vinci, and their *compagni* are a tough act to follow, but Tuscany and its ancient art cities and hill towns live up to their hype.

In spite of my lifelong attachment to Umbria, Tuscany remains the province I most frequently return to, ever since I biked through the countryside after finishing high school, waiting for the college term to begin.

The good news is that what I saw way back when still remains to delight today—that field of sunflowers, that hidden Romanesque church found along a country road, the Tower of Pisa, the walls of Lucca, medieval pageants and medieval towers, the curative waters of Montecatini, Market Day at Cortona, the art of a Renaissance master found in every town, and the garnet-colored *vino nobile* at Montepulciano.

A bottle didn't turn me into a wino, but made me a connoisseur for life of this noble grape. No bartender "carded" me, even though I was only a teenager. I asked the owner of a grottolike tavern why the Tuscans were so lax about such matters. "When a man is 17," he told me, "he is ready for life, and that means ready to enjoy all the pleasures that Tuscany has to offer, including good wine."

The point that long-ago tavern keeper made about Tuscany is still valid. Decades later, after seeing all the world, I would still be challenged to find a province that in such a condensed space offers isolated hill towns, beaches, cypress-studded landscapes, old *fattoria* (farmhouses), Guelf-Ghibelline medieval fortifications, and pecorino cheese.

Tuscany has attracted wave upon wave of artists, even poets such as Keats and Shelley. Each turn in the road evokes the bucolic backdrop of a Raphael Madonna or a Botticelli field of nymphs. Since there is fascination down every road, how do you go about seeing all of this wonder? Few visitors have more than 2 or 3 days—4 at the most—to wander about.

If you have only 1 day for Tuscany, head immediately for Siena, which basks in the glow of its heyday in the Middle Ages. Laundromats, for example, are likely to be housed on the bottom floor of a 14th-century *palazzo*.

In just 1 day of sightseeing, you can begin at the Piazza del Campo (the main square) and take in such stellar attractions as the Museo Civico in the Palazzo Pubblico, going on to the treasure-filled Pinacoteca Nazionale (Siena's picture gallery). You can also climb the Torre del Mangia for the greatest city view in Tuscany. For the afternoon, the Duomo or cathedral is the big attraction, with side visits to the nearby Battistero and Museo dell'Opera Metropolitana.

Another day? Head for San Gimignano, which also casts a medieval spell with a dozen towers still dotting its skyline from the 70 that were constructed in the 12th and 13th centuries.

With 3 days to spare, it's on to Pisa with its Leaning Tower and architectural glory. With yet a 4th day, you can explore the walled city of Lucca.

◀ *Tuscan landscape, near Siena.*

SPECIAL MOMENTS

1 **Chianti wine tasting.** Bacchus would agree: One of the great pleasures of a trip to Tuscany is to travel the winding Via Chiantigiana (the Chianti road) south of Florence for a taste of the grape on home turf. Tasting Chianti at a local estate takes you through a bacchanalian landscape of dusty-silver and spring-green olive groves, medieval wine castles, and fields of succulent grapes. Your best center for a launch pad is in the unofficial capital, Greve in Chianti, 27km (17 miles) south of Florence on SS222. The entire area is only 48km (30 miles) from north to south, so seeing its highlights in a day is easily possible. If you have time for only one wine estate, make it **Villa Vignamaggio** (Via Petriolo 5, Greve in Chianti; ☎ 39-055/854661; **www.vignamaggio.com**), a 15th-century Renaissance villa that was the home of Lisa Gherardini, known as *La Gioconda* to Italians, or more famously as the inspiration for Leonardo da Vinci's *Mona Lisa*.

2 **Siena: Medieval pageantry.** I must have seen it a dozen times, but each staging of Siena's medieval, no-holds-barred Palio is a different spectacle. It's too simplistic to call this competition a bareback horse race—it is, in fact, the most colorful, the most intense, and the most dangerous festival of Italy, taking place on July 2 and on August 16 of every year.

The festival has been attacked by critics around the world, who cite its violence and cruelty to horses. Many of these magnificent creatures are impaled on wooden guardrails. In spite of the critics, the Siennese will probably be staging their Palio 100 years from now. "To take away our Palio would be to remove bread from our table," said the mayor of Siena.

3 **Pisa: Climbing the tower.** Let's be honest: You don't dare return home and admit to friends that you failed to climb the Leaning Tower of Pisa. According to a Gallup Poll, the tipsy tower is the most recognizable building in the world. After being closed for major repairs for many years, this tower is open again to the public.

The moral of the tower is not to stack heavy layers of marble on unreliable alluvial subsoil. But, thanks to engineers, the tower leans only 4m (13 ft.) today as it did in 1838, not 4.6m (15 ft.), as it dangerously did in 1990. The tower is but one of the glories of visiting the Campo dei Miracoli (Field of Miracles) on which it precariously sits. This grassy lawn—to me, at least, the most beautiful square in the world—offered inspiration to Dante, Shelley, even Galileo.

There is no better place in Tuscany to sit out and enjoy a picnic surrounded by some of the province's most elegant buildings, the apogee of the Pisan-Romanesque style. These edifices include the Baptistery, the largest in Italy. Built in 1278, the Camposanto also stands here, built to house earth from Mount Golgotha brought back by the Crusaders. And there's also the Cattedrale, home to Giovanni Pisano's magnificent pulpit of 1302. As you eat and drink your wine, you're reminded of Herman Melville, who stood here waiting for the tower to crash. If it does, expect 15,000 tons of marble to rain down. If it doesn't, enjoy your crusty Tuscan bread.

4 **Biking atop Lucca's walls.**
Once the unofficial capital of Tuscany, the ancient Città Vecchia (Old Town) of Lucca is still enclosed by the best-preserved Renaissance defense ramparts in Europe. I know of no better way to enjoy them than to take the most thrilling bike ride in Tuscany. It's a journey of 4km (2½ miles) that stretches kidney-shaped past ilex, chestnut, and plane trees ordered planted by Marie Louise Bourbon in the 1800s. As you glide along the trail, you pass young lovers holding hands, "card-shark" octogenarians at tables, kids at play, and the strolling Lucchesi (notoriously known as the stingiest people of Europe). In all, 11 bastions and six ornate gates pass in review, each set against a backdrop of pine-studded mountains.

If you're not into biking, you can take the grand promenade on foot, striding along in the footsteps of the arrogant Castruccio Castracani, whom Machiavelli took as his model for *The Prince*. Puccini may have first conceived *La Bohème* while walking these walls.

ABOUT THE AUTHOR

DARWIN PORTER is one of the world's most prolific travel writers. His books for Frommer's include guides to the Caribbean, Italy, France, Germany, and England. A Hollywood columnist and a celebrity biographer, Porter is also a radio broadcaster; his shows on American popular culture are heard in all 50 states.

YOUR TRIP

General Information: For details on Tuscany in general, contact the **regional tourist office** in Florence (Via Manzoni 16; ☎ 39-055/23320; www.firenzeturismo.it). **Getting There:** The nearest major airport is Rome. From there it's 1 hour by plane to the small airports at Pisa or Florence, or 3 hours by train. For train schedules and pricing, go to www.trenitalia.com. For motorists, A1 links Florence both north and south. Florence lies 277km (172 miles) north of Rome; Siena, 230km (143 miles) north of Rome. **Best Lodging: La Certosa di Maggiano,** in Siena, is a restored 13th-century Certosinian monastery that is today the epitome of the style and luxury (Strada di Certosa 82; ☎ 39-0577/288189; www.certosadimaggiano.com; 400€–620€/$488–$756). **Best Lodging Value:** The **Piccolo Hotel Etruria,** in Siena, is a small, family-run inn with modern furnishings and rooms clean as a hound's tooth (Via Donzelle 3; ☎ 39-0577/288088; www.hoteletruria.com; 80€/$98). If you stay in Lucca, there's the **Piccolo Hotel Puccini,** your best bet within the city walls (Via di Poggio 9; ☎ 39-0583/55421; www.hotelpuccini.com; 85€/$103). **Best Restaurant:** In Siena, **Antica Trattoria Botteganova** (Strada Chiantigiana 408; ☎ 39-0577/284230; www.anticatrattoriabotteganova.it, Italian only; 22€–24€/$26–$30). **Best Restaurant Value:** A family-run Sienese local favorite, **Antica Trattoria Papei,** is just the place for simple but tasty local fare (Piazza del Mercato 6; ☎ 39-0577/280894; 7€–11€/$9–$13). **When to Go:** The best times to visit Tuscany are in the spring and fall. Starting in late May, the summer tourist rush really picks up, and from July to mid-September the country is teeming with visitors.

◀ *Countryside near Siena.*
© Peter Adams/Getty Images

ULURU, AUSTRALIA

Climbing it is not necessary—you can carry its image in your heart

The Aboriginal people of Uluru have a name for tourists. It is *minga*, the Pitjantjatjara word for ants, and aptly describes the tiny figures toiling up the vast face of the world's largest monolith, once known as Ayers Rock. I've never been one of them. And I never will be. This decision puts me at odds with some of my friends and family, who have climbed Uluru—or would, if given the chance. But I'm content in the knowledge that I'm not alone; indeed, I'm one of a growing band of travelers who choose not to scale this natural masterpiece in respect for the wishes of the traditional owners.

There are several good reasons for resisting the temptation to become one of the more than 200,000 people each year who complete the 348m (1,142-ft.) hike. The first—and most important—is that Uluru is a sacred site to Aborigines, who believe the path taken to the top is the traditional route taken by their ancestral *mala* (rufous hare-wallaby) men on their arrival here.

The presence of Uluru is all-pervading. It is difficult to describe to someone who has not seen it—photographs, no matter how good, cannot prepare you for the reality. This is truly a destination where the "spirit of place" is all around.

Anangu (or "the people," a term used by Aboriginal people from the Western Desert to refer to themselves) also want to keep you off Uluru because "The Rock" is dangerously steep and 35 people have died while climbing—either from heart attacks or falls—in the past 4 decades. Anangu feel a duty to safeguard visitors to their land, and feel great sorrow and responsibility when visitors are killed or injured.

While it would be worth coming all the way to Central Australia just to see Uluru, there is a second unique natural wonder to see, just 30km (18 miles) away. Kata Tjuta, or The Olgas, consists of 36 immense ochre rock domes rising from the desert, rivaling Uluru for spectacular beauty.

This part of Australia's red heart was first discovered in the 1870s by English explorers. Ernest Giles named part of Kata Tjuta "Mount Olga" after the reigning Queen Olga of Wurttemberg, while William Gosse gave Uluru the name "Ayers Rock" after Sir Henry Ayers, the chief secretary of South Australia.

By the 1950s, tourists and miners had begun to make tracks to Uluru and Kata Tjuta, and most of the Anangu scattered to other parts of Central Australia. In 1979, the Australian government recognized the existence of the traditional Aboriginal owners and created a national park to protect the sites.

In 1983, the traditional owners were granted ownership of the land. The park was leased to the Australian National Parks and Wildlife Service for 99 years, with the agreement that the public could continue to climb it.

Some areas of Uluru and Kata Tjuta are still considered sacred, and access is banned. Don't be upset, though. In the end it doesn't matter whether you climb Uluru or not, for once you have seen it you will carry its image in your heart and memory forever.

◄ *Uluru (Ayers Rock).*

SPECIAL MOMENTS

1 **Sunrise, sunset.** Never is the majesty of the desert more profound than as the changing light at the dawn and departure of the day falls on the ochre walls of Uluru and Kata Tjuta. There are viewing platforms established and areas to which bus tours carry their passengers for optimum viewing—and while this might sound unappealing, once the sun starts to work its magic, it doesn't seem to matter anymore. Visitors set up their camping chairs, or just stand transfixed, usually with a glass in hand to toast the beauty before them. Each moment brings a different shade of color to Uluru; at Kata Tjuta, where the tallest dome reaches 546m (1,791 ft.), the gorge walls blaze in the sunlight.

2 **The Liru walk.** Several guided walks run from the Cultural Centre, which is located inside the park on the main road to Uluru, about 13km (8 miles) from the entry gate and 1km from Uluru. My favorite is the Liru Walk, which covers the stretch of desert between the center and Uluru, and back again. Aboriginal guides speaking Pitjantjatjara, with translators, give you an insight into the history, lifestyle, and mythology of their ancient culture. You may be lucky enough, as I was on my first visit, to be guided by traditional owner Cassidy Uluru or one of his brothers. The 2km (1-mile) walk proceeds at a leisurely pace, as you stop along the way to discover more about *tjukurpa*—a word with no direct English translation, but which ties together the history, creation stories, laws, and beliefs of the Anangu. You will learn about the *mala* (rufous hare-wallaby), *kuniya* (woma python),

and *liru* (poisonous snake), all considered important ancestors. And always you will have Uluru as your backdrop.

3 **Base walk.** There are many ways to circumnavigate Uluru—by camel, by Harley Davidson motorcycle, by bus. But I think the best way to see it, to get up close and personal, is on foot. There's a track right around the base, and there's something about getting red dust on your boots that is very satisfying. The loop covers 10km (6 miles) and takes around 5 hours. To do it comfortably, you will need to get up before dawn and complete most of it before the heat of a Central Australian day sets in—no matter what time of year it is. Walk clockwise, starting at the Mala Walk. If you take a guided walk you will have the advantage of knowing

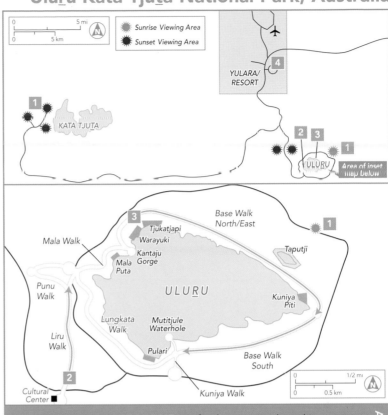

what you are seeing. As day breaks, you will hear birds calling and see the prints of animals, including dingo, in the dust.

4   **The sounds of silence.** The absence of city lights in the Red Centre—as Australians call this ochre-colored desert heart of their country—allows you to see the stars and planets as you may never have seen them before. The Sounds of Silence dinner is set up in style with white tablecloths and fine wines among the gently rolling sand dunes that form the landscape here, and the menu is undeniably different, featuring emu, kangaroo, and crocodile. A local astronomer will explain how the heavens work here—letting you view the stars and planets through a telescope, while explaining their significance in ancient mythologies and Aboriginal creation stories. The star of the show, of course, is the Southern Cross.

ABOUT THE AUTHOR

LEE MYLNE is a freelance writer based in Melbourne, Australia. She is the author of several travel guides and narratives and a passionate traveler who has been to more than 40 countries. She is a Life Member of the Australian Society of Travel Writers. Check out her website at www.leemylne.com.

YOUR TRIP

General Information: Contact the **Uluru-Kata Tjuta National Park** administration at ☎ 61-8/8956-1100; or the **Cultural Centre** (☎ 61-8/8956-1128; www.deh.gov.au/parks/uluru). A park-entry permit costs US$20/£11 for 3 days. **Discovery Ecotours** offers several tours of the Rock, as well as tours to the observatory (☎ 61-1800/803-174; www.discoveryecotours.com.au). **Getting There:** Uluru is 445km (276 miles; about a 5-hr. drive) from Alice Springs in the Northern Territory. You can fly from Sydney or Cairns in 3 hours to Ayers Rock (Connellan) Airport. Contact **Qantas** (www.qantas.com). Or take the long-distance luxury train **The Ghan** from Sydney or Adelaide to Alice Springs and fly from there (www.railaustralia.com.au/ghan.htm). **Best Lodging: Longitude 131°** is a clutch of 15 luxury permanent "tents" on the edge of the desert, each with an uninterrupted view of Uluru (Yulara Dr.; ☎ 61-8/8296-8010; www.voyages.com.au; US$1,440/£763). **Ayers Rock Resort,** run by the same company, has five other hotels in differing price ranges (www.ayersrockresort.com.au). For camping, **Ayers Rock Campground** is in the resort complex and even has grass (☎ 61-8/8957-7001; US$120/£64)! **Best Restaurant:** For dining outdoors, the 4-hour **Sounds of Silence** dinner can be booked through Sails in the Desert Hotel (in the Ayers Rock Resort; US$116/£62). In an outdoor clearing, you sip champagne as the sun sets over the Rock. For indoor dining, there's **Kuniya,** also at the Sails in the Desert Hotel (in the Ayers Rock Resort; US$31–US$40/£16–£21). **When to Go:** High season is July through November. Book well ahead.

◄ *The Olgas (Kata Tjuta).*
© Martin Harvey/Corbis

UMBRIA, ITALY

A visit to the art towns of Perugia, Assisi, Spoleto & Todi

When a waiter is shaving thin slices of *tartufi neri* (black truffles) over my hand-cut *strengozzi* pasta, I think I love Umbria more than the overrun Tuscany. The following morning, I return to my senses, knowing that Umbria can't compete with the Renaissance and medieval treasures of Florence and Siena. But the landlocked "green heart of Italy" casts a spell, as I travel its back roads where tableaux still look as though they were painted by Il Perugino.

In autumn it rains in buckets, but the rainbows and sunsets are spectacular, with an orange gold blanketing the land. Winters are cold and damp, but spring bursts forth and the wildflowers cover the dead fields.

A spoiled rich brat, Saint Francis was so moved by Umbria he switched lifestyles, ending up nursing lepers and converting bandits. I can't promise such ecstasy for you, but with its ancient cities of Perugia and Assisi, its chestnut-wooded countryside, its broad and rolling Tiber River valleys, its olive groves and vineyards, and its art and architecture, Umbria remains a potent lure.

"Tuscany is for the masses," a former mayor of Perugia once proclaimed, "Umbria is for the connoisseur."

You'll find yourself doing things here you'd never do back home—perhaps getting up before sunrise to watch a purple dawn chase away the Gothic mists hanging over the towns like giant spider webs.

If you're coming from Florence, as most motorists do, plan to overnight in Perugia, 154km (96 miles) to the southwest, where you'll quickly make Piazza IV Novembre your living room. All the major monuments lie within an easy walk, including the Galleria Nazionale dell' Umbria, home to masterpieces by native sons Perugino and Pinturicchio, plus dozens of other old masters.

The next morning, it's only a 24km (15-mile) drive southeast to the hometown of Saint Francis. Nuns dressed in brown *cappucci* robes still inhabit the place, looking like bats as they scurry about. You don't have to be seized with religious fever to appreciate the art-filled Basilica di San Francesco, the most visited site in Umbria, whose interior is sheathed with Giotto's celebrated frescoes on the life of Saint Francis.

The next morning, drive 46km (28½ miles) south from Assisi to Spoleto to spend pre-lunchtime wandering its Roman ruins, past buildings from the Middle Ages. By early afternoon, journey another 43km (27 miles) to the northwest, to Todi, for a taste of the medieval and an overnight. Make Piazza del Popolo your center, and wander the dimly lit streets at night. You'll feel like you're in a time warp, but you're at Umbria's prettiest hill town, often missed by most visitors. It'll be our secret.

The next morning continue for a final stop to that volcanic rock, Orvieto, 31km (19 miles) northwest of Todi. Built on an outcropping of reddish tufa stone, nearly 300m (1,000 ft.) above the big valley of the Paglia River, Orvieto looks like a mirage in the summer heat, the hot air waving in patterns like a bolt of moiré fabric. Its Duomo, with its dazzling facade, is a triumph of transitional Romanesque and Gothic architecture. The cathedral is but one of many treasures you'll discover before nightfall when you can sit outside at a cafe savoring a bottle of Orvieto Classico.

◄ *Fresco, Church of St. Francis, Assisi.*
© SuperStock, Inc./ SuperStock

SPECIAL MOMENTS

1 *Passeggiata* **in Perugia.** When in Perugia, do as the Perugians do, and join in the early evening stroll known as the *passeggiata*. Put on your best duds and join the locals as they parade up and down the wide boulevard, Corso Vannucci. The *passeggiata* began when families with marriageable daughters wanted to show off their beauties to eligible bachelors (not wolves). Link arms with your best friend, your lover, or even your wife or husband for this fancy stroll. You'll saunter to one end of the boulevard and back, and then the real fun begins. Take a break to sip cappuccino and bite into one of Perugia's chocolate delicacies, the best in Italy, at one of the classy joints lining the street. My favorite hangout is **Sandri Pasticceria** (Corso Vannucci 32; ☎ 39-075/5724112).

2 **Deruta stoneware.** Since the days of the Renaissance painters, the little town of Deruta, 19km (12 miles) south of Perugia, has turned out an array of stoneware products that have attracted buyers from around the world. Its most famous pattern is the traditional *arabascato blu* (blue arabesques) design. The town is also known for its handcrafted artisan designs. Raphael passed through one day and commissioned stoneware with a motif of cavorting dragons in the midst of flowers and vines. Guess what? Factories today, numbering some 300, still turn out his long-ago designs. The town itself is a virtual stoneware shop, with outlets lining both sides of the Via Tiberina, the main drag of the lower town. *Tip:* Avoid these hawkers and explore some of the artisan shops along the old back roads where craftspeople can be found hand-painting stoneware thrown with foot-powered wheels.

3 **Assisi.** There are good reasons why this town of pink and gray buildings hugging a mountainside ranks with the *palazzi* of Venice, the ruins of Pompeii, and the glory that was Rome as one of the major attractions of Italy. It draws some four million annual visitors. They come to walk in the footsteps of Saint Francis, who seems to rival only Jesus in inspiring devotion among Christians. In spite of damage caused by the earthquakes of 1997, lovers of art and architecture also flood into the city to see Giotto's *Life of St. Francis* frescoes, the resting place of Saint Clare, the medieval fortress, Rocca Maggiore, and the oak-studded slopes of Mount Subasio where Saint Francis retreated to meditate. My insiderish tip: Assisi is overrun with "pilgrims" from April to October, but if you visit off-season, you almost have Assisi's twisting, narrow alleyways to yourself.

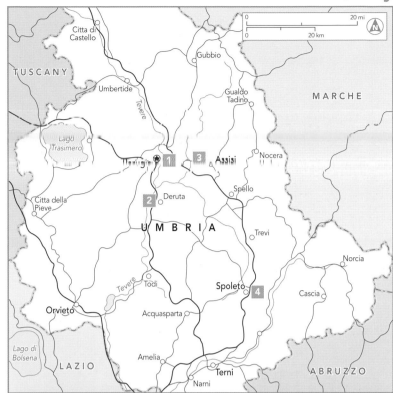

4 **Food and drink.** I've already extolled the glory of the black truffle, or *tartufi neri*. The Emperor Claudius claimed that he could service (or be serviced by) greater numbers of sex slaves after consuming large shavings of this delicacy. Spoleto is the best place for the black truffle. The culinary cognoscenti flock to Umbria for a gourmet holiday, and so do I. I always make at least one lunch out of the prized local salami, *mazzafegato*, made with pork liver, raisins, pine nuts, sugar, and fresh orange peel. Accompanied by a loaf of crusted country bread, the day is yours. On Sunday, the air is filled with the aroma of roasted whole suckling pig with wild fennel or else wild pheasant. The "green gold" of Umbria is the finest virgin olive oil in Italy, best sampled on bruschetta. Pliny the Elder was the first Roman to rhapsodize about the wines of Umbria. The Orvieto Classico is justly renowned, as are the bottles coming from the Torgiano vintners.

DARWIN PORTER is one of the world's most prolific travel writers. His books for Frommer's include guides to the Caribbean, Italy, France, Germany, and England. A Hollywood columnist and a celebrity biographer, Porter is also a radio broadcaster; his shows on American popular culture are heard in all 50 states.

ABOUT THE AUTHOR

YOUR TRIP

General Information: The two main **tourist offices** for the province are at Palazzo dei Priori on Piazza IV Novembre in Perugia (☎ 39-075/5736458), and at Piazza del Commune in Assisi (☎ 39-075/812534). For more information on Deruta, log on to the Italian-only website www.comune.deruta.pg.it. **Getting There:** Five different trains arrive daily from Rome (2¼ hr.), and two dozen trains link Assisi and Perugia. From Florence, take one of 12 daily trains to Terontola/Cortona (1½ hr.), linking with 35-minute trains going to Perugia. Log on to www.trenitalia.com for more schedule and pricing information. From Florence, motorists take the A1 south to the Valdichiana exit and the SS75bis on to Perugia. **Best Lodging:** **Hotel Brufani Palace,** in Perugia, is a deluxe bastion from 1884 towering over the town with grand panoramas (Piazza Italia 12; ☎ 39-075/5732541; www.brufanipalace.com; 352€/$457). **Best Lodging Value:** Cheaper but elegant digs are found at **Sangallo Palace Hotel,** offering luxury on a budget (Via L. Masi 9, Perugia; ☎ 39-075/5730202; www.sangallo.it; 126€–178€/$164–$231). Also expect first-class Umbrian cuisine at the restaurant. **Best Restaurant:** For Perugina cuisine at its finest, head for the atmospheric **Il Falchetto,** where the food is market fresh and classic (Via Bartolo 20; ☎ 39-075/5731775; www.ilfalchetto.it; tasting menu 30€/$39). **Best Restaurant Value:** In a medieval setting, **Il Cantinone** is cheap and good, including everything from savory pizzas to more classy Umbrian fare (Via Ritorta 4–8; ☎ 39-075/5734430; 6€–14€/$8–$18). **When to Go:** Apr–Oct.

◀ *Assisi.*

VENICE, ITALY

A destination of the spirit, a triumph of dreams over logic

Magic. It's a word travel writers are addicted to like cheap whiskey, and I pride myself on never using it . . . until, of course, I find myself writing about Venice. There's simply no other word to explain the spell cast by this moldering Italian city, floating above the encroaching Adriatic Sea, seemingly by sheer sorcery. Set on 118 separate islands dredged out of a polluted lagoon, Venice is in fact slowly sinking back under the water, some 2½ inches per decade, like some sort of exquisite Shangri-La. The sad fact is that Venice might not even be there for our children's children—all the more reason to see it as soon as you can.

Yet even without this tragic foreshadowing of doom, Venice has an air of mystery and melancholy that can't be explained in any rational terms. Oh, I've been to Venice, California, and to Venice, Florida, and I've even stayed at the Venetian resort in Las Vegas. Each imitator is lovely in its own way, and yet, when you come right down to it, they simply aren't Venice; they don't even come close. Nothing does.

Sure, other cities have canals, but Venice long ago committed itself totally to the mad idea of no streets at all, only canals (more than 150 of them) accompanied by a bewildering labyrinth of narrow paved stone walkways. Cars are useless; motor launches and anachronistic dragon-prowed black gondolas are the only way to get around town. Do not bother with a gondola—the fare is outrageous and you'll be poled along too slowly to get much of a thrill. Alluring as they seem, those gondolas are prettier to look at than they are to ride in, anyway. Instead, cruise the long S-curve of the Grand Canal by *vaporetto*, the Venetian equivalent of a city bus: Guidebook in hand, identify the succession of stately Venetian Gothic palazzi, each one more gilded and heavily ornamented than the next, all part of the age-old, status-seeking competition of this aristocratic city-state. Take careful note of the three bridges spanning the Grand Canal—the stone Ponte degli Scalzi, the marble Ponte Rialto, and the wooden Ponte Accademia—because once you're on foot, if you wind up on the other side of the canal, you may have quite a long walk to cross back. When at last you reach the Piazza San Marco, with its ornate Doge's Palace and shimmering basilica—well, you wouldn't be the first tourist to be absolutely awestruck by the sight.

Venice is expensive, no question, and the major tourist sites are jammed in the summer high season (when it's also wickedly hot and the canals begin to exude a distinctive rotting aroma). But so what? Venice isn't a checklist of must-see landmarks; it's a destination of the spirit, a triumph of dreams over logic. Wander about and let all your senses drink it in: the murmur of water lapping against stone, the faint scent of decay, a certain indefinable softness in the air. Abandon yourself to the magic . . . and hope you never wake from its enchantment.

A quiet canal near Piazza San Marco.

© Adrian Reynolds/AGE Fotostock, Inc.

SPECIAL MOMENTS

1 **Standing on the Piazza San Marco at twilight.** This marvelous colonnaded town square is perhaps the world's greatest stage set, culminating in the glorious gold-domed Basilica San Marco; just off to the side looms the exotic Doge's Palace, with its faintly sinister *Arabian Nights* facade. Packed with day-trippers and rapacious pigeons at noon, the piazza clears out surprisingly fast once evening softly descends; that's the time to stand here and admire one of Europe's most harmonious hodgepodges of architecture, as shadows begin to fill the arcaded walkways and lights wink on in the cafes.

2 **Getting lost.** Walking around Venice inevitably means getting tangled in a maze of narrow stone lanes, echoing palazzo walls, high-arched bridges, and sudden vistas of church towers. There's nothing like a logical grid, or even any main thoroughfare; streets twist, turn, and dead-end unexpectedly, and addresses are nearly meaningless. Yet somehow you'll always be able to find your way if you spot the yellow signs at every intersection, pointing you toward one of five landmarks: Piazza San Marco, The Accademia bridge, the Rialto bridge, Piazzale Roma, and the train station. Don't worry about "sights"; once you're out of the tourist center, look for stray cats, laundry hung out of upper stories, produce heaped outside greengrocer stands, children kicking soccer balls against 500-year-old walls. Discover the real city that hides from the tourist hordes.

3 **Visiting the lesser-known churches.** While every package tourist gapes at the glittering mosaics and treasure of the Basilica San Marco, I prefer to haunt the lesser-known churches (a great way to escape the brutal sun in summer, too). Begin in the Castello district with Santi Giovanni e Paolo (shortened by Venetians to Zanipolo), full of the doges' tombs. Across the Grand Canal, in San Polo, stands the church of San Rocco, loaded with Tintoretto paintings, and nearby is the wonderfully austere Il Frari featuring Titian masterpieces. But don't stop here—keep walking and pop into any church that strikes your fancy. For a few coins spent on lighting candles, you can rest in a pew and enjoy the paintings and statues without ever learning the artists' names (though many are by famous artists, indeed). Allow the dusky, echoing space to lay its centuries-old silence on your soul.

4 **Visiting the Guggenheims.**
There's so much Renaissance art
around Venice, it's almost a relief to
spend an afternoon in a modern-art
museum, especially since it's one
of the world's best—the Peggy
Guggenheim Collection. American
heiress Peggy Guggenheim lived
here from 1949 to 1979, and as you
stroll from room to room you'll not
only see priceless art, you'll also
get a sense of the life of a wealthy
expatriate with all the right avant-
garde connections. There's a whole
bedroom full of bold paintings
by her protégé Jackson Pollack;
Alexander Calder designed the
silver headboard in her bedroom,
as well as the mobile in her entrance
hall; there are several paintings by
Max Ernst, who was Mr. Peggy
Guggenheim for a while in the
1940s. The low-slung, white-marble
building itself is striking, the first
floor of an 18th-century neoclassical
palazzo that was never finished—
as if somehow it was always meant
to be the modern showplace it is
today.

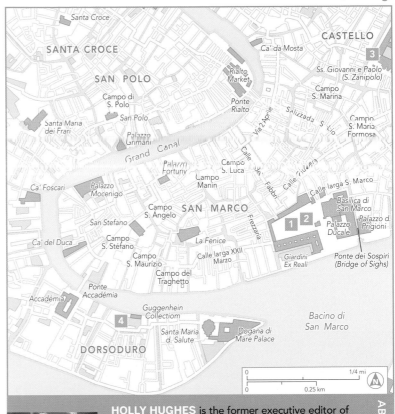

HOLLY HUGHES is the former executive editor of
Fodor's Travel Publications and author of *Frommer's
New York City with Kids* and *Frommer's 500 Places
to Take Your Kids before They Grow Up.* She's also
written fiction for middle graders and edits the annual
Best Food Writing anthology. New York City makes
a convenient jumping-off place for her travels.

ABOUT THE AUTHOR

YOUR TRIP

General Information: Visitor information is available at the **Azienda di Promozione Turistica** (San Marco 71/F;
☎ 39-041/5298711) or www.enit.it. **Getting There: Aeroporto Marco Polo** lies about a half-hour north of the city,
on the mainland in Mestre. **Delta Airlines** now flies nonstop from North America (www.delta.com). Venice is a
5-hour train trip from Rome and 4 hours from Florence. Check out www.trenitalia.com for train information.
Best Lodging: The **Hotel Danieli** is a fabulously luxurious palazzo on the Grand Canal (Riva degli Schiavoni,
Castello; ☎ 800/325-3535 in the U.S. or 39-041/5226480; http://danieli.hotelinvenice.com; 179€–2,000€/
$218–$2,440). **Cipriani** is more casual and resortlike, yet stratos-
pherically chic (Isola della Giudecca 10; ☎ 39-041/5207744;
www.hotelcipriani.com; from 499€/$608; closed Nov–Mar).
Best Lodging Value: Pensione Accademia is the ideal Italian
pensione, in a relatively quiet neighborhood (Fondamenta Bollani, Dorsoduro; ☎ 39-041/5237846; www.
pensioneaccademia.it; 80€–280€/$97–$341). **Best Restaurant:** The **Antico Martini** offers top-drawer gourmet
cuisine with a distinctly regional emphasis (Campo San Fantin, San Marco; ☎ 39-041/5224121; www.anticomartini.
com; 32€–79€/$39–$96). **Best Restaurant Value: La Locanda Montin** is a mellow neighborhood inn with a
bohemian pedigree (Fondamenta di Borgo, Dorsoduro; ☎ 39-041/5227151; 14€–26€/$17–$31). **When to Go:**
Summers are hot and muggy; winters are gray and wet, but not severe. The best months to visit are April through
June and September through October.

Gondolas on the Grand Canal.
© David Noton/Getty Images

WADDEN ISLANDS, HOLLAND

Holland's best-kept secret for bikers & beachcombers

In a survey, the Wadden Sea Islands, a chain of barrier islands between the Dutch coast and the North Sea, emerged as one of the least recognizable pieces of geography in Europe. Holland promotes them as the country's best-kept secret, even though that's not quite true. The Dutch themselves go here for their summer vacations, as do sun-seeking Germans fed up with the lethal prices of their own North Sea island of Sylt.

The Wadden Islands are the largest estuarine area in Europe, and they are kept afloat by the genius of Dutch engineers and their dike-building skills.

Each of the islands is easily reached from the Dutch mainland by ferryboat. In order of importance, the most intriguing islands are Texel, Vlieland, Terschelling, and Ameland.

On any of the islands, you can see mothers biking their way to market with flaxen-haired children riding in back. Follow their example. The bike is the way to explore these remote islands. Some of the bike trails are lined with honeysuckle. When the wind is right, you'll think you've strayed into a perfume factory.

I sometimes dislike the term "bird-watchers' paradise," but, in the case of the Wadden Islands, the term fits. Millions of migratory birds pass through here. Alfred Hitchcock, should he return to earth, could make a sequel to *The Birds* here, with its oyster catchers, spoonbills, eider ducks, avocets, and snow-white geese.

Unlike some other beach resorts in Europe, the Wadden Islands haven't yet been overrun. Farmers display produce for sale at unguarded stands—bouquets of sunflowers, fresh vegetables, cranberry preserves, freshly baked brown bread, even herb butter. The last time I visited, I secured the makings of a picnic at one of these stands. In an honor box at the stand, you leave what you consider a fair price. We wouldn't recommend this in Calcutta, or Manhattan.

The biggest thrill here involves walking on the seabed of the Wadden Sea when it disappears during the low tides. And, oh, those windmills, enough to make Don Quixote (or Quijote, as it's spelled today) and Sancho Panza abandon the plains of La Mancha forever.

Most of the locals are friendly. The place to meet them is in the local taverns, where you can acquire a taste for cherry beer.

Where to stay? The best place would be in a working farmhouse for 20€ ($26) a night, where "Mother Wadden" will prepare a hearty bowl of her Dutch split-pea soup for you and fry you some locally caught catfish, unless you request some of that aromatic and world-renowned Frisian lamb.

Forget Cape Cod. This is the place to go for salt marshes and sand dunes whose undulating shapes evoke woolly mammoths. There are fields of purple heather to rival anything in the Orkneys. I love the bright orange berries that grow on the rowan trees, the fields of marram grass, and the antique, half-timbered farmhouses under terra-cotta tile roofs.

Remote, tranquil, and utterly beautiful, the Wadden Islands get my vote for escapism.

◀ *The island of Texel at sunset.*

© Eddy Marissen/Foto Natura/Minden Pictures

SPECIAL MOMENTS

1 Texel. If you can visit only one of the Wadden Sea Islands, make it Texel, lying just 72km (45 miles) north of Amsterdam. It's the most visited and most westerly of the Dutch barrier islands, and it's only 24km (15 miles) long and 10km (6 miles) wide.

Within minutes you can escape from the commercialized town of Den Burg, the main village, after renting a bike at the ferry terminal. In all, there are some 134km (90 miles) of cycle paths, astonishing for so small an island.

Literally millions of orchids bloom in the wild in June, sometimes lining the roads. I gravitate to the green-winged orchid. As stunning as they are, though, nothing is as beautiful as the snowdrops that coat forest floors like white blankets in May. Past salt fens and heaths, you come across a colony of spoonbills, hundreds of grazing sheep, and clay mounds left over from the last Ice Age.

Nude beaches are found at Hoorn Horrnderslag, .5km south of Post 9, and at Den Hoorn Krimslag, 1km south of Post 28. Nude recreation is allowed on the beach and in the water, but not in the dunes. If you believe that law is enforced, then the Dutch tooth fairy will come to call on you at night.

2 Vlieland. If you ever dreamed of escaping to an isolated island, Vlieland is it. Yet it's reached by a 90-minute ferry ride from the Dutch mainland town of Harlingen.

Nonresidents can't bring cars over, so once you get to Vlieland you walk or bike (rentals available at the ferry dock).

The island is blanketed with meadows and forests of alders, maples, spruce firs, and Austrian and Corsican pines. But it's visited mainly for its 19km (12 miles) of unspoiled sandy beaches.

For me, there's much more to see and discover in the interior. Look for De Fortweg (The Fort Road) with bunkers left over from the World War I and World War II, an eerie sight.

Before crossing the water for a day trip, bring along a picnic lunch from the mainland just to be on the safe side.

3 Terschelling. With its nature reserves taking up 80% of the island, its endless sand dunes, some 28km (18 miles) of white sandy beaches, and its virgin forests, there is much to admire about this most accessible of all the Wadden Islands.

You can bike Terschelling, as the paths are excellent and stretch for 64km (40 miles). The Forest Service has mapped six walks, including three nature paths. The tourist office at Willem Barentszkade 19A in West Terschelling will give you maps before you set out. You can also pick up supplies along the main street here.

I prefer to head north from West Terschelling to see a series of picture-book villages along the eastern coast with names such as Midslands, Lies, and Hoorn. Finally you reach Oosterend after a leisurely stroll of 3 hours or so.

Car ferries leave from the port of Harlingen on the mainland, taking 2 hours, or else you can take a hydrofoil, putting you on Terschelling in just 50 minutes.

4 Ameland. Ameland was the last territory held by Nazi soldiers, who finally surrendered to the Allies on June 2, 1945, nearly a full month after the Germans surrendered. Perhaps

the remaining garrison was reluctant to part from such an idyllic setting.

A 45-minute ferry ride from the mainland port of Holwerd brings you to Ameland's capital of Nes, the prettiest town in the Wadden Islands.

Each of the other villages is also worth exploring, including Ballum, where 350 people live. Many old houses with wall anchors date from the 1700s. Ancestors of the present residents of the village of Buren once earned their living by lighting fires on the shoreline to mislead ships. When the ships wrecked off their coast, locals salvaged the plunder. Hollum, with its eye-catching, peppermint-striped lighthouse, is filled with beautiful old sailors' homes built with money made from whaling.

To end the perfect day, head for the best restaurant, **De Klimop,** in Nes (John Hofker Weg 2; ☎ 31-315/954-2296), for its salt-grazed lamb (*pré salé*), its garlicky fresh mussels, and a taste of the island's liqueur, Nobeltje.

DARWIN PORTER is one of the world's most prolific travel writers. His books for Frommer's include guides to the Caribbean, Italy, France, Germany, and England. A Hollywood columnist and a celebrity biographer, Porter is also a radio broadcaster; his shows on American popular culture are heard in all 50 states.

ABOUT THE AUTHOR

YOUR TRIP

General Information: When planning your trip, consult the **Dutch Tourist Board** (www.holland.com). For more information on the Wadden Islands, check out **www.wadden.nl,** which will lead you to the tourism websites for each island. The tourism office on Texel is at Emmalaan 66, Den Burg (☎ 31-222/314741; **www.texel.net**); on Vlieland, Havenweg 10 (☎ 31-222/451111); on Terschelling, Willem Barentszkade 19A (☎ 31-222/443000); and Ameland, Rixt van Doniastraat (☎ 31-222/546546). **Getting There:** All islands are linked to the Dutch mainland by ferryboat service. Boats leave from Den Helder for Texel; from Harlingen to Vlieland and Terschelling; and from Holwerd for Ameland. **Best Lodging:** A beautifully renovated skipper's inn, **Loodsman's Welvaren,** offers spacious, cheery rooms and a bar-bistro where sailors and pilots hang out (Herenstraat 12, Den Hoorn, Texel; ☎ 31-222/319228; **www.welvaarttexel.nl**; 66€–105€/$79–$126 double). **Best Lodging Value:** On the edge of the Duinen Van Texel Park sits **Hotel De 14 Sterren,** with its cozy charm in a romantic setting next to the 300-year-old barn-house restaurant, the De Worsteltent (Smitsweg 4, Den Burg, Texel; ☎ 31-222/322681; **www.14sterren.nl**, Dutch only; 55€–70€/$66–$84 double). **Best Restaurant:** The finest French/Mediterranean cuisine in all the Waddens is served at **Bij Jef** (Herenstraaat 34, Texel; ☎ 31-222/319623; **www.bijjef.nl**; 38€–65€/$45–$78). **Best Restaurant Value:** Texel's top fish takeout joint is **Vispaleis en Rokerij vd Star** (Heemskerckstraat 15; ☎ 31-222/312441; 6€–10€/$7–$12). Fish soup is their specialty. Ever had an eel sandwich? **When to Go:** May–Sept.

◀ *Sand dunes on Terschelling Island.*

WALES

Castles, mining towns & the fierce solitude of Snowdonia

Maybe it's the fugitive sunlight or the damp mists that trail around its rugged cliffs and secluded coves, but driving along the coastal highway of northwest Wales, I get an uncanny sensation that the ancient Welsh kingdom of Gwynedd never really went away, despite the Act of Union that forced Wales to become part of Great Britain in 1536. There's a particular fierceness to the landscape that I find spellbinding; escarpments plummet straight into the cold ocean, and small, sooty towns of gray stone cling like lichens to the hillsides.

The very town names around here are unpronounceable to outsiders; some 70% of the population are native Welsh speakers. Wales has more castles per square mile than any other country in western Europe, chiefly because English kings—most notably Edward I—had to keep building fortresses to maintain their rule. To pacify the Welsh, the heir apparent to the British throne is traditionally crowned Prince of Wales at the grandest of all of King Edward's castles, Caernarfon—but even Caernarfon Castle is a hollow, majestic ruin, as if to suggest that English sovereignty is a mere mirage.

After centuries of defiance, it took the Industrial Revolution to vanquish northern Wales. The great civil engineer Thomas Telford rolled out the London-Holyhead road (the A5 today) and a number of impressive ironwork suspension bridges (including the landmark beauty across the Menai Strait, leading to the Isle of Anglesey); once connected to the Midlands by road, Wales was gradually sucked into Britain's 19th-century industrial maw.

Amid all this natural beauty, I am captivated—and haunted—by the still-grimy mining town of Blaenau Ffestiniog, center of the slate-quarrying industry; for insight, visit the Llechwedd Slate Caverns (☎ 44-1766/830306; **www.llechwedd-slate-caverns. co.uk**) in Blaenau Ffestiniog, or the Welsh Slate Museum in Llanberis (☎ 44-1286/ 870630; **www.nmgw.ac.uk**). Yet even while the mountains of the interior were being ravaged, upscale Victorian-era resorts were cropping up along the scenic north Wales coast to amuse English holiday-goers—towns like Llandudno, with its gingerbread architecture and lacy iron amusement pier. I'm absurdly fond of these dowdy old resorts, with their fitful sunshine, outmoded amusements, and rocky shingle beaches. It's contrasts like this that give Wales its quirky character, more precious to me than manicured landscapes and sybaritic resorts.

Nowadays most visitors to North Wales are outdoorsy types keen on hiking, climbing, and rafting in Snowdonia National Park, which was founded in 1951 and sprawls across much of north Wales's highland interior. For all its popularity, Snowdonia still offers solitude and roughness. Rambling on Snowdonia's footpaths— a surprising combination of springy turf and gravelly scree—you may encounter wild ponies and free-ranging sheep, who don't seem surprised at all to meet hikers. (There are three times as many sheep as people in Wales.) A shadow flits across a rocky chasm, and you may wonder for a split second if there's a wizard hiding in that gnarled oak—or a stubborn Welsh chieftain brooding on the nearest hilltop.

◄ *A brooding Welsh landscape.*
© Lorentz Gullachsen/ Getty Images

SPECIAL MOMENTS

1 **Mount Snowdon.** Many visitors to Snowdonia National Park challenge themselves with a 5-hour round-trip climb up Mount Snowdon, at 1,085m (3,560 ft.) the highest peak in Wales and England. The view from the top is perhaps Wales's most breathtaking panorama—it's possible to see some 161km (100 miles) across the straits into Ireland, glimpsing the Wicklow peaks on a clear day. It's also possible to get to that spectacular Mount Snowdon view the easy way, via the rack-and-pinion **Snowdon Mountain Railway** (☎ 44-870/458-0033; **www.snowdonrailway. co.uk**) from the charming little town of Llanberis (1 hr. each way)—

a precipitous ride that's a thrill in its own right.

2 **Betws-y-Coed.** Set like a jewel in Snowdonia's Gwydyr Forest, a dense swath of oak, beech, and fir trees, Betws-y-Coed (pronounced "*bet*-us ee-*coyd*") is almost unbearably picturesque. It's little more than a main street, with its scrum of bed-and-breakfasts and neat small hotels, one lovely 14th-century church, and a series of no less than eight bridges arching pertly over the tumbling Llugwy and Conwy rivers. (Walk across them all for the classic Betws-y-Coed experience.) Just off the main street, a mile-long walking path climbs steeply from St. Mary's Church to Swallow Falls, a

stair-step series of chattering waterfalls where you can perch on the boulders and feel the mountain mist swirl against your skin.

3 **Conwy.** There's a definite medieval aura to the smart little cobblestoned town of Conwy, with a fine set of stately Edward I castle ruins thrusting crenellated towers heavenward from a rocky outcrop. Nearly a mile of city wall is intact, much of which you can walk along, and two half-timbered merchant's houses can be toured, one from the 14th century and one from the 16th. Only 8 miles south of town lies Bodnant Gardens, an elegant Victorian-era horticultural showplace; come early in the morning before the

day-trippers descend and you'll find dew still lying heavy on the magnolias in spring, and roses in summer.

4 **Portmeirion.** On the western coast lies Portmeirion, a glorious folly of a holiday village built in the 1920s by architect Sir Clough Williams-Ellis. Improbably, his whimsical vision of pastel Mediterranean villas tumbling down the rocky hillsides works superbly—so superbly, in fact, that it starred as The Village in the 1960s cult British TV series *The Prisoner,* a *1984*-ish political parable dreamed up by its star, Patrick McGoohan. Those elegant villas are now guest lodgings (there are no actual residents, though Sir Clough's original hope was to house a commune of likeminded artistic souls), though any visitor is welcome to wander around. Enjoy afternoon tea overlooking the Italianate central piazza; and then rummage around the shops for *Prisoner* souvenirs and beautiful Portmeirion pottery, designed by Sir Clough's daughter.

HOLLY HUGHES has traveled the globe as an editor and writer—she's the former executive editor of Fodor's Travel Publications and author of *Frommer's New York City with Kids* and *Frommer's 500 Places to Take Your Kids before They Grow Up*. She also edits the annual *Best Food Writing* anthology. New York City makes a convenient jumping-off place for her travels.

ABOUT THE AUTHOR

YOUR TRIP

General Information: For information to help plan your trip, go to www.visitwales.com. Also contact the **Snowdonia National Park** (☎ 44-1766/770274; www.eryri-npa.co.uk). The **Betws-y-Coed Tourist Office** is on Holyhead Road (☎ 44-1690/710426). **Getting There:** The inland A5 trunk road leads 402km (250 miles) from London to Caernarfon; the coastal highway, A55, runs 109km (68 miles) from Chester, England, to Caernarfon. London to Llandudno is a 4½-hour train journey. For train schedules, go to www.nationalrail.co.uk. **Best Lodging: Tan-y-Foel Country House Hotel** is a 16th-century manor with panoramic views of the Conwy Valley with Snowdonia looming in the background (Capel Garmon, near Betws-y-Coed; ☎ 44-1690/710507; www.tyfhotel.co.uk; £141–£155/$278–$305). The **Sychnant Pass House** is a country-house gem with great personality in Snowdonia's foothills (Sychnant Pass Rd., Conwy; ☎ 44-1492/596865; www.sychnant-pass-house.co.uk; £90–£170/$177–$334). **Hotel Portmeirion,** in Portmeirion, allows you to live overnight in the village (☎ 44-1766/770000; www.portmeirion-village.com; £167–£308/$329–$607). **Best Lodging Value: Ty Gwyn,** along the A5, Betws-y-Coed, is a charming old coaching inn (☎ 44-1690/710383; www.tygwynhotel.co.uk; £44–£100/$87–$197). **Best Restaurant:** All the above hotels have excellent restaurants open to non-guests; the **Groes Inn** (Tyn-y-Groes, Conwy; ☎ 44-10492/650545; £7–£20/$14–$40), and the **King's Head** (Old Rd., Llandudno; ☎ 44-1492/877993; £6–£18/$12–$35) offer traditional pub meals as well as upscale dining.

Pentre Ifan, 4,500-year-old dolmen, Pembrokeshire.
© Melissa Park/DanitaDelimont.com

YÁNGSHUÒ, CHINA

One of the most bizarre & haunting landscapes on earth

When I first saw them out of my taxi window I just started laughing. They were so ridiculously beautiful that it was difficult to believe they were real. They were hills, but hills like none I had ever seen. They seemed to rise up out of nothing in the southern landscape of China between Guìlín and Yángshuò: a range of stunning green peaks of the sort Gaudí might have created had he made mountains.

Those who saw these surreal shapes in ancient Chinese paintings and scrolls thought they existed only in the imagination. "I often sent pictures of the hills of Guìlín which I painted to friends back home, but few believed what they saw," complained the 12th-century scholar Fan Chengda.

More recently a *Star Wars* team spotted the alien potential of this bizarre landscape and used it as a backdrop in one of its films. The reality is, these hills are very much a product of earth, having been worn away over the centuries by naturally occurring acid rain.

Today it's not so much artists and film crews who flock here, but tourists and adventure-seekers. The town of Yángshuò, at the center of these strange hills, is a toy box packed full of adventurous activities, from climbing to river rafting, bridge jumping, road and mountain biking, zip-lining, and caving.

Of course, having all these activities available to you means Yángshuò is no longer an undiscovered hill town. If you want to be the only Westerner around, you had better go elsewhere. Yángshuò is still a real beauty, though, perhaps because of—rather than despite—the travel trade. While other Chinese towns have been allowed to get shabby through neglect, this assortment of ramshackle, white-washed buildings has been lovingly maintained.

The real snap-happy tourists tend to flock down from Guìlín along the Lí River—it's a full-day trip by boat—and then head back to Guìlín by bus or veer off to places like the Big Banyan Tree, where dressed up monkeys are paraded around for photo ops. Don't panic; all of this is easy to avoid and shouldn't put you off from coming here.

Your best bet is to stick around for a day or two, and head off into the hills, either on your own two feet, on a rented bike, or with a climbing company. The landscape deep in the countryside looks as though it were freshly invented for you. It even smells good: dark, tropical, green, and earthy. Climb up to one of the highest peaks, like Moon Hill for an extraordinary view of burnt-jade-colored limestone peaks rising up out of the mist and stretching off into nowhere.

Back at ground level, I wouldn't head back into town just yet. Among the best places to eat are the roadside shacks made of corrugated iron. Often they're family-run affairs with chickens running in and out of the door and rotund puppies rolling around on the floor. The local specialties are freshwater snails (*tiánluó niang*)—there are 18 types stuffed with all sorts of goodies, like pork mince and a minty herb called *bohe*—plus beer fish (*píjiǔ yú*). When you've finished, you'll be ready for your next adventure.

◄ *Sunset on the Li River.*
© Keren Su/Getty Images

SPECIAL MOMENTS

1 Walking up Moon Hill. Climbing is the hottest activity in Yángshuò, attracting enthusiasts from around the globe, but there's absolutely no need to hang from a rope to get high in the Yángshuò area. There are some far gentler gradients to take you up to the top of the karst peaks for some essential views. One of the easiest and most well-worn paths takes you up Moon Hill. It still requires a bit of stamina and a good pair of walking boots, but it can easily be done in 20 minutes, and the reward is the most amazing view of the dark green peaks, swaddled in mist, stretching on in all directions, for what seems like forever.

2 Head to Xīngpíng. One of the delights of basing yourself in Yángshuò is heading out to the less-developed villages and towns nearby. High on my recommended list has to be Xīngpíng (25km/16 miles northeast of Yángshuò on the Lí River), for its stunning mountain setting and its rambling wooden houses and shops. The journey here is magical in itself; with luck you'll see fishermen using cormorants to do their work for them (the birds catch the fish in their beaks but can't swallow them because of a collar around their necks). There is a 25km (16 miles) hike to Xīngpíng for the hard core who are planning on staying the night. Most, however, will probably prefer to make it a day trip, take a minibus there (leave from Yángshuò bus station or arrange a private vehicle at your hotel), and catch a boat back. There are some large boats packed full of travelers, but you can also hire your own motorboat down at the waterfront (be prepared to haggle hard or get your hotel to make arrangements), hitch a ride on one of the floating bamboo rafts, or take a bike. However you go, winding your way between the emerald hills is a once-in-a-lifetime experience.

3 Hiding from the rain in a restaurant. I love it when it rains in Yángshuò. When the clouds break, I scurry up to get a front-row seat on one of the second-floor restaurant balconies overlooking the streets. From here you can watch the deluge wash the streets clean. Later, when the skies clear, the activity starts up again in the market as plastic coverings are shaken off and trading continues. Meanwhile I chow down on burgers and fries. Yes, I know, I should be

Map

Guìlín
Pagoda Hill
Pierced Hill
Fighting Cocks Hill
Clean Vase Hill
Zhemu
Aged Banyan
Ertang
Father and Son Cave
Daxu
Chao Tian
Qifengzhen
Milestone Hill
Angling Terrace
Happy Marriage at Biya Hill
New Oxen Ridge and Three Islets
Liangfeng
White Dragons Playing with Water
Frog Crossing the River
Yearning for Husband Rock
Yanshan
Screen Hill
Caopingxu
Colorful Embroidery Hill
Liangfeng
Celestial Turning Millstone
Yangdi
Magic-Writing Brush Peak
Lion Peak
Tortoise Climbing Hill
Old Man Watching Apple
Nine Horses on Picture Hill
Eight Immortals Crossing the River
Glove Hill
Putao
2 Xīngpíng
Fairy Maiden Peak
Camel Hill
Snail Hill
Lion Mounted Carp
Puotang
Baisha
Dragon Head Hill
Yulong
3
Jinbao
Yángshuò
Fuli
4
Lion Hill
Green Lotus Peak
Snow Lion Peak
1
Aged Banyan
Moon Hill

0 — 5 mi
0 — 5 km

eating local food, but when you're soaked through, sometimes comfort food is just what you're after.

4 Cycle out between the hills.
The surprising thing about biking in and around Yángshuò is that the land around the huge karst peaks is relatively flat, especially if you follow the path of the Lí River. Geared, modern hybrid and mountain bikes are available for rent on and around West Street in town. Once in the saddle, you can stick to the roads, but there's really no need, as the dirt tracks winding their way between paddy fields and tumbledown rural villages are mostly solid, flat, and easygoing. It's best to go with an English-speaking guide (your guesthouse or hotel can easily arrange this, or simply ask in any cafe) who will know his or her way around the tracks. Otherwise, be willing to get lost or get a map from your guesthouse or hotel and head for Moon Hill, Yulong Bridge, or one of the small nearby villages like Longtang.

ABOUT THE AUTHOR

OLIVIA EDWARD is a British writer who began specializing in travel after living in Shànghǎi. She has written for *Time Out*, DK, and MTV guides, and for glossy publications for companies like American Express. Happiest when swimming in rough seas, she can be tempted onto dry land by rain, mud, and off-road motorbikes.

YOUR TRIP

General Information: You could try www.travelchinaguide.com for a brief introduction, but you may find you're better off speaking to the **China Tourist Board** directly. Call them at ☎ 888/760-8218. To get climbing or mountain biking, make contact with the Australian setup **ChinaClimb** (www.chinaclimb.com). **Getting There:** The nearest rail and air connections are from Guìlín, 65km (40 miles) north. Taxis from Guìlín take an hour. **What to See & Do:** Those preferring something more sedate can take courses on tai chi, Chinese cooking, calligraphy, medicine, or Mandarin at various places in town, including the **Chinese Culture and Art Promotion Workshop** (Diécuì Jiē 2; ☎ 86-773/881-1121). **Best Lodging:** There are no five stars in Yángshuò. **Magnolia Hotel** is clean, friendly, and airy with some great top-price rooms from which you can just see the peaks (Diécuì Lù 7; ☎ 86-773/881-9288; www.yangshuoren.com/magnolia02.htm; $25–$38/£13–£20). **Best Lodging Value:** Out of town there's the **Moon Hill Resort,** in Moon Village (☎ 86-773/8777688; $15/£8). **Best Restaurant:** Le Vôtre specialties include steamed mussels and grilled duck (Xī Jiē 7; $4–$10/£2–£5.30). **Best Dining:** Street food from the stalls on the corner of Shenshan Road and Diécuì Lù for a mere 30¢. **When to Go:** The spring or autumn. April to May and September to November are the best months for climbing and outdoor pursuits. In these months there is not much rain and plenty of sunshine; and it's not scorching hot, although you'll still need your sunscreen on the south-facing walls. The winter is cold but dry and summers are hot, rainy, and humid.

◀ *Yángshuò street scene.*
© Daryl Benson/Masterfile

YELLOWSTONE NATIONAL PARK, WYOMING

Hot springs, belching mud pots & steaming fumaroles

Surrounded by people from all over the world, we sit and wait. "When's it going to blow up?" a fidgeting young boy asks his parents. It's standing room only. The anticipation builds.

As sunset nears, a buffalo ambles up, as if on cue, and begins to graze on the grass surrounding the steaming hole in front of us, better known as Old Faithful. One of the icons of Yellowstone National Park, this is the world's most predictable geyser, erupting every 91 minutes, give or take a half-hour.

Water begins to spout from the ground, in fits and starts at first, which gradually grow into more powerful outbursts. The crowd oohs and ahhs. The top of the geyser scrapes the sky nearly 200 feet above us. During its average 3-minute eruption, Old Faithful expels about 6,000 gallons of boiling water. This blast might even be bigger.

My favorite spot for a walkabout in the wilderness, Yellowstone is one of only two undeveloped geyser basins in the world. (The other is on Russia's Kamchatka Peninsula.) Besides geysers, the park has thousands of peculiar and fascinating thermal features, including hot springs of every hue, belching mud pots, and steaming fumaroles. The reason for all this activity: The heart of the park is an active caldera, a massive volcano that erupted and collapsed into itself many millennia ago, leaving a crater 40 miles across and pockets of magma (molten earth) 2 miles beneath the surface—or, in geological terms, right next door. The annual spring snowmelt keeps underground aquifers full, and water trickles into magma-warmed hotspots and boils into steam. The pressure mounts and eventually results in aboveground thermal features like geysers and hot springs.

Old Faithful is the centerpiece of one of the many geyser basins in Yellowstone, and it's also the centerpiece of almost every Yellowstone vacation. From this starting point, the possibilities are nearly endless. In the park's vast confines—over 2 million acres—you can hike a mountain; fish for native cutthroat trout; look for black bears, grizzlies, or gray wolves in the Lamar Valley; or drive the 150-mile Grand Loop for an overview of the park's wonders. Or you could easily spend an entire weeklong vacation strolling the boardwalks at Old Faithful, waiting out Castle Geyser, Riverside Geyser, and the other unforgettable water displays with a camera and a good book, spending your nights in the civilized confines of the Old Faithful Inn.

I've been visiting Yellowstone since I was a child, but I still feel I've barely scratched the surface. There are still countless miles of trails I've yet to hike, panoramas I've yet to behold, and geysers I've yet to witness. I want to go snowshoeing in the park during the winter, when it's an otherworldly wonderland with plumes of geothermal steam puncturing the white blanket of snow. I want to go backpacking in the Thorofare and Bechler areas. I want to follow the route of Truman Everts, the accountant who became the first person to get lost here in 1870. Many Yellowstone vacations still await me—and all of us.

◀ *Grand Canyon of the Yellowstone River, Wyoming.*
© Muench Photography Inc.

SPECIAL MOMENTS

1 Yellowstone Association Institute. The best views of the park cannot be seen from inside of a car, behind a bug-stained wind-shield. Yellowstone is just the place to park the car and explore, and the Yellowstone Association Institute excels at helping people do just that. Its year-round curriculum includes classes covering park history, wildlife ecology, nature writing, photography, and much more. Some programs last a few hours, others several days or weeks, and many are good for families and children. I've personally taken a class about bison and gone on a guided backpacking trip, memorable experiences both. The 3-day bison class was split between lectures and field study, while the backpacking trip followed the historic Nez Perce Trail for 4 days. The Institute's main campus is on a onetime buffalo ranch in the wildlife-rich Lamar Valley in the northeast corner of the park.

2 Geyser gazing. The park has approximately 10,000 thermal features, including some 300 active geysers (about half the world's total). While the best known and most predictable, Old Faithful, is a must-see, it's just the first page in a geothermal epic. Among the numerous geyser basins, Norris is another highlight, with a wide range of thermal features (geysers as well as others like vents and hot pools); so is Steamboat Geyser, the world's tallest active geyser, sending 300-foot bursts skyward once a year, give or take. Many hotspots are deep in the backcountry: Seeing Lonestar Geyser blow is well worth the level 2-mile hike from Old Faithful. But bear in mind: The Yellowstone Caldera has historically erupted every 600,000 years, meaning a cataclysmic event is due any millennium now.

3 Mount Washburn Trail. From the summit of Mount Washburn, 10,243 feet above sea level, a sublime view of Yellowstone spreads in all directions. You can see the Absaroka Mountains to the east, the Gallatins to the west and north, and the Grand Canyon of the Yellowstone River and Yellowstone Lake, one of North America's largest Alpine lakes, to the south. On clear days, the view extends even farther south to the Grand Tetons. Start from the trail head at Dunraven Pass: The surprisingly mellow hike is about 3 miles one-way, gaining roughly 1,500 feet on its way to the warming hut at the top. The trail is not strenuous, but hikers need to be in reasonable shape. That said, I've also seen families with small children and folks on the far edge of 60 taking it all in at the top.

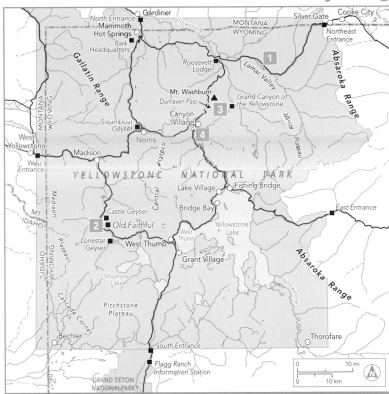

4 **Gawk at the Grand Canyon of the Yellowstone River.** For my money, the Grand Canyon of the Yellowstone River is just as dramatic and grand as its similarly named counterpart in Arizona. There are countless jaw-dropping views of the canyon and its superlative waterfalls, Upper Falls and Lower Falls. If you have time, I recommend hiking some of the trails in the area after getting a perspective from some of the overlooks just off of the road. I recommend the South Rim Trail with the loop trail to Clear Lake and Ribbon Lake (a moderately difficult hike of about 10 miles). Pack a picnic lunch and make a day of it. I also love Uncle Tom's Trail, which isn't really a trail at all but a steel 328-step staircase with a safe railing that drops you into the Grand Canyon of the Yellowstone River. The landing is a perfect perch from which to gawk at Lower Falls. From here you can feel the cool mist from the powerful 308-foot waterfall—nearly twice the height of Niagara's Horseshoe Falls.

ABOUT THE AUTHOR

A Denver-based freelance writer, **ERIC PETERSON** has written and contributed to numerous Frommer's guidebooks and *Ramble: A Field Guide to the U.S.A.* (www.speckpress.com). He's an avid camper and hiker, a lifelong Broncos fan, and a rock star (at least in the eyes of his nephew Mitch).

YOUR TRIP

General Information: For information before your arrival, contact **Yellowstone National Park** at ☎ 307/344-7381 or www.nps.gov/yell. For information on lodging and dining options inside the park, contact **Xanterra Parks & Resorts** (☎ 307/344-7311; www.travelyellowstone.com). Contact the **Yellowstone Association Institute** for information on education programs in Yellowstone (☎ 307/344-2293; www.yellowstoneassociation.org/institute). **Getting There:** Yellowstone is 91 miles from Bozeman, Montana; 129 miles from Billings, Montana; 52 miles from Cody, Wyoming; and 57 miles from Jackson, Wyoming. The nearest airports are **Yellowstone Regional Airport,** in Cody (☎ 307/587-5096); **West Yellowstone Regional Airport** at the west entrance in Montana (☎ 406/646-7631); and the **Jackson Airport** (☎ 307/733-7682). **Best Lodging:** The **Old Faithful Inn** is the apex of grand log national park lodges (at Old Faithful; ☎ 307/344-7311; www.travelyellowstone.com; $85–$450). **Best Lodging Value:** The **Roosevelt Lodge** is the most cowboy- and family-oriented property in the park (☎ 307/344-7311; www.travelyellowstone.com; $59–$102). **Best Restaurant:** On the north side of the lake, **Lake Yellowstone Hotel** has Victorian elegance with a lake view (☎ 307/344-7311; www.travelyellowstone.com; $8–$35). **Best Restaurant Value:** I love the retro vibe and hearty fare at the snack bar at the **Canyon Yellowstone General Store,** in Canyon Village; better yet, a picnic lunch. **When to Go:** May–Sept and Jan–Mar. The park is busiest in July and August; most of the lodges are open only from June to September or December to March.

◄ *Frost-covered American bison in Yellowstone National Park.*

YOSEMITE NATIONAL PARK, CALIFORNIA

Its scale, grandeur & beauty can overwhelm the senses

Atop Columbia Rock, I take a deserved break, and breathe deep. The short, steep trail up the wall of Yosemite Valley was a bit of a lung-burner, but the panorama now before me is the priceless reward.

The crown jewel of the Sierra Nevada, California's Yosemite National Park is home to some of the most visually stirring spots in the Western United States. Yosemite Valley is chief among them: Its scale, grandeur, and beauty can overwhelm one's senses.

I look around and soak in the sights. Directly across the lush valley floor is Half Dome, one of the park's most recognizable geological masterworks and a hiking and climbing magnet. Named for its appearance, the sheared 5,000-foot orb of granite dominates the southern horizon, flanked by the taller but equally aptly named Clouds Rest and the knifelike Sentinel Rock.

Blue sky, white clouds, steel-gray granite, foliage in shades of green: The views from here are breathtaking—so beautiful they defy easy description.

My heart rate slows and I continue up the trail. Soon I see Upper Yosemite Falls. Like the sight of Yosemite Valley from Columbia Rock, the view of the 1,400-foot ribbon of mist and water is worth the sweat. The strenuous hike to the brink of Yosemite Falls, traversing 7 miles and gaining over 2,500 feet in elevation, is not for everyone, but the park's extensive trail system runs the gamut from flat and easy to sheer and difficult. If hiking is your passion, Yosemite is a wonderful place to indulge—regardless of your ability.

The Valley Floor Loop Trail, for instance, is an easy 5- to 7-mile circuit with grand panoramas and plenty of places where you can get away from it all without a major workout. The mostly level trail is a great way for families and nonhikers to take in the sights and sounds of Yosemite Valley without a windshield in the way.

On my way down from Upper Yosemite Falls, I again stop to gaze from Columbia Rock. The moment feels like an eternity. Soon I am back in civilization on the valley floor, making my way on foot and in shuttle buses to the visitor center. In the midst of all of this dramatic scenery, bustling Yosemite Village offers lodging, dining, shopping, entertainment, and all sorts of other modern conveniences. But once you wander away from the roads, the bustle quickly melts into solitude, and almost every view is a great one.

In 1868, naturalist John Muir wrote of his first glimpses of Yosemite, and valued the experience as "enough for a great lifelong landscape fortune—a most memorable of days." These "most memorable of days" are still remarkably easy to come by in the park. Personally, I find them by lacing up my hiking boots and wandering where cars cannot.

But memorable experiences in Yosemite are not limited to hiking: Within park limits, one can raft a creek, ride a horse, climb a rock, or even enjoy 9 holes of golf followed by a five-course meal. In Yosemite, civilization is only as far away as you want it to be.

◀ *El Capitan, Yosemite National Park.*
© David Muench Photography

SPECIAL MOMENTS

1   Gazing at the waterfalls.
Yosemite National Park is home to three of the 10 tallest waterfalls in the world, not to mention many more that are not as statistically superlative but just as soul-stirring. The view of Yosemite Falls—2,425 feet tall, in three segments, making it arguably the longest waterfall in North America—is one of the park's most commanding sights, visible from the valley floor. There are also a number of waterfalls worth breaking a sweat to see. The Happy Isles Trail, which ascends from the west end of the valley between Half Dome and Sentinel Rock, offers something for all hikers: Beginners can venture a moderate mile and a half to the bridge for a great view of 317-foot Vernal Fall. Intermediate hikers can climb a more difficult 500 steps on the Mist Trail to the waterfall's brink for a closer look. Advanced hikers can continue up 2 more strenuous miles to the 594-foot Nevada Fall.

2   Getting away from it all in Tuolumne Meadows. Whereas heavy traffic is the status quo on the loop around Yosemite Valley, it is the exception in Tuolumne Meadows, the heart of the park's high country. Whereas the valley floor is around 4,000 feet above sea level, Tuolumne Meadows is a different world at 8,680 feet above sea level, making for a different ecosystem and a nice respite from the summer heat. Two of the park's tallest mountains, Mount Dana and Mount Lyell, are accessible via trail heads in the vicinity. For great views of the latter, hike to Dog Lake (easy, 3 miles round-trip), then cool off with a quick swim. This is also great backpacking country, whether you

stay within park boundaries (there are five High Sierra camps that provide food and shelter) or go on a longer route such as the John Muir Trail, my personal favorite.

3   Down time at the Yosemite Bug. My home away from home in the Yosemite area, the Yosemite Bug Rustic Mountain Resort is my favorite place to bunk and eat in the Sierra Nevada. Cozy but unpretentious, with a great cafe on-site, the Bug attracts a diverse mix of travelers from all over the world. Nestled on a wooded hillside, the

▶ *Towering trees in Yosemite National Park.*
© Lester Lefkowitz/Corbis

folksy hostel-turned-resort offers a full range of lodging options (from dorm-style bunk rooms to tent-cabins to themed private rooms), guided park tours, and a picture-perfect swimming hole just down the hill.

4 Get to know John Muir. Writer-naturalist John Muir has often been called "The Father of Yosemite." He first visited the area in 1868 at the age of 30, and subsequently spent much of his adult life exploring the park and the surrounding Sierra Nevada. His lively nature writing is some of the genre's best ever, spinning tales of his climbing a tree in a storm or exploring Lower Yosemite Falls by climbing behind them. Take some time to learn about Muir's words and deeds when you visit the park. At the Yosemite Theater, a regular show is presented with an actor portraying the long-bearded Muir. Area booksellers sell numerous titles and collections by and about Muir as well.

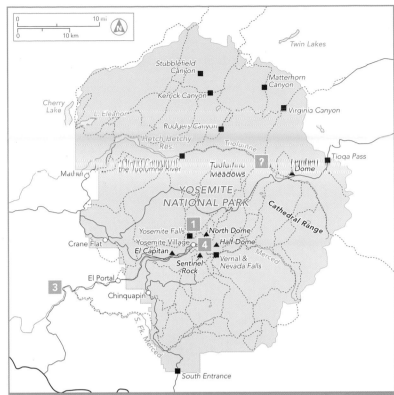

ABOUT THE AUTHOR

A Denver-based freelance writer, **ERIC PETERSON** has written numerous Frommer's guidebooks covering the American West and *Ramble: A Field Guide to the U.S.A.* (www.speckpress.com). He's an avid camper and hiker, a lifelong Broncos fan, and a rock star (at least in the eyes of his nephew Mitch).

YOUR TRIP

General Information: Call the 24-hour information line at ☎ 209/372-0200 or log on to www.nps.gov/yose. The primary concessionaire at Yosemite is **DNC Parks & Resorts,** which operates lodges and dining options inside the park itself (☎ 559/253-5636; www.yosemitepark.com). **Getting There:** The park is located 180 miles east of San Francisco, California. The closest airport is the **Fresno-Yosemite International Airport** (☎ 559/621-4500). Yosemite is a 3½-hour drive from San Francisco or a 6-hour drive from Los Angeles. **What to See & Do:** For guided tours of the park, contact: **Yosemite Guides** (☎ 866/922-9111; www.yosemiteguides.com); the **Yosemite Institute** (☎ 209/379-9511; www.yni.org/yi); or **Incredible Adventures** (☎ 800/777-8464; www.incadventures. com). **Best Lodging: The Ahwanee** is the flagship hotel in Yosemite Valley and a National Historic Landmark (☎ 559/253-5635; www.yosemitepark.com; $393–$863). **Best Lodging Value: The Yosemite Bug Rustic Mountain Resort** offers private cabins and hostel-style bunkrooms (6979 Hwy. 140; ☎ 866/826-7108; www.yosemitebug.com; $55–$115 private room, $18 dorm bed). **Best Restaurant:** The nationally acclaimed restaurant at luxury lodging Château du Sureau, **Erna's Elderberry House,** is known for its French-influenced cuisine (48688 Victoria Lane, Oakhurst; ☎ 559/683-6800; www.chateausureau.com; prix-fixe $92). **Best Restaurant Value: Happy Burger Diner** has fast food better than any franchise (Hwy. 140 at 12th St., Mariposa; ☎ 209/966-2719; www.happyburgerdiner.com; $3–$13). **When to Go:** Year-round, but avoid holiday weekends.

ZERMATT, SWITZERLAND

A four-season resort in the shadow of the Matterhorn

Visiting Zermatt is all about seeing and succumbing to the allure of the Matterhorn. No other mountain on earth enthralls you in this way, completely engulfing all of your senses. The first time I saw it, I was spellbound by its jagged profile and the way it sits, solitary, crowning the horizon, as though no other mountain would dare to stand beside it. The mountain mesmerizes you. You stare and you stare and you stare.

Zermatt is a hamlet, 1,620m (5,310 ft.) above sea level, in the small, German-speaking portion of the predominantly French-speaking *canton* (province) of Valais, adjacent to the Italian border. I always hear a jumble of languages floating around town—mainly German, French, English, and Italian—typical for a fashionable mountain resort and de rigueur in cosmopolitan Switzerland. Zermatt is also one of Switzerland's many car-free resorts; the only forms of transport are electric taxi vans with jingling bells, and ornate, horse-drawn sleighs and carriages. In Zermatt, I always feel like I've been plopped down in postcard Switzerland: Dark timber chalets line narrow, cobblestone lanes and dot the valley; snowy peaks jut out beyond rolling hills; and just when you think Heidi is going to come skipping around the corner, you hear the soft sound of Alphorns, played by locals in traditional Swiss dress.

The town teems with energetic visitors year-round. In summer, the mountain biking, Nordic walking, paragliding, hiking (400km/248 miles of trails), and mule trekking make the area an outdoor enthusiast's utopia. Rock climbers and mountaineers from every continent come to scale the rock and conquer the four-thousanders (peaks above 4,000m/13,120 ft.)—the area around Zermatt possesses a whopping 36 of them. Naturally, the Matterhorn is the ultimate summit. But if all you want to do is kick back and do nothing, you can hop on a cable car to one of dozens of restaurants above Zermatt and spend the afternoon on a sunny balcony overlooking the panorama of peaks, listening to the gentle clank of cowbells in the surrounding pastures. In winter, the slopes around Zermatt are my slice of bliss: three prime ski and board areas with a total of 313km (194 miles) of marked pistes. I've skied here for an entire week and never skied the same run twice. If I start the day early enough, I can ski to Italy for a midday plate of spaghetti *bolognese* and return to Zermatt just in time for an après-ski cocktail.

Whether I visit Zermatt in summer or winter, there are always three certainties: I relax; I inhale fresh, unpolluted Alpine air; and I stop, mid-ski run or mid-hike, and surrender to the most iconic mountain on earth. The thrill of seeing the Matterhorn in person seizes me every time.

◄ *Traditional Swiss mountain hut with view of the Matterhorn.*
© Hans Peter Merten/Getty Images

SPECIAL MOMENTS

1 Ascend the Rothorn. Getting to the Rothorn is half the fun. First, zip up to Sunnega Paradise (Swiss-German for "Sunny Corner") via a 5-minute underground funicular ride, and then hop on a snazzy eight-seater cable railway to Blauherd. Here, transfer to a big red cable car that hoists you up 3,000m (9,840 ft.) above sea level to Rothorn. The entire trip takes only about 25 minutes, but you'll wish it took longer because the views along the way are astounding. They're not as awesome, however, as what you see at the top: Over 30 colossal four-thousanders frame the horizon up here. This vantage point is the most photogenic place to gape at the Matterhorn.

2 Explore the Hinterdorf. Wandering down the bustling Bahnhofstrasse (main street) is fun and entertaining in summer and winter—but the real treasures line the side streets, in an area of the village known as the Hinterdorf. Veer off Bahnhofstrasse onto Hinterdorfstrasse and let yourself get lost in the meandering lanes crammed with miniature chalets and *mazots:* worn, wooden barns oddly propped up on multiple round, stone disks and thick stilts to keep the rodents out. The chalets enchant, regardless of the season: In summer, their window boxes spill over with vivid, thriving flowers. In winter, the snow drifts pile up against their dark, ancient wood walls.

3 Embrace the chocolate and the cheese. Something happens when you set foot in this country: You buy chocolate and find yourself eating it everywhere: on the train, on the ski lift, during your picnic, and probably before you go to bed. It doesn't matter what brand you buy, it's all fantastic, creamy, and satisfying. But somewhere in between your chocolate fixes, you'll crave another Swiss specialty: cheese. And the best way to appreciate it is warm and melted, in two basic dishes: fondue and raclette.

Cheese fondue is a mixture of two or three cheeses (usually Gruyère and Emmental or Vacherin), garlic, wine, and/or a shot of schnapps melted in a cast-iron pot. You dip cubes of bread into the concoction and savor the flavor. This is a heavy load on your stomach, so do as the locals do and pair the meal with herbal tea or white wine (preferably locally produced Fendant, a light-bodied wine made from the chasselas grape). If you're up for it, sip or do a shot of Swiss fruit schnapps like Kirsch (cherry) or Williams (pear) while you eat; the theory is that this burns a hole in the cheese and makes way for more. I think it is just an excuse to drink locally made distilled spirits. Whatever your poison, don't

drink water (it coagulates the cheese in your belly and makes for an unpleasant ache).

Raclette is slightly more complex in terms of the cheese-melting procedure. Large rounds of raclette cheese are cut in half and screwed onto a special contraption that heats the flat side of the cheese. As it melts, the oozing cheese is scraped off onto a plate over boiled potatoes. Cornichons and pearl onions join the mix, and the result is heavenly, addictive comfort food.

4   Drink Glühwein. Glühwein is hot mulled wine—a mixture of red wine, sugar, cinnamon, and cloves, usually served with slices of fresh orange and lemon. In winter, you'll find it for sale at slope-side restaurants, from tablecloth-and-fine-silverware lodges to ramshackle huts with a few creaky chairs. It is the perfect warm treat to sip on a break between ski or snowboard runs. Year-round, you'll find Glühwein served at most traditional Swiss restaurants or bars in the village.

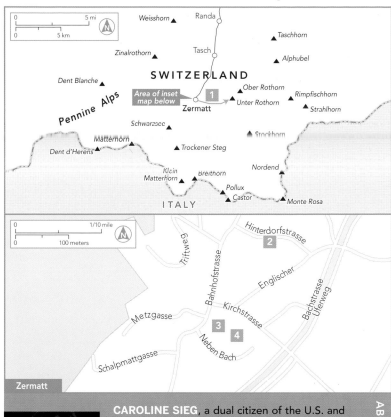

CAROLINE SIEG, a dual citizen of the U.S. and Switzerland, has spent most of her life moving between Europe and North America. She travels in search of fabulous food, fine wine, spectacular hiking trails, and awesome ski slopes. She lives in London, where she occasionally hosts midwinter fondue and Glühwein parties.

ABOUT THE AUTHOR

YOUR TRIP

General Information: Contact **Zermatt Tourism** (☎ 41-27/966-8100; www.zermatt.ch) or **Swiss Tourism** (☎ 41-800/100-200-30, or 877/SWITZERLAND in the U.S.; www.myswitzerland.com). **Getting There:** Hourly trains depart from Brig and stop in Visp and Täsch. The route is scenic; on the way up, sit on the left for the best views. Travel time from Zürich or Geneva to Brig is 2 to 3 hours. If you must drive, park in the large lot in Täsch (the closest town that allows cars) and travel the rest of the way by train. **Best Lodging:** Splurge on a room with a view of the Matterhorn at **Seiler Monte Rosa,** a traditional, character-filled hotel in the center of Zermatt (Bahnhofstrasse 80; ☎ 41-27/966-0333; www.zermatt.ch/monterosa; $351–$454/£186–£240). **Best Lodging Value: Hotel Weisshorn,** a snug and cozy chalet near the train station, has clean rooms and a friendly staff (Aufdenblatten; ☎ 41-27/967-3839; www.holidaynet.ch/weisshorn, German only; $97–$127/£51–£67). The best lodging value for groups of three to eight people on winter ski/snowboard trips is to rent a furnished apartment—many are in renovated chalets. Contact **Zermatt Tourism** to view properties and make reservations (see above). **Best Restaurant:** The **Grillroom Stockhorn** serves fondue, raclette, and other local specialties in a chalet with a roaring fireplace (in Hotel Stockhorn; ☎ 41-27/967-1747; www.grill-stockhorn.ch; $18–$35/£10–£19). **Best Restaurant Value: Walliserkanne** serves Italian and Swiss specialties in a rustic and informal space (Bahnhofstrasse 32; ☎ 41-27/966-4610; $14–$43/£7–£23). **When to Go:** You can ski/snowboard in the Zermatt area year-round, but the main ski season runs from late November to late April.

◀ *The town of Zermatt at dusk.*
© Ed Collacott/Getty Images

INDEX BY COUNTRY

For more than a decade, **RICHARD FOX** has been senior photo editor for Frommer's. In 2006, Richard received the Wiley Outstanding Accomplishment Award for his contribution to the Frommer's *Day by Day* series. He is also an oil painter and watercolorist, and has exhibited throughout the U.S. View his artwork at www.strata-art.com.

ABOUT THE PHOTOS